Man and Nature in China:
Gender, Natural Resources Management and the Chinese State in an Inner Mongolia Village

Hu Yukun

Paths International Ltd

中国社会科学出版社
CHINA SOCIAL SCIENCES PRESS

ABSTRACT

The process of China's rural modernization over the past half-century was punctuated by an ambitious attempt to transform the natural environment. "Wars against nature" were long a nationwide characteristic in rural China during the collective period. After decollectivization, rather than being reversed, overexploitation of nature intensified due to rapid economic development and increased inequality. Meanwhile, the rhetoric of "man can conquer nature" was replaced by "rehabilitate beautiful landscapes," seeming to embody a shifting conceptualization of people's relationship to nature.

In the background of the twin campaigns of "war against nature" and "rebuilding beautiful landscapes," this dissertation provides a firsthand understanding of natural resource management and environment changes from a gender perspective in the context of larger economic and ecological transformations in a peasant community over the past five decades. It examines how village men and women managed, viewed and negotiated environmental resources in their everyday lives along lines of wealth, ethnicity, age, marriage status, and livelihood. The ethnographic methodology of this study triangulates complementary qualitative and quantitative techniques of participant observation, informal conversations, in-depth interviews, oral histories and life stories, with household census and survey, archival materials, and local government statistics and documents.

The daily experiences of men and women in natural resource use, agricultural development and environmental conservation in Ao Village where I did my ethnographic study, were heavily shaped by multiple gendered forces. It mirrored many dimensions of a multilayered bureaucratic control, combined with local cadres' malpractice. The simultaneously "gender-blind" and male biased "development," based upon false notions of femininity and masculinity, as a consequence, had extremely negative impacts on women. Indeed, the Chinese State and its local agents still treated the "household" as a unit of policy assessment without looking at the differentiated relations between men and women inside a household. Institutional supports beyond the household for female farmers in the form of extension services, training, information and input supply were elusive or even worked to their disadvantage. Apparently, social inequalities—particularly gender inequalities—were interwoven with poverty, declining natural resources, degraded environments and unsustainable development, from Liberation to collectivization and continuing after de-collectivization.

Contents

Figure and Table List

Figures

Tables

Measures, Weights and Abbreviations

Measures and Weights

1 *mu*=1/6 acre=0.067 hectare

1 *chi*=0.33 meter

1 *catty* =1/2kg=1.1 pounds

1 *cent*=0.01 *yuan*

1 US $=8.3 *yuan* (in 2003)

Abbreviations

AQG	Aohan Qi Gazette
AQPG	Aohan Qi People's Government
ASB	Aohan Statistics Bureau
GYV	Greater Ao Village
HRS	Household Responsibility System
NRM	Natural Resource Management
SARS	Severe Acute Respiratory Syndrome
SFA	State Forestry Administration
UNEP	United Nations Environment Programme
UNDP	United Nations Development Programme
WTO	World Trade Organization

Man and Nature in China

Chapter One

Engendering Rural Development and Environmental Changes

The process of China's rural development over the past five decades was punctuated by a vigorous attempt to transform the natural environment. It is fair to say that this was long a nationwide characteristic in the Chinese countryside during the collective period. After decollectivization since the late 1970s, rather than being reversed, overexploitation of nature was intensified by rapid economic development and increased inequality (Muldavin, 1996b; Williams, 2002). I entitled the dissertation "From 'Man Can Conquer Nature' to 'Rebuild Beautiful Landscapes'," using two official slogans, to embody a shifting conceptualization of people's relations to the physical environment. It was true, the lived experiences of village men and women in natural resource use, agricultural development and environmental conservation in Ao Village, as an integral part of regional practices and a larger Chinese pattern, was shaped by multiple forces differentiated village men and women inside and outside the household.

The objective of this study is to provide a first-hand understanding of natural resource management and environment changes from a gender perspective in the context of larger economic and ecological transformations in a peasant community over the past five decades since 1949. More specifically, it examines how women and men conserved, managed, viewed and negotiated environmental resources in their everyday lives along axes of wealth, ethnicity, age, marriage status, and livelihood.

Theoretically, this localized and politicized feminist study focuses on the trajectory of men's and women's daily lived experiences and their agency embedded in multiple institutional dynamics. In this dissertation, I treat gender—that is the contested meanings assigned by local and external actors to being male and being female—as a power process interacting with other power hierarchies to structure complementarities, cooperation as well as negotiation and contestation among various social actors. These power hierarchies interact in multiple political sites, from the household, to the community, market and state. Each was a site shaped by—and also producing—ideas about masculinity and femininity where competing and conflicting interests and struggles were waged over resources, labor, power and authority. By integrating micro and macro dynamics of gender-environment interactions, the connections were made among the individual, household, community, regional, national and even international scales.

This chapter first lays out the national and regional historical context, in which the local gender-environment nexus occurred, and then introduces the theoretical perspective and the structure of the study.

Rural Modernization, Ecological Legacy and Gender

Rural Development and Its Environmental Outcomes

Chinese rural development over the past half-century was characterized by the contrasting development strategies of collectivization and decollectivization, each of which shaped the fate of both nature and people. The collectivization of agriculture was essentially completed with the establishment of the people's communes in 1958. Under a quarter century of the three-tier commune system, the people's communes, production brigades, and production teams owned all major productive assets and provided almost all administrative, social, and commercial services for the rural population. The Chinese State determined production, pricing, and distribution of goods and services, which was known as a planned economy. The commune system was dismantled when a series of rural reforms initiated since 1978 swept across rural China.

The most important reform was the creation of the "Household Responsibility System" (HRS thereafter), which has been followed by some more market-oriented reforms initiated since the mid-1980s. The revolutionary changes with environmental ramifications brought about by the rural reform, in my view, include: (1) decollectivization: communal land was contracted out to individual households and restored the household as the basic unit of production. The management of many other community-based resources was shifted to small householders as well; (2) privatization and diversification: the reform gave rural social actors more options to maximize their well-being through decisions about growing and marketing agricultural products, starting up businesses, or migrating to towns or cities, which resulted in a diversification of employment opportunities and sources of income; (3) commercialization: rural households were linked to the market in one way or another, and consequently, subsistence and market economies coexisted in rural landscapes. The HRS substantially improved the well-being and livelihoods of the rural poor and dramatically transformed the agrarian economy (Judd, 1994; Netting, 1993; Potter and Potter, 1990; Putterman, 1993).

Despite astonishing economic development, there has been an enduring paradox of unprecedented national economic growth rates and accelerated environmental resource degradation due to wide-scale and unremitting exploitation in rural areas (Edmonds, 1994; Muldavin, 1996a, 1997, 2000; Smil, 1993; Xu et al., 1992). Numerous environmental challenges loomed large on the rural horizon, which took a variety of forms, including deforestation, shrinking agriculture land, increased use of marginal lands, intensified cropping patterns, increased and uncontrolled use of destructive chemical inputs, a decline in agricultural infrastructure investments, industrialization and accompanying pollution (Edmonds, 1994; Muldavin 1996b; 1997; 2000; Smil 1993; Xu et al., 1992).[1]

China has manifested an awareness of environmental challenges ever since Liberation in 1949. Given severe human-nature conflicts in rural China, the continuous "Mao's wars against nature" became one of the priorities of the governments at various levels under the collective regime (Shapiro, 2001). In these efforts, effective political control also permitted the government to deal with human-land collision with modern, innovative measures (Huang, 1989). In the early 1970s when preparing the UN Conference on the Human Environment (Stockholm, Sweden, 1972), the Chinese Government started to awake to the significance of preservation of the environment. An increasing awareness of the economic

1 For a comprehensive discussion of China's environmental crisis, see Vaclav Smil (1993) *China's Environment: An Inquiry into the Limits of National Development,* Armonk, N.Y.: M. E. Sharpe and Richard Edmonds (1994) *Patterns of China's Lost Harmony: A Survey of the Country's Environment,* London: Routledge.

and social outcomes of rural environmental crises gave rise to a series of laws intended to control and ultimately reverse the worsening trend of environmental degradation.[1]Since the early 1990s, the top Chinese leadership expressed growing concern about environmental protection and conservation. During the UN Conference on Environment and Development held in 1992, China approved the 21st Agenda. Environmental protection wassoon established as a fundamental state policy.

Paralleling the agrarian reform, one of the largest re-afforestation efforts in history by a developing country (Rozelle et al., 2000)—a state sponsored regional shelterbelt initiative—was simultaneously launched in 1978 to combat increasingly severe erosion and desertification in arid and semi-arid regions in northern China. The Three Norths Shelterbelt (*san bei fang hu lin*) widely hailed as "the Green Great Wall" would continue to be introduced into approximately 550 counties, 13 provinces and autonomous regions in the northern, northeastern and northwestern "Three Norths" areas, which covered 4 million km^2 or 42 percent of China's total territory.[2] Since the late 1970s, the vigorous agroforestry scheme significantly altered the landscape in many rural localities like those in Aohan (Moore and Russell, 1990; Richardson, 1990; Rozelle et al., 2000).

Land erosion and desertification have long been serious problems in large parts of northern China. It was widely acknowledged that the degraded area brought under control had been far exceeded by the size of newly-eroded areas. This was captured by an expression of "rehabilitating partly and worsening overall." Since the late 1990s, the severity of the newly emerged transboundary problem of dust and sand storms has provoked widespread attention. The fourth phase of the "Three-Norths" Shelterbelts Project continued, but it was overwhelmed by two other field projects: the national Cropland Conversion Campaign, or "*tui geng huan lin*" and the Source of Sandy Wind Programme around Beijing and Tianjin Area. The former was a national

1 The laws enacted since the 1980s dealt with different aspects of natural resource use, management and conservation. They include: *The Forest Law* (1984; revised 1998), *The Grassland Law* (1985 and revised in 2002), *The Law of Land Administration* (1986), *The Water Law* (1988, revised in 2002), *The Environmental Protection Law* (1989), *The Law of Water and Soil Conservation* (1991), *The Agriculture Law* (1993), *The Desertification Prevention and Control Law* (2001), *The Land Contract Law* (2003) and the like.

2 It embraced Gansu, Guizhou, Qinghai, Shaanxi, Sichuan, Yunnan, Guangxi, Inner Mongolia, Ningxia, Tibet, Xinjiang, and Chongqing.

afforestation effort initiated in 2000, and the latter a regional campaign against desertification launched in 2000, involving Beijing, Tianjin, Hebei, Shanxi and Inner Mongolia.

Despite the shrinking of the agricultural sector, China was an overwhelmingly agrarian society, and approximately 70 percent of its population remained categorized as peasants. As Chinese agriculture was increasingly embedded in national and international markets, it became "an unprofitable, unattractive and even redundant economic activity" (Croll and Huang, 1997). China had nearly 1.3 billion people, over one fifth of the world's population (Donald and Benewick, 2005), yet only 7 percent of the world's arable land.The arable land per capita was 0.11 hectares, which was merely 43 percent of the world average (Rozelle et al., 2000). Given the precarious position of Chinese peasants, land was still their ultimate source of security in case they failed in shifting to non-farm employments or migration.

There was increasing evidence of causal connections among multiple driving forces of economic growth, population pressures, poverty, gender inequities and rural environmental problems. The combined effect constituted one of the most formidable challenges to the sustainability of China's rural development.[1]After two decades of development, the well-known "three agrarian questions" or "*san nong wen ti*"—the three interconnected dimensions of farmers, agriculture and rural areas—were still extremely harsh. They provoked serious concerns among scholars and policy makers alike, and became a top priority of academic research and policy interventions.

Economic Restructuring and the Making of the West China

Since the mid-1980s, China's growth pattern has led to broad regional development disparities between the affluent urbanized coastal areas in eastern China and the poorer rural interior in western China (World Bank, 1997). The coastal areas experienced dramatic industrial growth (Rozelle, 1996). To address the remarkable

1 The terms "sustainable" and "sustainability" in this dissertation are used in the same sense as those of the Bruntland Report (World Commission on Environment and Development, 1987:43), where sustainable development is defined as "meeting the needs of the present without comprising the ability of future generations to meet their own needs." There was a wide range of debates on the exact meaning of sustainability such as what was to be sustained, for who and by what ways were highly contested (see Rocheleau, 1998).

east-west disparity in China's development at the national level and ultimately achieve common prosperity, the Central Government launched the West China Campaign in March 2000 as a key initiative, widely known as "the Great Opening of the West" or "*xi bu da kai fa*". Twelve provinces, autonomous regions and municipalities, predominantly in west China were incorporated into the "West China Campaign".[1] Given the fragility of the environment in west China, environmental rehabilitation was identified as a top priority, embracing large-scale infrastructure and water and soil conservation projects through mass mobilization efforts.

Since China opened its door to the outside world in the late 1970s, radical changes bearing the imprints of capitalism occurred, which were widely articulated on the landscape of everyday life through labor, market and prices. In December 2001, China became the 143rd member of the World Trade Organization, which marked a new stage of China's opening to the globalized world economy.

Under the economic re-structuring, rural people—particularly poor rural women in west China—were brought into the global system on unfavorable terms. As a result of subsidy cuts and trade liberalization, it became increasingly difficult for China's small-scale farming to survive competition with global agribusiness corporations (Deckers, 2004). Farmers in China's western regions were hit the hardest, since they produced low yields of crops lacking of international comparative advantage (Huang, 2003). The penetration of capitalism was not a uniform phenomenon, nor did it affect all women's lives in the same way. There was no question that global capitalism dramatically altered the political economy of small farming households, as it affected social relations within the household and beyond it. An analysis of gender-environment interactions, therefore, must never be segregated from this historical and geographic specificity of globalization.

Gender-Environment Nexus in Chinese Contexts

The introduction of the HRS, in combination with the burgeoning of gendered rural industrialization and large-scale migration, has had far-reaching effects on gender divisions of labor, responsibility, space and authority within the household and beyond. However, these effects were not evenly distributed across gender, age and wealth categories, as gender-based roles were modified and renegotiated

1 It embraced Gansu, Guizhou, Qinghai, Shaanxi, Sichuan, Yunnan, Guangxi, Inner Mongolia, Ningxia, Tibet, Xinjiang, and Chongqing.

constantly as households responded to changing livelihoods and sustained the family (Cartier et al., 1998; Jacka, 1997; Judd, 1994; Bossen, 2002). It was estimated that in some regions, the widespread migration of men resulted in over 70 percent on average of the farm labor being performed by women (Cartier et al.1998; Jacka, 1997). Gender, therefore, became a significant dimension of economic, social and ecological re-structuring in rural China. Without question, globalization impacted upon gender relations in complex and contradictory ways.

The dismantling of the commune system and the reliance on market forces resulted in a re-structuring of the rural labor force and labor relations. Many peasants were diversifying their survival strategies by shifting out of agricultural work and pursuing non-land-based livelihoods. The gender division of labor responded to internal and external forces within and outside the household, which reflected the decision-making strategies of men and women for sustaining their livelihoods and undoubtedly interwove with power and authority. For some social groups, their overarching involvement in agricultural work and natural resource use—especially in West China—stemmed primarily from their lack of access to other more lucrative activities. This social exclusion carried very important policy implications for natural resource management and rural sustainability. As a result, the gender-environment nexus was in a dynamic and complex process of change and played out differently by region and place as well as by the socioeconomic characteristics of the peasant household and the woman herself—class, ethnicity, migratory status, the family life cycle, and livelihood systems in various locations.

Despite the everyday essential roles of female farmers in managing natural resources, producing food, and sustaining livelihoods, as Judd (1994: 2) points out, agrarian reform and its policy changes "have had wide ramifications throughout rural society, and none can be viewed as gender-neutral. Each of the policy changes and the program as a whole has been officially presented as changes in political economy without reference to gender or to the specific interests of women." In Ao Village as elsewhere, women were more than "half of the sky," and constituted a key part of labor force in the countryside. In real rural life, as Croll and Huang (1997) observed in their fieldwork, it was frequently stated only those who were "not capable" of undertaking any other agricultural or non-agricultural jobs were left in the fields to cultivate, which demanded little skill or education. As a consequence, agricultural laborers were deemed unworthy of any training or further education. This view virtually pervaded in rural China.

In the context of Chinese WTO entry, how could we pit the vulnerable, small household farms predominated by the ill-equipped "386199" troops[1]against hi-tech multinational companies? Farmer women's subordination, therefore, must be understood within the context of the subordination of Chinese peasants, especially farmers in west China. This clearly sharpened the trade-offs between economic growth, gender equity, and sustainable development in the long run.

Contested Terrain: Gender, Natural Resources Management and Institutional Matrixes

The theoretical framework of this study was motivated and informed by several strands of scholarly legacies, including among others, women's studies, development studies, environmental studies, Chinese studies, and institutional analysis with respect to gender and the environment. This work seeks to address knowledge gaps, and to advance beyond existing theory and application.

Gender and Its Relevance in NRM and Environmental Experiences

In rural societies all over the global "South", women and men are key resource users and managers, but they face different roles, responsibilities, opportunities, and constraints in managing natural resources both within and outside the household (Momsen, 2000). Gender, therefore, is "central to positioning both men and women vis-à-vis institutions that determine access to land, to other resources, and to the wider economy" and essential to disaggregate and interpret the functions of the households and the community in NRM (Slocum et al., 1995). In the same vein, Leach et al argues that, "gender relations are integral to the social and economic organizations which mediates people's relationship with particular environments" and thus "a key dimension of social difference affecting people's experiences, concerns and capabilities in natural resource management"(1995:1).

Following Joan Scott's (1988) theorization of gender, I address three inseparable and mutually reinforcing components of gender: gender ideology, organization and identity. The first category refers to the dominant cultural representations of sexual differences. Gendered organization means the role of gender in the

1 The "386199" troops referred to the feminization of agriculture in rural China. March 3rd is the International Women's Day, June 1st is the International Children's Day and September 9th is the Elderly People's Day in China.

functioning of social institutions. Gender identity refers to the multiple experiences of femininity and masculinity. As is well-known, gender does not exist in isolation, but interacts with other structures of inequality in shaping local processes of agrarian transformations and ecological outcomes.

In this study, I argue for a more localized and politicized understanding of these three interconnected aspects of gender in everyday rural landscapes and see gender as a power process governing the negotiation and contestation between women and men within the various political sites of the household, community, state and market, which are always gendered spaces of struggles over labor, property, power and authority.

Since the early 1980s, various brands of feminist scholars and practitioners have started to engender environmental debates, resulting in a spectrum of insightful perspectives. Gender and the environment became a crosscutting focus and concern of the United Nations and many other donor programs and projects in the 1990s, which revealed the significance of gender in (1) empowering women; (2) protecting the environment; and (3) creating sustainable development.[1]Among many feminist formulations, I found the somewhat overlapping perspectives of feminist environmentalism and feminist political ecology most inspiring and useful for my research. The feminist environmentalism perspective represented by Bina Agarwal (1992; 1994; 1997a; 1997b), situated land and property rights as well as environmental degradation and action in broader institutional settings. The political economy of natural resource use was viewed as the result of gender, class, ethnicity-based divisions and distribution of labor/power/privilege/property relations. The

1 The convergence of interest in gender, the environment and development emerged within the context of the rapid restructuring of economics, ecologies, cultures, and politics from global to local levels (Rocheleau, Thomas-Slayter and Wangari, 1996). The UN Conference on Environment and Development (Rio, 1992), followed by a continuum of conferences such as International Conference on Population and Development (Cairo, 1994), the Fourth World Conference on Women (Beijing, 1995), and their series of follow-up conferences all recognized the crucial role of women in NRM and sustainable development. *The Beijing Platform for Action* specifies that "economic development, social development and environmental protection are interdependent and mutually reinforcing components of sustainable development" and "equitable social development that recognizes empowering the poor, particularly women living in poverty, to utilize environmental resources sustainably is a necessary foundation for sustainable development" (United Nations, 1996:10).

crux of her analysis was a compelling argument for the material basis of gender-environmental interactions.

Feminist political ecology(cf. Carney, 1993; Leach, 1992; 1994; Thomas-Slayter, 1992; Rocheleau,1991) documented the empirical realities of gendered political ecologies through case studies. The framework suggested by Rocheleau, Thomas-Slayter and Wangari (1996) expanded the mainstream political ecology approach1 both topically and theoretically. It treated gender as a critical variable in shaping resource access and control, interacting with class, caste, race, culture, and ethnicity to shape processes of ecological change, the struggle of men and women to sustain ecologically viable livelihoods, and the prospects of any community for "sustainable development" (Rocheleau, Thomas-Slayter and Wangari, 1996: 3-4). In addition, it "builds on analyses of identity and difference, and of pluralities of meanings in relation to the multiplicity of sites of environmental struggle and change," (ibid.: 287) focusing particularly on gendered sciences of survival, gendered environmental rights and responsibilities as well as gendered environmental politics and grassroots activism. This school of feminist scholarship also highlights the need to understand and interpret local experience in the context of global processes of environmental and economic changes. This framework also had the virtue of alerting us to be more sensitive to various axes of social relations and power structures in men's and women's lives in the context of social, economic and ecological restructuring at different geographic scales.

The formulations of these two feminist schools were not entirely free of weaknesses. Feminist environmentalism focused primarily on the material reality of women/environment interactions and institutional basis of gender inequality, while it gave less account of social construction of meanings and identities. Agarwal's brilliant formulations also lacked of contextual nuances and subtleties of women's everyday lived experiences. As for the feminist political ecology perspective utilized by Rocheleau, Thomas-Slayter and Wangari (1996) and Thomas-Slayter and Rocheleau (1995), the institutional dimensions of gendered resource use and allocation were coalesced to its framework, yet this school did not push its insights

1 The political ecology perspective focused on the socio-economic hierarchies and power relations regulating land use and management by class and ethnicity, yet paid little attention to the gendered and gendering dimensions of environmental practices and outcomes (cf. Bryant and Bailey, 1997; Peet and Watts, 1996).

far enough. For example, it predominantly focused on the organizations rather than institutions, on the community-level interactions instead of inter-and intra-household dynamics (cf. Thomas-Slayter and Rocheleau,1995; Rocheleau, Thomas-Slayter and Wangari, 1996).

Both formulations dealt mostly with the gender-environment nexus in the context of private ownership of land and property. In rural landscapes all around the world, women rarely owned the land that they cultivated. But in Chinese property regimes, private property was abolished during the long collective era, and only partly restored during the reform era. Even in places where other commune capitals were privatized in the re-structuring, land was mainly owned by the collective, and the distribution of ration land was relatively fair along gender and other social markers, resulting in very complex and hybrid outcomes. Apparently, the theorization of environmental rights and tenure regimes by those working in the tradition of feminist environmentalism and feminist political ecology must be scrutinized contextually in the specific context of transitional China.

There was generally a dearth of comprehensive geographically anchored and empirically-based studies on the topic of gender-environment interactions except for a few select works by Carney (1988; 1993), Leach (1994), Rocheleau and Ross (1995), Thomas-Slayter and Rocheleau (1995) , Schroeder (1999), among others. Most authors working on this topic were preoccupied predominantly with gender-based conflicts over natural resources, relatively neglecting the intersections of gender, class, ethnicity and other social markers (see Carney 1988; 1993; Carney and Watts, 1991; Schroeder, 1999).

The most systematic and insightful ethnographic study concerning gender and the environment (more exactly agroforestry) were probably the case studies of Melissa Leach (1994) and Richard Schroeder, respectively, conducted in rural Sierra Leone and the Gambia. The former focused on how men and women in a rainforest community use, manage and view forest resources. The latter highlighted intra-household and inter-household gender politics in the context of the rise of garden boom and environmental rehabilitation. Both provided remarkable ethnography of gendered political ecology of resource use and control in local people's everyday lives embedded in the larger political economy structure, and thus made critical contributions to our understanding of the gender-environment connection. However, neither addressed certain dimensions essential to an understanding of agrarian transformations in the Chinese countryside, most notably, the state. What was lacking was also the multiple matrixes of social structures and local men and women's resistance to those structures. As we shall see later, excluding the institution of state, it was actually impossible to explore natural resource access, use and management in rural China. The study takes up where the previous feminist scholarship, especially Leach (1994) and Schroeder's (1999) case studies have left off.

Everyday Politics at Institutional Matrixes

Over the past 30 years, feminist scholars and practitioners broadened the very notion of politics, which contributed tremendously to contemporary feminist praxis as well as various spheres of social sciences. During the second feminist wave, "the personal is political" figured prominently in feminist movements. In the 1990s, feminist scholars illustrated that not only was the personal political, the impersonal was political, too (Elson, 1995). Instead of referring narrowly to formal political areas, political participation in particular, as Hart (1991:95) summarizes, "Politics has increasingly come to be used in a broader sense to refer to the processes by which struggles over resources and labor are simultaneously struggles and bargains over socially-constructed meanings, definitions, and identities" (Carney, 1993; Berry, 1989; Jackson, 2000; Rocheleau, 1995).

Since gender referred not simply to the social roles of men and women and the sexual division of labor, but also the ways that abstract qualities such as strong/weak were defined as masculine/feminine, namely referring to biology and nature, gender representations were often used to naturalize inequality and to obviate dissent within as well as beyond the household (Hart, 1991: 95). Taking work for example, the politics of what was viewed as work, what and which work was valued or devalued ideologically, whose labor and how work could be mobilized, how notions of skilled/unskilled, heavy/light were gendered, and what processes and mechanisms influence division of labor might lead to a great deal of contestation and conflicts politically. This was a discursive terrain of what Ong (1988) calls "cultural struggles" and Scott (1985) terms "the war of words" or "everyday forms of ideological struggles."

Institutional matrixes as mediators of people-environment relations became a flourishing domain in both mainstream and feminist scholarship. As Hanson (2000) rightly argues, "sustainability is fundamentally a political rather than a technological or design problem, in the sense that the greatest barrier to sustainability lies in the absence of institutional designs for defining and implementing sustainable practices in local contexts." The new institutionalism, represented by North (1990), emphasized the role of institutions, both formal and informal, in economic growth. According to him, institutions were distinguished from organizations. Social institutions were sets of formal and informal rules and norms that shaped interactions of the human with each other and with nature, which included social rules of tenure, property rights and labor mobilization, etc. Formal institutions were shaped by laws and policies made by higher-up governments, while a large part of social and economic life was governed by informal norms (North, 1990; Posner 2000). North stressed that informal rules provided legitimacy to formal rules, because whether a formal institution could succeed depended to a large extent on whether it was supported by informal institutions such as customs, traditions, and codes of behavior.

Gibson et al (2000) have developed the institutional theory in a context of forest ecology. According to him, institutional factors at a micro level include, but are not limited to the following variables: specific rules-in-use about who could harvest, when and how, and how much harvesting of different products was authorized or forbidden; the types of afforestation activities or other protection activities that were encouraged and by what means; the types of subsidies provided; the methods of monitoring and sanctioning forest use and investment practices; the level of common understanding of what rules were used, monitored and enforced; the degrees of organization among users. At a macro level, the institutional forces included national legislation authorizing diverse types of forests and their restrictions or subsidies; the types of private or communal land and tree tenure authorized; taxation laws on land, extraction rates; the availability of courts to resolve disputes over land or tree tenure, and disciplinary actions within public agencies.

The analysis of institutional dynamics in the context of community-based natural resource management proposed by Leach et al was even more inspiring. In their view, "diverse institutions, both formal and informal, and often acting in combination, shape the ways in which differentiated actors access, use and derive well-being from environmental resources and services and, in so doing, influence the course of ecological change"(1999:240).

Feminists identified and offered insightful analysis of four inseparable and interwoven gendered institutions—the household, the community, the market and the state (Agarwal 1994; Kabeer, 1994; Kabeer and Subrahmanian, 1996; Geotz,1997)

—and demonstrated how institutions could shape relations of power and authority. As conceptualized in different societies, patriarchy, state bureaucracy and even capitalist logic in these multiple terrains of confrontations often took the forms of institutional forces that defined and sustained the domination of some social groups, while reinforcing the subordination of others (Berry, 1989; Hsiung, 1996; Lee, 1998). As of 2003, a comprehensive analysis—especially empirical accounts—of institutional dynamics at multiple levels of household, community, state and their accompanying conflicts and struggles were almost non-existent and dismissed in Chinese study; this contrasted sharply to the lived experienced in west China. As we shall see in the following chapters, new gendered patterns of intra-household and inter-household cooperation, reciprocity, and exchange of labor, goods, or services evolved within and outside the community so as to ensure household survival and promote individual well-being. In the pages that follow, I will outline institutional analyses more fully.

Unearth the "Black Boxes"

Due primarily to feminists' efforts, the idea that the household was not a unit of congruent interests and preferences gained fairly wide acceptance. Empirical evidence from the global "South" indicated that bargaining and negotiation within the household played key roles in terms of access to and control over resources and labor. Familial social relations—once supposed to function around "material altruism"—were increasingly viewed as governed by various bargaining models such as the "conjugal contract" (Whitehead, 1981; Jackson, 1995) or "cooperative conflict" (Sen, 1990), intra-household subsistence budgets (Folbre, 1986; Guyer, 1988; Dwyer and Bruce, 1988), access to land and property (Davison, 1988; Agarwal, 1994; Schroeder, 1999) and the allocation and remuneration of intra-household labor (Jones, 1986; Carney, 1988; Carney and Watts, 1990; 1991) were seen as the outcomes of negotiation and renegotiation between men and women. Despite the intentional denial of domestic conflicts, there was no reason to believe that rural China was immune from these phenomena. The present study indicates gender politics at the domestic sphere was an integral part of political ecology dynamics in the village landscape.

Under the reform, the HRS was implemented on a household basis, which initially resulted in the expansion of the power and authority of the male head of the household (Davin, 1995). But this study indicates that discrimination against women was executed more obviously through external institutions rather than the household. Under the re-structuring, the community-level power structure reconfigured itself and a greater share of decision-making and authority went to a few elite men. Every so often, tensions and conflicts between women and men within the household and outside rooted in everyday lives were downplayed in China. The absence of research on these issues should not be equated with the absence of struggles and resistance. The rising rates of female suicide[1] and divorce were merely two of the most telling indicators of potential and actual domestic politics between generations as well as conjugal arrangements. The widespread assumptions of maternal altruism among Chinese women in both literature and the media, therefore, need to be reconsidered in day-to-day rural practices. The assumption of aggregate and harmonious rural communities in the Chinese countryside is another terrain that needs to be challenged so that difference and conflict can be acknowledged as an inseparable part of rural life (Guijt et al., 1999).

"Unpacking the State"

The most important non-household institution embedded in everyday practices of rural people was the state. Compared with the household, the institution of the state exerted even stronger influences on farmers. The agrarian reform launched in the late 1970s was a multifaceted program, which set the context for diverse choices and experiences among differing social groups, and thereby played a significant role in class formation as well as gender stratification. Based upon the neo-liberal tenets advocated by the World Bank, the state institutionalized the privileged positions of male social actors under the political slogan "to let a few get rich first," expecting the most prosperous to "trickle down" to their less fortunate counterparts.

The most pronounced negative outcomes of China's agrarian reform over the past two decades, in my view, were not only severe environmental destructions but also the widening disparities between west and east China, urban and rural areas, the rich minority and the poor majority, and women and men in terms of income, labor,

1 China was the only country that reported a larger percentage of female suicides in the world. According to a study by Harvard University, the World Bank and WHO, around 56 percent of the world's female suicides occurred in China, which accounted for more than 30 percent of the deaths among rural women aged 15-29. Quite typically, family conflicts were the major reasons.

resources, and well-being, with poor women in rural west China being hit hardest. This fact was never starker and more geographically pervasive than in the new century.

As virtually in all countries, past and present, the state was gendered in complex and apparently contradictory ways through gender-blind or male-biased policies, laws, programs, and practices. Although environmental protection, family planning, gender equality, and openness to the outside world were juxtaposed as fundamental national policies for China's social development, women were obviously marginalized from the policies and programs intended to manage the environment and foster sustainable development by governments. For example, on the eve the 1995 World Conference on Women, the Chinese Government promulgated *The Program for the Development of Chinese Women 1995-2000*, the first comprehensive agenda for women's development ever developed in China. Women and the environment, one of the twelve critical areas in *The Beijing Platform of Action* of the United Nations women's conference, had not been translated directly into this Program with 11 targets.

The HRS was created on the notion of a unitary male-headed household, with land titles being granted to men. The dominant assumption was that the family was an undifferentiated unit governed primarily by altruism and land parcels owned by the male head would benefit the whole family. The land tenure rights privileging men were embedded in the policy, but reflected in everyday practices (Croll and Huang, 1997; Bossen, 2002; Judd, 1994; Li, 1999). From time to time, village to village, women were particularly discriminated against in land allocations. The Chinese state was complicit with the forces of economic globalization and its role in protecting women from the negative effects of global capitalism was called increasingly into question.

Apparently, it was crucial to deconstruct the patriarchal/class nature of any state under Chinese circumstances. As Alvarez (1990), Kabeer (1994) and other feminists argued, we needed to "unpack the state," examining its multiple institutional and ideological instances (Alvarez, 1990). Scholars needed to go beyond the official goals and ideologies by examining the actual relationships and processes by which they were constituted (Kabeer, 1994:281).

When Arun Agrawal et al (2001) theorized community-based conservation, they insightfully dealt with three critical aspects: the multiple interests that make up communities, the processes though which these actors interrelate, and the institutional arrangements that structure their interactions. Environmental politics in sustaining rural livelihoods and shaping processes of ecological change within the community escaped their analytical scrutiny. In environmental literature, community was sometimes treated as a panacea for problems concerning conservation, and an artificial boundary separating communities from the market and the state were always assumed. Only after living and observing in the village community for an extended period of time, did I realize markets and states in the Chinese context were inextricably embedded inside and outside the community, and manifested themselves in local people's lived experiences of environmental resource use, management and conservation.

Gender-Environment Studies in Chinese Settings

Scholars within and outside China responded to the dramatic transformations in rural China by producing a large amount of scholarly works. Generally, gender was systematically excluded from considerations in both environmental studies (see Richardson, 1990; Edmonds 1994; Williams, 2002; Yin, 1998) and agrarian research (Huang, 1985; Putterman, 1993; Yan, 1996). As of 2003, women's studies scholarship was totally silent about natural resource use, environmental changes and their implications for gender relations or vice versa. Despite a burgeoning scholarship on women in the context of agrarian transformations within and beyond China, relatively few village studies were conducted by Western or Chinese scholars and even fewer regarding gender or the environment, let alone the gender-environment nexus.

The work on rural women and gender by Western scholars initially relied on documents produced by higher administrative levels. The studies along this tradition generally represented homogeneous rural women at the aggregate level, either as the beneficiaries or victims of the state policy and program.[1]Even in the post-reform era, due to the political restrictions for them to do independent field research, relatively

1 Some of the most influential English-language work on rural women by western scholars included: Margery Wolf (1985) *Revolution Postponed: Women in Contemporary China*, Standford University Press; Judith Stacey (1983) *Patriarchy and Socialist Revolution in China*, University of California Press, Berkeley; Elizabeth Croll (1981) *The Politics of Marriage in Contemporary China*, Cambridge: Cambridge University Press; Elizabeth Croll (1985) *Chinese Women Since Mao*, International Labor Office, Geneva; Key Ann Johnson (1983) *Women, the Family and Peasant Revolution*, Chicago: University of Chicago Press; Phyllis Andors (1983) *The Unfinished Liberation of Chinese Women, 1949-1980*, Bloomington: Indiana University Press.

few ethnographically-based works were conducted, with only some of them touching on gender relations permeating rural life (see Gates, 1996; Potter and Potter, 1990; Pasternak and Salaff, 1993; Ruf, 1998; Watson, 1991). Very few studies based upon firsthand fieldwork systematically examined gender, with only a few exceptions such as Bossen (2002), Croll (1995), Croll and Huang (1997) and Judd (1994; 2002). Foreign researchers were prevented from staying in a single site for a relatively long time or even were denied to live in the village (Judd, 1994; Bossen, 2002) and thus they were in varying degrees prevented from intensive interactions with local people. Perhaps for this reason, subaltern/marginalized voices and gender subjectivity often astonishingly went unrecognized (see Judd, 1994; Jacka, 1997).

Feminist Chinese scholars were preoccupied with the impact of the rural reform on women's status and roles, agricultural work and the sexual division of labor, education, marriages, families/households, family planning, reproductive health and rights, etc. However, few development-related studies were devoted to the topics of environmental experiences and outcomes.

A wave of scholarly publications on rural environment by Chinese and westerners alike were concerned about how recent economic growth fueled environmental degradation such as pollution, desertification and shrinking of agricultural land taking place in the Chinese countryside. Generally, little was studied ethnographically. The "macro", homogenizing discourses were not based upon first-hand or eye-witnessed accounts, which were often presented out of context. As a result, they focused predominantly on aggregate level analysis, and ignored not only how macro-level policies and processes were articulated on a day-to-day basis at the grassroots level, but also the complexity of historical and geographic specificity of everyday practices of natural resource use and environmental changes. By neglecting the interactions between the micro and macro levels, they offered only a partial perspective.

As far as Inner Mongolia was concerned, the few existing community-based studies on the environment either gave priority to Mongols in the pastoral region or were silent about the implications of environmental changes on gender relations or vice versa (Ma,1987; Williams, 2002). For example, the village-level ethnography of a pastoral community by Dee Mack Williams (2002) explored how state-imposed policies led to severe environmental consequences in the past two decades. The centerpiece of his argument was that the post-1980 privatization process, coupled with Chinese government policies of barbed-wire fencing of grasslands, led to enormous ecological and social the social transformations such as fragmentation and economic stratification. Little was touched on the long-neglected aspect of gender. Pasternak and Salaff's (1993) village studies emphasized how environment/ecology shaped the choice of farming or pastoralism, but was less concerned with ecological changes per se.

Against the above backdrop, this study aimed to answer the following core causal questions:(1) How did economic and ecological transformations over time affect the content, extent of, and possible distinctions between women and men's heterogeneous participation in NRM? And how did this participation differentiated by gender, wealth, ethnicity, age, marriage status, and occupation shape local ecologies and rural women and men's lives? (2) How did ever-changing institutional dynamics at multiple scales of the state, market, community and household impact on men's and women's access to, management, and control over environmental resources? (3) How did women and men as differently positioned social actors negotiate and contest the politics of resource use and management in both material and ideological terms? (4) How were assumptions regarding "femininity" and "masculinity" historically constructed, maintained, negotiated and transformed in local landscapes?

By taking seriously the actors', particularly women's perspectives of changing environmental experiences and their gender dimensions in a community setting, this site-specific, historically situated study identifies many inappropriate policies and practices to address women's empowerment, environmental conservation and sustainable development. The study demonstrates that if runaway environmental degradation and ever-growing poverty are to be controlled, not only academic research, but also policy and intervention must be reoriented to increase equity—particularly gender justice and equity—as well as effectiveness of agricultural work and natural resource management.

Agricultural development that integrates environmental sustainability with gender equity became an urgent and critical challenge, not only for rural livelihoods and development, but also for China's long-term human development.The multiple theoretical and methodological orientations of the study have relevance to various disciplines: women's studies, gender and development, ethnography, development studies, environmental studies, and Chinese studies.

Major Structure

The dissertation is divided into three parts. The first part is devoted to an account of socio-cultural and historical contexts at both macro and micro levels. Chapter one sets the macro socio-historical context in rural China, followed by a review of theories connecting gender, environment and development. Chapter two outlines the politics of ethnographic fieldwork and the methodology of the study. Chapter three traces the local and historical-specific contexts for an understanding of gender-environment linkages, past and present, in a peasant community. All these chapters set the stage for subsequent discussions of gender-environment interactions.

The second part delves into the on-the-ground gendered experiences of natural resource use, management and conservation as well as the processes of environmental changes from within. The gendered experiences of local actors' in natural resource use, management, agrarian changes and environmental conservation had shaped and continued to shape men's and women's intersections with each other and with the natural environment. Chapter four chronicles the continuities and changes in the nexus of agricultural production, both crop and livestock farming, and their ecological implications from gender perspectives. Chapter five sketches the village history of environmental conservation implemented and enforced at the local level, disclosing the conservation dilemmas in the rural scene of contemporary China. It casts doubt on the universal claims of conservation succession from grassroots perspectives.

The last part is dedicated to a gendered analysis of institutional matrixes structuring NRM and environmental changes, focusing, respectively, on the social dynamics of the local state, marriage and the household, and the market. I argue that dynamic and changing institutional arrangements determined men's and women's access to and control over resources, which, in turn, influenced resource use and the process of environmental change. Chapter six traces the political aspects of community-based natural resource management at the village level—formal political structure, community-based natural resource management, gendered resistance politics. Chapter seven describes marriage strategies and the gender regimes inside and outside the household refashioned into environmental resource use and the local environment changes. Chapter eight traces three interconnected dimensions of the market-driven economy—the commodity market, off-farm work and socioeconomic differentiation, which carry policy implications for both gender and natural resource use, and hence for the environmental changes.

The concluding Chapter returns to some of the key issues raised throughout the text concerning the theoretical and policy implications of gendered NRM practices and institutional mechanisms. Apart from a chapter on fieldwork, the following chapters lay out the on-the-ground gendered experiences of natural resource use, management and conservation, the process of environmental changes, as well as the corresponding institutional mechanisms from within.

Chapter Two

The Politics of Fieldwork

In western feminist scholarship, Haraway's (1991) theorization of knowledge as "situated, embodied, and partial" inspired many feminists to state their situatedness based on gender, class, race, and other social markers. Indeed, as Townsend et al (1995) admitted, the knowledge that they presented was incomplete, because it was limited by their own personalities, understandings, cultures, languages, ethnicities, classes, and perhaps even gender. Some feminist ethnographers creatively analyzed the positionalities, power relations, and the embedded biases in the research process, as well as their field dilemmas in the Third World context (Hsiung, 1996; Townsend, 1995; Visweswaran, 1994).

Most foreign scholars doing fieldwork in rural China, feminist or not, mentioned the fieldwork limitations imposed by officials from on the one hand, and their active interactions with ordinary villagers on the other (Bossen, 2002; Croll, 1995; Judd, 1994; Wolf, 1985), yet no one ever systematically described how the multiple social locations based upon difference and identity shaped their field experiences. Following some feminists' formulations, I included my own social locations in fieldwork into the interpretation of the research process and brought my own self-reflexivity into the text. This chapter begins with the site selection and the initial visits. It then proceeds to a discussion of multiple power operations in fieldwork interactions. The last part describes the methodology of this study.

The Site Selection

As I drafted the dissertation proposal, I was attracted by the so-called "Green Great Wall"—the "Three-Norths" shelterbelt in north China. At that time, I was concerned with gender and agroforestry practices in the "Three Norths" area. More exactly, my original motivation was to study the dynamic interactions of gender and environmental changes in a community in the context of agroforestry. Inner Mongolia was in charge of building one third of the "Three Norths" shelterbelt, and its total area of afforestation and planted grassland ranked first in the shelterbelt region.

When I returned to Beijing from the United States in 2002, I learned Aohan Qi was quite successful in incorporating the forests into its farming system. The outstanding contributions of Aohan to environmental conservation won it national recognition as a model and ultimately the award of the UNEP's Global 500 Roll of Honor in 2002. This honor, I then thought, could serve as a benchmark by which to measure its past efforts and continuous struggles under the shadow of "model" county. Choosing Aohan, of course, was also out of more pragmatic considerations. It was 560 kilometers from a train station in the county to Beijing—merely a night's trip of ten hours.

Almost from the very beginning of locating a field site, I was introduced immediately to the political sensitivity of the fieldwork. Learning that All China Women's Federation once organized a course of lectures on the topic of "Three Norths" program for senior female leaders, I made contact with a former colleague to seek a connection to the co-organizers in the State Forestry Administration(SFA, i.e. the Former Ministry of Forestry) for my field research. The colleague was hesitant at first to tell me about it, and frankly confided to me shortly after that there were a great deal of troubles with the shelterbelt. "Since you have returned from the United States, I should introduce your 'double identities' to them," she added. She meant that I was an ex-researcher of All China Women's Federation as well as an overseas graduate student. This seemed like an implicit message that the field research—and the environmental study in particular—was politically sensitive, running the risk of "releasing state secrets." Such episodes in practice emerged and remerged in the later fieldwork.[1]

1 While I was staying in Aohan, one encounter surprised me most concerning the local cadre's vigilance against outsiders. The editor-in-general of a local government newspaper once told me that he could not allow me to read any of their newspapers unless I had local government connections. He continued that, no official could assume the responsibility of disclosing "certain" data to strangers, which might, unfortunately, turn out to run against him. This event, among many others, pointed to the political sensitivity of fieldwork and the research project. To protect the privacy and anonymity of the villagers and cadres whose stories were told, pseudonymous place names were used for the township and village, even in the references.

Women's Federations at various levels—national, provincial, municipal and county—helped greatly to clear the stones on the path to access to the field site. I had worked in the Women's Studies Institute of China, All China Women's Federation[1]for about ten years before studying in the United States. It was from this connection that I was able to draw on the top-to-bottom hierarchical network of Women's Federations to gain access to the study village and complete the fieldwork.

After a night's travel by train, on an early spring morning of late March in 2003, I arrived at the train station of Chifeng City. Just passing through the exit, I saw somebody holding a board with my name on it. Three staff members from the Women's Federation of Chifeng City were waiting for me in a freezing spring wind. During that day, I visited their offices, learning some general information on women's work and the ongoing projects at the prefecture and county levels. On the next morning, accompanied by one staff member, the driver drove me to the county seat of Aohan Qi.

The field site was chosen in consultation with a host of county and township officials, for which the director of Aohan Qi Women's Federation played a key role. During the four days that I stayed in the county, the director took time to accompany me to visit various county government departments, including the Propaganda Office, the Forestry Bureau, the Statistics Bureau and other government agencies, from which I was able to harvest much expected and serendipitous information. In the Forestry Bureau, for example, we met a female deputy director, who was the only leader left in the office while the other three male directors had gone down to the grassroots to guide the upcoming mass conservation campaign. During the talk, she complained about the obstacles lying in the road of female's political participation. She described her own promotion by using a popular Chinese saying, "It takes ten years to finish grinding a sword" (*shi nian mo yi jian*).

The selection of a village site was not unproblematic even for a native Chinese. After many comparisons, the director of Qi Women's Federation accompanied me to visit a village one day. The intended host family was situated on a roadside near the

1 The Women's Studies Institute of China was affiliated with All China Women's Federation founded in 1949, the largest semiofficial women's organization in China functioning as "a bridge connecting the governments to women." It had a huge staff member across China to initiate various activities as well as to advocate policies from very high to member grassroots levels.

village headquarters, where only about 20 houses lined both sides of a highway. This cluster of households separated itself from the rest of the villagers, which inevitably would prevent me from interacting with other villagers on a daily basis. With such concern in mind, coupled with my own preferences and theoretical considerations, I certainly was not satisfied with the site. At that time, I was more interested in visiting Lan Township—a Mongolian ethnic township—had been incorporated into a micro credit project sponsored by the United Nations Development Programme (UNDP), yet the director told me that she had tried to solicit the consent from the township Party secretary, However, the latter implicitly rejected it. I further learned that only a year earlier, a social scientist from Beijing came to investigate the problem of peasants' tax burdens, and in the end brought the issue to outside attention. The Party secretary got quite angry about it, and became wary of outside visitors. Using the words of the director, "The presence of strangers is, nowadays, not warmly welcomed by local authorities, since no one would like to make trouble for oneself."

Frustrated by the difficult trade-offs, I suggested to the Women's Federation director why not go directly to the township seat for a visit to see if it was possible. When we arrived at the building compound of the township government, the Party secretary—a Mongolian official working in this township for over ten years—was working in his office. After introducing my research purposes, I was at first treated with great suspicion, yet he did not refuse totally, probably because he thought women's issues were not so politically threatening, probably due to the standing and personal authority of the director in the county, or perhaps both. He began to think over the possible sites, and finally suggested to me to go to the "average" Ao Village,[1]for its ethnic composition[2]as well as its level of economic development falling in the lower-middle range in the township.

The Initial Visits

Accompanied by the super authorities of the township Party secretary and the

1 I thereafter used a fictional name of Ao Village. Pseudonyms were also used for all personal names in the village.

2 To identify Ao Village as a research site was not purely opportunistic. As I planned to do a research in Inner Mongolia, I initially hoped to seek a chance to examine the interactions of ethnicity and gender. Therefore, a minority village with a mix of Han-Mongol had originally been on my research agenda. In addition, Ao Village was not a model village in terms of environmental conservation or other aspects.

county women's director, I visited my research village for the first time on a sunny late March afternoon. It was about 4 kilometers away from the township seat. After about a kilometer's driving on an asphalt national highway, we turned right into a relatively narrow, rugged village road, with a patch of poplar near the left side of the village entrance. The village road stretched out zigzag for about 3 kilometers to the residential area of Ao Village. After entering the community, we soon stopped inside a walled compound with a big iron gate. This was the headquarters of Greater Ao Village, under which Ao Village was administered.[1] The village Party secretary, village director and other village cadres happened to be in their office that afternoon. After I was introduced to them, I briefly explained the nature of my research and my interests in women and environmental issues. They seemed to issue a perfunctory greeting. In front of the superior authorities, the village officials, or cadres, accepted me into their village without explicit rejection, demonstrating neither questioning nor warmly welcoming in their reactions.

Nobody seemed to believe that I could stand living in a rural setting for at least half a year and bear the harsh physical conditions. The village cadres promised to find a suitable household with a vacant room. The village women's director—a young woman—was soon called in. She was in her mid-thirties with a son of fifteen years old. "You must have married and given birth early," the Qi Women's Federation director joked. All in the room laughed, and the atmosphere changed immediately, the Party secretary responded, "What should young women do if they do not get married and give birth to children early?" We did not stay long since the township Party secretary had a meeting that afternoon. I told them that I would settle in the village a week later before a national scheme of cropland conversion started in this village.

A week later in the early morning on April 8, I arrived at the train station of Chifeng City again, a staff member from Women's Federation came to greet me, and the same driver drove me to Aohan that morning for a second time. After lunch, the Qi Women's Federation director, the driver and I headed again to Ao Village. When

1 I knew later a former school building was converted into the village office building after the primary school in the village was closed in 2002. A pre-school class organized by residents for little kids still occupied a classroom. The previous village headquarters built in 1994 was sold to a villager.

we arrived at the village headquarters, it was past 12 o'clock and no one was at the office. The director called the Party secretary who was then outside the village. While waiting, we soon met an old man in his mid-sixties, and knew immediately that he was a cook for village officials. He volunteered to show us to the chosen household where I would live. We followed him along a somewhat sandy path, and soon stopped in front of a walled courtyard standing on the main street about 50 meters away from the village headquarters.

As we approached a wide iron door, a tall, middle-aged woman came over to meet us and guided us to her house. She was my hostess, Song Ling, whom I later called *da sao*, meaning an elder brother's wife, a term of respect commonly used for a woman a little bit older than oneself. My host, Hong Xiang whom I called *da ge*, meaning elder brother, a polite address for a male a little bit older than oneself, was not at home then. While we were waiting for the Party secretary, we talked and looked around. The house was built of red tile and brick eight years ago, with the inside wall being whitewashed. The spare room that I would live in was on the west side of the building previously used by their elder son, Hong Jun, and his wife.[1] Two years ago after they married, the wife of Hong Jun joined her husband to migrate to a place in Beijing, where he had already worked for 5-6 years. The room looked very clean and bright with a big glass window.

After the Party secretary arrived, he required Song Ling to cook a welcome meal for us, even though we had already eaten. A middle-aged woman, Zhang Hualan, happened to come here, and she helped Song Ling to prepare the meal. Zhang Hualan was some kind of distant relative to my host family. As usual, she came over for "*chuan men*", meaning to drop by somebody's home. During my ethnographic presence in Ao Village, she came over to my host's house almost every day, and

1 They had two young adult sons. The second son, who was unmarried, was working in Beijing as well. The daughter-in-law came from a wealthy rice-growing village near a town about 16 kilometers away. About four years ago, their elder son Hong Jun helped others to transport grain to a purchasing station owned by his prospective parents-in-law, who picked the handsome migrant young man for their third daughter aged 17 then. Although Hong Jun's registration was transferred to the rich village of his parents-in-law's through connections, Hong Xiang and Song Ling insisted that Hong Jun was not uxorilocally married, because the wedding banquet was held in Ao Village rather than "brought in" by his parents-in-law.

sometimes with her husband Liu Xing. The two households had worked together for crop cultivation for two years and they had intimate cooperation in other spheres as well. During the course of fieldwork, I got quite familiar with the daily activities of these two households. Soon after the arrival of the Party secretary, Hong Xiang came back. He spoke little and looked quite honest. While Song Ling was still busy in the kitchen, we were invited to sit on the *kang*[1]around a small square wooden table with short-legs, and were most hospitably entertained with a meal. After several rounds of Chinese white wine, Song Ling was required to come over to drink a cup of wine with us, she did so with dignity, and then went back to the kitchen. I found out later that whenever the male guest was present, women seldom ate together with them on the *kang*, even if the guest came from their own natal families. Only after men finished drinking might they join in the meal.

As elsewhere in rural China, the Party secretary was always the highest seat of village power. The then Party secretary was a township official. By the time we met, he had just assumed the position in Greater Ao Village for 83 days. As a native to one of its hamlets, he was appointed to the highest-ranking position by township leaders to tackle knotty "problems" in Greater Ao Village, where his two immediate predecessors were removed from their positions ahead of time. Over the meal, the Party secretary repeatedly expressed his unwillingness to be a Party secretary here, and mentioned more than once that he did not fear anybody from Beijing (referring to me) or the city (the driver from Chifeng City), but instead was afraid of the county authority (referring to the director of Qi Women's Federation). My first encounter with the Party secretary left certain negative impressions in my mind, an initial sign of difficult cooperation.

After the meal, we soon left the village. In the next afternoon, the director again escorted me to my host's house. After her departure, I talked with *dasao* Song Ling for a whole afternoon. That night, when Hong Xiang returned home, they moved a big chest into my room for me to lock-up my belongings such as my computer, I actually never locked anything, even when I returned to Beijing for a short time. "We only have two persons in the house, and no child will interrupt you. If you do not dislike our food, you are welcome to eat with us," Song Ling said. Ever since then,

1 *kang* was a kind of built-in brick and cement bed typically found in the countryside of north China. For more accounts of the *kang*, see the next chapter.

we "lived together like a family." Song Ling occasionally entered the room to chat, and most of the time we ate and chatted in their room on the east side of the building.

Different from foreign feminist ethnographers (Bossen, 2002; Judd, 1994; Wolf, 1985), as a native scholar, I was allowed to reside with local people in the village and participate in their everyday life. I was more than lucky to have taken up residence with this ordinary family.[1] My host couple was widely considered as "good people," who were merely marginally better off than average villagers.[2]Hong Xiang was aged 49 and Song Ling 47 in 2003. As most of the residents in their age, they both grew up poor. During the collective years, Hong Xiang once served as a team leader for less than a year, for he was "too honest to control the complex team matters."

I was hosted in their house not merely because they had an empty room, but also because they were known to villagers to be kindhearted, hardworking and keep the room clean.[3] Inhabitants repeatedly mentioned that the rooms in my host's home were the cleanest in the hamlet. To intensively participate in the everyday lives of ordinary folks like them made it possible for me to learn and observe their opportunities and constraints, happiness and sufferings. In our daily contact, I was also able to stay informed of the village happenings as well as the latest local news.

My initial discomfort with the strong wind with sand, coupled with unbearable coldness, hard *kang* and monotonous diet in a rural northern community, were soon dissipated by warmth, hospitality, and the constant help from my host and hostess. Song Ling warmed the *kang* for me every day even during the summer. I was told if one slept on the cold *kang* for long time, s/he would suffer from rheumatism. "You

1 As a national gender specialist for a Sino-Britain rural water supply and sanitation project, whenever we lived in the villages in Yunnan and Sichuan provinces, we were always housed in the houses of village officials or their relatives so that our payment could create an additional resource of income for them.

2 If there was anything special to distinguish this family from others, it was that Hong Xiang's fourth elder sister was married to a young man sent down from Beijing in the "Up to the Mountains & Down to the Villages Campaign (*shang shan xia xiang*) operated during the period from 1970-79 and later she worked and lived in Beijing. I was constantly told that my host family benefited greatly from having "good relatives". Song Ling admitted that they got many old clothes from the sister, who also initially helped Hong Jun to find a job in Beijing, "but no more than this."

3 A few residents hinted to me that my stay in my host's house increased their income–generating chances from the village leaders.

have never slept on the *kang* before, you might be especially vulnerable to it," Song Ling always warned. Although Hong Xiang did not like rice very much, they always cooked rice when we ate together and tried to make the diet as diversely ample as possible by making dumplings, noodles and steamed breads. I only occasionally cooked instant noodles myself when they both worked outside. During the summer and early autumn, we had enough vegetables from the garden to eat. I always brought back vegetables, meats, biscuits, cooking oil, and the like to share. No matter how late I came back from my interviews, they always waited for me to eat together. We often watched TV together and exchanged ideas.[1]

The first research trip was made in late spring when the farming season was coming, which broke the idleness of the long winter. Inhabitants were busy with preparing the forthcoming spring planting, digging manure out of the pigsty, transporting it to the fields, purchasing seed and fertilizer. When I walked around, I could find heaps of manure piling up outside their courtyards along the street. The strong dry wind frequently stirred up clouds of fine dust and even flying sand. When I came back from outside, I felt the dust blown all over my face. The scene was commonplace, as the village had windy days much of the year.

Due to the increasingly severe spread of the Severe Acute Respiratory Syndrome (SARS, thereafter) pandemic, I retreated from Ao Village on April 22, after staying in the community for about two weeks. Not until the World Health Organization cancelled the traveling warning on SARS in China did I return to the village again on July 9, over two months later. As elsewhere, although not a single SARS case was discovered in Aohan, a large-scale political mobilization was launched. During some time of the SARS spread, officials from the county and township levels took turns staying in the village to deal with the emergencies. Village officials were stationed at the village entrance, and no outsider was allowed to enter. In those days, villagers, male or female, seldom dropped by each other's houses. On my first fieldtrip, I realized there was less agroforestry in practice in the village than I had originally anticipated. As I resumed my project, I had decisively switched the topic of my research to gender and natural resource management on a daily and local basis, and the consequent environmental changes over the past five decades.

1 Local inhabitants spoke only Chinese, more exactly, an Inner Mongolia dialect with a Shandong accent, which was not quite different from Chinese, and thus was easy to understand.

Given the immense heterogeneity and variations in Chinese village communities, no single village in fact could be considered "typical" of regional dynamics as well as those of rural China as a whole. This was as true of the interactions of gender and rural environment as of anything else. There were a total of 325 administrative villages in Aohan, the divergent climate and geographic characteristics largely structured local land use patterns and accompanying conservation practices at different localities, which certainly prevented any generalization within the boundary of the county. This case study is, therefore, not claiming to be representative of rural China as a whole. Quite the contrary, it emphasizes the highly place-specific processes occurring in a village setting. Ao Village was not in any sense extraordinary. The value of studying it was that we can use it as an exemplar to reflect the intricate pattern of development and change in this part of rural China probably with more dramatic environmental transformations than anywhere elsewhere.

An Ethnographic Gaze: Power in Operation, Power in Transition

Many western scholars, Stacey (1991), Patai (1991), Wolf (1996), among others, focused on the unequal power relationships between ethnographers and their informants, highlighting the intrusion of the ethnographers into the lives of their female informants, the deployment of informants' stories, and the dominant position of the researcher in presentation and representation of the researched. Later, some feminists started to challenge the dichotomous conceptualization of this power relationship, which merely assigned the ethnographer as the agent. For instance, Ong (1995) asserted, if one considered power as a decentralized, shifting and productive force, animated in the networks of relations rather than possessed by individuals, then ethnographic subjects could also exercise power in the production of ethnographic knowledge. She rightly argued that the ethnographer-informant relationship was, after all, enacted and portrayed in different fields of power, including the informant's home and their native community.

Doing fieldwork in the Chinese countryside was a process full of negotiations of a political nature, which were encountered not only by western scholars (Bossen, 2002; Huang, 1989; Judd, 1994; Wolf, 1985), but also by native Chinese (Cao, 2000; Liu, 2000). As any other ethnographer, I certainly could not escape the complex constellations of power embedded in local structures of authority and power.

Despite certain privileged positions that I occupied—urban, middle class, educated, versus rural, poor, minimal education of villagers, in the ethnographic field, I interacted not only with ordinary villagers, but also bureaucratic officials at various levels. Even as a project staff member working on his project activities, Schroeder (1999: xvi) professes that he "certainly held no monopoly on power"; both men and women were equally involved in "political maneuvers". This was true in my field trips.

The intertwined power hierarchies of gender, age, class and other social identities were complexly and even contradictorily woven into the relationships between me—a female ethnographer—and my male and female subjects. The triangular relations among ordinary folks, village officials and me, in many senses, significantly shaped what I did and observed as well as how I was perceived during the fieldwork. As indigenous feminist Hsiung experienced in her fieldwork in Taiwan's factories, I was similarly "seen, treated and approached simultaneously as an insider and outsider" (1996:5) and multiple identities played a part in shaping my insider/outsider status. Description of multiple power relationships, therefore, could provide a contextual framework in which the feminist researcher could explore how power structures were constructed and contested through everyday interactions between the dominator and the dominated (Hsiung, 1996: 8-9).

Privileged with the consent as well as direct introduction of the township Party secretary, and accompanied by the director of Qi Women's Federation, my entry into the community went smoothly without great obstacles. However reluctant village officials might be about my presence, they did not question it directly in front of the officials from the higher levels. This way of entrance into the community had an implication for my encounters with village officials. From the very beginning, the village Party secretary did not show me great enthusiasm and friendly cooperation. From our first few encounters, I was quickly introduced to bureaucratic state powers and the power of their agents. The village officials[1] exercised their power through refusing my access to village records. It proved always a challenge for me to obtain

1 I do not mean all current and former cadres were unfriendly. The village women's director, along with a few recently retired village leaders, virtually were quite helpful, who viewed and recounted village affairs from the vantage point of their former posts, and thereby provided valuable insights into the official viewpoints.

village data from them, with the exception of the Family Planning Roster kept by the women's director.[1] My requirements were regularly rejected under various pretexts. I was told that all relevant village records were kept in the hands of the accountant, yet no accountant was available in the village.[2] Yet I seldom pushed them too hard to avoid jeopardizing my relationships with them, and consequently the study itself.

It was understandable why village cadres deliberately hid information. As is well known, direct bureaucrats in China tended to warp any unfavorable figure. Greater Ao Village was trapped in severe debt, and thus the antagonism between ordinary folks and village cadres dominated village life, which added additional complexity to the political characters of this ethnographic research. As a sympathetic outsider, sometimes I could hardly help questioning village cadres for the wrong things done. They surely did not like me to know or expose their "dark sides," individually or collectively, particularly because they all knew I had good connections with higher authorities. As a result, they always responded by correcting my "false" impressions or views. Several current and former cadres confronted me, "Who will read your dissertation?" "Will you submit it to the Chinese Government?" "The village matters are too complicated to comprehend in such a short time"; "What ordinary people have told you is often not true at all."

This frustrating fact challenged me to turn to building good rapport with some officials at the township and county levels. It was true, as many residents put it, "it

1 Fortunately, I was able to gain access to the Family Planning Roster via the women's director. Similar to the Household Register (see Judd, 1994:173 for the contents of it), the Family Planning Roster contained a host of data on individual villagers and their households, including the household head, name, sex, year of birth and death, ethnicity, education, marital status, year of marriage, numbers of children, native place of birth, family planning measures, and so forth. What distinguished it from the Household Register was that it contained the newest information about birth and death, and some of long-absent migrants, whereas the Household Register would have been valid for a period of twenty years since its initial construction, and it did not update its information very often. In addition, it had no information about migration. In Greater Yangzi Village, the Household Register held by individual households or the copy kept by the village committee was issued on 31 December 1988 and updated on 6 October1996. For this reason, the Family Planning Roster functioned as the foundation of decision-making by village officials.

2 To prevent severe village corruption, a new policy was issued by the county government, for a village under 1700 populations, no village accountant would be assigned, and village officials were supposed to render their accounts to township accountants.

is far easier to deal with higher officers than with lower ones." Generally, I gained easy access to certain information from township officials, which was enhanced partly by my comparatively high prestige as a doctoral student in the United States. A few cadres liked to talk with me about the larger outside world. In the Qi Archive Bureau, the staff member allowed me access to the documentary materials as I requested. Most of them were women, they told me that they could understand how hard it was for a woman to be far away from her own family to do research in a poor community.

My connections with the director of Qi Women's Federation and other county authorities gave me much power and authority inside the community and at the township and county levels. During my presence in the village, no restriction was imposed directly upon me. I had the liberty to visit and interact with any resident at my will without any intervention from cadres, which contrasted sharply with what foreign researchers encountered in rural China. Many foreign researchers mentioned they were always steered toward wealthier places or households. In practice, I myself had such experiences previously when I conducted research in Yunnan and Sichuan provinces. In all the communities studied, even when poor women's participation was especially highlighted, some relatively literate, young or not so poor residents were usually selected by village leaders to attend the focus groups. This proved to run the risk of recording certain dominant perspectives while neglecting the voices of the real poor (Hu, 2002). In this sense, my insider's position permitted me to observe something that foreign researchers might not.

On my first research trip, the more people I came in contact with, the more it became clear to me that there were remarkably antagonistic relations and tensions between cadres and ordinary villagers. My "thick" involvement, coupled with the interactions with both sides, allowed me to perceive directly community-level politics, the operation of power at the grassroots, as well as how officials' powers were challenged and contested in everyday life in a "natural" setting. Many adult people whom I encountered for the first time, regardless of sex, voluntarily expressed their dissatisfaction towards corruption, real or alleged, and the injustices associated with the mass conservation project. At the outset, their discontent and complaints often dominated our conversations, they did so probably to hope I could publicize their plights or expose the corruption of village officials openly, or probably just to take the opportunity to vent their dissatisfaction.

This was sharply contrasted with what I encountered in Yunnan and Sichuan provinces. As Davis Mosse (1994) puts it, when group or collective activities involved influential outsiders, the community tended to exhibit particular solidarity. Indeed, when I visited some communities as a national gender specialist, villagers often expressed their collective needs and priorities rather than their own. In other words, they understood what they expressed would have implications for the future of the community. Local leaders tried to manipulate us for economic advantages as well. This helped explain when some sensitive questions were asked, even those concerning the discrimination against women, residents tended to point out that such things did not exist in their villages, or those things only happened in the past. In a Yunnan village, a Party secretary constantly told his fellow villagers, "This cannot be said and that cannot be mentioned." We certainly could not mistake it for an absence of conflicts and even struggles within the community.

But in Ao Village, no longer were villagers instructed by cadres on how to answer questions "correctly" to outsiders, and village cadres themselves were not afraid of losing their reputation capital for their misbehavior. As the inhabitants unanimously claimed, the village was in a state of disunity, seeming to be "a sheet of loose sand" (*yi pan san sha*).

In contrast to village officials' subtle reactions to my presence, as with my host and hostess, ordinary villagers generously welcomed me into their home and community, showing great curiosity and hospitality. Since there was no formal introduction, it took some time for me to get familiar with most of the inhabitants in the neighborhood. My initial exposure to Ao Village sparked many discussions. Throughout my stay, many residents stopped by for a chat. Until now, I was still full of the memories of the interesting interactions with local men and women. Working as an ethnographer, I was keenly aware of my own positionalities.

My multiple identities—female gender, age and marriage status—were useful for an affinity with the residents, while my class, urban origin, educational performance and other factors that might isolate me from them provoked a great deal of curiosity, admiration and questions throughout the course of my fieldwork. At an initial stage, many were curious about what I told them about my personal life in Beijing and my experiences in the United States. One day, a forty-three year old woman curiously asked me, "Do you take planes to the US?" she added immediately, "You must laugh at me for asking such a stupid question. I had never even seen a train before my son married into a village near a railway station." On another occasion, a woman said to me, "Even your body smells sweet. Look at our dusty faces, we live just like small ants." A girl once told me when her mother knew I was only one year older than her, she felt so upset and refused to speak for a whole night. Some expressed their admiration for my education and my good memory. They were struck by the fact that I knew the names of most adult men and women, for which they themselves actually never knew.[1] My familiarity with villagers' names served to bring our relations close.

As I got familiar with various residents, the forms of my address were subject to change in different contexts. I was first treated as a visiting stranger. As the project proceeded, they inquired with more questions about my research: "Why do you choose to come to this poor village?" "What do you want to look at?" "What is useful to know about our village and our lives?" I am often called by elders as *lao* Hu (old Hu) or *xiao* Hu (little Hu). People younger than me addressed me as elder sister (*da jie*). Most of the time, I was referred to as teacher Hu or Dr. Hu. Little boys or girls called me *yi* (mother's younger sister) or *gu* (father's sister). When I talked privately with a women almost the same age as me, they sometimes might say to let us *jie liang* (between two sisters) have a good chat with each other. On numerous occasions, an elder woman would say to let us *niang liang* (between mother and daughter) have a good talk. A boy of eleven years old lost his mother due to a traffic incident, since I was very sympathetic to his case; his grandmother once asked whether I could adopt the boy as a godson. Ostensibly, my inside/outside status was interwoven into these addresses and interactions.

There were a variety of responses among residents to my power, resources, and assistance. Although I identified myself as a PhD candidate at a US university and a former researcher working in the All China Women's Federation, I was variously treated as a reporter, a writer, a teacher, or even a "big official" from Beijing. On numerous occasions, villagers approached me to seek my help and advice. In their eyes, I understood the law and state policies so that I could help them with their problems such as agricultural taxes, retirement pensions, children's education, material compensation and so forth. Some hoped that I could help them to find a job in Beijing in the future, while others wished I would bring funding and money into

1 As elsewhere, married women in the village were essentially nameless. Except for some native women, adult women were known in reference or were addressed by the kinship terms such as "mother or wives of so-and-so." For an excellent discussion about it, see Rubie Watson (1986).

the community.

In this peasant community, I found that my married status and age of over forty mattered in specific ways, whereas my middle-class status was a limitation as well as strength. From the perspectives of the locals, people in their forties were quite "old." who would soon become grandparents, as most young men and women were usually betrothed around twenty years of age. As a local saying goes, "If someone is forty years old, it marks one day has already passed the noon" (*ren guo si shi ri guo wu*). In this circumstance, my gender identity was relegated to a less important position, which otherwise should have implications for a study in rural Chinese society. I could interact with anyone of the opposite sex of all ages on household visits with no fear of causing awkward situations.

Some residents came over merely to ask me to take photos for them. I was always happy to do so since this was the only way that I could "help" them temporarily. Apart from the identity card, many elderly people had never taken any other picture in their whole life. One day, I went with a group of elder people to collect a kind of shrub seeds; I took several pictures for them while they were getting together. After I brought back the pictures from Beijing and gave each of them a copy, they were all so excited. One woman said to me, "We have never been to Beijing, it's great our pictures have been there." On several occasions, male villagers required me to take pictures for them to use as "evidence." I took many pictures for the inhabitants, as they required. Several women commented, "You are staying in the village to 'serve the people'."[1]Before my departure, many of my friends requested, "Could you give us the photos of your family? When we miss you, we can see them."

As ethnographic interactions progressed, I developed deep friendships with many inhabitants. I was treated to dinner in my honor in many households and I consistently enjoyed certain privileges. For example, whenever I rode their livestock-drawn carts or motorized tricycle, they always gave me a cushion to sit on or reserved a "best seat" for me. On cold winter days, when I paid a visit in their home, I was often urged to sit at the head of the *kang*. My vulnerability as an outside visitor was identified. Even if I took a flashlight with me, many people always accompanied me all the way to the door of my host's house. I was told that my multiple arrivals and departures caused disappointments among them. Toward the

1 This was one of Chairman Mao's quotations, which was commonly used in the past.

end of my fieldwork in 2003, many asked, "Will you come here again?" "We will miss you if you leave"; "When will you come back next year?" In my 2004 revisit, an elder woman told me, "I really missed you after you left. If I had ever gone to school, I would have written to you."

A few of them volunteered to help me with my research. I remembered, one afternoon, the oldest resident in the village, a man of eighty-two years old, came over to my host's house. He told me that he had thought over several days before stopping by. He just could not eat my candies and biscuits without any reciprocity, and he wished to help me to win a "writing prize". He was a shepherd for over half a century, and was unable to see clearly because of long exposure to the weather. In the end, he sang a couple of pastoral songs, and was so pleased that I had a "treasure" (tape recorder) to record what he had sung. My favorite time was the numerous hours when we were relaxing on the warm *kang*, with villagers sharing with me their lives and memories, and I sharing with them the faraway affairs of the outside world.

In this face-to-face peasant society, people long settled into the village community, they knew each other quite well through an efficient mouth-to-mouth communication network. At a later stage, the formal guarantee of confidentiality on my part was always met with responses like: "I don't have any privacy"; "I tell you as it is"; "My life is no secret"; "Who does not know whom?" and "Nobody's life is a secret". As time went on, we touched on more sensitive topics such as resource or domestic conflicts. As a sympathetic and patient listener, I was sometimes treated as "*zi jia ren*", or one's own family members. Several times, a newly married ex-widow told me with tears in her eyes about her conflicts with her husband's younger brother.

Although I was working very hard on my part on the project, yet from the perspective of some natives, I enjoyed a great deal of leisure time, "Since you have nothing to do, just sit for more time," they always suggested. One afternoon, I came across a woman in her early fifties on a village path. After talking for about 20 minutes, I knew so much of her life stories. In the end, she said frankly, "We are not familiar with each other, while we do not talk like strangers"(*ren sheng hua bu sheng*). After we separated, she returned and added, "Mountains will never meet with each other, but people do." Some women were so articulate that I just could not interrupt them, and thereby sometimes had to listen to whatever things they told me.

Subtle or unexpected misunderstandings occurred as well. One day, when a group of women sat on the *kang* for a chat, one woman mentioned another woman helped her a lot by borrowing some money with relatively low interest for her outside the village. An expression of worry suddenly shown on the face of the mentioned helper. I later learned that the helper herself was actually a moneylender. Perhaps money lending in her mind was an illegal practice. Probably she was afraid she would not receive the relief from the village committee if her "secret" leaked. Her family was one of the poorest households in the village, and occasionally received something like sacks of grain or old clothes donated by urban residents via the village government. For some time after that, she always issued uncomfortable greetings to me. This example was a clear reminder of the importance of understanding local specificity.

In short, the site selection as well as ethnographic fieldwork was filled with politically charged events. My multiple identities played a significant part in shaping my insider-outsider status, which in turn, profoundly shaped my field research. As mirrored in many other ethnographic reports (Hsiung, 1996; Ong, 1987; Tsing, 1993), the ethnographic gaze was never neutral and value-free. Instead, it was embedded in asymmetrical power relationships among village cadres, higher-level officials, ordinary villagers and me. In the context of fluid powerfulness and powerlessness at the grassroots, my work with local women and men profoundly shaped my understanding of indigenous people's lives and their relations with the natural environment—past and current environmental practices, kin networks, marriage patterns and conjugal relations, livelihood strategies, everyday resistance and resource struggles. I could not control and manipulate their information, because they had their own choice whether or not tell their stories, or what kinds of stories to tell. In this sense, as Ong (1995) hinted, even ordinary villagers were not merely powerless.

Being acutely aware of this point, throughout the dissertation I interwove the views of local men and women with those of my own representations, making the agency and subjectivity of social actors central to the explanation of NRM and environmental changes.

Methodology

To explore the topic of gender, NRM and environmental changes in a rural community in the context of a changing political economy, both qualitative and quantitative paradigms were used in my ethnographic fieldwork in 2003-2004: participant observations, informal conversations, in-depth interviews, oral histories, life stories, household census and survey, archival materials, and local government statistics and documents. A total of six months' field research was carried out in Ao Village from late April to December 2003. To further catch up on new changes, I made a short return trip between September and October in 2004. To live among villagers physically for a prolonged period of time gave me the advantage of looking at everyday interactions in a rural Chinese society from within.

Before I knew the community very well, I primarily relied on informal, open-ended conversation. Some initial interviews were intended to yield general information about gender regimes and environmental changes. After living at the site for some time, more focused, open-ended interviews were conducted with specific persons who were believed to have specialized knowledge on some particular topics under investigation. Since I was denied access to the written statistics on village records, a demographic and economic census of the whole village was carried out from September to November in 2003 to collect structured data. A second semi-structured survey was conducted in 2004, and 30 random households with at least a married couple were interviewed. Through oral histories and life stories, I particularly used the lens of women's lived experiences to analyze the intersections of gender, the environment and development. As Tsing (1993:231) pointed out rightly, "Stories of individuals have been very helpful in theoretical projects that point to sites of exclusion, struggle, and creativity beyond the scope of dominant discourses."

The ethnographic presence, coupled with the consistent encounters with villagers through participation in their daily lives, provided me with a greater chance to understand the grassroots' insights into the trajectory and rich reality of gender-environmental interactions. During my stay in the village, I was constantly reminded that only to live among locals for extended periods of time could one learn the truth about what exactly occurred at the local level. The intensive ethnographic interaction enabled me to weave men's and women's critical narratives into my own interpretations.

Departing from most studies on Inner Mongolia, the present study explores the historical processes as well as the on-going reality by combining both 'vertical' and 'horizontal' processes. A long time framework was vital in understanding the trajectory of environmental changes, which after all, were continuous and accumulative. From a gender perspective, this project examined the history of NRM and environmental transformations in a peasant community from the pre-Liberation period through the long collective era, and into the post-reform era, spanning over half a century, yet it focused on comparing the collective and post-reform periods.

Meanwhile, the present study highlights day-to-day gender-environment dynamics that were occurring at the local level in 2003. By directly participating and observing the daily routines of local inhabitants, I was able to gain an intimate view of their sufferings, strengths, and "weapons of the weaker" (Scott, 1985) in terms of access to and control over natural resources. In particular, I explored the problems and conflicts in the community that I might otherwise have never known without an interactive experience and ethnographic study. By incorporating both 'vertical' and 'horizontal' aspects, the study combined both micro (individual, household and community) and macro (county, region and nation) scales in a broader historical and global context.

The household-level demographic and economic census allowed for a systematic study of each resident household in the community. Most residents were visited and interviewed in their homes by using structured and unstructured questions, which mainly covered the following topics: demographic characteristics of the household members such as age, gender, formal education, on-farm and off-farm work, sources of income, the size of farmland, woodland and pastureland holding, the area of house and courtyard, heads of various livestock, crop area and species. I also relied on the official Family Planning Roster to choose a random sample of 30 households for interviews. The topics involved gender division of labor, the pattern of intra-household decision-making, inter-household cooperation, previous and current resource conservation practices, determinants of environmental changes, chemical fertilizer application, and incomes and expenditures. Many residents were interviewed repeatedly to probe relevant questions further.

During the field research, I used a tape recorder occasionally. I took notes sometimes on the spot, and sometimes at night from what I learned during the day. Respondents were assured of confidentiality. The oral histories, especially life histories of both men and women were collected. The archival materials collected contained vivid narrative information, including various work summaries, memos to superiors, proceedings of local meetings and so on. My research, undoubtedly, was constrained by not living in the community over the entire agricultural year. In addition, I initially assumed that the bias of my presence could be minimized through residing in a given household continuously for a relatively long time, yet one of its disadvantages was that if certain residents did not have good relations with my host family, they might treat me with suspicion as well. Fortunately, my host family basically had good relations with their neighbors and relatives.

The discrepancy of data was a challenge that I encountered constantly in the field. Villagers' memories were sometimes unreliable, not only was what they said occasionally different from the actual situations, as evidenced by interviewing divergent people, but also they offered different versions for the same thing. I was even more puzzled by local government reports and statistics. From the very outset, I realized that official data at various levels was unreliably twisted, either being exaggerated or reduced. This was almost an "open secret"[1] in rural China, especially in those radical years such as the Great Leap Forward and the Cultural Revolution. The triangulation of multiple methods allowed me to crosscheck various figures and testimonies. Throughout the text, I problematize some dubious statistics and obvious inconsistencies.

1 One township official once told me, since Aohan was a state-designated poverty county, the statistics figures at various levels were sometimes constructed to fit the criteria of poverty.

Chapter Three

The Setting: Land and Its People

A Peasant Community in Northeastern China

A narrow, rugged village road stretched out zigzag for about 3 kilometers from the residential area to the highway cutting through the eastern edge of Ao Village, where I sometimes took the bzus to the county town. This made it somewhat more isolated than those communities located along the highway. I went along this village road again and again during my stay in the village. Sometimes I took a taxi, or sat on animal-drawn carts, and sometimes I walked by myself. Ao Village was located in a place north of the Great Wall in eastern Inner Mongolia. It was 4 kilometers away from Lan Township under which Ao Village was administered and approximately 100 kilometers east of the Chifeng City (the seat of Chifeng Prefecture) in Inner Mongolia.

Figure 3.1 the Map of China, Inner Mongolia, Chifeng City

Figure 3.2 the Map of Chifeng Prefecture, Aohan Qi and Lan Township

The Chifeng Prefecture-formerly known as *Zhaowuda Meng*—was located in eastern Inner Mongolia, one of the five provincial-level Minority Autonomous Regions in China. *Meng and Qi,* literally means league and banner, were the Mongolian terms used for the prefecture and county, respectively, in Inner Mongolia.[1] Aohan—a Mongolian name—literally means "*lao da*" or the eldest child. This name has been used since the seventeenth century in the Qing Dynasty (1644-1911). Bordered by three counties in Liaoning province to the south, Aohan was historically closely connected to this neighboring province. A railway station in a market town connected Aohan to some large cities such as Shenyang and Dalian in Liaoning province, as well as Beijing located 560 kilometers away. Aohan and its vicinity was one of the major sources of the sandstorms affecting Beijing at the turn of the century. The geographic proximity to these big cities rendered Aohan ecologically significant in north China.

Situated in a semiarid region, Aohan has a temperate continental climate with

1 In the Qing Dynasty, the league-banner was the basic administrative, economic and military unit under a feudal-like system. For details about its origin and evolution, see Jagchid and Hyer (1979).

extremes in temperature. The winter (from November to April) is cold, with the lowest extreme temperature reaching 30.9 centigrade degrees below zero. The summer (from July to September) is hot and short, with the highest extreme temperature being 39.9 centigrade degrees. The average yearly temperature is about 7.5 degrees centigrade. The spring is arid and windy, and frost comes early in the autumn. The frost-free period ranges from 130-143 days. Pan evaporation is 2000-2600 mm, 6-8 times that of precipitation, with the average annual rainfall ranging from 310mm-460mm. In addition, over two thirds of the total precipitation occurs between July and August. Almost all growth of vegetation takes place during the period from May to September. In Ao Village, the short growing season means all land is singly cropped, which ostensibly precludes the same multiple cropping pattern and thus intensive agriculture that occurs in many other areas of rural China.

Aohan was a state-designated poverty county in 2003. Like most village communities in west China, agriculture dominated its local economy. Although Inner Mongolia was best known as a pastoral area, Aohan was basically an agropastoral area. It was sometimes referred to as a semi-agricultural and semi-pastoral region. Only one out of its 29 townships (*xiang zhen*) was a purely pastoral region. The increasingly higher percentage of livestock production since the late 1990s could be attributed to the successive droughts sweeping the region. According to official data, the net per capita income among farmers and pastoralists in Aohan was 1541RMB in 2003, ranked the last among 12 districts/counties in Chifeng Prefecture (on average 2056RMB), much lower than 2284RMB in Inner Mongolia and 2622RMB in the nation as a whole (ASB, 2004:14). The gross output of agriculture and industry was, respectively, 66.8 and 33.2 percent in 2003. Historically, the gross output of crops was higher than livestock.

Rapid population growth in the county resulted in heavy, if not extreme, pressure on the land. According to official data, its population jumped from 0.25 million in 1949 to 0.587 million in late 2003, a 134.8 percent increase. Around 90.7 percent of its total population was rural. Meanwhile, the per capita farmland was reduced from 11.36 *mu* in 1949 to 4.29 *mu* in 2003, a 164.8 percent reduction. In the last two decades, much of its land was devoted to conservation purposes such as alfalfa and trees. However, the real situation of both the resident population and cropland access was far more complex in different localities, as demonstrated by the case of Ao Village.

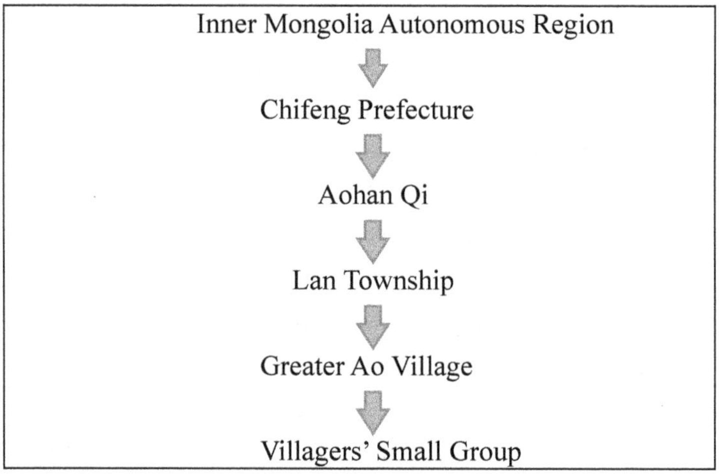

Figure 3.3 Administrative Structure

As shown in figure 3.3, the political structure of China was broken up into many levels. The administrative levels below the central state include provincial/city/autonomous region, prefecture/municipal, county, township, administrative village (*xing zheng cun*) and villagers' small groups (*cun min xiao zu*). Strictly speaking, the township, administrative village, and villagers' small group belong to the rural collectives,[1] which were equivalent, respectively, to the people's commune (*ren min gong she*), the production brigade (*da dui*) and the production team (*sheng chan dui*) during the collective period from the 1950s-1970s. Despite the demise of the people's commune over twenty years earlier, many villagers still habitually called themselves "we commune members" (*wo men she yuan*).

Greater Ao Village[2]—one of the 12 administrative villages under the jurisdiction of Lan Township—was composed of four dispersed hamlets widely called "natural villages" in China.[3] There were eight official villagers' small groups in Greater Ao

1 The township and administrative village shared some government functions. The term of 'local government" referred mainly to these two levels throughout this dissertation.

2 Greater Ao Village was amalgamated with an adjacent village—during the land reform, and they separated in 1961.

3 "Natural villages" (*zi ran cun*) were isolated from each other due to disruptive terrains. In many localities, several geographically scattered natural villages made up an administrative village, which was tended to highlight the political rather than spatial location. In other localities, as Judd (1994) observed in Shandong province, a single natural village might constitute an administrative village.

Village.[1] The four groups in Ao Village were amalgamated into two in 2000 to "save administrative expenditure": with the west group (formerly Team One and Team Two) occupying the west village and the east group (formerly Team Three and Team Four) the east village.

Selection of the Village Site

To justify why I singled out Ao Village as a case study site, it is necessary to look at the broader context of Greater Ao Village. To avoid confusion, I named the remaining three hamlets B, C and D, which were, respectively, 3, 4 and 3 kilometers away from Ao Village (see Figure 3.4). Hamlet D was located in close proximity to the highway. In contrast, it took almost an hour walking on a bad village road from Hamlet B to Ao Village to gain access to the highway. According to *The Greater Ao Village Economic Development Plan (2003-2005)* (GYV, 2003b),[2] by mid-2003, Greater Ao Village as a whole had a population of 1161 living in 312 households.[3]

Figure 3.4 the Map of Greater Ao Village and Its Constituent Hamlets

Although the four geographically separated hamlets shared some identifiable

1 The collective organization at the level of villagers' small groups existed nominally, which had had almost nothing except for the group leaders who were known locally as team leaders.

2 *The Greater Ao Village Economic Development Plan (2003-2005)* formulated by the village committee in June 2003 was based primarily upon estimation. Although most of the socio-economic data derived from the Plan were the estimated figures, it could basically reflect the official views of the situations in Great Ao Village and its hamlets. It gives us an idea of rough, if not real, situations.

3 *The Year-end Statistics Forms* (GYV, 2003a) produced by the village committee records 1239 persons in 323 households in Greater Ao Village.

commonalities such as policy environment, climate, or agricultural technology, they were distinguished from each other in many aspects: local history, livelihood strategy, development trajectory, access to agricultural infrastructure, and above all, natural resources base. Hamlet B and C were endowed with large patches of farmland and pastureland on more sandy soils. To make a comparison, the socio-economic profiles of each hamlet are tabulated below in table 3.1. Judging from the ratio of the gross output of crop vs. livestock farming, Ao Village and Hamlet B might be judged as a mixed crop and livestock economy in 2003. By comparison, Hamlet C had a clear dominance of livestock rearing, accounting for over two thirds of its agricultural production. Hamlet D was a small community with only 19 households, where herding was virtually nonexistent. In 2002, 17 out of its 19 households were engaged in raising meat chickens for an agribusiness company. This helps to explain why it had the highest per capita income. Each village apparently interacted with nature in different ways. With the availability of irrigated fields, Ao Village was once more prosperous than the remaining hamlets.With the decline of well irrigateel fields, but by 2003, it had lagged behind with the lowest per capita income in Greater Ao Village.

Table 3.1 Socioeconomic Profiles in Four Hamlets

Hamlets	Population (person)	Cultivated land (*mu*)	Livestock (head)	Net Per Capita Income (RMB)	Gross Yield Value of Crop vs. Animal [1] (%)	
Ao Village	547	2628	576	1423	52	48
Hamlet B	189	1034	801	1502	45	55
Hamlet C	350	1888	1350	1517	31	69
Hamlet D	75	340	46	1733	13	87

Source: *Greater Ao Village Economic Development Plan (2003-2005)* (GYV, 2003b).

Note: The Livestock gross output value includes the income from meat/laying chickens and pigs.

Field observations illustrated that all close-knit social networks and everyday interactions took place within the boundary of each hamlet. Historically, Ao Village, Hamlet B and C were originally occupied by different Mongol lineages. As any other multi-surname community, each village had its own lineage structure with a number of different surname groups. Residents in Ao Village linked themselves to other hamlets only on certain occasions such as events in mass conservation campaigns. Yet co-inhabitation played a key role in shaping their sense of identity. For the inhabitants in Ao Village, the residential area was their "own village" or *ying zi,* in local usage. Also noteworthy was that there was little intermarriage among these hamlets. As will be discussed in Chapter seven, the residents in Ao Village rarely intermarried with persons in the other three hamlets, nor did the remaining hamlets with each other.

For researchers of rural China, to cover an administrative village, undoubtedly, offers the most convenient channel to utilize available official data, as most village studies do, however, the aggregate information at the level of an administrative village does not necessarily reflect the reality in each of its hamlets. One can make a trade-off between an in-depth exploration of a single hamlet and a broader coverage of the administrative village as a whole. For a study of gender-environment dynamics in rural China, it is obviously misleading to treat the administrative village as a single rural locality. As far as natural resource use is concerned, Ao Village was worthy of a study in its own right. This site made it possible to systematically survey each household, and thus contributed to gaining a more nuanced understanding of the village. In this study, my scale of analysis focused on Ao Village, while referring to the remaining three hamlets wherever appropriate.

In Aohan as a whole, Ao Village was a poverty-stricken peasant[1]society. The village was poor by regional and national standards, but it was not so "deprived" as other west China communities that I visited in Yunnan and Sichuan provinces. Villagers derived their livelihoods predominantly from the soil, with a mix of subsistence and commercial crop-livestock farming, supplemented by seasonal wage labor on farm, migration or other off-farm work. *The Greater Ao Village Economic Development Plan (2003-2005)* (GYV, 2003b) provides a rough official idea of the village economy. It offers the percentage of the expected income from various sectors in Ao Village in 2003 as follows: crop (38.1 percent), livestock[2] (35), forage crop (9.2), forestry (0.7), migrant laborer (10.2), industry, commerce and transportation services (3.9), and others (2.9). It demonstrated that households in Ao

1 Here, I reserve the pejorative term peasant (*nong min*), which was a label frequently used by local inhabitants in their everyday lives. Quite often, they added an "old" (*lao*) before the peasant. They often employed the "old peasants" to distinguish themselves from the *zhi gong* such as teachers and workers or the *cheng li ren*—the urban folk. For a detailed discussion about this concept as a metaphor of the disadvantaged status of peasants, see Myron Cohen (1993) "Cultural and Political Inventions in Modern China: The Case of the Chinese 'Peasant'," *Daedalus* Vol. 122. No.2. This official status still utilized in 2003 did not necessarily indicate a person's actual place of residence or occupation.

2 The livestock industry included the raising of meat and egg-laying chickens and pigs.

Village depended predominantly upon the natural world for subsistence and cash.

Ao Village lay under a chain of four hills. The highest hill within its boundary was about 700 meters above sea level. Seen at a distance, the land appeared relatively flat, in contrast to rugged mountainous terrain in Yunnan and Sichuan Provinces. The surrounding landscape of the village was a matrix of pastureland, shrubland, cropland, woodland, gullies and hills. The settlement was surrounded by semi-sand and semi-soil croplands to the north and east. According to knowledgeable villagers, about two fifths of its territory was sandy, laying primarily in the southern and western parts. A large gully lay to the south of the settlement, stretching in a rough east-west direction. A newly paved path spanned the large gully for about 50 meters, connecting the settlement to a large patch of pastureland in the south. On the right side of the path lay a reservoir; on its left side, not far away from the reservoir was a huge pit, almost the same size as the reservoir. Above it there stood a brick kiln. Clay was dug from this site and fired into bricks when a brick factory operated there from 1994-2000. Along both sides of the large gully, immense stretches of land were punctuated by a kind of sand-fixing shrub, locally called *ning tiao*.

Ao Village was a beautiful place for me. Even poverty could not totally hide its natural beauty. Different plants occupied divergent ecological niches. Large patches of fields were cropped with both cash and subsistence crops: corn, millet, sorghum, rice, sunflower, soybean, sesame and so forth. The scenery changed over each season. In the summer, seen from a distance, the settlement seemed to be punctuated by green trees. The most common trees included poplar, apricot and elm, which were mainly dotted in certain localities. With the change of the season, a large patch of alfalfa turned from green, to purple, and then to dark brown.

As shown in figure 3.5, there was a dense settlement in the interior of the village. Within the memory of senior generation, there were two scattered dwelling clusters within the settlement, with one occupying the east village and another the west village. The middle section so densely settled in 2003 was free from habitation. The walled courtyards-mostly attached to each other with only a few separated from the rest-lined the sandy streets. Three basically parallel streets stretched from east to west for approximately one kilometer;[1] They were crossed by a single rugged road stretching from the north to south. This road divided the neighborhood geographically in half. In local usage, the east village was known as "*dong ying*

1 Strictly speaking, the streets are not exactly in east-west direction.

zi" and the west village as "*xi ying zi*". Even for an outside observer, there was a distinguishable east-west separation in intra-community relations.

The village headquarters lay on the east-west main street, which was approximately the geographic center of the community. Just opposite the north-south road, there stood a grocery store and a small grain-processing mill. There was an old pool table in front of the store. Posters were sometimes put on the outside wall. The stock on the display shelves was not impressive for an urban individual. Men and women, old and young, often came here to buy daily necessities; a group of men always stayed here to chat, smoke, drink wine or beer, exchange news and rumors, or watch TV at night, especially during the slack season. This masculinized public space was, in a sense, the heart of the community'ssocial life. Since there were no grocery stores and mills in the other three hamlets, their residents sometimes came here to process their grains.

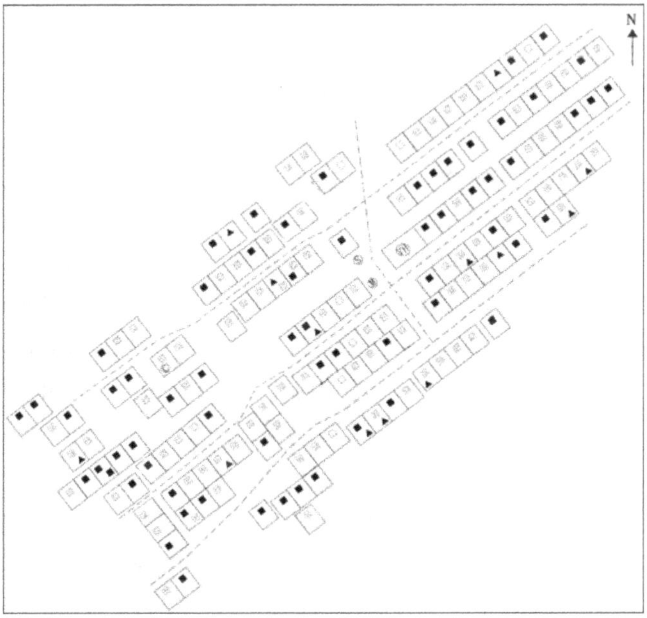

Figure 3.5 Streets and Houses in the Residential Area

Source: 2003 field observation and interviews

Note: □ courtyard
mud house
mud-brick house
■ brick house
□ abandoned house
▲ undecorated house (means a framework without ceiling, windows or even a door)

----- motorable street and road
VH: Village Headquarters
M: Mill
C: Clinic
S: Store

The figure shows a general layout of the houses and streets. The actual size, shape, and conditions of the courtyard and that of houses were much more complex, and certainly were not neatly arranged as the map shows.[1] The courtyard ranged from 0.5-4.0 *mu*. During the collective period, the houses were mostly built of mud with thatch. Since the last few years of collectivization, the thatched roofs gave way to tiled ones. In the early 1980s, a few rich households used some bricks in the front wall of their houses. Following the operation of a brick factory in Ao Village in 1994, the construction of new homes and renovation of old ones boomed, which somewhat changed the landscape of the neighborhood. In 2003, most villagers lived in mud-brick or pure brick houses. Some people lived in the principal house, while others lived in the wing house before they could afford a principal house. Almost all principal houses, without any exception, were not directly facing the south, but instead faced slightly towards a southeastern direction so as to let in as much sunshine as possible.

All households had the built-in brick bed, called the *kang,* widely used in the countryside in northern China. The platform of 0.70-0.80 meters in height, 4.5 meters in length and 2 meters in width, occupied almost half of my host's main room.[2] The *kang* had multiple functions: to sit, eat and chat on it during the day, and to unroll their mats to sleep at night. The *kang* was a femininized site of social and family activities. For a woman like *da sao* Song Ling, who seldom dropped around, she spent most of her time on the *kang* doing something or watching TV during the slack agricultural season. Zhang Hualan came to my host's family for a visit almost every day, especially at night. She always sat on the *kang* to chat with Song Ling. In contrast, men had more widely reaching activity areas beyond the house. During the winter season, Hong Xiang was busy with hunting, while Liu Xing continued his transportation services. Two big brick ovens built on the concrete floor in the cooking area were connected to the *kang*. When cooking food on the stove, the heat

---

1 For example, my host's courtyard is recorded as 884.95 square meters or 1.33 *mu* by the *Certificate of House Ownership* issued by the Qi Bureau of Land Management in 1999. The principal house totaled 90 square meters. The east wing served as a stock shed and the rest of it functioned as a storage room for grains. The west wing was used for agricultural tools and fodders. Inside the principal house, there were two main rooms, which were the all-purpose space, serving as the living room, bedroom, dining room or many other purposes.

2 Only some newly married young couples have modern beds.

of a fire went directly to the *kang*. In this part of China, residents long relied on the *kang* for warmth in the long unbearably cold winter. The heating of *kang* usually cost a large quantity of firewood, which once imposed enormous pressures on the vulnerable local ecology as well as huge labor burdens on village women. In what follows, I turn to certain aspects of the social and environmental dynamics in the village.

A Village in Flux: The Intersections of Class, Gender And Ethnicity

Ao Village could be characterized as an ethnic mosaic, with a high concentration of ethnic minority Mongols, the numerically largest ethnic minority group in Inner Mongolia. This became more apparent when looking at the statistics. In 2003, there were 134 Mongols residing in 43 households, accounting for 23.8 percent of the total population of 564 persons and making up 26.7 percent of the 161 households, a percentage much higher than the overall ethnic compositions of Lan Township, Aohan Qi and China as a whole.[1]Other non-Han minority populations included 10 Hui Muslim Chinese living in three households and a married-in woman of Manchu. Han Chinese comprised 73.9 percent of the village population. The distinctions made in the local dialect were the Han people (*han min*), Mongol people (*meng min*) and Hui people (*hui min*).[2] This helped to explain why Ao Village was often recognized as an ethnic minority village.

The Birth of a Mongol Village

Ao Village could trace its origin to a male Mongolian founder, who settled in the village during the emperor Qianlong (1736-1795) of the Qing Dynasty (1644-1911) (AQPG, 1987). The village name was a Mongolian name, which was originally

1 Mongols constituted a tiny fraction of Aohan population ever since the Liberation. As early as 1949, Han Chinese accounted for 97.2%, and Mongols 2.39%. Due to the implementation of ethnic minority policies, by 2003, Mongols had increased to 4.67%. The Lan Township was the third largest Mongol settlement in the county, with 12% of its population being Mongols (ASB, 2004). According to China's Fifth Population Census (2000), 91.59 percent of its 1.295 billion people were identified as ethnic Han, and the remaining 8.41 percent consisted of ethnic minorities. There were fifty-five officially recognized ethnic minority groups residing within the Chinese territory. In Inner Mongolia, approximately 84% of the total population was Han Chinese, as against over 15 percent of the population being Mongols.

2 There were nine Mongolian surname groups and 36 Mongolian households with a household head of Mongol. In Lan Township, there were a total of 12 Hui people and thus they were the "real" ethnic minority from local perspectives.

named after an imperial title in the Qing Dynasty.[1] This indicates that the pioneering Mongols settled in this place for over 200 years. There existed divergent legends of the ancestral origin. Some elder men maintained that the founder came from Hohhot, Inner Mongolia, with his family, while others claimed he was formerly a prefecture magistrate in Jinan, Shandong province. He came here by himself and married a Mongolian woman and later became a Mongol himself. Since no genealogical record was available, no one knew exactly what happened.

The descendants of this same ancestor remained the largest Mongolian lineage in the village. They were often called by local people as "the oldest native settler" *(lao di hu)*. According to the eldest man of seventy years old from this clan, at least 6-7 generations of his ancestors were buried in a site to the west of the settlement. Assuming 20 years for a generation, it attested to the fact that the original inhabitants settled into the place about 200 years ago. The lineage reached its peak at the time of this man's grandfather, having as many as 50-60 persons living in a big extended family. After the death of his grandfather, the family was divided and its fortune began to wane. Local bandits repeatedly made off with the lineage's property through means such as direct attack or kidnap for ransom.[2] This man's father was a heavy gambler and lost almost all his land before Liberation. His family was ironically classified as a poor peasant during the land reform, two of his uncles were assigned as rich peasants, but no one was labeled a landlord in this lineage.

The second lineage settled in the village was also a Mongolian lineage. It was said the original settler ancestor originally came here as a daughter-in-law of the first lineage. There were some legends about the conflicts and cooperation between these two clans. One well-known doctor from this lineage later became a landlord. The other two Mongolian landlord households resided in the village over one hundred years, arriving a little bit earlier than the first group of Han Chinese. The Mongolian lineages were mostly indigenous to the region.

Han Migration and the Onset of Environmental Change

Han inhabitants were the latecomers with a relatively short history of less than

1 Hamlet B was founded by a Mongol at the period of the emperor Xianfeng (1851-1861) of the Qing Dynasty. Hamlet C was founded at almost the same time as Hamlet B by another Mongol. Hamlet D was created in 1963 (AQPG, 1987).

2 Elder residents mentioned that in the pre-Liberation years, the bandits in the region occasionally kidnapped the richer for ransom.

a hundred years of settlement in Ao Village. The Han settlers primarily came from Shandong province. My own survey indicated that 108 out of 123 Han households could trace their origins to Shandong province, a place of dense population and intensive agriculture. The rest of the Han households came from a few neighboring provinces such as Liaoning, Hebei or Tianjin. About eight Han households moved into the community before the Liberation, followed by some who came here in the early 1950s to "escape famines" (*tao huang*) in their native villages. In some cases, husband and wife came together. In others, men came first and then brought their families or married local women of Han Chinese descent. As we shall see below, the influx of Han Chinese was not a distinctive history of Ao Village, but a regionally shared characteristic.

The massive influx of Han Chinese into Inner Mongolia has deep historical roots.[1] Inner Mongolia is located in a border area of great strategic importance. In the nineteenth century, Russia moved eastward, posing a severe threat to China's frontier areas. Meanwhile, many Chinese peasants in the interior of China lost their lands and livelihoods because of natural disasters and famines. For the purpose of strengthening border protection, the Qing state launched a policy called "borrowing the land to support the people" (*jie di yang min*), actively encouraging the migration of Han farmers into the Mongolian frontier. Aohan was not a real frontier in terms of its geographic location, yet it experienced a historical process of intensive influx of Han Chinese since the early nineteenth century. During one of emperor Kangxi's (1654-1722) expeditions outside the Great Wall, he found the land in Aohan very fertile. From that time onwards, Han farmers were actively encouraged to pour into this thinly populated area.

Environmental conflicts in the region have long been related to ethnic divisions. Ever since Han migrants ventured into the Mongolian land, Mongol-Han confrontations over natural resources have occurred. The conflicts between land-owning Mongolian elites and poor Han peasants are well documented in *A History of Lan Township Development* (LTPC, 1960).

Here is one such example: the Mongolian ruling class occupied large patches of fertile land and allowed no Han poor migrants to touch it. They even drove the latter out of this territory through violent means. A poor farmer named Wang Wen

1 For a detailed account, see Jagchid and Hyer (1979), Owen Lattimore (1962) and AQG (1991).

witnessed numerous such cases with increased hatred for Mongol elites. One day in 1876, he and his wife reclaimed a tract of a pastureland owned by a local Mongol prince. The prince's followers discovered them. A fierce physical battle followed between the Wang couple and the prince. Their brave struggles frightened the ruler and inspired many other poor people. The Chinese migrants finally were allowed to use this patch of land. Environmental transformations in Aohan were closely associated with this process of Han migration, land reclamation and the consequent pastureland degradation.

There were originally large stretches of pastureland in Ao Village owned by Mongols. In the years before the Liberation, it was still a demographically sparse community. As elsewhere in this sparsely populated region, since the earliest settlements, Mongols have not practiced nomadic pastoralism. They were sedentary livestock farmers, simultaneously practicing a crop cultivation method locally known as *"man sa zi"*, which means to broadcast seeds widely by hand. After planting, they just waited for the harvest without putting in any further energy, and there were not so many weeds then. According to elder people, Mongols then drove their herds to the rangeland in the morning and returned to the settlement when the sun went down. This traditional land-use pattern started to change with the influx of Han Chinese. The newly arrived Han Chinese mostly came from Shandong province, and were familiar with fairly intensive cropping systems in their native communities. As more and more non-indigenous Han people moved in, crop production gradually shifted from an extensive form to an intensive one, and land use was intensified. Ever since then, dramatic landscape changes have occurred.

Mongols hired Han migrants to work full time either in the fields or in their homes, which were locally called *"kang huo"*. The laborers received cash or grains, mostly millet, after a year's work. Mongols also lent out their land to sharecroppers, which was locally called *"pang qing"*. In the latter case, the landlords normally loaned out a certain amount of grains ahead of time at an interest rate of 50 percent for ten months. After harvest, the farmers, in turn, repaid both the capital and the interest, with the remaining amount being shared between them usually on a 50-50 basis. According to an elder woman named Jiang Mei, an able-bodied worker earned merely 2-3 *dan* of grain (1 *dan* equals 350 liters) after a year's hard labor, being far from enough to feed their families.

Generally, there was strict class stratification and an ethnic hierarchy in the pre-revolutionary society. Male Han settlers came as landless tenant farmers or hired laborers to work for the landowning Mongols and lived in the houses owned by Mongols. Originally, the ethnic boundaries were strictly maintained. Cultural identity was expressed in the use of land, the settlement system, and, of course, the language. The social construction of hierarchical differences between Mongols and Han, material or cultural, existed as part of a community experience, which was utilized to establish or maintain the dominance or hegemony of Mongols over Hans.

Before Liberation, agriculture, either crop or livestock farming, was characterized as a male activity. The classical formula in China's history of "men till and women weave" never existed in this part of rural China. Both Mongol and Han living elder women claimed they never had the experience of weaving cloth, but instead bought a kind of narrow cloth from the market. Unlike their counterparts in south China, who did the bulk of farm work in the field (cf. Bossen, 2002),[1] most women only did some field work during the planting, weeding or harvesting seasons. We must acknowledge that the role played by women in agriculture was one of heterogeneity and complexity, varying with social classes and ethnic groups, with gender, class and ethnicity being intricately intertwined.

The interview of a small sample of the living members of the most senior generation indicated that women from landlord families, Mongolian and Han Chinese alike, were not engaged in agricultural work, and they were even rarely seen by outsiders. Unmarried Mongol girls from these households preoccupied themselves with making and embroidering shoes and sleeping pillows, which they would carry with them when they got married. Only a few elder women from these families might occasionally come out to supervise the laborers working in the fields. They primarily lived indoor lives and took the livestock-drawn cart when they

1 Many feminists have revisited the quantitative evidence derived from John L. Buck's vast surveys conducted in the 1930s. Bossen (2002), among others, challenged Buck's arguments that women in southern rice-growing regions of China had contributed only small quantities of labor to farming, and women in the northern China almost none. In this village, both elder men and women unanimously claimed that women seldom worked in the field, which was locally called "*shang shan*", literally meaning to go to the hill, as this region was characterized by hilly land. This demonstrated the regional variation of women's involvement in agricultural practices.

went out. The norm of female seclusion was only limited to a small minority of the relatively rich landlord households. This seclusion was not monolithic even within the same county. An elder woman from a rich peasant family in a village in the same county recalled, she had helped to milk cows, and to herd cattle in her natal village before marriage. She also occasionally cut opium for others to earn some extra money. Mongolian girls in her native community could go anywhere they wished.

By contrast, while their husbands or fathers worked outside as day laborers or sharecroppers, poor women, Han or Mongol, unmarried or married, preoccupied themselves with a series of reproductive tasks, much of which was closely connected with natural resources access and use: collecting firewood, fetching water, gathering wild plants to supplement the meager grains won by their male family members on an almost day-to-day basis. They also engaged in grinding grains, cooking meals, raising children, and doing all the needlework. Obviously, women's reproductive work was an essential component of family survival. The wives and daughters of tenant farmers sometimes worked side by side with their male family members, but their percentage in the village was very small. The life story of a widow of seventy years old, Jiang Mei, whose parents were among the earliest Han settlers in the village, shed light on women's productive and reproductive practices in the pre-Liberation period.[1]

> I was born in 1933. I feel extremely sad at the thought of those days before the Liberation, the hardest times in my life. I was born in the crotch of my mother's trousers as she came back home from collecting firewood. My mother just lost two young adult sons (they died of diseases) of eighteen and twenty years old, respectively. Seeing a little female baby, my mother desperately threw me into a heap of ash before my father returned home from working for a landlord. A poor neighbor heard my cry and picked me up from the ash.
>
> Life was so bitter during the period of Manchukuo under the Japanese

1 Many scholars eschewed the term of the "Liberation" to refer to the Communist triumph nationally in1949. I kept the expression because the residents used it frequently to interpret their historical past.

occupation.[1]We had no land at all, not even a small garden. We lived in a tiny hut owned by the Mongolian landlord for whom my father and brother worked. We did not have enough grains to feed ourselves. Since around 7-8 years of age I began to fetch firewood and collect wild vegetables to eat. In those days, we could not even find grass seeds to eat, which pigs are unwilling to eat today. We were not allowed to enter the fields owned by the landlords, they were afraid it might damage their crops.

When I was small, we covered ourselves with a grass curtain at night and I often woke up because of the unbearable cold. My father owned a worn-out fur-lined jacket, and my whole family often huddled together. When I was eight years old, I went with my mother to weed for the landlord. I could not sleep at the thought of working for them. I missed the two meals so much offered to our laborers, which for me, was almost equivalent to celebrating the lunar New Year. As a matter of fact, what they supplied was a meal of ordinary coarse grains, primarily sorghum. At that time, even the landlord families could not afford to eat rice and wheat flour very often. Several times as soon as I returned home from the work, I fell asleep in the courtyard. We were paid for our labor one or two liters of coarse grains or sometimes a little money of 0.25 or 0.50 yuan per day. We had little meat or lard to eat. If we bought one catty of lamp oil, we usually used it for a whole year. I still remember when I was a small girl, one day my older brother stole three pieces of salt for livestock from a landlord family and melted it in a bowl, I came back home from collecting firewood and drank the bowl of water without realizing its salty taste. My brother almost beat me to death for this. I had a narrow escape from death several times and was not destined to die.

I was still struggling after marriage. I married into a family of three adult Han brothers at fifteen years old and my mother only required five deciliter (*dou)* of coarse grains. Since two young members of my husband's household were hired out to work for the landlords, I needed to worry so much about food, but I had to do so much work at home. Sewing and

1 Japan occupied China's northeastern provinces in 1931 and established the State of Manchukuo from 1932-1945.

repairing shoes and clothes was then one of the biggest burdens among women. We could not afford to buy the thread; I had to go out in search of a wild hemp in the hill to weave it into thread to make shoes. Before the dawn at about 2 or 3 o'clock, I got up to cook for my husband and his brothers, who had to arrive at the fields before it was fully light. I was feeling so sleepy at the beginning; I could not wake up and even fell asleep when I was cooking. My husband sometimes hit me hard using his shoe. Wife beating was an acceptable practice in those days. They beat women as they wished and men exploited us women. Most women at that time were afraid of their husbands. During the day, I often went out to fetch firewood and water almost every day.

After Liberation, my life improved a little bit. We started to have more grains and did not need to collect wild vegetables. I gave birth to a son at sixteen years old and went outside to work a few days after the delivery. In total, I gave birth to 13 children, with only five living ones. I bore children one after another like a mother pig, with nobody available to help me. You could not imagine how much work I had to do. I grew up poor, and had experienced so much hardship without sufficient food and firewood. Until a few years ago, I still picked up firewood, small pieces of cloth or other items scattered on the ground when I walked along and saw them. I have never dreamed of the good life like today, which seems like living in heaven.

The dismal picture of Jiang Mei's early life mirrors gender and class-based environmental experiences and poor women's daily struggle and coping strategies. She sighed deeply when she was talking of how "we women were exploited by men." Her use of the term "exploitation" caught my attention. Seeing the puzzle on my face, she explained further, "it was typical in those days in the region." After Liberation, she once sought divorce, yet she finally abandoned the idea for the sake of her children. The testimonies of other men and women of her generation confirmed that the pre-Liberation period was the hardest time for residents, especially for women.

The "nei ren dang" Case: An Episode of the Cultural Revolution

The campaign, locally called "to dig and purge" or "*wa su*", was a turning point shaping ethnic relations between Mongols and Han Chinese in the region. The residents who lived through the campaign remembered it as a time of tremendous disruption. The trauma of this experience had a profound impact on Mongols in the village. After the launch of the Cultural Revolution (1966-76), which was officially dubbed "ten years of great calamity" (*shi nian hao jie*) in China, Ulanhu, the paramount leader of Inner Mongolia as well as the vice premier of the State Council, fell from power. He allegedly organized a counter-revolutionary organization of "the New Inner Mongolian People's Party" or "*nei ren dang*", as locally termed, to split Inner Mongolia from China. A political campaign against the party was introduced in 1968 and swept quickly over many urban and rural areas of Inner Mongolia. The political struggle took on the character of ethnic conflicts, which gave rise to a witch-hunt and cost many lives in Inner Mongolia.[1]

At the beginning of the Cultural Revolution, two village school teachers with "bad" class labels like former landlords were first singled out as the special targets, followed by a few Mongolian cadres. A Mongolian brigade Party secretary was thrown out and replaced by a Han man, and then a Han woman, who served shortly as the director of the Han-controlled Revolutionary Committee. When the campaign reached Ao Village in the autumn of 1968, a few cadres from the people's commune were sent down to mobilize villagers. Not long after, many ordinary Mongol men were imprisoned and pressured to confess their alleged affiliations, followed by some Han men who were suspected of supporting Mongols. The relations between Mongols and Han Chinese suddenly became very tense. Around 40-50 residents were targeted and arrested, 90 percent of them were male Mongols. Only a few Mongol adult men escaped that fate.

At the climax of the campaign, a group of former landlords and rich peasants, a group of village officials, and a group of "*nei ren dang*" members were all locked up in separate rooms. Some of them were confined for about 50 days. The rest of the team members continued to work during the day, but were called upon to attend the

1 The Inner Mongolian People's Party was in practice officially dissolved in 1946. For more discussions about this campaign, see William R. Jankowiak (1988) "The Last Hurrah? Political Protest in Inner Mongolia," *The Australia Journal of Chinese Affairs*, No.19-20 and David Sneath (1994) "The Impact of the Cultural Revolution in China on the Mongolians of Inner Mongolia," *Modern Asia Studies*, Vol. 28, No.2.

criticism meetings at night. This campaign persisted well into March the next year. During the ordeal of almost half a year, few Mongolian households could readily detach themselves from the influences of the campaign. The mishandled cases were eventually redressed by the government in 1978, ten years after it was launched.

Interviews revealed the traumas of violent struggles on local men and women. The gendered collective violence gave rise to the death of three Mongol men: one was tortured to death, another committed suicide and the third one dropped to the bottom of a well.[1] As for women, only two Han women were labeled as "*nei ren dang*" members, yet many more had painful experiences when their male family members were punished. One Han woman of sixty-three years old in 2003 came to seek my help one day with her case for possible compensation.

Thirty-five years ago, on the very day she gave birth to her youngest daughter, her husband, a Han Chinese, was targeted and punished before her eyes. When she protested, somebody hit her harder. Shortly afterwards, primarily because of her connections with the wife of her younger brother—the then women's director—who had already been announced as a "*nei ren dang*" member, she was soon labeled as such as well. She told me that in those days, she was really driven mad. On that same day, she showed me her redress certificate issued by the county government in 1978 and many pages of medical receipts. She hoped the local government would compensate her further. Rural women in relation to men were marginalized political actors, who seemed to be less severely influenced by the political campaign. However, when their male family members experienced the punishment or torture, they too suffered.

I was puzzled by how residents in a small village like Ao Village were mobilized to take part in the alleged political case that originated at the provincial level. When asked whether there were any severe intra-community ethnic conflicts among inhabitants, the common answer was "not exact". Villagers were prone to point out that the political case was entirely orchestrated from above and there was no denying a few residents took the opportunity to betray their actual or potential opponents

1 After the mishandled political case was depurged in 1978, a few children of the dead were granted permanent employment at the county town and became city residents. A man, who enforced beating and torture and eventually led to the death of a Mongol man, was imprisoned for five years. The woman, who once served as the director of the Revolutionary Committee, was discharged from her job.

out of personal revenge. After the political campaign was halted, the government propaganda emphasized the fault on the part of the higher-ups. Official discourse, consequently, created powerful rhetoric of ethnic equality and unity to minimize the negative impacts of the prior campaign. This political event exposing the hidden tensions and contradictions among residents, ironically, signaled a turning point in ethnic interactions between Mongols and Han in this part of China. Since then, as we will see below, there was increasingly less perceived difference between Han and Mongol people.

Ethnic Interactions

Despite a major demographic difference in ethnic composition, as of 2003, Ao Village was a fairly homogeneous community in terms of language, customs, dietary habits, income, and livelihoods. After so many years of daily interactions, my impression was that Mongols and Han Chinese were culturally identical with each other. All residents spoke only Chinese, more exactly, the Aohan dialect of mandarin. Several Han Chinese told me that Han villagers were sometimes treated by outsiders as Mongols due to their way of pronunciation, but they themselves did not realize the difference. Beneath the cultural commonalities, there remained certain minute distinctions between them in everyday life, particularly on some ritual occasions. In official discourse and some scholarly work, there always existed the romantic accounts of "ethnic integration" in the region. For instance, Ma Rong (1987) writes,

> It is more likely that Mongolian natives and Han Migrants are 'melting' into a new cultural system...each of the two groups adapted some cultural norms and values from the other. Not only do in-migrants change their norms and values because of the influence of the Mongolian community, but native Mongolians have also been strongly affected by the cultural system and behavior patterns of the Han majority brought into Inner Mongolia by the Han migrants.

However, as Pasternak and Salaff (1993) observed in farming communities in Inner Mongolia, Mongols "adopted the north Chinese mode of farming and the Han manner of life...they live interspersed with the Han and have become culturally indistinguishable from them. In architecture, clothing and activity, we find few indications of a major departure from the Chinese Way. They make their livings much the same way and enjoy much the same income. Like the Han they favor early patrilocal marriage, two to three children, and stem families" (Pasternak and Salaff, 1993: 265). Indeed, as an ethnic minority, the intrusion of the "Chinese Way" and that of the powerful state overwhelmed Mongols in this part of China. The following narrative offered by a male Mongol teacher in his early forties illustrated his frustrations and powerlessness beneath the "ethnic integration":

> For native Mongols here, the greatest misfortune is, undoubtedly, losing their own language. Before the mid-1960s, children were required to learn both Mongolian and Chinese at school, which was interrupted during the Cultural Revolution. Although the practice was restored again in 1978, things have somewhat changed. Taking my own family as an example, the generation of my parents spoke Mongolian quite well. When we were small, our parents taught and used Mongolian at home. After attending school, we began to learn and speak Chinese, but continued to use Mongolian at home. We now still can understand, but cannot speak it. Our four brothers have six children; none of them can speak Mongolian. We grew up with increasing exposure to Chinese influences. The people we encountered, dealt with, and interacted with were mostly Han-speaking Chinese. Even if we bought things at the supply and marketing cooperative, we had to use Chinese. I remember when I was a child, two kinds of characters of Mongolian and Chinese were used on some important occasions. If your own language is lost, your heritage and culture must be devalued.
>
> Generally speaking, when Han outnumbered Mongols, the latter were assimilated by the Han majority. They lost much of their originally distinctive cultural heritage and followed the Han way of life and Han folk customs (*feng su xi guan*). For the generation of my parents, Mongols all had Mongolian spouses. But three of our four bothers took Han wives. Realizing the next generation of mixed marriage is clever, I married with a Han woman as well. When I was small, indigenous Mongol men sometimes wore robes and belts. Nowadays no man wears Mongol gown or sashes here. Previously when we were sick, my parents used to turn to the Mongolian lama for help. The way we pay respect to our ancestors was different from Han before. Han offer the sacrifice to their ancestors at the grave before

> the lunar New Year, while Mongols used to do it on the very eve of the New Year at home. By comparison, we realized the advantages among our Han neighbors. In last the few years, many of us have shifted to the practice of sweeping the tombs ahead of time.
>
> In my mind, I was previously proud of our heritage and had prejudices towards Han. During the *"nei ren dang"* case, the Mongolian culture and Mongols came under brutal attack. Fortunately, my grandmother, who died in 1988, was a welcomed folk practitioner in the village, and my father was such an honest person, he never argued with other people, thus, my own family members luckily escaped the beatings. Anyway, I felt hurt by this campaign.

Indeed, the decades-long collectivization played an important part in exposing Mongols to the influences of Han's culture. After Han Chinese settled in the village, they dispersed and lived in houses owned by Mongolian landlords. When Mongols constituted a majority, Han settlers learned the Mongolian language. A few Han elder men and women became excellent Mongolian-speakers. Jiang Mei picked up Mongolian from her girlfriends of poor Mongol descent when they played and worked together. During the period of collective agriculture, Mongols and Han of each production team sometimes worked in gender specific groups, and sometimes in mixed groups on a day-to-day basis; this contributed greatly to level many of the traditional differences among residents. With the passage of time, most of the differences were absorbed into the innate fabric of the community through working and cohabiting in a locality.

According to residents, the perceived or actual differences continued to exist prior to the *"nei ren dang"* case. Mongol men sometimes wore Mongolian clothing on important occasions. Mongols and Han Chinese seldom intermarried across ethnic boundaries. In the entire Greater Ao Village, only a few Mongol ex-soldiers initially brought their Han wives home from the outside. There were increased intermarriages between Han and Mongol villagers from the 1970s onward. In 2003, among 160 living couples, there were 23 Mongol-Mongol marriages and 22 Mongol-Han marriages. Among the mixed marriages, seven Han men secured Mongol wives and 15 Mongol men obtained Han wives.

In China, people with the status of ethnic minority nationality (*shao shu min zu*) sometimes enjoyed certain favorable treatment.For example, over much of the period of collectivization, the minority communities in this region could access more cloth tickets and minority persons more wine than others. When family planning programs were intensified, Mongols could legally bear more children than their Han counterparts. In 43 households with Mongols, the average household size was 3.74 persons, slightly higher than that of the village as a whole (3.5 persons). As Jankowiak (1992) summarizes, being Mongolian promises political and economic advantages, and even Han invent Mongolian ancestors to change their nationality status. These gains include disproportionate political representation, favored admission to educational institutions, and the prospect of avoiding the more severe constraints on reproduction imposed on Chinese families under the strict 'one child' family limitation program (Jankowiak, 1992, cited in Pasternak and Salaff, 1993: 15). I heard about the "switching" of Mongol nationality by those originally classified as Han in Hamlet D, but know of no such case in Ao Village.

Some ethnic minority people were sometimes scorned as poor, dirty, uneducated and "backward", which often had ramifications in the real world. In Sichuan province, a female scholar of Yi ethnic nationality once told me that they tended to avoid choosing ethnic minority names for their children to avoid being marked by an ethnic label, since such labeling often had negative effects. This is because some people still look down upon ethnic minority members.I heard such stories in rural Yunnan province as well. Unlike some peripheral ethnic minority groups, it seems that Mongols in this region do not actually suffer from such ethnic discrimination.[1]In this region, if either the mother or father is a Mongol, their children can be officially classified as Mongol. No wonder, children with a Mongol mother or father in Ao Village all take Mongol ethnic classification without exception. Historically, Ao Village was a site of ethnically defined migrations, in and out, which not only resulted in fluid ethnic composition, but also shaped the pressures on local natural resources. In the pages that follow, I explore the movements of people in and out of the village, an important factor affecting environmental changes in the village.

1 Compared with "shrewd" Han Chinese, Mongols were generally renowned for their honesty, single-mindedness or straightforwardness, locally termed as "*shi chen*", which carried both positive and negative characteristics.

A Village on the Move

According to elder villagers, ever since Han migrants settled in the village, almost half of Mongols had moved out of the community to the pastoral areas further north. They probably hoped to continue their livestock farming, or perhaps did not want to live with a growing number of "shrewd" Han migrants, as some villagers mentioned. An elder Mongol man recalled, when he was young, he joined the flock to migrate to the northern pastureland. He finally came back because he could not bear the more inhospitable weather there.

Even during the collective era when inhabitants were tied to their native community and there were extremely strict limits for rural-urban migration, to move from one rural area to another was relatively easy. It was said if only you had good connections with brigade or team leaders, your relatives would be allowed to move in without any obstacles. Because Ao Village was desperately poor, relatively few in practice moved in. With the advent of the rural reform, a small minority of Mongols continued to move out of the village. Only after Ao Village became relatively prosperous with the availability of irrigated fields in the late 1980s and early 1990s, eight Han households moved in.

The official data regarding village population varied greatly. According to one source submitted by village cadres to the township government in the spring of 2003, there were 579 persons in 134 households. According to *The Greater Ao Village Economic Development Plan (2003-2005)* (GYV, 2003b), the village consisted of 547 persons. I was always puzzled by the discrepancy in various sources. This inconsistency might arise from the fact that the figures are often created to serve specific purposes.[1]The dynamic and shifting nature of village population further complicated the problem. Doubts about the accuracy of official statistics prompted me to recalculate village households and population myself, based primarily upon my own demographic and economic census carried out at the end of 2003, in combination with the data in *the Family Planning Roster*.

The dwelling pattern and family relations were quite complex in Ao Village,

1 I was told that official calculation was sometimes based upon the amount of villagers registered in the village, sometimes on those who actually had access to their ration land, while at other times on the actual presence, or even different criteria combined.

coupled with increased mobility, which rendered the counting of households very difficult. Anyone who is familiar with rural China knows that parents are supposed to live with one of their sons, usually the youngest son, sharing a house as well as the Household Register. Despite popular household division, not all divided households were granted a separate Household Register. However, the simplistic official counting normally only treated the households owning a Household Register as an administrative household or *hu*, which ostensibly did not reflect the actual departures and household divisions. For my research purposes, I calculated the households in two ways: one included all those registered in Ao Village, whether present or absent, since they were all entitled to a share of ration land, with only one exception.[1]Since the household is a residential, consumption, production and labor unit, I treated those households that occupied separate dwellings and ate separately as two households. According to these criteria, there were a total of 161 households in Ao Village in 2003, higher than the official figure. For some purposes, I sometimes only counted the 146 resident households, excluding 15 households (51 persons) that had entirely moved out of the village.[2]

Similarly, for the purpose of this gender-environment study, I calculated village population in two ways: one encompassed both de jure and de facto members of Ao Village. Some of them might not be officially identified as village members.[3] According to this method, the villagers, absent or present, with or without official registration, were 564 in total; 269 of them were females, accounting for 47.7%. In most cases, I only counted the people, de jure and de facto residents, in 146 resident households.

In 2003 and 2004, the migration to and from Ao Village was still quite dynamic.

1 To my knowledge, a one-person household lost its share of ration land, because no one helped him to complete the task of mass conservation labor after he moved out of the village.

3 They registered in Ao Village, but had no family members being left behind.

3 These included 16 persons: (1) five college students (although their residence registration had been transferred out of the village, they were allowed to keep their ration land until they eventually obtained fixed jobs. Furthermore, their financial source was often the greatest pressure on their parent);(2) six male teachers with nonagricultural registration in Ao Village; (3) two former widows without formal registration in the village and thus they had no access to a share of village land; (4) a couple holding nonagricultural registration elsewhere, who returned to their previous rural home upon retirement in Ao Village ten years ago; (5) a baby born in late 2003.

The population composition was fluid between my fieldwork in 2003 and my return visit in 2004. In late 2003, three young women married out. During my stay there in 2003, a man died of disease and a new baby boy was born. During my return visit in 2004, I learned that two elder people had passed away and another new baby was born. An elderly couple had joined their married daughter in a more wealthy area outside the county with no intention of coming back again. In addition, another two teacher households had moved to Lan Village. During my ethnographic project in 2003, at least three elder women, who registered elsewhere, were staying with daughters in the village for a relatively long period of time. By the same token, there were a couple of villagers away for reasons other than employment.

Considering migration, the composition of villagers was even more fluid and dynamic. Of the 146 resident households, a significant proportion of single men and women were away from the community in search of non-farm jobs inside and outside the county. In 2003, at least 69 individuals (50 males and 19 females) were away from the community to work elsewhere for at least four months.[1] The year of 2003 was rather special, a large number of migrants returned to the village in early May when the SARS epidemic spread in China. Some of them did not flow out again after they returned but instead worked locally. The four month period of migration was almost a farming cycle in this region. On the other hand, a few college students, some high school students studying in the county town, and a few visitors who lived outside of the village seldom or never came back in 2003. There were 141 persons, or one fourth of the total population, away from the village for whatever reason for at least four months. Among them, 101 persons, or about 18 percent, had been away for almost one year[2] and some of them were long-absent migrant laborers. Those who migrated to other places in the same township or within the county made frequent trips in and out of villages. Many of them still came back to till their land. These findings alerted us to the dangers of using available village data, as most village studies did.

1 It was misleading that the Family Planning Roster only counted some people who left the village for a long time as migrants. That helped to explain why the Year-end Production Statistics Forms (GYV, 2003a) produced by the village committee only report a total of 76 migrant laborers in Greater Ao Village, which apparently severely underestimated the real situation in the administrative village.

2 Most of the migrants might return home for a short time for the lunar New Year celebration.

Figure 3.6 Distribution of Population in Ao Village by Gender, Residential Status and Age Cohorts (2003)

Age Cohorts	Females	Males
70 and above	---±+++++++++	++++++++++++-
65-69	++++++	+++++++++
60-64	+++++++	++++++
55-59	-+++++	++++++++++++-
50-54	-++++++++++++++++++	++++++++++++++++++++++±--
45-49	-±++++++++++++++++++++	+++++++++++++++++++---
40-44	-----++++++++++++++++++++	+++++++++++++++++++----
35-39	----±+++++++++++++++++++++	+++++++++++++++++++++-----
30-34	-±+++++++++++++++++	+++++++++++++++++++++++±±±±±----
25-29	-----±±+++++++++++++++++	++++++++±±±±±±±-------
20-24	------±±±++++++++++++++++	++++++±±±±±±--------------
15-19	--------------±±±+++++++++	+++++++++++±±±±±±±---------
10-14	--±+++++++++++++++++	++++++++++++++++±--
5-9	--++++++++++++++++	++++++++++++++++++--
0-4	-+++++++++++	++++++++++++-

Source: 2003 household survey.

Note:

each "+" represents one person who resides in the village throughout the year of 2003. Each "–" represents one person who lives almost totally outside the community either for work or for visit, s/he may never come back during the year, or returned just for a short period of time. "±" denotes one person who lives outside the community for at least four months, but less than a year.

We can see from figure 3.6, among teenagers of the 15-19 cohorts, girls were as active as boys in migration, while in the age cohort of 20-24, male migrants were about twice those of female migrants. This was because young women mostly married in their early twenties, and they seldom migrated out of the village immediately prior to or after marriage; but married young men continued to move out of the village to seek wage labor. In the cohort of people over 25, there were more male migrants than females. Unlike some villages that I visited in Sichuan Province, where the large-scale male migration resulted in, on average, 70 percent of farming being performed by women. In Ao Village, most adult men and women still worked on the farm and a large percentage of men relied on natural resources to graze their livestock. These are some important policy findings with gender implications. They demonstrated although migration somewhat reduced population pressures on local ecology, it had not provided a viable livelihood for many residents. For a more detailed discussion about gendered migration, see Chapter eight.

Landscape Dynamics And Environmental Challenges

Over the five decades from 1950-2003, tremendous environmental transformations occurred in Ao Village as the life experiences of village men and women shaped its local history, which in turn, structured its development. This ethnographic research demonstrates that the landscape dynamics in the village were highly variable in time and space. Ao Village witnessed a significant change switching from one type of land use to another during the past half century. In this process, the pastureland—originally the dominant land use pattern—shrank gradually and was ultimately replaced by a myriad of other land use types, which in turn brought new dynamics to the local ecosystem. The heterogeneous vegetation niches in the contemporary village scene—rain fed and irrigated cropland, woodland, pastureland, and shrubland—were thereby indicative of a twin mixed trend of both destruction and improvement of the natural world. By 2003, the natural pastureland had almost entirely disappeared. As a consequence, the common grazing lands were, ironically, confined to two patches of the perennial shrub *ning tiao* under which few grasses grew. As farmers, livestock rearers, gardeners, as well as gatherers of firewood, medical herbs, and grass, village women played a pivotal role in shaping the local landscape.

The Ecological Dynamics of Pastureland: A Retrospective View

As a great yurt are the heavens
Covering the steppe in all directions
On the plain of Ch'ih-le (*Chile*)
Under the mountains of Yin

Blue, blue is the sky
Vast, vast is the steppe
Here the grass bends with the breeze
Here are the cattle and sheep.[1]

1 The translation quoted here derives from Jagchid and Hyer (1979:10).

The conventional wisdom about the pastureland in Inner Mongolia is vividly captured by this classical folk song handed down from the North Dynasty (A.D. 439-534). Aohan was historically famous for its landscape described by this famous poem familiar to many Chinese. Oral histories and documentary evidence suggest that before local Liberation in 1947, most of its land surface remained well endowed with abundant vegetation coverage. This fact was widely confirmed by elder villagers in their sixties and seventies. When I witnessed sheep browse on an almost barren land interspersed with sparse and short grasses, I could hardly imagine this was once a place of beautiful pastureland.

Elders' reminiscences were always embroidered with a world of immense grassland with perennial wild shrubs, dense grasses, and wild animals. Both men and women nostalgically mentioned the thickly vegetated pastureland, "Some grasses grew to the height of a house in the gullies. As soon as we entered into certain grazing land, dense vegetation obstructed us from discovering where our sheep were. We had to listen carefully for the breath of sheep to locate them." Male elders remembered with nostalgia they had to take shepherd dogs with them when they grazed sheep, since there were so many wolves around. Jiang Mei noted, "When we were cutting grasses for fuel,it seemed like chopping down trees."

Many elders offered intriguing anecdotes about the vanishing biodiversity. Foxes, wolves and other wild animals as well as some Chinese medicines disappeared completely under their eyes.Elder residents' recollections also testified to dramatic ecological changes during their lifetime. A striking case in point was the large gully. It was merely a groove over a half-century earlier, but in 2003 it was almost 50 meters wide in one section. The pastureland transformation was part of local history, which served as "a reservoir of detailed ecological knowledge and a repository for the memory of the past events" (Brosius, 1997: 95).

The trajectories of landscape change figured prominently in the accounts of some residents, who were fully aware of nature's revengeresulting from the startling destruction of vegetation cover. According to them, in the pre-Liberation years, although there was sand blown by the wind from the north pastoral area, sand storms were still not so severe. The removal of the vegetation on large tracts of pastureland led to severe sand storms in the years around 1970. Many residents recalled, on spring mornings, "You often found heaps of sand piled high in the doorway and you just could not open the door." In 1980 and 1981, large tracts of loose soil were exposed to the wind. "In spring planting, if you made ridges one day, it might be totally lost under a thick layer of sand the next day. When the winds rose up, it looked like smoke." From a historical perspective, the environmental challenge was most serious in the years immediately before and after decollectivization. It was reported that the sand heaped roughly one meter in height in certain fields near the highway in the spring of 1981. Entering the 1990s, as in Aohan as a whole, severe sand storms were somewhat brought under control by immense planting of shrubs, forage crops and trees in the region.

As we shall see below, social and ecological dynamics have been mutually conditioned and interacted with each other. Among a multiplicity of factors responsible for environmental changes, the legacy of successive political campaigns during the radical years of collectivization imposed profound impacts on the local environment as well as men's and women's livelihoods. As regards the negative impacts of the two episodes of the Great Leap Forward (1958-1960) and the Cultural Revolution (1966-1976), many scholars have stressed that the negative socio economic consequences of the Great Leap Forward were more profound than those of the Cultural Revolution.[1]

However, in Aohan as a whole and in Ao Village, the opposite might be true. In the1958 iron and steel campaign, many village students were called upon to construct "backyard steel furnaces" to melt down "iron and steel" from stones. They ran the crude blast furnaces for 2-3 months for nothing.[2] Adult men and women were mainly required to collect and mill low-grade ore and deliver it to the commune seat after washing. The campaign lasted for several months. From the winter of 1959 through 1961, residents "ate in two mess halls" for one and a half years. Although no death was reported in the aftermath of the Great Leap famine, residents experienced an extremely severe food and nutritional crisis during the communal eating. Many recounted that they relied mainly upon watery gruel, bran, tender grain stalks, young

1 The excess mortality caused by the Great Leap Famine of 1959-61 ranged between 15 and 30 million nationally. See Judith Banister (1987) *China's Changing Population,* Stanford, CA: Standford University Press and Jasper Becker (1996) *Hungry Ghosts: Mao's Secret Famine,* New York: Free Press.

2 The devastating effects of the Great Leap Forward on the local environment were reported elsewhere. For example, in a Sichuan county, Ruf (1998:103) writes, "Much of the forest cover of the county had been cleared for fuel to use in the 'iron and steel' furnaces and for the canteens."

leaves and other wild plants. "The steamed bread fell apart easily and we had to eat by holding it in both hands." According to an order from the people's commune in 1959, all livestock herds in the whole brigade were pooled and driven to Ao Village, home of the brigade headquarters. The disastrous "husbandry big plan"(*xu mu ye da ji hua)* resulted in a great deal of ecological damage in a single winter. It was reported that the area was denuded of wild trees and grasses, and did not recover for many years.

By contrast to the Great Leap Forward, the political struggle of the Cultural Revolution left bitter images and even deeper scars on villagers—particularly Mongols—in Ao Village. The chaos of the Cultural Revolution and its aftermath also placed an enormous burden on local ecology. After the inauguration of the Cultural Revolution, the collectives at both brigade and team levels were broken down. As noted above, at the height of "digging *nei ren dang* members", many men, Mongols in particular, were confined and abused. The changes in local leadership and frequent political struggle sessions disrupted both production and social order. As a result, village life was often in severe disarray. In those days, people competed to chop down wild trees on the surrounding hills. A man aged fifty-six recalled, when he was a child, there were wild elm and apricot trees all over the hills. With the advent of the Cultural Revolution, all the wild plants disappeared and nobody took care of it. In the late 1960s, male villagers had to steal firewood from Hamlet B and C.

The land cover changes were, undoubtedly, triggered by multiple historical processes in the context of dramatic political and economic transformations. Table 3.2 gives us a local view of the temporal and spatial pattern of grassland degradation in Ao Village. The grassland in the village had long been under threat throughout its history, resulting both from direct use such as grazing, harvesting of fuel or fodder, and from a wider pattern of grassland conversion to cropland, pastureland, and woodland. In the eyes of villagers, incredibly low agricultural productivity and desperate poverty forced local men and women to rely heavily on natural resources for survival. During the collective period, the excessive harvesting of grasses as firewood and fodder, combined with population pressure and mismanagement, resulted in dramatic reductions and degradation of grassland. After decollectivization, the expansion of livestock production and uncontrolled grazing had progressed at a much more rapid pace and increasingly became a key factor hastening grassland destruction. In addition, more grassland was cleared to make space for alternative uses. These interactive processes and their effects were cumulative. In the following chapters, the study will offer a more nuanced understanding of the historically situated and often mutually reinforced forces shaping land use and land cover changes.

Table 3.2 Major Determinants of Grassland Degradation in Ao Village

The Collective Period	
Major Reasons	**Percentage (N=24 respondents)** [1]
Fuel collection	92
Grasses collection	42
Population pressure	38
Mismanagement	21
Soil erosion	8
Grazing	8
The Post-reform Period	
Major Reasons	**Percentage (N=30 respondents)**
Overgrazing	93
Lack of rainfall	77
Mismanagement	57
State intervention [2]	53
Land reclamation	37
Soil erosion	13

Source: 2004 sample survey.

Note:

[1] This figure represents the percentage of informants reporting about the major determinants of grassland degradation in Ao Village. Six respondents, who were mostly young married-in wives, did not offer their view about the situation in the collective era.

[2] It refers to shifting government policies to convert grassland into pastureland, woodland or other reserves, which had led to grassland reduction and decreased mobility of livestock.

The Natural Environment at the Crossroads

The ecological challenges confronting Ao Village were still overwhelming in 2003. Even to an inexpert eye, it was an area of environmental vulnerability and ecological instability, facing multifaceted environmental crises—wind and water erosion, desertification, loss and lack of pastureland, water supply shortage, and recurring droughts.

In this drought-stricken semi-arid environment, it was popularly reported "out of ten years there will be nine drought;" "what one eats depends upon nature" and "what livestock grazes relies on nature." "Natural" catastrophes have afflicted the region more frequently since the late 1990s. By 2004, drought had plagued the county for six successive years. When the most severe drought first occurred in 1999—the worst in living memory—most households desperately abandoned their land to livestock herding. People sat outside everywhere in groups playing poker and most residents had little harvest that year. From the following year onward, despite a slightly less severe drought, inhabitants could not afford to abandon their land any longer. Local men's and women's lives were made more precarious by adverse climatic events. In the summer of 2003, I witnessed the scene of locals waiting eagerly for the rainfall. When I revisited the village in 2004, on the day before the Mid-Autumn Festival, I went with a group of women to a fair in Lan Village. Taking a shortcut through a large tract of fields, I was told that the crops ripening in the fields were threatened by the approaching frost. Those crops were planted later due to spring drought and barely had time to come to maturity. In 2003, a localized hailstorm swept in and damaged large tracts of crops. Again in 2004, two heavy summer rains washed away seedlings in many fields. Many residents believed the tendency of drought and erratic rain was not transitory.

Both water and wind erosion characterized the landscapes in Aohan within this ecologically vulnerable region. The northern section of the county was primarily an area of wind erosion, and the south of water erosion. Located in the middle, Ao Village was threatened to different degrees by both soil and water erosion. Due to the arid climate, sand-bearing wind swept through almost all year round, and often lifted the topsoil into the air.[1]Chicken claw-like gullies were scattered throughout the surrounding slopes. Despite the dry nature of the area, a sudden flood could not only destroy crops and terraced fields, but also widen the gullies overnight. Farmland was badly dissected by erosion into many crisscrossing gullies, up to a depth of about ten meters. Animal and vehicle tracks, followed by heavy rainfall, further enhanced gully formation.

On a summer afternoon during the harvesting season in 2003, Hong Xiang drove Song Ling and me to their fields to the north of the settlement to harvest buckwheat. Before a deep gully in the middle of the field, the mule-drawn cart stopped. We were obliged to walk down a steep dirt path (just constructed for the harvest) to the bottom of the gully and then walk up. When I headed home myself, I originally tried

---

1 Aohan was among the main localities where wind erosion and sand dunes caused the dust storms in Beijing.

to find the newly built stone bridge across this gully that had been constructed not long ago and was bitterly complained about by the residents.[1] I walked along the gully cutting through an expanse of the cropland. After walking ahead for some time, I had completely lost my sense of direction. In the end, I had to search for the man-made dirt path again to return home.

The severe erosion of surface was complicated further by new human interventions. As we shall see in Chapter five, successive waves of conservation campaigns were launched in response to the environmental challenges. Residents were constantly called upon to dig large tree planting pits throughout the surrounding hills and slopes. The scars of previous interventions were clearly observable. If you walked around outside the settlement, you could not miss the profusion of tree planting pits. Some pits had trees in them, while others didn't. After the small watershed project under the "rebuild beautiful landscape" campaign was basically completed in 2003, even more pits appeared on the project sites. I marveled at the broken topography, which had dramatically transformed the local landscape, and in some sense, worsened the ecological crisis. It is simplistic to assume increased environmental interventions necessarily lead to ecological improvement.

In 2003, most men and women were eking out their livelihood under harsh eco-environmental conditions. Apart from a very unfavorable agro-ecological environment, Ao Village also confronted other formidable environmental threats such as overuse of chemical fertilizers, poor irrigation practices, overexploitation and mismanagement of agricultural land and other natural resources. All these environmental challenges, coupled with a low level of technical capacity among local people as well as institutional weaknesses, set up a cycle of declining productivity and increasing environmental degradation, and thereby threatened the sustainability of village development and local men's and women's long-term welfare. Against this historical background, the following three chapters are devoted to the lived experiences of village men and women in natural resource use, a series of conservation campaigns, and the consequent environmental implications from a gender perspective.

1 Half a dozen men were paid to build this bridge, yet its site was chosen by township and village cadres. Two bridges were originally planned, only one was finally completed due to lack of money. The bridge was located too far away from the fields of most residents, and therefore, was complained about severely by residents.

Chapter Four

Agrarian Changes and the Crusade against Local Environment

As elsewhere in rural China, agricultural development in Ao Village over the past half century, particularly since decollectivization, suffered from China's shifting policy priorities—rural development strategies in general and specific agricultural initiatives in particular. More specifically, village political economy in the development drive went through drastic social and environmental transformations triggered by state priorities under two distinct regimes—collectivization and decollectivization. In this larger political-economic process, as we will see below, gender-differentiated roles in local agriculture systems, more exactly, men's and women's divisions of labor, rights, responsibilities, and space in multiple productive and reproductive activities shifted over time in the last 50 years. The results had a complex set of consequences for sustainable or unsustainable patterns of natural resource use, and hence on the rural environment. Gender-specific roles of men and women, therefore, are essential to understanding the gendered field of agriculture, whether crop or livestock production (Sachs, 1996).

Ao Village has long been an agricultural community. During the collective period, crop cultivation was the villagers' main means of livelihood, which remained the backbone of both the household and village economy in 2003. With the return of household farming, since there were few viable ventures outside agriculture at the local level, an overwhelming majority of households made their livings by crop production, in combination with livestock farming. Since the late 1990s, environmental challenges—particularly recurrent droughts—have created new sources of tension over natural resources among residents, especially for those who depend on agriculture as their sole means of survival. As elsewhere, women in Ao Village related to agriculture as farmers, as farmers' wives, daughters and mothers, as farm workers, or as rural residents. In all of these roles, which were structured by socioeconomic characteristics of the household, and of women as a group, women's interwoven productive and reproductive work[1]has helped shape natural resource conditions and environmental changes in dynamic and shifting ways.

State policies were practiced locally in heterogeneous ways. It is, therefore, significant to situate farming as well as environmental practices in a specific historical and geographical context. This chapter pieces together a picture of the interactions of gender and the environment in a context of agrarian changes. The issues that I examine are the continuities and discontinuities in farming practice and their gender and environmental aspects. Through tracing a variety of gendered forces over which local people had little control, I describe how agricultural practices shaped men's and women's everyday experiences, which in turn, impacted the rural environment.

The chapter begins with the environmental legacy of collective farming, followed by smallholders' intensive commercial agriculture. In the rest of the chapter, I chronicle livestock development in an environmental context. I argue that the trajectories of agricultural development and accompanying environmental changes have fundamentally altered men's and women's connections to their immediate environments, and thereby their interactions with each other.

Agricultural Collectivization and Itsenvironmental Impact

Land Tenures in the Context of the National Political Agenda

As elsewhere in rural China, the land tenure system in Ao Village has undergone four major stages since the Liberation: the land reform, the co-operative system, the people's commune system, and the household responsibility system. The land tenure regimes not only have shaped the organization of agricultural production, but also influenced local men's and women's interactions with their social and physical landscapes.

1 The concept of reproduction in this dissertation means not only biological reproduction, but also all the activities required to maintain a household, including cooking, cleaning, childrearing, collecting fuel, water and fodder, health care, making clothing and shoes, and other "support".

In Ao Village as in the rest of Aohan, land originally belonged to a handful of Mongolian landlords who practiced extensive livestock and crop production. On the eve of Liberation, land concentration was remarkable. Rigid class divisions led to little social mobility with few exceptions. In this early-liberated community, a party work team was sent down to carry out the "rent-and-interest reduction schemes" (*jian zu jian xi*) in September 1945, followed by the land reform campaign, locally called the "big storm" or "*da feng bao*" in the winter of 1947. During the land-reform campaigns, all village families were classified as "landlords", "rich peasants", "middle peasants", "lower-middle peasants" and "poor peasants". The landlord class was the principal target of this political and economic movement. The poor—previously marginalized—were pushed to the front stage, with a few of them serving as the judges in the mass court. Three Mongol men and one Han man were finally classified as landlords, and two other men as rich peasants in the village. These class labels later became a permanent and hereditary component of each family's identity until the end of the collective era.[1]

Land reform dramatically transformed ethnicity-class relations based upon landed wealth. Agricultural land, houses, livestock, and other property owned by landlords were confiscated and allotted to the poor according to their economic conditions. The landlords were expected to become self-supporting through labor reform (*lao gai*). The so-called "penniless loafer" who previously owned little or no land acquired land and draft animals from the landlords. The land reform made it possible for "tillers to have their own land". Land was allocated on a per capita basis of approximately 10 *mu* in the village, almost the average number of 11.4 *mu* per person in Aohan as a whole (AQG, 1991). Land, as a result, ceased to be a marker of wealth and social status. The land reform fundamentally transformed farmers' relationships to the land as well as to each other.

Although the "poor masses" got some land, houses, draft animals and implements, the small-scale peasant economy was especially vulnerable to drought and disease.

1 A person born after the land reform inherited the class designation of his/her father. During various political campaigns, some of those with "rich peasant" or "landlord" labels were subject to public humiliation and condemnation (Cohen, 1993). These political labels had great influence in determining a person's prospects of admission to the armed forces, colleges, universities, local administrative posts and even marriage chances (see Cohen, 1993; Croll, 1984; Bossen, 2002).

Some households began to hire laborers, buy land, lend money for high interest, and consequently, new inequalities emerged. As in other parts of rural China, Agricultural Co-operativization Movement through a series of campaigns—from "Mutual Aid Groups" ("*hu zhu zu*") through the "Elementary Agricultural Producers' Cooperatives" ("*chu ji she*") to "Advanced Agricultural Producers' Cooperatives" (*"gao ji she"*), and finally to the large-scale "People's Commune" ("*ren min gong she"*)—were initiated in the 1950s. Peasant households were correspondingly incorporated into various collectives, and their land, draft animals and labor were pooled in different combinations.[1]

The agrarian reforms culminated in 1958 when the co-operative system was replaced by the commune system.It was alleged that further collectivization could increase rural capital formation, which was conducive to local public works though mobilizing rural surplus labor so that output and productivity could be greatly enhanced. Large-scale people's communes were established across rural Aohan in 1958. The people's commune was initially the owner of all assets, including land, livestock, large and medium-sized farm implements. *The Revised Draft Regulations on Rural People's Commune Work* released by the Central Government in 1962 established the three-tiered ownership system of the people 's commune, production brigade and production team. The production teams owned arable lands, draft animals, and farm implements. The production brigade owned the machinery and organized local public works, whereas the people's commune served as the grassroots government body. China vigorously promoted collective agriculture for almost three decades. The three tiered ownership system was finally replaced by the Household Responsibility System in Ao Village in 1980.

Dividing the land and going it alone (*fen tian dan gan*) was a term widely used by locals to describe the dramatic transformations brought about by the last wave of rural reforms. The pillar of the reforms was land tenure changes, which separated land ownership rights from use rights through the establishment of the HRS. Under this system, the use and management rights of collectively owned land and other

1 There are two excellent works regarding the collectivization process: Vivienne Shue (1980) *Peasant China in Transition: The Dynamics of Development Toward Socialism, 1949-1956,* Berkeley, CA: University of California Press and Edward Friedman, Paul G. Pickowicz and Mark Selden (1991) *Chinese Village, Socialist State,* New Haven & London: Yale University Press.

assets were devolved to individual households, and thereby established households as the primary unit of production. The reforms, as a result, turned the clock back thirty years to the point where the land reform left off in the early 1950s when farmers were sharecroppers (Hinton, 1998). It was true, as Bossen (2002: 92) asserts that, "households can be seen as tenant cultivators because they do not have rights to buy or sell this land, and because the village itself is, in a sense, the collective owner and rent collector." The HRS was even applauded as "a second Liberation" by some peasants.

A Note on Pre-collectivization Agriculture

As shown in Chapter three, before the Liberation, farming was basically constructed as a masculine occupation and agricultural work was predominantly carried out by men, with poor women mostly working in the fields seasonally for some labor-intensive jobs such as planting, weeding or harvesting. Village women were then essentially "villagebound, homebound and even stovebound." From the very beginning of the Liberation, the outside world has been a powerful influence in organizing village agriculture as well as other aspects of social and economic life. In this early-liberated region, many young men rushed to join the revolutionary army.[1] Women were correspondingly mobilized to work family fields, sew cotton shoes for the revolutionary army, and help military-dependent households with their fieldwork.

As throughout rural China, women's participation in economic activities at that time was reinforced by ideological and political drives. As a huge "reserve army of labor," rural women's employment and labor participation beyond the household was propagandized as the precondition for improving their status and for gender equality. As a result, for some time, girls and young married women were empowered by attending village schools, whereas other adult women were encouraged to take part in literacy campaigns. No wonder, Hershatter (2002) argues that, "any inquiry into the lives of women in socialist China cannot abandon concern with the state, for the Chinese Party/state moved rapidly and forcefully in its early years to rearrange rural gender relations (those of both production and reproduction) and the categories

1 Aohan was liberated from Japanese in 1945, four years earlier than the founding of the People's Republic of China. In 2003, there were still four living veterans who once fought in the revolutionary army before the national Liberation.

through which they were understood."

All these forces set the stage for women's participation in collective labor shortly afterwards. Elders' memories and archival records suggested that the collectivization drive from 1952 to 1958 had profound influences on gendered agricultural practices and rural life. As members of co-operatives, young married wives often worked together in the field when necessary. Many women continued to gather wild plants from communal lands to supplement meager grains. They were also involved in creating new fields out of pastureland. Yet some lines between agricultural femininities and masculinities were still clearly drawn. Women were usually not allowed to thresh in the yard. It was popularly believed that women's presence in the threshing ground could spoil the crops in the coming years.

"Eating Rice Out of a Big Pot" (chi da guo fan)

The organization of agricultural production under collectivism was often referred to as "eating from a big pot", a metaphor that meant everyone could get the same rewards regardless of one's work performance. It ultimately led to indifferent work habits, bad crop care, low productivity, poor rewards, and in the long run, prolonged poverty. Under the collective regime, the team-based production system prevailed. Team leaders were made responsible for labor, land and field management, income distribution, and marketing arrangements. From 1962 through 1980, the production brigade in Greater Ao Village functioned as a basic accounting unit. Although brigade leaders often came down to inspect the work of the constituent teams, they had little control over most decisions, including agricultural practices and financial affairs at the team level.

The organization of labor was differentiated along gender lines. Relatively restrictive gender division of labor in the labor process, consequently, led to gendered village spaces. All able-bodied adults were expected to contribute their labor to the collective with little choice in work assignments. Male team leaders divided the tasks each morning or the day before, and men and women frequently worked in separate groups. Women's groups were always led or supervised by a female team leader, who often had little say in the team committees, but bore the responsibility of guiding women to do their work *(ling zhuo fu nv gan huo).* As documented in many studies across rural China, men's and women's work assignments varied from place to place. There was generally a task-specific division of labor, for instance, weeding was popularly designated as women's work. More often than not, women assumed very demanding and difficult activities during the transplanting, weeding and harvesting seasons. Even if men and women worked in the same field, when they took a break, they often sat far away in spatially separated groups. Women in later stages of pregnancy or with newborns were allowed to stay at home. The working mothers with small children were sometimes permitted to work nearby so that they could return home to nurse their babies. During the winter when agricultural tasks were at a minimum, women were assigned little work, while men worked around team headquarters, cutting short grass or stalks, cleaning pens, and building or repairing sheds.

The authority of male team leaders was absolute. All team cadres were required to take part in physical work regularly, but in reality they were often preoccupied with meetings or other business. Not only did they control women's daily work assignments, male team leaders were sometimes involved in the direct supervision of women's farm work. On several occasions, women mentioned that the male team leader in Team One always sat or even laid down under a shady tree with a fan covering his face while they were weeding under his supervision. Occasionally, he walked around. If the work was not done properly, any woman could be rebuked if he was in a bad mood. On many occasions, he seized a young woman by her ear and forced her to do her work over again. A woman commented to me, "If you had a thin-skinned face (one who did not want to be blamed publicly), you were obliged to work hard and conscientiously under such circumstances." No one dared to challenge him to his face. In another case I was told, when a newly married woman worked in the collective field, she was too shy to ask permission from a male team leader to take a break to urinate. As a result, she continued to work with wet trousers until the morning session of work was finished.

The distribution of power and authority disproportionately favored men. Men occupied almost all management, animal husbandry or other technical jobs, which were consistently better rewarded than those of women's work characterized as "worst rewarded and technically least demanding." The team committee normally consisted of a team leader, a female team leader, an accountant, a treasurer, a storekeeper and a militia leader was overwhelmingly dominated by males with the exception of the female team leader. In the whole community, not a single woman ever acted as a big cart driver, tractor operator, or herdsman. The male orientation, interwoven within social and political relationships, was reflected most clearly in the allocation of the privileged positions of tractor operators. When the brigade was granted tractors through state assistance in 1978, four men in Greater Ao Village were sent to technical school to learn the relevant technology. Three of them came from Ao Village. Liu Xing was chosen when he was eighteen years old. He admitted the reason why he was selected was because his father—a veteran—had long worked as a cook in the brigade. Similar to his case, the selection of two other men had to do with their powerful male family members: the brother of one man was then a key brigade leader, while another man's father was a team leader. After decollectivization, all three men continued to benefit from the skills they learned.

This masculinized work arrangement imposed remarkable income inequality between men and women,[1] as the work points in Ao Village did not often accurately reflect either the quality or the quantity of men's and women's collective labor. Men and women were often assigned differing tasks, which largely prevented the implementation of the principle of equal pay for equal work between the sexes. Women were usually not considered equally productive compared to men. Therefore, the tasks where women dominated were always assigned relatively low work points, while men's tasks were granted higher work points. For instance, in the busiest planting season, young men who spread manure—being perceived as the most strenuous work—earned the full 12 points per day; old men pulled the plow and earned 10 points; while women sowed the seeds and received 10 work points. As with male team leaders, cart or tractor drivers earned 3600 work points and herdsmen 4500 work points per year—the maximum work point rating under collectivism. A male carpenter could receive 14 work points each day working for his teammates, who in turn, were expected to submit 20 work points to the team. Women's work was often perceived as "lighter", and consequently "naturally"

1 As was practiced throughout rural China, in the pre-1980 collective economy, labor input was measured by the work-point (*gong fen*) system. The total profit available for work remuneration among team members came from the income a production team could earn in a year after deduction of taxes, investment and welfare funds. All farm or off-farm tasks were priced at a certain number of work points, which took into account specific labor intensity, technical and skill characters, the degree of willingness, and their comparative importance. It was also determined by personal characters of the laborer—his/her physical strength, capability, age, and gender.

worth fewer points than men's work (Andors, 1983; Bossen, 2002; Johnson, 1983; Pasternak and Salaff, 1993). This earlier generalization applied to Ao Village as well. Additionally, agricultural chores during the winter were normally left in the hands of men and thus most women earned no work points at all. As a result, fewer women could earn over 3000 work points per year.[1] It deserves mention that only in the case of mass conservation campaigns, did both women and men earn the same work points for the labor that they contributed.

At the end of collectivism, some responsibility systems such as the output-and-work contracting work (*bao chan bao gong*) under the piece-rate system were introduced. Women rarely had the opportunity to assume these tasks on their own, although they might join men to complete certain work. Individual income derived from the total number of work points earned. The work points of all household members were finally converted into a cash payment as well as grain, fuel or other necessities, which were lumped together to and handed over to the head of household at the end of each year. This fact was mainly the result of cadres using the household as their unit of measurement and policy assessment. This practice, undoubtedly, made invisible women's economic contributions to the household. As a consequence, as will be seen in Chapter seven, if a wife functioned as a "family manager" to control money, her husband might become an object of ridicule.

The way female labor was deployed and undervalued in agricultural production in collective labor largely shaped gender roles inside and outside the household. Many anecdotal accounts illustrated that gendered power relations in public space structured men and women's roles at home. Not only senior males enjoyed certain decision-making authority over team matters, most household heads, young or old, had power over women and youngsters. This pattern clearly dominated the collective period. Women's time-consuming reproductive work was never regarded as part of production work, nor equally shared by male counterparts. One woman recalled

1 The fact that women got an unfair share of income and work points was confirmed by empirical evidence from other parts of rural China. For example, Ruf (1998:105) writes, "throughout the collective era, the work point system undervalued the labor of women by at least 20 to 30 percent, and arguably much more. An able-bodied male laborer could generally earn up to ten work points a day, whereas his female counterpart could earn only seven or eight at most. Moreover, as suggested in the account above, women received no labor credit, for the time-consuming tasks of cooking, cleaning, laundry and childrearing"(Wolf, 1985).

that her deceased husband seldom took the burden of childcare or other household chores. He occasionally "helped" her with taking care of the baby. If someone happened to come for a visit, he immediately put down the child to prevent loss of face and perceived masculinity. This was typical among village men. If a man did much housework, he could be viewed as "henpecked" and not manly.

Although the wives of team cadres might be exempt from collective labor and shared some of their husband's resources, I got the impression that they seemed to assume heavier workloads and lower status vis-a-vis their husbands inside the household. For instance, Zhang Guisheng, who served as an accountant for a long time during the collective era and was also a public figure in the community, was widely reported to be seldom involved in domestic work. In 2003, I witnessed only his wife fetching water and firewood. One day I paid a visit to them, and they happened to be eating their meal. I observed that only Zhang Guisheng was eating pork-filled dumplings on the table, a rare diet for the poor elder couple, and his wife was not touching the dumplings at all. She consumed only a bowl of millet rice with salty vegetables. Out of curiosity, I later asked others about it. I learned that for a long time in this family, relatively higher-grade food had been prepared and served to Zhang Guisheng only. As a matter of fact, it was not an isolated case in the community. I noticed that village women always ate least and last. I was told this was especially true in times of food crises during the collective period.

Men and women in the village shared the same lot of engaging in inefficient and low productive farming, year in and year out, for little material gain. The economic security of residents was bound up with their respective teams, upon which they depended to procure cash payment, ration grain, firewood, meat and vegetables. Almost all these provisions would be deducted from their work points. According to residents, in the constituent teams of Yangzi Village, an average value of 10 work points earned in a day was equivalent to 0.40-0.60RMB.

Although a household's income depended directly on how much male labor resources they had, in the notoriously poor team—Team Three—even if the household had a plentiful supply of labor, they still had no way to improve their material conditions. The 82-year-old shepherd in Team Three, introduced in Chapter two, recalled that he earned 4500 work points after working a full year, yet in many years, the value that he got did not exceed 45RMB. He earned merely 3.5RMB in one year and nothing at all in another year. Two of his sons had difficulty finding a mate. One of his sons, fifty-three years old eventually married a widow of fifty years old in 2003. It was rumored since he "lived" on the hills to graze sheep the whole year, his deceased wife had an affair with one of his teammates. She even had illegitimate children with the man, who in turn, helped her a lot to struggle for the survival of her children. If the man borrowed two bags of grains, he would deliver one bag to her. A woman commented to me, if his wife had behaved properly, her children might have suffered from starvation in the chronic grain-deficit that afflicted Team Three.

The remarkable differences in economic performance among teams conditioned the well-being of its members. Team Three was for a long time in serious trouble in terms of food self-sufficiency. From 1963 to 1980, it depended predominantly on state assistance for survival, whereas the rest of the teams required food imports only one or two years in the case of crop failures. The desperate impoverishment stemmed not from a real labor shortage but rather the weakness of the collective economy, which structurally limited the potential efficiency, enthusiasm and resistance among team members. Many resident members—especially women—pretended to be sick and excused themselves from collective labor. The team was composed of over twenty households and there should have been at least 20 women to work for the collective, however, more often than not, only 4-5 women showed up. It was not until decollectivization that some women began to learn farming. To avoid being tied to the poor team, young men tried hard to move out of the village to escape the local scarcity. A former brigade cadre from Team Three explained to me, in the latter years of collectivization, among five of his adult brothers, the oldest one worked in a mine, he himself served in the brigade, the fourth was a tractor driver, and the fifth enlisted in the army. Consequently, the grain that the team produced was not even as much as a big farm household reaped after decollectivization.

The same inefficiencies that plagued Team Three were widespread in other teams as well as other peasant communities (cf. Friendman et al, 1991). Many men and women felt cheated by powerful local elites, but had limited means to express their opposition. This was vividly captured by a local lament, "Team leaders held power, accountants controlled money, the storekeepers were too full, whereas ordinary commune members went hungry." The collective production regime dampened the work incentive among team members, which was ultimately detrimental to the collective economy. In those days, the grain output was unbelievably low. A popular local sayings put it, "To cultivate a tract of slope, to harvest a cart of grain, to harvest a dustpan of grain, to cook only a pot of food." Typically, the average gross yield was approximately 100 catties per *mu*, with 200-300 catties in sorghum, and a little bit over 100 catties in millet in a normal year. As an elder woman noted, "People trapped in desperate poverty do not want to work, just as skinny horses are unwilling to eat. If you were hungry, how could you till the field?" Even if they presented themselves in the field, most of them did not make serious efforts. At the end of collectivism, many households were trapped in debt to their team, which in turn, went into debt to the bank, a phenomenon locally called "a debt chain of three parties" (*san jiao zhai*). Debt-plagued inhabitants had no money to earn back the entire grain ration guaranteed to them. Many unanimously claimed, "If the collectives remained, most commune members would die of starvation."

Surviving in the Center/Margin Nexus

The bitter memories of collective agriculture were imbued withan alarming food shortage, which persistently haunted almost all team members over much of the collectivization period. Many constantly mentioned that the whole family had to share the burden of household food supply. Boys and girls were obliged to quit school and helped their parents through hard times. Teenage girls tended to enter the collective physical labor to earn work points earlier than boys, since they had less chance of attending school. During the Great Leap Forward, when there was nothing to eat, many lived on grain chaff, watery coarse porridge and even wild plants, as an everyday diet. Especially in those households with many mouths to feed, it was said that hungry children with swelling faces sometimes became weak and even faint.

Women, who assumed the major responsibility for food-preparation, always found themselves trapped in constant struggles to search for food and bore the brunt of material deprivation. To cite an example, among a few residents wandering as beggars, there was a desperately poor woman in Team Three, who had six daughters and two sons, and whose husband was extremely lazy. She sometimes went begging with her daughters and always carried back whatever relatively good food they had collected for her husband.

The following testimony offered by Song Ling underscores more clearly the gendered nature and outcomes of food scarcity in this historically poor area:

> The team allocated the grains to us three or four times each year in case we would eat too much at a time. More often than not, households exhausted the grains before the next allotment. Almost all households faced chronic grain deficit and many residents experienced hunger. Fine grain hardly existed and we often ate coarsely ground millet. Only on festivals did we have a little white flour and rice to eat and we only ate a meal of dumplings on the eve of the lunar New Year. We were then too poor to afford to raise a pig or to buy cooking oil. It was not unusual that we did not boil vegetables for a whole month, and relied merely upon salty vegetables and even salty water. We felt quite happy if there were soybeans or soy sauce to eat. If you had no grease in your empty stomach, you could eat an elephant. An able-bodied young male could consume two catties of coarse grains per meal. Although households with more daughters might save on some grains, girls meant less chance to earn more work points. It was women who took charge of cooking, so they had to carefully calculate the family's grain consumption. We worked fruitlessly for a whole year, but were unable to meet the family's grain needs year round. Sometimes what we earned was not enough to earn back our ration grains. During the pre-harvest time, the busier you were, the less grain there was left to eat in my big family with four male siblings. That's why many residents competed to sell grasses to their teams in exchange for grains.

As is well known to all, grain production in rural communities under collectivism was enmeshed in the larger planned economy. At the beginning, I was indeed puzzled by their narratives and always asked curiously, "Why was that so?" In the modernization drive of the 1960s and 1970s, China's agriculture was long regarded as a necessary precondition to pursuing heavy industrialization. Especially since the mid-1960s, food self-sufficiency and the grain-first policy known as "take grain as the key link" (*yi liang wei gang*)—ardently advocated by Mao Zedong—eclipsed all other concerns. This, ironically, led to the exclusion of cash crops, the neglect of animal husbandry, and the detriment of collective or individual off-farm ventures. For instance, in the campaign to "cut the tail of capitalism" during the ultra-leftist period in the mid-1970s, here as elsewhere, the small amount of private plots were withdrawn from villagers, who were not even allowed to grow anything in their own courtyards. Meanwhile, "the grain first campaign" led to rampant, destructive "agricultural reclamation" in the grassland. During the period from 1966-1976, over 50 percent of pastureland were converted into farmland in Aohan (AQG, 1991). The resulting environmental degradation unavoidably imposed negative impacts on agricultural production.

During the collective period, residents in Ao Village predominantly practiced subsistence crop production. The cropping plans, including the size of the crop area and the estimated needs for local consumption, were made by commune officials in response to higher-level requirements for grain quotas to the state.[1] In an ordinary year, agricultural taxes paid in the form of grain by the team was determined based upon the normal yield from fixed tillable fields, locally called "*chang geng di*", which was approximated 5 *mu* per person in Ao Village. After deducting the annual per capita grain rations, seeds and feedstuffs, the remaining grains were required to be delivered to state agencies at the price imposed. Once determined, the quota remained unchanged for a fixed period of time. Locals distinguish between "*gong liang*" (i.e. agricultural tax) that they were obliged to deliver and "*gou liang*" that was the extra compulsory low-price grain marketed to the state.

The annual per capita grain rations were, on average, 320-360 catties of coarse grains. Two or three catties of subsidiary grains per day were often allocated to each worker during the weeding and harvesting seasons or in the case of mass conservation labor, as an incentive to encourage participation.[2]Under such circumstances, ongoing covert and overt struggles surrounding grains arose among team leaders and ordinary folks, team leaders and brigade leaders, and brigade leaders and higher-level officials (see Chapter six for local resistance).

Apparently, deprived peasants and communities lost control over the resources for their own growth and development. Under strict central control, failures in food

1 The economic planning system was initiated in the 1950s and consolidated in the early 1960s. As evidenced in the Yearly Statistics Forms submitted by the production brigade to higher-up administration in county archives, all production activities were put under strict quota regulations, which encompassed detailed cropping patterns, planting acreage, seed selection, field practices, output targets and delivery requirements.

2 The surplus allocated to residents as subsidy grains was saved from the seed quota. The team was allowed to keep 5 catties of seed per *mu* of cropland, yet in a good year, one catty was enough.

production were almost a nationwide characteristic of rural China. As Friedman et al (1991:175) rightly points out, "In China, the rural hinterland was the periphery; the state was the exploitative center. The leadership's view was that the countryside was temporarily sacrificing itself for industrialization. The transfer of critical resources from the countryside to urban heavy industry, and from the peasantry to the state sector and the city, deprived many rural communities of the margin of surplus required for their development and prosperity."

The overwhelming reality of food shortage and desperate poverty confronting villagers was interwoven into their memories of the collective past. No data was available for Ao Village itself, but the low value of work points as well as low land/labor productivity in rural Aohan as a whole can be seen clearly from table 4.1, taken from official sources.

The history of rural people in Aohan under the collective regime was characterized by a desperate need of sustenance. A then popular local expression "relying on selling-back grains for feeding, counting on loans for cash, and depending on relief for daily existence" vividly captured the plight of the rural population. After paying agricultural taxes, if a team's crop harvest failed to reach the members' level of subsistence ration grain, it was qualified to purchase the remainder from the state. This was locally termed as "selling-back" grains *(fan xiao liang)*. If they could not even buy *fan xiao liang*, they had to rely upon state relief for survival, which was called relief grains (*jiu ji liang*). Towards the end of the collective era, Aohan suffered from severe scarcity of grain. In 1972, for example, the total yield of grains was 45 million kilograms, in the same year, it was granted 55 million kilograms of "selling-back" grains by the state (ASB, 2004). As was true for most rural communities in the county, residents unable to earn their subsistence through collective labor were obliged to resort to the local ecosystem beyond the farm as a survival strategy.

Table 4.1 Per Capita Net Income, Grain Availability, and Crop Yield in Aohan By Decades/Years

Decades/Years	Per Capita Net Income (RMB)	Average Work point Value1 (RMB)[1]	Grain Availability[2] (catty)	Output/*mu* (catty)
1940s (1946-49)	—	—	—	37
1950s (1950-59)	25.5[3]	0.61[3]	435.4	78.5
1960s (1960-69)	34.7	0.55	333.5	85.1
1970s (1970-79)	40.0	0.44	365.6	152.6

contd.

Decades/Years	Per Capita Net Income (RMB)	Average Work point Value1 (RMB)[1]	Grain Availability[2] (catty)	Output/*mu* (catty)
1980s (1980-85)	150.8[4]	0.26[5]	497.3	187.3
1990s (1990-99)	950.4	–	–	–
2000-2003	1080.5	–	–	–
2003	1541.0	–	–	438.0

Source: This table was adopted from information in Liu (1989: 139-40, table 4 and 164-66, table 8); Li (1991: 61); ASB (2003:221) and ASB (2004:14).

Note:

[1] In rural Aohan, there was a great divergence in daily work point earnings, ranging from over 2RMB per day to several cents and even nothing. The work point value per day was, on average, 0.50-0.80RMB in the county as a whole. The grain yield averaged around 150 catties per *mu* in the 1970s.

[2] The annual per capita grain availability among farmers included both ration grain and selling-back grain. The figure in the 1950s was modified from the average number of the years from 1953 to 1959.

[3] The per capita income and average workday value in the 1950s were derived from selected years from 1956 to 1959.

[4] The income of 150.8RMB was the average amount from 1980-1989.

[5] The work points in 1980—the very year of the collapse of collectives—were 0.26RMB.

"If the Hill is Green, Nobody Will Die of Starvation"

Since villagers were locked within the community, where no other subsistence options or cash sources were available locally, the most critical strategy for coping with hunger and survival was to resort to the overexploitation of natural resources in the village landscape. When village women and men struggled with the daily pressures of grain and firewood shortage, they compelled to turn to the local ecosystem in one way or another on a near-daily basis—collecting wild plant products to tide over grain shortfalls, gathering firewood for subsistence or cash sales, and cutting saleable grasses and Chinese herbs—to supplement their meager income from collective work. A local expression, "if the hill is green, nobody will die of starvation" (*shan qing e bu si ren*), vividly conveyed the importance of off-farm resources in the surrounding environment to their lives. In this context, as noted in Chapter three, the greatest threat to pastureland came from the convergent impacts of unchecked firewood and grass collection. In this sense, impoverishment among villagers played a significant part in the damage to the environment.

During the collective period, the historically situated practice of grass collection, both as forage and as fuel, was once the heaviest burden on the village pastureland.

In those days, when there was rain or snow, livestock were fed in team headquarters, and some weaker sheep were stall-fed the whole winter and early spring. Whenever there was a scarcity of crop residues, oxen or other highly valued animals were also fed hay as supplementary feed. Teams sometimes assigned the task to its members to supply a specific amount of grasses for corresponding work points. Without other income-generating alternatives, poverty-stricken inhabitants counted on selling hay to their team to earn some extra money. The team purchased hay at 2-5 *cents* per catty.

The collection tended to follow a gender-specific pattern. During the period of fodder harvesting, almost every one would cut some grasses before or after collective work. A day's harvest sometimes could yield them 70-100 catties, earning at least 2RMB per day, an amount much higher than the work points earned from collective labor. A woman could shoulder back a large bundle of grasses of about 20 catties. When all able-bodied laborers were forced to work in the collective fields, some older women, who were free from collective labor, focused on the job of grass collection. What they earned was often much higher than their family members working for the team. A few of them often rode donkeys and carried food with them. Large quantities of forage grasses usually piled up "like a hill" in the courtyards of each household, awaiting purchase by their respective teams. An elder woman proudly told me that she harvested so much grass that occasionally she would trade the grasses collected for a baby animal from her team.

During the collective era, the unsustainable and excessive harvesting of grasses as fuel constituted one of the most important sources of human impact on the natural environment. In comparison to other parts of rural China, firewood scarcities have continuously afflicted the region ever since Liberation. During the long frigid winter, fuel was in high demand and a great deal of fuel was needed by each household to heat the *kang*.[1] During the entire collective period, only sorghum, millet, soybean and buckwheat were planted in this village. The lower crop yield was accompanied by fewer crop residues. All millet or soybean residues were kept for livestock

1 As of 2003, a main source of indoor air pollution in Ao Village came from cook stoves with poor ventilation, which were mainly fueled by crop residues. The whole house sometimes was filled with fumes and smoke. Another indoor polluting factor was smoking, which increased dramatically after decollectivization. Women were in more danger from indoor air pollution of fumes and dust since they were responsible for cooking and stayed at home longer.

consumption, while the yearly repair of livestock shelters, along with individual house building, exhausted much of the sorghum stalk. Shepherds and others slept on the *kang* in team headquarters each night to take care of the animals. There were also meetings almost every night for team members to assess their work points or for other things, and they warmed themselves by burning *kang*, which consumed a large amount of buckwheat stalk during the winter. In this context, there was not sufficient buckwheat stalk to share among individual households.

Without enough grain stalks or other alternative sources, grasses on the grassland became the main source of energy as cooking or heating fuel to meet their demands. Local people, particularly women, were desperate to secure fuel to last the long freezing winter. Before the 1960s, people used a kind of bamboo rake to gather up the hay, but by the 1970s, a kind of iron rake was widely utilized, which often uprooted grass roots. After the ground was frozen when little collective work was assigned to team members, almost the entire village rushed to gather up hay repeatedly. "At the end of collectivism, after raking together grasses in half a *mu* of pastureland, you could merely obtain a bundle of hay, which could only cook a single meal or two. A day's yield often lasted only one or two days, especially for the larger families," a woman remarked. During the winter, hay was usually piled high like a hill in the courtyards. Although it is hard to quantify total consumption, it is easy to imagine that to meet daily fuel needs was a big challenge for local people. Animal grazing, followed by cutting and raking of grasses, often left nothing on the bare pastureland.[1]

As witnessed in other rural communities throughout the global "South", hauling firewood by women as "a key icon of the gender, environment and development literature" (Schroeder 1999: 5) was once part of the social landscape in Ao Village. Women and children usually bore the brunt of fuel shortage and even fell victim to environmental deterioration. Many women

1 After returning to household farming, especially since corn cultivation, a variety of crop stalks have provided residents with large quantities of smoky biomass fuels. Some households had their own trees and could harvest branches. Many households owned electric cookers or bottled-gas stoves. Electricity was readily available, but was still too expensive for most villagers to use for heating or cooking. To my knowledge, only a few prosperous households have turned to imported commercial energy sources—coal for cooking or heating. Despite the ban against the cutting of shrubs, many inhabitants continued to risk cutting it for subsistence uses.

assumed the major responsibility of fetching firewood almost on a daily basis. Some women recalled that they never returned home from the collective field empty-handed. Lacking access to beasts of burden, they would carry heavy loads of firewood or fodder on their backs or shoulders, sometimes from sites far away from home. They had to spend more time and walk increasing distances in search of fuel on steep slopes and in remote parts of the landscape. Even boys and girls were burdened with carrying heavy bundles of firewood beyond their physical capacity. As a consequence, a few of them suffered from physical handicaps. An elder woman told me that her granddaughter of thirty-nine years old in 2003, suffered from internal injuries caused by firewood collection far from home when she was only about ten years old.

Not only did uneven relations of power between men and women shape gender divisions of labor, they also structured gender-based roles in access to and use of natural resources. Women, relative to their male counterparts, utilized a variety of very arduous, labor-intensive strategies to sustain their families, and to change their own life and the lives of their children. This experience still loomed large in the memories of female villagers.

For instance, an elder woman aged 81 told me in 2003 that her husband passed away 43 years ago, leaving behind six mouths to feed, three daughters and three sons, ranging in age from 2-15. For the sake of her children, she decided to raise them on her own. With the help of her two elder daughters, she painstakingly supported her large family and sent all her sons to school. One son later became a state teacher, and another a village cadre. Apart from working for the collective, she relied predominantly upon the extra money derived from the selling of grasses and Chinese herbs. She spoke of chronic pain caused by carrying heavy loads of grass, fodder, firewood, and water in her youth. This story indicated how women's daily productive and reproductive practices were closely linked with the processes of local ecological change. It also demonstrated the differential opportunities for male and female children, and the way that people used natural resources to negotiate difficulties.

"Politics Were In Command"("*zheng zhi gua shuai*")

As elsewhere in rural China, the recurrent political campaigns after the Liberation, particularly those launched during the Cultural Revolution, created persistent tensions in village life.[1] Those with negative class labels (*chu shen bu hao*) such as landlords, rich peasants, and their descendents were periodically recognized as targets of struggle, and were subjected to discrimination, criticism, humiliation, class struggle sessions and even physical abuse. In the most radical period, everything personal was in some sense overtly political. Under this political environment, a child born into a "bad" class family was unable to escape the shadow of his/her family background. For instance, they were often assigned less rewarding jobs.

The Story of a Woman with "Bad Class Background"

Before I encountered Yang Baoqin personally, I learned that her deceased father was assigned the class label of rich peasant before her parents moved into the village in 1949. As a punishment, one year, her father was humiliated by having to collect urine each morning from the chamber pots of his team members to be used as manure. Her father was often accused of being too vocal when he was criticized, and he even severed the tip of his own tongue one time after a class struggle meeting. Her mother came from a middle peasant background. Her own good class status, more or less, provided a kind of buffer for herself. As a daughter, Yang Baoqin made many contributions to her native family inside and outside the household. To cultivate good relations with their team leader as well as to escape discrimination against them from their teammates, her father arranged her engagement to a son of the team leader,[2] three years younger than herself.

After the advent of household farming, her husband, a former tractor driver, long worked as an absentee worker outside the community. Yang Baoqin single-handedly made decisions about all agricultural production and domestic matters and was never idle. The long physical separation gave her a strength that other women lacked. Like most other women of her generation, Yang Baoqin never attended school, yet she was quite vocal and could always figure everything out clearly in her mind. She was a capable and talented household manager. Through her skillful budgeting, her household became relatively prosperous. Her capable work earned her admiration as a "female team leader". She was an energetic woman, who looked older than her

1 For a discussion of community politics under the collective regime, see Chan, Madsen and Unger (1992), Siu (1989), and Potter and Potter (1990). The class label was finally abolished in 1979.

2 In a report kept in the county archives, I discerned that her father was criticized for corrupting a team leader through affinity.

actual age. Her own narratives offer valuable insights into some of the key themes in this dissertation.

> I was born in 1956. I have four brothers and a younger sister. Male supremacy was rather strong when I was a girl. All my brothers, younger or older, attended school more or less. Like most other women of my generation, I never went to school for a single day. Because of our negative class label, when we were children, small kids in the neighborhood did not want to play with us and even bullied us. We were often called as "sons of bitches" (*gou zai zi* or *di zhu gao zi*). My siblings thus united and worked very hard to improve our lot.
>
> I began to work in collective fields when I was about 7-8 years old. If an adult finished a whole row, I did only half of it and was granted 5 work points for a whole day's work. I sometimes went herding for the team with my father and gathered firewood simultaneously. As a child, I learned female skills from my mother. I began to make shoes at the age of thirty. We had eight members in my native household, if each one needed an average of three pairs of shoes, I needed to make a total of 24 pairs of shoes in a year. It took about 6-7 days to completely finish one pair of shoes. In those days, we were dressed in clothes heavily patched, which required continual mending. I often stayed overnight and sometimes carried the sewing work with me and did it during the break. That's what life was then.
>
> After I grew up, I worked for the collective for about 300 days each year. In the spring, I labored side by side with men to transport manure to the fields, even during the winter I did whatever work I was assigned. Life was so bitter, but I worked like crazy inside and outside the home, and did not feel weary. I participated in building a reservoir in Hamlet D when I was seventeen years, old and later worked in a specialized team for two years. I also took part in various mass conservation campaigns such as digging irrigation canals, constructing dams, building roads and railways outside the community. Occasionally, most able-bodied youth, males and females, were sent to construction sites.
>
> Apart from working for the collective, my family members worked hard

to generate income. During the grass-cutting season, we devoted much energy to gathering grasses. We did not waste any time, collecting it before and after the communal work. I even refused to stay idle during the 10-minute break or approaching the end of a row when others sat for a rest. Quite often, we brought lunch with us to avoid losing time for the noonday meal. A bundle of grasses weighed about 20-40 catties; I sometimes collected three bundles per day.

During the heyday of the Cultural Revolution, our whole family became quite nervous and we were afraid of saying anything publicly. Income-generating activities often rendered us more vulnerable to attack. To avoid unwanted criticism, we even did not dare to gather a bigger bundle in front of other workmates. When we sold more grasses, made *kang* mats and wove baskets, some residents became jealous of us and viewed us as a threat.

Although my father suffered from mistreatment outside the household, he held absolute authority at home. We all had to do what he said. My father arranged me to be betrothed at the age of seventeen with the son of our team leader; he was then just turning fourteen, merely a kid. Since then, I also assumed the responsibility of making shoes for my prospective husband's household, since he had no mother when he was young. We married when he reached the age of twenty, the minimum age for legal marriage. The betrothal money was 300RMB, and a further 270RMB was offered for clothes before the wedding (no money would be given if clothes were provided by the groom's household). My parents used most of the payment for my brother's marriage and could not afford much for me. As a local saying goes, 'To sell daughters to live a humble life,' which was typical in my time.

After decollectivization, my husband had long been hired out to work as a tractor operator, and all matters at home had been left up to me. I did all the farming work by myself during the long period of physical separation. In 1992, I arranged the building of our new brick house myself, which was then the first pure brick house in the village. My husband seldom involved himself in my business. Even if he stays at home now, he still relies on me to make various decisions. He always says, 'Do as you please, and just treat it as if I were absent like before.'

The freezing of class status caused a great deal of trouble for other villagers as well. A Mongol male with a landlord family background told me, although his biological father had fought and died in Korea, he would never have a bright future. He was designated as a "*nei ren dang*" member when he was merely seventeen years old. In those days of 'never forgetting class struggles,' he felt his future was doomed and hopeless, and his inherited family label made him look inferior to others. No matter how hard he worked, he was nothing! He thought he would never be able to change his fate and win emancipation unless there was a change in regime. To overcome the disadvantages of their class background, some residents like Yang Baoqin worked extremely hard to prove their abilities and improve their lot.

The Onset of Agricultural Intensification

Agricultural intensification was already visible under the collectivist regime. Despite the fact that little room was left for the villagers' own initiatives, more innovative team leaders often mobilized their male and female teammates to expand acreage through land reclamation.[1] Fallow farming and crop rotation techniques were applied to these lands. Before the approach of each autumn, some team members were devoted to turning green grasses under on the grassland to fertilize the land and crops were planted during in the next spring. Since no manure was applied to this type of field, after tilling it for one or two years when crops no longer grew well, they gave up the land and reopened other tracts of "wasteland". As soon as grasses grew high again, another team might reclaim it.

After collectivization, small plots of cropland were granted to individual households as private plots. Corn at one time was commonly cultivated on such private plots (to eat green corn). Many residents, male and female, saved their energy for family-run private fields, and therefore the marginal return from their small private plots was often much higher than that from collective land. This was

1 Since its establishment, the history of Ao Village has had a distinctive thread of "land reclamation" to increase its grain production. With agricultural expansion, more and more pastureland, even marginal land, was put under cultivation. This process reached its first climax after local "Liberation" in 1947. The second wave of massive land reclamation occurred in the earliest years of decollectivization and even a year before it. As evidenced in the county archives, Ao Village was one of the places in Lan Township where land reclamation was rampant. Since the 1990s, large patchworks of marginal plots such as those on the slopes, and at base of the large gully, have been brought into private cultivation under land contract.

not a localized phenomenon.

A Chinese version of the Green Revolution was propelled locally from the late 1960s into the 1970s. "The Eight Characters for Agriculture" (*nong ye ba zi xian fa*)—widely advocated and practiced across rural China—were familiar to local people. Improvement in the following eight aspects was strongly promoted: soil improvement (*tu*), rational application of fertilizer (*fei*), water conservancy (*shui)*, improved seed species (*zhong*), rational close planting (*mi*), plant protection (*bao*), field management (*guan*) and improvement of farm implements (*gong*). In spite of the lack of specific village data, archival materials at the county level illustrated that management and conservation of arable land—the main natural resource used in agriculture—was always put on the local agenda. Although land was less intensively cultivated in those days than in 2003, fertilization, both chemical fertilizer and manure, was actively promoted in the late years of collectivism. Soil and water conservation activities were intermittently applied to agricultural land. Villagers tried out irrigation development several times.

The Chinese government also actively pursued and promoted agricultural mechanization in the rural modernization drive. Mao's statement, "the ultimate solution of the agricultural problem lies in mechanization"—iterated and reiterated in the national propaganda—found its local expression in local government efforts to promote mechanization. At the end of the 1960s, Greater Ao Village got its first tractor as a state gift, and in 1978 it got another chain-style 802-tractor with 75-horse power. In 1964, Mao's call "To Learn from Dazhai in Agriculture" was echoed across the nation. Dazhai was a village in Shaanxi province, which became relatively wealthy through improvement of harsh physical conditions. Its conservation-based agricultural practices called for better forage supply, afforestation, and rangeland management and had a positive impact on Chinese agriculture (Ho, 2000b). I found that the movement to emulate Dazhai made a frequent appearance in the county archive materials. In Ao Village, the campaign was a big push for local people to put their energy into improving their land so as to create "high-and stable-yield fields" and to build the physical infrastructure necessary to support increased productivity.

Apparently, here as in other parts of rural China, collectivized agriculture failed to win "common prosperity" for farmers, male and female. On the contrary, it led to a vicious cycle of disincentive, low productivity, women's marginalization, food shortage and ecological damage. The collective organization of production under the planned economy began to be abandoned across the Chinese countryside at the end of the1970s. Rural reforms set in motion the reorganization of agricultural production. In what follows, I look locally at smallholders' practices with mixed consequences for villagers, male and female, and for the local environment.

Plunging Into Smallholder Patterns: Agricultural Intensification, Technological Changes and the Gendered Labor Regimes

The year 1980 marked a watershed in the shift of the local political economy, as Ao Village switched from the decades-long collective regime into a smallholder's production system under the HRS. Since the household functioned as a principal unit of agricultural production and management, the household heads in most cases became leaders themselves. The changed political environment, coupled with dramatic social and economic transformations, set the stage for equally dramatic agrarian changes. Agricultural intensification had been reinforced, which in turn, was strengthened through technological changes (Boserup, 1965; Netting, 1993).[1]In the context of global re-structuring, Ao Village witnessed an increasing penetration of capital (chemical fertilizers and hybrid seeds) into different aspects of the production process. "Chinese agriculture, as it [became] further enmeshed in national and international markets, [shared] the rural problems experienced all over the world" (Muldavin, 2000: 249).

As elsewhere in rural China, agricultural production and NRM have changed over time after decollectivization in response to changing market opportunities, labor relations, and different actors' interests and priorities. Villagers intensified their farming practices through utilizing modern farming equipment techniques: chemical fertilizers, pesticides, hybrid seeds as well as tractors and irrigation systems. A new reservoir was built, which brought about a short period of economic honeymoon. Crop production was extended into marginal areas. Large tracts of farmland were terraced and the shelterbelt network on farms was constructed, which would have had a positive effect if managed properly. There were also more water supply and organic fertilizer inputs. The driving forces behind sustainable or unsustainable land management practices did not resemble those in the collective period. As Muldavin (2000: 236) correctly points out, "Since the introduction of reforms in 1978 and with

1 For a further analysis on China's changing farmland, see Vaclav Smil (1995) "Who Will Feed China?" *The China Quarterly*, No.143.

intensification of production, the use of land in China has become a short-sighted affair, with rare exceptions." As a consequence, the gender-environment nexus was re-structured with the advent of household farming.

Gendered Labor Regimes in Smallholders' Farming Practices

Smallholder farming in the post-reform period was characterized by the inroads of privatization, modern technology, and new social relations of agricultural production, including gender relations. Contrasting with the pre-1980 regime, smallholders controlled the disposition of the plots' use, the deployment of domestic labor as well as the production processes. These were mostly beyond the direct control of the state; this was a sharp departure from the collective production system. Smallholder farming was a household enterprise, which involved the input of household members with complementary responsibilities. The HRS and other rural reforms effectively boosted the enthusiasm of individual households to intensify land and labor use at the household level. The increased demand for land and labor has also changed agricultural labor relations (see Chapter seven for a more detailed discussion). Men's and women's roles in farming practices and livelihood systems were radically reconfigured in response to agrarian transitions unfolding at the household and village levels.

Household-based farming laid the foundation for a radically different deployment of domestic labor as well as unparalleled intensification of crop cultivation. Like most farmers in the west interior, labor was the main productive asset for most households in Ao Village. In the early post-1980 years, villagers arduously toiled the fields with amazing intensity from dawn to dark even in the most extreme heat of the day. Some women mentioned that they carried food with them to the fields without taking a midday break in the scorching months. Even in the year before the threshold of decollectivization, many residents started to channel their labor into "land reclamation." Lacking access to animals, many men and women initially opened up the "wasteland" by hand. Due to overwork, some women and men suffered from permanent physical ailments. As witnessed elsewhere in rural China, there was an impressive crop yield in the years immediately after 1980.[1]When it came to the succession of drought, men and women frequently pointed out, "If it remained under

1 For an excellent discussion of the efficiency gains of the HRS, see Chapter seven and the appendix in Louis Putterman (1993), *Continuity and Change in China's Rural Development*, New York and Oxford: Oxford University Press.

collectivism, everyone would have been reduced to starvation, but today people still can handle it, because they make a 100 percent effort."

Agriculture intensification at the household level also manifested itself in gendered-differentiated labor diversification. Since the 1990s, there were at least three forces shaping women's productive and reproductive work: the commercialization of agricultural production, the rise of off-farm work and migration, and technological changes. In the earliest reform years, to handle labor shortage, some boys and girls were taken out of school in order to help with farm work or livestock herding. Many children contributed substantially to the household economy when they were growing up. As I observed, in some Yunnan villages where this labor allocation strategy was still used by local peasants, the high drop-out rate among children, particularly girls, was still a serious problem that plagued rural education.

After the return of household farming, particularly since the 1990s, diversified allocation of family labor emerged as a family strategy and figured prominently in village life. As we will see in Chapter eight, men had disproportionately diversified out of crop production into other pursuits: sheep herding, off-farm activities, and migration out of the village. The number of women who engaged in full-time crop production (130 persons) was almost twice that of men (77), while the number of men who pursued part-time crop production (58) was almost six times that of women (10). The gendered migration of 50 men vs. 19 women was also remarkable. Field observations suggested that even if adult men remained in the community, village women were widely acknowledged to be more over-worked than men, exploiting themselves more heavily for their families, above all, for their children. The exodus of youngsters to the city, and the departure of adult men in particular, greatly reduced the source of domestic labor, and thus often intensified labor shortages at the household level.

The gendered labor mobilization could not be viewed as a complete rupture with the collective past. Jacka (1997) traces the changes and continuities in gender divisions of labor in domestic work, agriculture, and the cultural values underlying some stereotypes in rural China. When she elaborates the social construction of women's work, Jacka defines three dichotomies of "outside" and "inside", "heavy" and "light" and "skilled" and "unskilled" work, and argues that the first phrase in each pair is associated with men while the second pair is associated with women.

I only partly agree with her argument. Such articulations, I believe, need to be examined in specific local contexts. In Ying Village, as we will see in Chapter five, women long played a significant part in the "heavy" mass conservation labor. Furthermore, the local concepts of "heavy/light" and "skilled/unskilled" altered with the availability of specific technology and changed over time. Since the advent of household farming, the distinction between outside and inside became increasingly blurry. In Ao Village, women's productive and reproductive work was interwoven in complex ways beyond any simple dichotomy.

Village women in Ao Village did not form a homogeneous social grouping. The factors that structured the extent of women's agricultural participation included: age, wealth, ethnicity, migratory status, family life cycle, household enterprises, the presence and absence of male household members, the sex and occupation of their children and the like. If we disaggregate village women into different age groups, we can discern a dynamic picture of intergenerational differences. Although women over seventy no longer worked in the fields in 2003, yet they continued to work around the courtyard. Most elderly women in their sixties still engaged in field labor, either on their own plots or helping to work their children's fields in the peak labor season. Middle-aged women of 40-50 years old were the group who worked most strenuously. Most of them struggled hard to earn a large sum of money for the marriage of their son. On numerous occasions, I heard women in this age category said, "I am doomed to work constantly. When I relax in the slack season, I always fall sick." Unlike before, young new wives enjoyed a period of leisure without working the fields when they were pregnant or had small children, especially those who lived together with their husband's parents.

A feminization of agricultural labor has been reported widely in differing contexts in the Chinese countryside (Davin, 1999; Bossen, 2002; Judd, 1994). In some rural communities, as I found in many villages in Sichuan province, the male labor force almost entirely vacated the village. Only some adult women, the very old and very young, the so-called "38 61 99 troop" (it refers to the feminization of agriculture in rural China)were left behind in the community. As noted above, although we cannot say agriculture was entirely feminized in Ao Village, women were indeed more likely to be left behind to undertake crop production, formerly the responsibility of the entire household. Migration as a last resort required many sacrifices by both members of the couple. In over half a dozen households with married men migrating out of the village for wage labor, women carried out agricultural work exclusively or predominantly. In female-headed households, an intensification of female labor was extremely pronounced. Without men to take care of the heavy work, women were always overburdened. If they sought help with their work from other men, there might be village rumors about them. With their husbands being absent, young married women sought out the companionship of other women at night.

Xiao Yang was a smart woman who headed one of the female-headed households in the village. She was forty with two children, a daughter aged 15, who quit school before completing her sixth grade in 2002, and a son aged 13, who was attending a junior high school. The couple was trapped into debt trouble for several reasons. After their son's birth in 1990, they were fined about 6000RMB for violating a family planning policy of proper spacing. Following many others, they purchased a tricycle in 1998 for approximately 8000RMB on credit in the hope of earning extra money, which ended up creating little money from transportation services. They desperately sold it off in 2002 for about 3000RMB. In 2002, using the bricks that her husband earned from a neighboring brick factory, they built a house framework, which has further placed them into debt. This family of four lived in a one-room house and shared a *kang*. Much of their debt was charged 30 percent interest rates for ten months. As Xiao Yang bitterly complained, what they earned each year was not enough to pay back the loan "with legs".

Xiao Yang sought various ways to get rid of the family debt. In 2003, she persuaded her husband to migrate to the city to search for a job. She cooperated with her younger sister in the same village, whose husband was absent as well, to till their fields. The departure of adult males led to a severe labor shortage. The two women were often obliged to intensify their own labor. Xiao Yang lived not far away from my host's house. I observed that her door was always locked when they worked outside. She told me that they were so scared at midnight when they were waiting for their turns to irrigate the fields; they took a small child of her younger sister's with them, who finally fell asleep in the fields. With help from her daughter, Xiao Yang also raised a pig, two sows, a horse and a donkey. She earned about 2000RMB from the sale of an adult pig and two litters of piglets. In spite of tremendous pressures on her time and energy, she grasped every opportunity to work for wages. Immediately following painstaking weeding, she and her daughter both worked on a road construction project for half a month and earned about 1000RMB.

She sometimes also worked on the farm of others. When 5 *mu* of her paddy fields were polluted by the dust deriving from the road construction, she made every effort to defend her own rights to gain compensation (see Chapter six). Her experience of being overwork was most notable when her husband was absent.

A fraction of women like Yang Baoqin and Xiao Yang did not hesitate to take over the role of their husbands in their absence. Women's agricultural contributions, as a result, gave rise to changed assumptions about the conjugal contract (see Chapter seven). However, some conventional agrarian femininities and masculinities remained unchanged. One example may serve to illustrate this point clearly. Wu Dong, fifty-three years old, was the oldest male migrant in 2003. He was a carpenter during the collective period and sometimes worked as an electrician after decollectivization. This couple borrowed heavily for the marriage of their son in the mid-1990s. When they divided the household in 1996, they assumed a debt of 7000RMB, and spent another 8000RMB to build a simple house for themselves. Most of their earnings each year went to repay their loans. In 2003, Wu Dong decided to try his luck in the city in the hope of changing their plight. He finally found a job of unloading stones in a quarry in the suburbs of Tianjin. He was forced to return home after his nephropathy recurred, and brought back home only about 1500 RMB after working outside for eight months.

When he was working far away, his wife Zhao Suyun ran a farm of 17 *mu* on her own. She also did everything possible to repay their loan little by little whenever she earned some money. She raised a pig as well as a sow for the sale of piglets. She sold two litters of them for 1100RMB. Like most of her peers, she never went to school when she was a girl. When her husband was absent, Zhao Suyun decided to plant a new variety of seed corn on their 6 *mu* of reclaimed contracted land at the base of the large gully. Extension agents from the township seed station took charge of showing them specific techniques. They recommended a spacing of 2 by 2 *chi* for a stand (3 *chi* equals 1 meter) without paying attention to the specific situation of soil quality. Without any prior experience in the cultivation of seed corn, she consulted many residents in the neighborhood who had tried the planting before. She finally chose 3 by 2*chi* as suggested by experienced villagers.

When faced with labor shortage, she hired a few women to help her with her fieldwork. While some other households failed due to improper spacing, she won a bumper harvest and thus contributed greatly to relieving the family's indebtedness. I met Wu Dong soon after he returned to the village. When talking about his wife's performance, he boasted that he was a teacher of his wife, "I think hard about crop cultivation, while she doesn't. She knows nothing but to weed. I am always her teacher. If I had stayed in the village, we would have harvested more." Indeed, as we shall see in Chapter seven, the bias against women and devaluation of women's economic contributions were not unusual in Ao Village.

The above stories draw attention to a regional pattern of migration and the experiences of female-managed split households. In these split households, all productive and reproductive work fell on the shoulders of women. Physical separation also gave them the power to make decisions themselves about what to grow or raise, how much to grow or keep, and whether or how much to sell crops and animals. In the few cases like Yang Baoqin and Xiao Yang, women became de facto farm and household managers on their own. This helped explain the economic autonomy of many village women.

In sharp contrast to what was practiced before 1980, women exercised greater agency than they could in the collective era. Women's roles in agricultural practices, including daily decision-making increased remarkably. Although there was little institutional support from the outside in the form of extension, credit, training or input supply, a small minority of women was quite successful in crop and livestock farming. It was my impression that even if they were not literate, a sizeable proportion of women were quite familiar with farm operations—daily agricultural practices, labor inputs, and to some extent, market prices, indicating their deep involvement in domestic decision-making. Some non-literate women, like Song Ling, could always offer more accurate information than men about the concrete time that an event occurred[1]and the amount of money spent. In our daily conversations, women's identities and sense of pride surfaced and resurfaced frequently in their own narratives. This pattern was clearly part of a larger picture in rural China.

There were "peaks and troughs" in crop production , and thus the work routines

1 As most women in her peer group, Song Ling often used some specific events to describe the time, such as "when I was thirteen," "the year I married," "the year my son was in the hospital," "the year that the brick factory was established" and so forth.

differed in winter and summer.[1] The winter months lasted from November until April the subsequent year. In contrast, animal production proceeded all the year round without remarkable seasonal shifts. The rhythm of their daily, seasonal and yearly labor arrangements largely shaped their everyday lives. In the pages that follow, I will outline household farming operations with the cycle of crops, and refer to my host family and that of their farming partner, Liu Xing and his wife, in many cases. Both households had only two present persons, tilling 15 *mu of* cropland-a typical household size and landholding in Ao Village. Since 2001, the two households cooperated with each other in crop production. In 2004, the two couples—all were experienced farmers—described to me the gendered process of farming practices in Ao Village that I mostly observed in the previous year. It took at least four months for local crops to grow and ripen from April through October, and farm households experienced approximately two months of intense activity during the busiest season. It took about 100 labor days (on average 10-12 hours per day) to till 15 *mu* of cropland, which meant that each *mu* required 6.7 days of labor. If wife and husband both took part in all stages of farming, they worked roughly 50 days each on the plots.

The Planting Season: The annual farming cycle started in early April. When the weather got warm, villagers began to clean up manure in the shed or remove the stubble in the fields. The land was plowed either by hired tractor operators or by themselves. After the tractor plowing, they needed to level the fields using the hoe. One *mu*'s work took about three days. To remove the remaining stumps took one day per *mu.* If plowed by animals, one *mu* took 4-5 hours, averaging 2 *mu* per day. Plowing was historically defined as "masculine work." Although tractor operation was still a male preserve, with the return of household farming, both men and women were likely to be involved in plowing, using animals.

Irrigation began immediately after the Tomb-sweeping Day (April 5 in 2003). When watering the field, villagers had to wait for their turns day and night and showed up in the fields to guide the water to their own fields. If there were enough

1 As elsewhere in rural China, in their daily farming practice, residents never relied on the western solar calendar, or *yang li*. Instead, they depended upon the traditional lunar calendar or *yin li*, and particularly the traditional solar calendar or *jie qi,* which were always on their lips, but this was totally unfamiliar to me, as an urban person. In the text, I converted them all into the western solar calendar.

water, it took about two hours for watering 2 *mu* of fields. Both sexes might take part in the task. If their turn happened to be at night, men were more likely to take the responsibility. To deliver the compost to the fields was always tough work. If an animal cart was used (about 1000 catties per load), to deliver over 30 loads was quite normal in most households. It required 5-6 days to finish it. Even if a tricycle was used, it took at least a day to deliver 7-8 loads. Motor transportation by tricycle was widely used for delivering compost (A load of manure weighed about 4000 catties).

The cultivation of annual crops began with corn cultivation in irrigation fields, which often took place 5-6 days before or after May 1. The crop cultivation in rain fed fields occurred after May 20 when the rainfall arrived to make the ground moist enough. The spring planting was the busiest time for farmers in this part of China. The planting procedure normally included the following gender-specific tasks: (1) to dig ditches (men); (2) to drop seeds (women); (3) to apply fertilizer (women); (4) to apply compost (men), and (5) to drive animals to draw the roller so as to make the soil solid (women). A team of two animals was usually yoked to a plow. Men usually held the plow. Following the furrow that men made, women poured seeds into it and dropped chemical fertilizer powder. It was usually men who applied compost to cover the seeds. This backbreaking labor was traditionally a male job. Hong Xiang bought a seeder for 120RMB in 2000, which made it possible for them to finish the first three tasks-to dig the furrow, apply fertilizer powder and drop seeds-at one time. The use of the seeder saved them much time going back and forth several times, and they could plant 4-5 *mu* of fields per day. As Hong Xiang commented, the seeder could save almost two persons' work. Inspired by their improved productivity, by 2003, this implement was widely purchased and used by other villagers.

The Weeding Season: In a "good" year with sufficient rainfall, weeding began about ten days after planting. To weed 15 *mu* of land three times took almost a month. There was thus always a labor bottleneck in June and July. Hand weeding, a traditional female territory, was labor intensive, tedious work. Women used a kind of short hoe to thin out the seedlings and pull out the weeds. After crops had grown for about two months, farmers weeded again by using a harrow drawn by animals, which was locally called *yun*. This was followed the second hand weeding about 4-5 days later. After crops had grown for about three months, farmers weeded again by using another harrow drawn by animals, locally called *tang.* Both *yun* and *tang* aimed to turn over grasses, upturn the fertilizer spread around the plant stand, and to loosen the ground so as to increase water absorption and retention. Men usually performed the tasks of *yun* and *tang*, yet many women learned to weed with a donkey, for better or worse. The labor demand of weeding different crops varied greatly.

The Harvest and Post-harvest Activities: The harvest was carried out around the Mid-autumn Festival, which lasted for about a month. During or even before the harvest, some women prepared the courtyard for threshing. They reaped crops with the sickle, which basically took one day for one *mu* of land. In the case of corn harvest, after removing corn from its stalk, they cut and packaged the stalks into bundles. Both corn and stalk bundles were carried back home soon afterward. After ears of millet or sorghum were stripped from their stems, a practice always done by women, they were usually trampled by driving an animal cart or a tricycle over them. Men often did winnowing. Grains were ultimately bagged in sacks and stored in the room, or readied to be sold soon.

Apparently, the deployment of domestic labor was quite flexible. Gender division of labor in crop production showed remarkable continuities and discontinuities with the collective past. In many households, particularly those with men working off-farm inside and outside the community, women had become the mainstay of field-based activities. After the harvest and post-harvest activity was over, villagers were preoccupied with exchanging labor to cut short stalks as feed, or repairing sheds or houses. Some people had more leisure time for sleep, gossip, and entertainment, but men and women in sheep-owning households usually became even busier.

As in many other regions in rural China, in spite of a remarkable increase in agricultural productivity in smallholder farming, crop cultivation increasingly became an unrewarding activity. As will be seen from the following two tables, the gross crop value in my host family in 2004 amounted to 3650RMB, about 1594RMB higher than that in 2003. The farming expenses including fertilizers, irrigation fees, seed, and the agricultural tax equaled 867RMB. After deducting farming inputs of 867RMB, they could net an estimated income of 2783RMB. Divided by 16.5 *mu*, the net gross value per *mu* was 169RMB. The daily net income per person within a space of 50 days approximated 28RMB. Obviously, they received low profits compared to the high costs of inputs and smallholder's grain earnings were marginal. It seemed impossible for smallholders to produce substantial surpluses for the market. Many farmers resorted to diversification of the household economy through other pursuits.

Table 4.2 Crop production in My Host Family (2003)

Plot	Land (*mu*)	Distance from Home (km)	Year Allocated	Types of Crops	Yield (catty)		Incomes (RMB)	
					per *mu*	Gross	Per catty	Total
A	2.0	2.5	1990	Millet	240.0	480.0	0.70	336
B	7.1	2.0	1998	Buckwheat[1]	83.6	600.0	1.10	660
C	2.0	0.5	1990	Black bean	54.0	108.0	1.45	156
D	2.0	1.5	1989	S/M[2]	26.0	52.0	2.00	104
E	1.0	2.5	1990	Corn	600.0	600.0	0.50	300
F	1.0	3.0	1991	Corn	1000. 0	1000. 0	0.50	500
								2056

Source: 2003 interview.

Note:

[1] This tract of land was converted from hitting melon, which was a king of local melon. When opening it, villagers hit it with their fist. Its seeds rather than the melon itself were sold for cash.

[2] S/M: one *mu* soybean and one *mu* millet.

Table 4.3 Costs and Returns of Crop production in My Host Family (2004)

Plot	Land (*mu*)	Crops	Yield/per *mu* (catty)	Gross Value of Yield (RMB)	Expenses Items(RMB)	
A	2.0	Sun Flower	40	160	Amine	210.0
B	7.1	Hitting Melon	94	1660	Urea	285.0
C	2.0	Millet[1]	200	630[1]	Chicken Manure	140.0
D	2.0	Corn	500	300	Seeds	40.0
E	1.0	Corn	500	300	Plowing	52.0
F	1.0	Corn	1000[2]	600	Agricultural Tax[3]	97.7
G	1.5	Millet	200		Irrigation Fee	42.0
Total	16.5			3650[4]		867.0

Source: 2004 interview.

Note:

[1] 200 catties of husked millet per *mu* yielded roughly 180 catties unhusked millet, which meant 700 catties could yield approximately 630 catties.

[2] The corn yield with sufficient irrigation water could reach about 1000-1200 catties per *mu*, which would be reduced by half if not irrigated.

[3] Agricultural taxes for the year of 2003 collected in November 2003 was 124.61RMB, but they refunded the overcharged tax of 26.96RMB in May 2004.

[4] Actual cash income was less than this figure, since almost all corn was used as fodder.

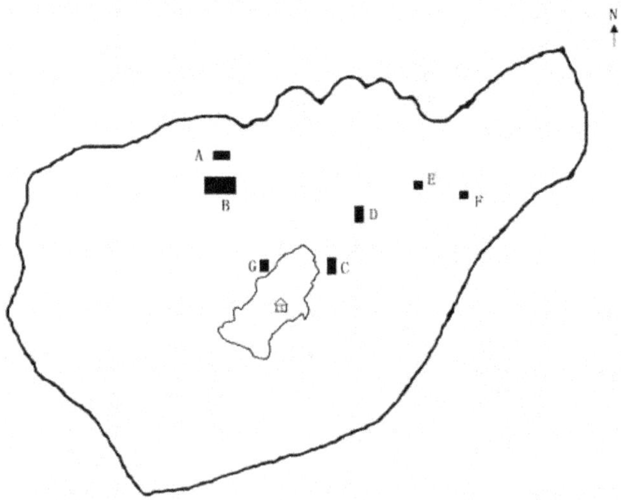

Figure 4.1 Land Parcels of My Host Family (2003)

From 1980 to 2003 in an attempt to maximize land use to increase productivity, more capital-intensive technology was utilized in crop cultivation, and soil conditions were altered, to a significant extent, through fertilization, irrigation, cropping pattern and other land use practices. Many residents were quite sensitive to the outcomes of environmentally damaging practices.

A Sketch of Fertilizer Use

A "Green Revolution" style of farming in Ao Village was clearly reflected in the sharp increase of chemical fertilizer uses. Household farming, coupled with an increased use of manure and a growing dependency on chemical fertilizer, supported relatively high yields, which, in turn, triggered an unprecedented rise in the demand for chemical sources of fertilizer. Under collectivism, villagers used to apply a certain amount of animal manure to collective fields. In the 1970s, chemical fertilizer supplied by the state was basically refused. Even in the initial years after decollectivization, no one considered fertilizer as essential. Lin Hui, a woman married into Ao Village from Hebei province, recalled, when she came to the village in 1985, residents relied only on manure. When her mother came for a visit, she once persuaded her husband to try a little bit of chemical fertilizer to raise the yield. Yet, her husband insisted that fertilizer was not of much use in the sandy fields in Ao Village. Only 3-4 years later a few well-informed males started to try it in their sorghum fields.

Not until the availability of the irrigated field did the use of chemical fertilizer spread. In 1989-90, a few creative men experimented with a small quantity of fertilizer to spring wheat planted in the irrigated fields. From the third year onwards after all irrigated fields were put into corn cultivation, an increasing quantity of fertilizer was applied there. At the beginning, no chemical fertilizer was used in the field with organic fertilizers. Shortly afterward, both fertilizer and manure were applied simultaneously. The amount of chemical fertilizer applied per *mu* was initially about 2-3 catties, which had reached over 10 catties of amine and around 20 catties of urea (see table 4.4). The situation was even more severe in a village like Lan Village where fewer livestock were raised. It deserves noting that prosperous residents were more likely to use more purchased fertilizer. Villagers also used more fertilizer on the crops that yielded the highest return. Commercialization was, undoubtedly, a strong motivation to turn to heavy use of commercial fertilizer to their fields, particularly to the large tracts of contracted land geared toward market production.

There was a widely shared concern over the heavy use of fertilizers among village men and women.[1] It was clear to them that higher farm yields could only be achieved by supplying more fertilizers, and no fertilizer meant a waste of land and labor. As elsewhere, Ao Village suffered from the loss of soil fertility and productivity due to overuse of and dependence on agro-chemicals. The soil deterioration was indicated by the fact that the soil became "harder and harder", as they frequently complained. The increased weed growth due to fertilizer use also required more intensive weeding on the part of women. In the eyes of some women, chemical fertilizers were poisonous and many diseases occurring in rural areas could be attributed to their uses. When they gave me various products to bring back to Beijing, a few of them

1 More and more scholars believe that imbalanced fertilizer use is a hidden time bomb in rural China. If it is not corrected, soil productivity, and thereby the welfare of rural population, and ultimately food security for China are in jeopardy. The organic matter in the soil has also been depleted by other causes. The prevalent practice of removing and using crop residues for fuel and fodder led to the loss of fertile land. The "pesticide treadmill" (e.g., the growing dependency and increased cost of pesticide use) reported in many other localities, where farmers used the pesticides to minimize the time spent on weeding, did not seem to happen in Ao Village. The available seeds sold in local markets, whether vegetable or grain, had already been mixed with pesticides. Villagers only applied a small quantity of pesticides to rice and some vegetables.

emphasized what they offered was "valueless, but are real 'green food' grown for their own use without putting any fertilizer".

Table 4.4 Fertilizer Application on Cropland in My Host Family (2004)

Crop (*mu*)		Fertilizer Use Per *mu* (catty)		
		Base (amine)	Top(urea)	Livestock Manure[1]
Corn	4.0	18	25	Chicken
Millet	3.5	8	15	Chicken/Donkey
Hitting Melon	7.1	13	16	Donkey/Pig
Sun Flower	2.0	8	17	Pig

Source: 2004 interview.

Note: They bought two cubic meters of chicken manure, and put most of it in their corn fields and the rest of it in their millet fields.

In this part of rural China, the application of organic manure has increased simultaneously with the boom of livestock development. Animal manures, the by-product of livestock management, was collected from pigs, chickens, sheep, donkeys, mules and horses. The ashes were always thrown to the animal pens and were mixed with manure. The best manures like chicken manure, were applied to the fields that could bring the greatest cash returns. In the case of Ao Village, that was the cornfields. Many villagers turned their former fourth-class irrigated land into the most productive parcels, even better than their previous first-class plots. Some households bought chicken manure to fertilize their ration fields. In a small proportion of household fields, where much chicken manure was used consecutively, little mineral fertilizer was used.

"Green Revolution" Seed Varieties and Cropping Patterns

Ao Village was endowed with abundant, albeit low quality, land, and farmers practiced single cropping in its relatively flat fields. The croplands in the village were distinguished locally as dry land (locally called *shan di*), irrigated land (*shui jiao di*) and paddy fields (*dao tian*). Ao Village combined dry and irrigated farming after the construction of the reservoir. Less than ten years earlier, over 100 *mu* of lower wastelandon both sides of the highway was converted into rice paddy fields, depending on the water flowing from the base of the large gully.

The cropping history during the collective period was characterized by low yield coarse grains, which mainly included millet, sorghum, buckwheat and others. With the availability of the reservoir, farmers tried double cropping of spring wheat, followed by buckwheat in the irrigated fields in the first two years. Intensive cropping was also supported through planting crop varieties that had shorter growing seasons. They also introduced drought-resistant high-yielding hybrid varieties of seeds. After decollectivization, agricultural land use shifted from an almost total concentration on subsistence grains to a mix of food and cash crops.[1]

Table 4.5 Crop Area and Its Percentage at Village Level (2003)

Crops	Area (*mu*)	Percentage (%)
Corn	818	21.7
Seed corn	190	5.1
Millet	755	20.1
Sorghum	565	15.0
Buckwheat	335	8.9
Hitting melon	299	8.0
Sun Flower	206	5.5
Back Soybean	184	4.9
Soybean	97	2.6
Sticky broomcorn millet (*shu zi)*	80	2.1
Rice[1]	78	2.0
Mung bean	73	1.9
Sesame	66	1.8
Unstuck broomcorn millet (*mi zi*)	16	0.4
Total	3761[2]	100.00

Source: 2003 household survey.

Note:

[1] Less than ten households cultivated rice. The actual acreage of rice should be greater than this figure, because not all the villagers who planted rice lived in the village.

[2] Based upon my survey, the total cultivated land was 3761 *mu*, which was still a conservative figure. At least the fields cultivated by those villagers who lived nearby were not incorporated. To my knowledge, at least seven households lived beyond the village, but their members returned to till their land. Village records reported 2628 *mu* of cropland sown in Ao Village. If each person was entitled to 5 *mu* of ration land, the total cultivated land would be 2820 *mu* (564 person in total). The gap between the official and actual figures shows an approximate one-third underestimation in the acreage sown. In early 2003, about 1300 *mu* of farmland was lost to a cropland conversion project. This indicated that the acreage sown in the preceding years should be much larger than the figure of my survey.

1 The cropping pattern in Ao Village was similar to that in Lan Township as well as in Aohan as a whole. The acreage of the first five crops sown in Lan Township in 2003 were: corn, millet, sorghum, buckwheat and rice. The order of the first five crops in Aohan was: corn, rice, millet, sorghum and buckwheat (ASB, 2004).

Since the third year with irrigated fields, residents used the same tract of land for corn cultivation over and over again without crop rotation. The corn patch accounted for 21.7 percent of all cultivated land in 2003. Corn was mainly used as an animal feed for pigs, sheep or chickens, or sold off for cash instead of for direct human consumption. Corn has been particularly favored by local men and women for a couple of reasons. Corn yields were higher than other varieties of grain per unit of land. High-straw varieties were popular in Aohan, which provided the villagers with substantial benefits including fodder and firewood. Villagers sometimes intercropped corn with kidney bean, and the corn plants provided support for the climbing beans. From the early 1990s, farmers tried various new varieties of corn with different maturation rates. No one could tell exactly how many times they had changed varieties. As they reported, "We plant whatever the local seed station is selling and spreading." Regardless of varieties, the repetitive monocropping contributed to exhaustion of the soil.

Except for corn, the remaining crops were all planted on the rain fed land. Husked millet, locally called *gu zi*, was long a predominant grain crop. Unhusked millet, locally referred to as *xiao mi*, was historically the mainstay of local subsistence and was still the staple that formed the bulk of the daily diet in 2003. The acreage of millet was as large as 818 *mu*. Sorghum ranked the fourth in acreage only after corn, seed corn and millet. It was primarily sold to be converted into alcohol. Buckwheat was a late season food crop. Many residents turned to this crop after their hitting melon was damaged by a heavy hailstorm. Several leguminous crops such as soybeans, black beans, and oil-bearing crops like sesame and sunflower were also planted each year, but only a small proportion of land was devoted to these crops. Hitting melon was a kind of small melon, locally called *da gua*. Residents also ate the melon as a fruit. In 1994, a young male electrician working for the township government then, who frequently traveled within and beyond the boundary of the township, experimented with the melon planting in 10 *mu* of contracted land. The seeds that he harvested were sold for a cash income of approximately 6000RMB. From that year onward, hitting melon was grown as a major cash crop in the village.

After the launch of household farming, individual men and women were left to make largely unregulated planting decisions by themselves. Cropping choice at the household level in a given year depended on different combinations of factors: grain self-sufficiency, crop yield, growth cycle, market price and profit, crop rotation cycle, sex and age of household members and their consumption. The millet-legume combination was widely practiced to improve soil fertility. Crop varieties created differing demands for the labor of women and men. In this sense, the crop choice itself was gendered. When faced with a labor shortage, particularly with the absence of women, households avoided planting labor-intensive crops. A few young bachelors who tilled large tracts of land continually planted less labor-intensive crops such as corn and sorghum instead of high density crops like millet or sesame. By the same token, a couple of men whose wives worked outside the area, chose to plant crops with minimal labor input.This practice was not so notable among women, even for those whose husbands were absent for a long time.

Generally, local people tended to choose a more diverse cropping pattern than under collective regimes. The increasing amount of land sown with cash crops reflected a growing responsiveness to the larger economy. However, the significant shift to high-value crops was still constrained by an unpredictable market and many other factors. Given fluctuating prices in local markets, the crop choice was often opportunistic. There were wide discrepancies in the crop yield per *mu* at the household level, which depended on the nature of various inputs,[1] including the amount and type of animal manure, gender, the skill and initiative of family laborers, and the use of modern technology. Even in normal years, low and unstable grain yields characterized rain-based agriculture. The successive drought from 1999-2004 made it even harder for villagers to grow crops profitably.

Gender and Agricultural Technology

As in the past, women were often marginalized from the technologies that shaped their lives, meanwhile they also benefited from some of those technological advances. As in the rest of rural China, agricultural technology spread slowly. Although some farming techniques such as deep plowing, plastic film mulching and irrigation were promoted, non-mechanized labor-intensive production still dominated agricultural practices. Most farm tasks were still performed manually through traditional techniques in 2003. Hand tools such as the sickle and hoe were widely used. One household bought a new small tractor with 28-horse power in 2000. To my knowledge, in 2003, only about 180 *mu* of seed corn was sown by the machine, and

1 Inputs in this dissertation refer to many components of production, including land, labor, seed, fertilizer, machinery, tools, and irrigation water.

no crop harvested by it. After electrification in 1979, many labor-saving technologies were introduced into the village. Compared to men, women were marginalized from modern technology, which had profound impacts on men's and women's work. As of 2003, all electricians were males, as were the operators of different varieties of food and feed processing equipment.

One telling example of uneven benefits by gender from new technologies was men's and women's different access to more productive vehicles. As has been commonly discovered elsewhere, all drivers of the big cart, tractor and power-driven vehicles in Ao Village were males. During the collective era, village men initially controlled the ox cart. After the late 1960s, each team owned a big cart, locally known as *da che*. It was pulled by four horses or mules, and could load up to 5000-6000 catties of grains, or a maximum of 20 persons at a time. The cart managers earned 3600 work points per year. They were sometimes hired out to earn extra income for their teams and often involved in long-distance travel. Whenever there was a mass conservation campaign, cart managers might take part in it by driving their carts; they also carried brides on engagement or marriage occasions. One of the car managers proudly told me, "In those days, brigade cadres were first-class citizens, while cart managers were second-class."

Following decollectivization, villagers in Ao Village switched to more productive vehicles, unlike the more economically deprived hill villages in Yunnan and Sichuan provinces which I previously visited, where both men and women still carried heavily laden baskets on their backs even with manure in them up and down steep village paths. This phenomenon was rarely seen in Ao Village. After decollectivization, villagers initially owned a kind of small iron-wheeled cart without axles, followed by a more efficient animal-drawn cart locally known as No.3 cart. By 2003, most households in Ao Village owned this type of cart made of a wooden framework with two rubber-tire wheels. A single animal, either a donkey, mule or horse, could draw it. Most women could handle the donkey cart, but only a few could harness the mule or horse on their own. It was not uncommon that women walked to and from their private fields or other places if males in their households were not available to handle the mule/horse cart. Elder people normally did not have draft animals of their own.

In the early years of the collective period, bicycles were few and far between. If a man rode a bicycle—locally called "a foreign donkey" then—passing through the village, residents might rush out to look at it. In 2003, over twenty village men owned and rode motorcycles, which had become a sign of masculine success in off-farm work. Two women owned their motorcycles, they were both public figures and rode them for their business: one was an UNDP micro-credit worker, and another one was the village women's director. Three male petty traders each drove a five-wheel truck on a regular basis. A young man who co-managed the grocery store also owned a minibus and used it as a taxi. My qualitative observations also indicated that the act of driving, along with related knowledge and skill, was associated with masculinity.

A kind of diesel-powered agricultural tricycle locally known as "*san lun che*" made its first appearance in the village in the late 1980s. In 2003, over 30 households owned this kind of diesel fuel tricycle. It had a carrying capacity of up to two tons of coal. It was also used to thresh millet, rice, or alfalfa seeds on the ground.[1] The power-driven vehicle was much more productive than the No. 3 cart. The use of motor transportation was a site of gender differentiation. The vehicle was commonly sought after and driven exclusively by young and a few middle-aged men, and driving it was socially constructed as a masculine job. Buying a tricycle was actually beyond the means of most households, yet over the past ten years, many households with young men available even paid an exorbitant interest rate of 3 percent per month to secure a loan of 7000-8000RMB to purchase one. As a result, some households were ultimately trapped in severe debt. To keep a tricycle was costly. If they wanted to drive it on a highway, all expenditures charged amounted to a total of about 1300RMB for each vehicle, excluding the fuel fee. In 2003, only 7-8 households could afford to pay the entire fee so as to drive their vehicles beyond the village. Liu Xing was one of the few lucky men who still earned a considerable income from their vehicle services. During my stay in the village, he frequently drove his tricycle to pull loads of bricks, coal, building material, manure, grains and even persons within and outside the village.

The Livestock Economy in an Ecological Context

Being endowed with relatively favorable conditions for livestock production,

1 I observed male villagers putting millet on the ground in large circles and then driving the tricycle around to trample it. It took much less time to thresh millet this way than driving an animal to do it.

the agrarian economy in Ao Village had long held a comparative advantage in developing pasture-based livestock production. Compared with most other villages in the agricultural zone. In this part of rural China, the number and species composition of grazing animals, pasturing practices,[1] commercial orientation, gender divisions of labor in livestock production, and many other factors, interacted with each other to shape the local environment. Some livestock-environment problems were intertwined with economic, political and cultural factors, which in turn, interplayed with ecological and physical forces. As with the vicissitudes of crop production, the environmental issues associated with livestock farming cannot be addressed in isolation from the larger political economy and local socio-cultural factors. The following section will outline the burden of livestock production on natural resources, gender-specific roles and experiences of livestock farming, and the implications of environmental conservation for the livestock economy.

The Livestock Economy in From a Historical Perspective

Livestock production has long played an important part in the village and household economy in this part of China. In the pre-Liberation period, native Mongols were not pastoralists, yet animal husbandry was their dominant agricultural activity. With the influx of Han migrants, crop cultivation was gradually integrated into the local farming system and later became the mainstay of local livelihoods. According to the recollections of elder villagers, on the eve of the local Liberation, four male shepherds herded approximately 500 head of sheep, 100 head of cattle, 30 mules or horses, and over 50 head of donkeys for Mongolian and Han Chinese elites. During land reform, an overwhelming majority of livestock was allocated to poor households on a per capita basis.

During the collective period, although each team was obliged to meet state delivery quotas for animal production, due to the deep-rooted national commitment to grain self-sufficiency, the economic role of livestock production was generally disregarded. The pattern was very similar to what Ho (2000a) describes in neighboring Ningxia province: (1) the prices for wool and mutton were set by the state; (2) rural collectives had to produce according to the annual quotas for state procurement; (3) self-subsistence rather than profitability was the main driving force for livestock production. Over most of the period under the collective regime, the

1 For the purpose of this dissertation, the livestock other than browseable species was not discussed here.

four teams in the village owned, respectively, about 100-200 head of sheep, 20-30 non-draught cattle, around 10 oxen, and a small amount of horses and donkeys. Adding privately owned animals, the livestock number ranged from 800-1200. In those days, private ownership of livestock was kept to a minimum. Only relatively rich households owned 3-5 sheep herded by team shepherds. Livestock was kept at a subsistence level, and the practice of animal-raising was delegated to a few males.

With the onset of decollectivization in 1980, all large livestock were allocated to small farming groups, and small livestock to individual households. Since the late 1980s, a boom in livestock production occurred. Compared to crop production, livestock production in 2003 was still a relatively lucrative livelihood strategy, a critical means for local people to generate a consistent source of income from natural resources beyond their ration land.

According to my survey in 2003, 135 out of 146 resident households, or 92.5 percent, raised some kind of animals, large or small.[1]The rapid expansion of livestock production after decollectivization was embedded in the regional political economy. Livestock development in this part of rural China was often treated as a popular poverty-fighting measure.

Different animals do not utilize the pasture in the same manner, nor do they consume the same type and quantity of forage, and therefore have divergent impacts on the natural environment. In Ao village, apart from sheep and goats,[2] grazing animals included cattle, horses, mules, and donkeys. Even indigenous pigs were historically adapted to grazing. By the time of decollectivization, the ox was still a highly valued animal for local people. Many recounted with excitement having had an ox of their own after the return of household farming. In a few years following the reform, almost all households kept oxen and many other large animals. According to knowledgeable residents, from 1984-1988, there were approximately 130-150 head of cattle, and 40-50 horses and mules. Since the late 1980s, residents gradually shifted to more powerful livestock—horses, mules or donkeys—as a source

1 In the remaining 11 households without animals, ten of the households were elder singles or couples.

2 Goats, characterized as relatively prolific and profitable, were long raised in Ao Village. Since goats were more destructive in their grazing habits, beginning in 2002, the grazing of goats was formally forbidden in Aohan. In 2003, only 3-4 households, respectively, kept a goat as milk animal for their lambs.

of draft power. A local saying vividly captured the sharp change happening at that time, "No ox was used in plowing and no oil was used in lighting." In 2003, only one household of ethnic Hui raised 34 head of cattle, because they enjoyed good connections to the market. They hired a village boy to graze the flock for them.

As with sheep, the number of large livestock was in constant flux. During my survey period in late 2003, there were 51 horses, 26 mules, and 216 donkeys. Among them, donkeys accounted for 73.7 percent of large livestock, which closely approximated the villagers' estimation of 80 percent. During the collective era, only a small minority of affluent households raised a donkey for transporting water or firewood, grinding grain or for riding. Since the mid-1990s, donkeys have become increasingly profitable in local markets. Because donkeys were easy to handle, the use of donkeys as beasts of burden was also particularly favored by women.

The combination of livestock and crop production benefited local men and women in significant ways. Draft animals—horses, mules, and donkeys—provided an important source of draft power. Certain field work such as plowing, planting, off-field work like post-harvest activities, and local transportation depended heavily on the power of draft animals. Stall-fed animals also provided manure as organic fertilizer, which was an important input for improving soil fertility and increasing crop yields. The mixed farming of crops and livestock also enabled local people to provide their animals with a large quantity of grain stalks as forage.

Prior to 2003, all livestock, large and small alike, were allowed to graze the communal land. Since large livestock was not grazed on a day-to-day basis, in the following section, I will particularly deal with sheep-raising, which was always identified as a main reason responsible for pastureland degradation in Aohan. Faced with reduced rewards from crop cultivation due to prolonged droughts, combined with limited alternative economic activities beyond crop production and uncertainties in migration, inhabitants increasingly turned to sheep-raising as a last resort to scratch out a living. This gave them at least some security, to use a local expression, since sheep "ensure stable yields regardless of drought or excessive rain (*han lao bao shou)*". The modest profits were primarily derived from the sale of unproductive adult animals, wool, or their offspring. Despite the ever-changing local and global markets, the selling price of sheep was relatively stable, being around 3RMB per catty in 2004, the same as the preceding year. The heaviest sheep amounted to approximately 140-150 catties.

Household sheep-raising developed dramatically after the dismantling of the collectives. About 5-6 sheep-owning households continued the pursuit without pause. For example, a marrying-in woman brought two head of sheep with her as her dowry to husband's family in 1985. The couple expanded their herd size gradually. In 2003, they owned over 60 head of sheep. The household, with the largest herd (104) in 2003, also started with only two sheep. A small percentage of commercially minded stockowners kept as many sheep as possible to maximize their income. In 2002, the largest number of sheep in a household amounted to 150 head. A small minority of sheep-owning households accumulated conspicuous wealth through sheep-raising, which was termed by local people as "making a fortune out of sheep (*fa yang cai*)." Sheep-raising became an important determinant of income level among households, contributing to local socioeconomic differentiation.

The distribution of sheep among households was differentiated by wealth, ethnicity and other factors. According to my survey, the highest total number of sheep was 1336 in 2003. There were a total 38 sheep-owning households. The head of sheep among them ranged from a minimum of four to a maximum of 104, averaging 35 sheep per household. Disaggregating the figures by ethnic composition and settlement location, I found that ten out of the 38 households were Mongols (26.3 percent), who kept 359 sheep, accounting for 26.8 percent of all sheep herds. Two were households of Hui ethnicity, and the remainder were Han Chinese. Eleven households had a herd size exceeding 50, among them, three were Mongols, one was a Hui household, and the remainder were Han Chinese. This indicated that Mongols did not have an advantage in sheep raising. Besides, a large percentage of sheep-owning households were concentrated in the west village. They owned 1110 sheep, making up 83 percent of the total herd.

In the post-reform period, sheep-raising became increasingly commercial. Two kinds of sheep were raised in Ao Village: a local breed of "Aohan fine wool sheep" (hereafter, sheep) and an imported breed, locally termed "tailed-small *han* sheep" (*xiao wei han yang*, hereafter, *han* sheep).The native fine sheep were once quite famous even beyond this region. According to elder villagers, throughout the 1950s, improving the genetics of sheep was strongly promoted by the county government, and the genetic improvement campaign was carried out like "waging a battle". The improvement work persisted for about 30 years. Each brigade was sometimes required to set up its own breeding station. At that time, wool rather than mutton was the government's priority, and consequently, the fine-wool sheep breed developed quickly and spread to other regions as well. Not until the invasion of the coarse-wool *han* sheep, as in Aohan as a whole, were the upgraded stock of sheep dominant in Ao Village.

Aohan introduced han sheep-a very adaptable breed-from Shandong province in the early 1990s. Since this breed was more prolific than native sheep, it spread quickly. A mature breeding female could produce 2-6 offspring per annum in contrast to native sheep that usually produced one offspring annually. About 20 days after delivery, the ewe might get pregnant again. As a result, there was an increasing demand for mature breeding females, which in turn, stimulated the quick expansion of sheep production. After shifting to mutton-focused han sheep, the quantity rather than the quality of the stock was stressed.

These "extra" animals provoked multiple problems—a growing workload among women, increased grazing pressure on pastureland resources, the reduction of the native breed, and above all, the loss of purebred sheep. Seeking quick gains, many residents made a quick switch from native sheep to han sheep. In Ao Village, the intrusion of han sheep dated back to 1997 when a couple purchased 10 han sheep on credit for a total of 8000RMB. They sold all of their sheep for approximately 9000RMB in late 2003. In a space of about seven years, they totally earned around 30000RMB, which was clearly more profitable than crop production. According to some herders, in 2003, there were more han sheep than local variety sheep in the village. This was apparently motivated by the desire for immediate returns on investment.

Livestock Management and Gender Divisions of Labor

Herding has long been socially constructed as a masculine job. Many male villagers constantly mentioned they lived a long herding life. The oldest male resident, mentioned above, worked as a shepherd for a total of 57 years, from eighteen years old when he settled into the Village in 1939 until he was seventy-five years old in 1996. He started herding sheep owned by landlords before Liberation, a few years after Liberation he herded the flock owned by his large family. He took care of sheep in Team Three during the collective period, and sheep owned by individual households after decollectivization. He was once a famous shepherd in the vicinity of Ao Village, being honored as a second-grade labor model at the county level and as a first-grade laborer at the township level. Yet he did not even know how to till the land. This was also true for many other village men.

The transformation from the collective "pig pot" system to the HRS dramatically changed livestock management patterns. Prior to 1980, collective livestock farming was long a masculinized field, which was assigned to a few males only. The shepherd, locally called *yang guan,* and other stock raiser, locally called *niu guan*, respectively, earned 4500 work points per year, the highest rate of work points under the collective regimes. They normally "lived on the hill" during the day and slept in team headquarters at night. In 2003, an overwhelming majority of households raised livestock, large and small, for subsistence, and above all, for the market. This meant residents had to combine these two labor-intensive activities-crop and livestock farming simultaneously. It was widely admitted among inhabitants that after decollectivization, privately owned animals were better cared for than collectively owned animals under the previous regime.

Distinguished from crop production, which was characterized by the busy and slack period, livestock production imposed a continuous labor demand on men and women all the year round. It required household members—men and women, boys and girls—to split duties among themselves. The predominant pattern in Ao Village was that men took care of large livestock, while women were responsible for the care of pigs and poultry. Men herded sheep outside, while women took care of them at home. The large stock was normally corralled, tethered and did not herd on a day-to-day basis. Despite a new policy of zero grazing issued by the county government in 2002 (see Chapter five), residents sometimes still grazed their horses, mules or donkeys on village commons or in private fields after the harvest, except for the three-month confinement from April 1 to July 1, Unlike sheep that needed close supervision, large stock often pastured without the presence of their owners. In 2004, after the large patch of pastureland was opened to herding, as before, stockowners drove their large livestock there in the morning and drove them back before dark. Only in rare cases did villagers herd their sheep with large livestock. In the summer of 2003, I sometimes observed a shepherd grazing a flock of over 50 head of sheep as well as five donkeys simultaneously.

There was a clear-cut gender division of labor between men and women in sheep-owning households. Men were preoccupied with herding, while women assumed the major responsibility of animal care at home. Shepherding had long symbolized masculinity at the local level. The time-consuming sheep herding was mainly undertaken on an individual basis. Before the new policy of sheep confinement was imposed in 2003, there was an ongoing, repetitive herding routine throughout the year until heavy snowfalls completely covered the ground, preventing sheep from eating grasses beneath the snow. The grazing days amounted to almost 300 days. Subtracting the three-month confinement imposed from April1 to July 1, the grazing days still approximated 200 days in 2003. Grazing hours were normally quite long. It often took 10-12 hours in the summer, 8-10 hours in the spring and autumn, and 6-8 hours in the winter. The herders normally traveled with their stock for 10-15 kilometers per day within a circumference of 3-4 kilometers.

Almost all sheep-owning households grazed their own stock. To use their own expression, "There is one shepherd per household." There were actually a few exceptions. One man hired an elderly man to graze his flock for 2400RMB a year. Another owner left his small flock to his neighbor for 50RMB per head per year since his wife and son had migrated out of the community. About eight households with relatively small herds shared the herding responsibility with each other on a rotating basis, some seasonally and some for the entire year. Only when men went out of the community, or under "emergency" conditions did women "help" to herd for a short period of time. To my knowledge, only 5-6 village women herded sheep once in a while in 2003. A few women mentioned to me, since they felt sleepy when they went herding, they preferred to keep busy at home. Male herders often got together to herd; they cooperated and negotiated sale prices, and exchanged knowledge and skills, from which women were clearly excluded. Many women clearly had no idea about relevant skills and market prices.

Men's and women's cooperation was fundamentally significant in their daily practices. This was reflected in the fact that women were widely treated as "stock raisers." Looking after sheep penned at home, particularly in winter and spring, `required a substantial amount of female labor. Women assumed the bulk of responsibility of feeding and watering sheep when they returned home each night. It was also women who were in charge of collecting grasses, preparing forage, cleaning pens and courtyards. The combination of these two labor-intensive regimes of crop production and sheep-raising kept these women much busier than other women all the year round. In sheep-owning households, men usually shared some fieldwork for only a few days in the peak season, whereas women tended to bear the triple burden of crop production , running the household and taking care of sheep and other animals simultaneously. During the winter, young lambs or weak sheep were always moved into their main rooms with *kang* since not a single "warm pen" was available in the village. On many occasions during my household visits, I found lambs were kept on the straw scattered on the floor near the *kang* and the room was full of an unbearable sheepy odor. For this reason, there were always both positive (hardworking) and negative (dirty) images of sheep-owning households. The spatial division of labor by men and women reflected the gendered impacts of livestock management on the natural world.

Proper herding by men was key to the survival and growth of adult sheep, so was the careful tending of ewes and lambs by women. From late December to March the following year when ewes gave birth to lambs, women could never relax. If an ewe was going to give birth at night, household members had to stay up, otherwise the newborn could be ruined by its mother. The local breed of sheep had only one offspring each year, and occasionally twin babies. If a mother sheep had no babies at all, or if the only lamb died, this meant a great loss to the owner.

Higher survival, therefore, depended heavily upon the capability of women to deal with all the potential problems in a timely way. Women needed to grind soybean into flour and slip it into the mouths of lambs one by one, three times a day. It was important not to feed the lambs too little or too much. Only one month later could they feed grasses to the lambs, and after May when the grasses turned green could they herd them outside. The health of the lambs had to be overseen carefully, feeding them medicine if necessary. Raising the new breed of *han* sheep exacerbated the labor burden of women. As *han* sheep produced more offspring throughout the year and required supplementary feeding of breeding females during their gestation period of about 150 days. A few middle-aged women became well-known "sheep raisers" with special skills in the care of ewes and their lambs.

The Myth of Herd Size

Ao Village witnessed a rise in its stock numbers from the 1950s to 2003, particularly since 1999 in response to the recurrent droughts. The rise of stock numbers put increasing pressure on the local ecology. However, the stock numbers in Greater Ao Village were open to local interpretations. When I checked the Year-end Production Statistics Forms (GYV, 2003a) submitted by the village committee to the township statistics unit, I was surprised to find that livestock size was reported as unbelievably low. As recorded in the forms, there were a total of 1471 head of livestock, large and small in Greater Ao Village at the beginning of 2003, which increased to 1893 at the end of the year (a 28.7 percent increase). This was clearly a severe underestimation, far below the actual number. In Ao Village alone, the number of livestock approximated the figure for Greater Ao Village. As described in Chapter three, the agrarian economy of Hamlet B and Hamlet C were more livestock-oriented and they raised many more grazing animals.

According to some knowledgeable herdsmen, the overall number of livestock in Ao Village was approximately 2000, a figure unparalleled in the history of the village. As far as sheep population was concerned, the sheep herd of 1336 head, by my own survey, was probably a little bit lower than the real situation, because some informants might underreport their total amount or ignore the small lambs. The figure of 1500 offered by many herders was perhaps a more accurate estimation. With respect to large animals, my statistics (293 head) only covered those animals that residents owned during my survey period in late 2003. The actual number throughout the year would be greater than this figure. Several men told me, the average number of large animals per household was 2.5 and the total number of large livestock was 400. Villagers' statements were almost consistent with my own survey. Taken together, the assessment of 2000 head, large and small, should be taken as a number of relative accuracy.

Then, why was there such a notable discrepancy with official reports? What created the incentive for the village authority to under-report rather than inflate the figure? Many possible factors might explain the significant underreporting. The village committee was supposed to produce *the June-end and Year-end Statistics Livestock Reports*, which theoretically were derived from the vaccination records of the village vet. However, residents had a strong incentive to underreport their livestock numbers to avoid higher taxes in the past, and the excess vaccination fee in 2003. In addition, by the end of June, all sheep had already given birth to lambs in the past. If all animals were calculated, the figure should be accurate. With the intrusion of *han* sheep, ewes bore all the year round, making it impossible to count the number correctly. Furthermore, the number of livestock varied between months and throughout the year due to marketing activities and other reasons. The fluctuation also added complexity to the reliability of the village statistics. Another key factor was probably that the status of a poor village could qualify Greater Ao Village for certain benefits not extended to other better-off communities. And finally, the artificial under-reporting of its grazing animals could also hide its problems with overgrazing.

This inconsistency mirrored a problem in the statistical reporting system in rural areas. The village statistics were sent to township statistical officials, who were in charge of adding them up to form the township's estimated figures, which in turn, were submitted to the county statistics unit. It was impossible for higher-up officials to verify the accuracy of these reports. In this sense, we could not even guarantee the accuracy of data quality at the county level, and more broadly at the national level. Such fake figures were misleading, and might not represent the real magnitude of the grazing pressure.[1]This revelation not only had profound policy implications, but also warned of the hazards of merely relying on official data, and the importance of case studies in scholarly research.

Livestock Grazing and Environmental Conservation

Over the past five decades, despite dramatic shifts in the livestock economy in the context of rapid social changes, indigenous sheep-herding practices remained relatively unchanged. To use a local expression, it was "to depend upon nature for herding (*kao tian fang mu*)." This attitude towards animal grazing had long governed villagers' herding practices. Before Liberation, the daily existence of livestock relied almost entirely on the exploitation of grass resources on the grassland. During the collective era, pastureland was still the predominant source of feed. After decollectivization, the forage consumed continued to rely upon the native grassland, yet other sources of feed such as crop residues and forage crop were also used as supplementary feed. To cut the costs and maximize earnings, livestock, large and small, were seldom kept in stables. After the liberalization of the market for livestock and their products, individual producers intensified the exploitation of the communally held pasturelands. As a well-known local saying put it, "entirely free-ranging of animals after lunar September 9 (*jiu yue jiu da sha shou*)."

As in Aohan as a whole, destructive herding practices without corresponding conservation, coupled with continued overgrazing on an increasingly limited space, worsened the availability and quality of the pastureland, and imposed

1 The average forage requirement per animal, especially for large livestock, was substantial. For example, an adult donkey consumed an average of 30 catties of hay or 50 catties of fresh grasses each day. An adult mule might consume between a minimum of 40 catties and a maximum of 60 catties of fresh grasses.

tremendous pressures on local ecologies. Grazing, and particularly overgrazing, was increasingly identified by the county government as the greatest threat to pastureland development and environmental conservation. Unlike many other pastoral areas in Inner Mongolia, where privatization of pastureland resources was implemented after decollectivazation (Williams, 2002), common pasturelands in Ao Village were never allocated to individual households. Despite numerous environmental initiatives launched by the county government, Ao Village as elsewhere in Aohan witnessed a "tragedy of the commons."[1] Local people grazed an increasing amount of livestock on already-overgrazed spaces.

At the same time, the county government strengthened the control of pastureland rehabilitation. As the woodland, pastureland and cropland free of animals increased, the physical base for grazing dramatically shrank, which in turn, forced livestock into even more limited spaces. In other words, the closing of large patches of formerly communal land, ironically, led to further destruction of the available pastureland, where continuous intensive grazing allowed no time for natural vegetation cover to grow. While I was staying in the village in 2003, I witnessed a series of recent environmental interventions that were imposed simultaneously—a scheme of zero grazing of large livestock, periodical confinement of sheep, the farmland conversion project, and the launch of the small watershed project (see Chapter six for a more detailed discussion). As a consequence, livestock were further forced out of many spaces previously open to grazing, and natural pasturelands disappeared almost entirely.

All these factors inevitably imposed an even greater challenge on stock-rearing households. The immediate impacts of this radical reduction were clearly enormous. Households with sheep responded to this "crisis" in three ways in 2003: reducing their sheep and keeping only a small number of high-quality animals; to disposing of sheep and switching to other pursuits; and overusing the remaining little commons left. In late 2003, the number of sheep in the village was cut almost in half. Before my departure, the de-stocking caused severe concerns among some residents. When I returned nine months later, I was told that compared with 2003, the households

1 This is a theoretical thesis popularized by Garrett Hardin (1968), who contends that when individual people graze their livestock on communally owned land, they have an interest in raising increased numbers of animals even if the land is facing overgrazing and degradation.

with large herds reduced, yet those with small herds remained and even increased in 2004.

Although the imposition of environmental interventions temporarily restricted people's access to the controlled areas, as will be seen in Chapter seven, the sharp reduction of grazing lands and more strict patrolling created unanticipated conflicts between hill keepers and livestock owners. Despite being frustrated by trespassing fines imposed on them, some sheep owners resisted by adopting opportunistic herding practices. For instance, they grazed their flocks at night, if not during the day, or encroached on the protected areas when there was an opportunity. Under such a scenario, there was a higher incidence of grazing violation. Throughout my fieldwork in 2003, I frequently heard the gossip that so-and-so's sheep were caught on the scene or the trees and the alfalfa plant had been attacked. In a sense, the failure of grazing-control measures was more a reflection of improper management strategies rather than the act of grazing itself. As of 2003, no requirement had been imposed to reduce the total population of livestock to a sustainable level at both the household and community levels.

The individual motives of some livestock producers clearly ran counter to the government's objectives of protecting the environment. Some attitudes were so firmly entrenched among stockowners that they seemed to pose an insurmountable obstacle. My study indicated that most villagers were reluctant to give up their rights of access to the communally owned land and refused to transform their decades-long herding practices. They responded opportunistically to the available natural resources and did not appear to care much about the impacts of their practices on the environment. Many of them viewed the introduction of environmental interventions as a threat to their livelihood. After the ban period was over or patrolling was relaxed, their behavior remained largely unchanged.

To cultivate some fodder could potentially relieve the pressure on the grazing area. One feed source was silage, locally called *qing zhu*, literally meaning to store and ferment the plant when it is green. Ammoniated corn stalk was strongly advocated by the government to increase the nitrogen content and palatability of the fodder. It was widely reported that confined sheep could fatten more quickly than free grazing animals. It was technically feasible, and proved to be an economically viable venture in many localities throughout Aohan. Hamlet C in practice was rather successful in utilizing ammoniated fodder since 1998. At the beginning, they built only clay vaults. In 2002, sheep owners started to build a standardized warm pen under the subsidy of the county government. Almost all households with sheep (over 30 households in total) invested in silage in 2003. Yet, the benefits of silage were not yet appreciated by villagers in Ao Village. I found little evidence to suggest they were enthusiastic about it. Only sporadic efforts were ever attempted.

While I was staying in the village, I managed to convince many of them this could be an appropriate way to replace the time-consuming herding practices. Much to my surprise, my proposal received no active responses. They were almost unanimous in claiming that, "What you say may be right, but we have so little land, who would be willing to sacrifice their own ration land for fodder planting?" Another reason that they cited was that they "dare not try for fear of spoilage." They also mentioned they had no time to dig the vault, but I was told it took only 3-4 days of work per vault. A few of them noted that if they had time to dig vaults, they would rather cut some grasses. Apparently, there existed a difference of opinion among residents. The Ao Village case indicated that although its resource base had great potential for commercial livestock production, the prospects of livestock development were limited by a multitude of interwoven factors.

Concluding Remarks

In light of the findings from Ao Village, it was quite clear that almost all local developmental interventions in the name of modernization, from "grain first and self-sufficiency," to "crop-livestock integration (*nong mu jie he*)" after decollectivization, were largely accompanied by greater damages to natural resources, and thus to the environment. The political economy of subsistence during the collective period and the proliferation of commercial production in the post-reform era both radically shaped local resource bases upon which agriculture depended, as well as gender divisions of labor, tasks and responsibilities in access to land and other natural resources in divergent ways. The social organization as well as policies pursued under collectivism imposed extremely negative ecological and economic impacts on local men and women. Grain shortage resulted in severe fuel deficiency, which in turn, led to pastureland degradation. The same was true for agricultural intensification in the context of zealous pursuit of commercial objectives. After the advent of household farming, capital-intensive farming practices—intensified land exploitation, increased dependency upon chemical fertilizers, irrigation and monoculture came at the expense of local ecology was well as local people, particularly women, who were more likely to be left behind in the field and the community.

This chapter examined the centrality of gender in local economic life as well as the effects of trajectories of agrarian change on the gendered practices and outcomes of production and reproduction among village men and women, as well as their relationships with the natural world in a community setting. As was common in many regions in the global "South", macro structural factors of the political economy in large part constituted roadblocks to achieving sustainable agriculture. Although smallholder farmers were often blamed for having caused environmental problems, as with the rest of the rural population in China, men and women in the village could not in any way change the broader state policies regarding land tenure, land use practices, and larger economic forces such as prices and markets, all beyond the village's boundaries.

Chapter Five

Voices from the Grassroots: Gender, Bureaucratic State Power and the Mass Mobilization Conservation Campaign

Since the early 1990s, Aohan has won national recognition as a model for its persistent environment-centered efforts. The following awards were cited as a reflection of its accomplishments in environmental initiatives: in 1991, the National Afforestation Committee, the Ministry of Forestry and the Ministry of Personnel jointly awarded Aohan "the Advanced Unit of National Afforestation" and "the Advanced Unit of Combating Sand." In 1994, the Ministry of Forestry granted it "the National Demonstration County of Technological Forests Construction." The SFA granted Aohan "the Advanced County of National Forestry Ecology Construction" in 2000, followed by "the Advanced Qi in Rebuilding Beautiful Landscapes" given by the National Afforestation Committee and the State Environmental Protection Administration. Above all, Aohan won the UNEP's Global 500 Roll of Honor award in June 2002 for its extraordinary contributions to environmental conservation.[1]

This hallmark indicated that Aohan's experiences had become part of a growing environmental movement flourishing around the world. This was a landmark in the county's history, which also made Aohan a showcase for the rest of China. These figures and honors were, of course, very impressive. As a result, we were often left

1 Aohan was one of eight individuals and organizations receiving this prestigious environmental award in 2002. As of 2002, 727 individuals and organizations had been honored with the Global 500 Roll of Honor award since the inception of the award in 1987.

with an assumption of virtually universal success in Aohan. At the beginning, I accepted this myth myself. Only after working with the residents of Ao Village for a prolonged period of time did I realize it was wrong to totally accept these official figures and reports at face value.

Late in the summer of 2003, when a large-scale small watershed project coordinated by the county government was underway in Ao Village, a dozen men were paid to build four huge Chinese characters—"*xiu mei shan chuan*", which literally means beautiful landscapes. They laid stones on the slopes of the chain of four hills-under which the village was located—to make the characters, with each character being placed on one hill. Being brushed with white lime, the four characters of 20 by 20 meters could be seen clearly at a great distance from the national highway. To protect the site from damage, livestock were denied access to the grass-covered hills that had previously been used as a grazing ground. The work was part of the newly launched environmental initiatives in the village.

One day soon after the characters were finished, I met a man who had joined the construction team. When I mentioned the work, he immediately responded, "To do this kind of work is totally of no use, but just a waste of time and money, as time passes by, all stonework deteriorate. This is merely a show. You will see it later, if you still doubt it right now. No cement was used, do you believe it can last long?" He then offered me an example. When an adjacent village lying beyond the hills became a model for its terraced cropland, and a place of pilgrimage for patriotic education as well as for leaders' inspection, residents in Ao Village were mobilized to construct a road with a parking lot on the same hillside, which was not far away from the site where they built one of the characters. He continued, "It is a ridiculous decision, you know! The road has never been used for that purpose since its completion, which actually has been of no use at all." When I returned to Ao Village in 2004, much to my surprise, the four characters had already begun to fade from view. I was told that lime was washed off by rain and some stones moved out of place. As usual, the work was launched without paying attention to local men's and women's needs and once a project was completed, no one cared to preserve it.

As noted earlier, China's rural modernization over much of the past 50 years was accompanied by a vigorous effort to transform the natural environment, in which the mass mobilization conservation campaign (thereafter, *da hui zhan,* as locally termed) played a key role. However, massive labor investments in large-scale infrastructure for collective benefits had become increasingly difficult, and community activities declined remarkably (Liu, 1996; Yan, 1996). As Liu Xin (2000: 131) observed in his field research, "Any ethnographer of northern rural Shaanxi in the 1990s would note that after decollectivization, there was very little activity of any kind sponsored or organized by the community as a whole. Wedding and funeral celebrations, prepared by each family relying on its own network of relations and connections, became the only form of collective activity."

Meanwhile, in the national discourses, the well-known slogan "man can conquer nature" was in large part replaced by rhetoric such as "greening the motherland" (*lü hua zu guo*) or "rehabilitating beautiful landscapes," embodying a changing conceptualization of people's relations to nature. This was a widespread phenomenon across rural China. Aohan was distinct in that it continued *da hui zhan* in the post-reform period without stopping.

In this chapter, I piece together the mass mobilization conservation campaign—a crucial aspect of state-peasant relations almost ignored in Chinese studies—in the specific geographic and historical setting of Ao Village over the last 50 years. It starts with the campaign's unfolding in Aohan in general and in Ao Village in particular, from the early years of Liberation to the present, followed by the story of a Party Secretary, who imposed drastic conservation activities when he was in power. The last section reconstructs a new round of conservation efforts in the making of "beautiful landscapes", brought in by a flux of development interventions under the West China Campaign. These four elements constitute a complete village-level picture of the mass conservation labor embedded in the context of larger political, economic and environmental changes.

The questions that I explored include: How were the conservation projects connected with and implicated in larger social processes? How could the conventional conservation methods be put into practice in this part of China after decollectivization when the Chinese state had weakened in rural China?What were the differences and similarities in the mobilization campaigns before and after the reform? What were the strengths and inherent weaknesses of *da hui zhan*? How did conservation practices relate to gender? What were their impacts on the local environment and local people along gender lines? Did local men and women participate voluntarily or were they just coerced to be a source of cheap or free labor? Had they enjoyed the fruits of their labor? To better understand the larger picture of which the village was a part, I will first outline a local tale at the county level.

Environmental Action as a Mass Mobilization Conservation Campaign: a Local Tale

The Call of Green

Aohan was among the places in Inner Mongolia where the ecological conditions had been changed thoroughly since the Qing Dynasty (1644-1911). The long intensive influx of Han Chinese into the county, coupled with the Japanese occupation and the Civil War in the 1930s-40s, dramatically transformed the local landscape (AQG, 1991). Following the Communist victory, as elsewhere in China, the crusade against nature persisted. However, the reliance on *da hui zhan* to carryoutlarge-scale environmental initiatives signaled a new departure.

Shapiro (2001), among many others (Murphey, 1967), tended to highlight the political causes of environmental change. She argued that the political violence raged side by side with violence against nature during the Mao era. I only partly agree with this argument. Although politics were highly relevant in the context of Aohan, the local processes of environmental transformation during the collectivization and decollectivization periods, mostly had a logic and dynamic all their own. As we know, when the political movement and policy intervention filtered down to different localities, they tended to take on different styles in response to specific local circumstances. A glimpse of Aohan in general and Ao Village in particular should have borne this out.

I believe that the local origins of *da hui zhan* in the county need to be put in the context of overwhelming poverty and the vicissitudes of nature at the local scale. Aohan had been notorious for its severe desertification as well as soil and water erosion in the region. Immediately after Liberation, as in most areas in rural China, local people were highly vulnerable to the calamities imposed by nature. Aohan started to declare war against nature in the early 1950s when the vagaries of weather gave rise to disastrous floods every year. The *da hui zhan* had the potential to deploy mass participation to transform nature, and thereby get rid of poverty. At that time, Aohan aggressively carried out projects of irrigation works along the main rivers within its boundary (AQG, 1991). Almost identical stories were sporadically recounted in some other studies. It was true, as Elizabeth Economy (n.d.) rightly argues, "Mobilization campaigns in China often have served a dual purpose of consolidating power and developing the economy." In the following section, I will reconstruct what happened in Aohan where the conservation practices were long rooted in its specific historical, geographic and environmental contexts.

As stated above, Aohan was long plagued by extensive ecological degradation—desertification, soil and water erosion, and water scarcity, which posed serious threats to the local economy and rural people's lives. By the time of Liberation, there were 1.1 million *mu* of sandy lands, with most of them being fixed and semi-fixed sand dunes. There were merely a total of 0.16 million *mu* of forestland, the scene beautifully described by the poem, "Blue, blue is the sky, Vast, vast is the steppe, Here the grass bends with the breeze, Here are the cattle and sheep" (cited in Jagchid and Hyer, 1979:10) was still prevalent in most areas of the county. From the 1960s to mid-1970s, population growth, overgrazing and land reclamation combined to accelerate local ecological degradation. By 1975, there were semi-fixed and moving sand dunes of approximately 2.59 million *mu*. In the years around 1980—the most severe period in Aohan's history—the topsoil often became a ready source of sand in sandstorms, and numerous farmlands were buried by this sand. In the spring of 1981, the very section within the boundary of Aohan of the newly opened Jingtong Railway (connecting Beijing and the city of Tongliao to the north of Aohan) was submerged by moving sands, and as a result was shut down for 72 hours. It was reported that in a few localities, heaps of sand were piled as high as a house, and consequently animals stepped onto and fell down through the roof.[1]

These oft-quoted legends in official discourse were frequently found in the accounts of Aohan's physical conditions in the past. Ao Village shared the ecological challenges described above. Many residents whom I interviewed vividly described to me a similar surrounding world that they faced in the early 1980s. As a married-in wife from a neighboring province, Lin Hui still had clear memories of the predicament that she faced when she came to the village in 1985.

> When I came here, the neighborhood remained plagued by the sand blown by the wind. The rustle of the "flying sands" hitting on our windows covered with the transparent plastic film constantly penetrated my ears at

1 The datum of this paragraph came from government reports and county archives.

> night. In the morning when you got up, you would find grains of sand all over the top of the stove, inside the pot and even in the food. Whenever I ate a meal, I always wanted to weep. I thought I had never eaten such bad food before. I missed my parents so much and I wanted to go back to my natal community. Even chickens did not like to stay in the courtyard. Occasionally, you were even unable to see clearly during the day, and we had to light a lamp at home. In the first few years after we got married, we were desperately poor. We shared a mud house with another young couple. At that time, we had little firewood to cook or warm ourselves; I went out to dig a kind of dispersed sand-fixing shrub for fuel. I ate so much bitterness at the beginning. Now, I have become accustomed to living here.

Because of the harsh agricultural environment, the grain output was unbelievably low. A popular local saying accurately captured the real situation then, which was so typical of the area at that time "to cultivate a patch of slope, to harvest only a cart of grain; to harvest a dustpan of grain, to cook only a pot of food" (*zhong yi po, da yi che, da yi po ji, zhu yi guo*). Crop and livestock production were especially vulnerable to various disasters. In such circumstances, local people struggled to survive on severely degraded land, and a large percentage of rural people had to rely upon state relief.

Taking Up the Challenges

A combination of pressures forced the county government to take conservation actions without any delay. Since around 1965, with ecological challenges looming particularly large on the horizon, the Aohan government started to embark on large-scale ecological constructions on the already fragile land. Land degradation was singled out as the biggest threat to local economic survival and rural development. As a consequence, water and soil conservation were perceived by the county government as a major engine of enhancing agricultural productivity and improving living standards.

Since the rural reform beginning in the early 1980s, a relentless battle against "nature" was waged in two ways: to coercively impose *da hui zhan* on the one hand, and to overexploit natural resources mostly at the household level on the other. The deployment of labor resources initially focused on bringing water and the hill under control, which had shifted to integrated small watershed management in the 1990s.

After three decades of continuous afforestation efforts, Aohan ranked first in China in terms of afforestation and green crop planting, with a large portion of its land area being "greened". In the whole county, by the end of 2002, the accumulating area being put under control for the purpose of water and soil conservation had added up to 3300 km² or 51.4 percent of the total area affected by soil and water erosion (ASB, 2003). In the late 1970s, the forest cover accounted for 10 percent of its land, but by 2003 it made up 42.5 percent of its total territory, a figure thirty-three times that in the early years of Liberation, and four times that of 1978. Furthermore, Aohan had 8000 hectares of green crop planted[1]and approximately 381300 hectares of the small watershed areas were managed in an integrated way (ASB, 2003).

Given the notable differences in topography and ecological variations, the reality in Aohan was far more complex than expected. Depending upon specific physical environments and inputs, some localities might be more successful than others in their conservation practices. As a consequence, the distribution and quality of forest and grass resources differed from place to place. I had no intention of making a generalization about the success or failure in the whole county. Only when viewed from the vantage point of the grassroots, especially, when seen with careful attention to vivid women's lives, can we comprehend the real implications of its honor.

As of 2003, environmental challenges still loomed large in Aohan, an ecologically vulnerable region in semi-arid northern China. It included several climate zones and soil types, showing considerable diversity in its landscape. Located at the southern edge of Keerqin (Horqin) Sandy Lands, where sand soil and moving dunes occupied 90 percent of the region's land area (NSRZ, 1991:1, cited in Williams, 1996), sand was increasingly approaching Aohan from the north. The total area of Aohan was 8294 km², with 77 percent of all its territory being affected by water and soil erosion (ASB, 2003). There remained over 200000 hectares of eroded land, 80000 hectares of desertified land, and 120000 hectares of degraded grassland.

As any other outsider who had visited the county, Premier Wen Jiabao was amazed by its accomplishments in environmental conservation as well as its desperate poverty. On September 4, 2002, he wrote down the following instruction featured inthe Aohan Statistics Yearbook (ASB, 2003).

---

1 According to a government report, the areas of forest and green crop accounted for 53 percent of Aohan's territory, and both of them ranked first among the counties in the whole country.

> Decades of years' painstaking struggles by Aohan people—tree-planting, afforestation, mountain and water control—have transformed the ecological conditions here, and thereby won the UNEP's Global 500 Roll of Honor award, which has not been easily won. We must make persistent efforts through formulating long-term objectives and plans to build beautiful landscapes in Aohan. The relevant departments in Inner Mongolia Autonomous Region and the Central Government should show care for and give guidance and help to this good model.

Inspired by Premier Wen's second visit in 2002—and his instruction in particular—the Aohan government formulated a new conservation policy entitled *The Aohan Qi Ecological Construction Plan (2001-2010).* It was released by the county government in February 2003 and was designed as a blueprint for the period between 2001 and 2010. As in any other official account, in its historical construction of the undesirable past and current success, the document unfortunately omits a critical aspect—the role of local men and women in the long-standing tradition of grand-scale mass campaigns in the service of its environmental priorities. It highlights instead how the county government had led cadres and masses of various ethnic groups to achieve celebrated ecological accomplishments. Apparently, this document was a brief expression of what local authorities had long had in mind.

Da hui zhan: Changes and Continuities

The meaning of the mass mobilization campaign is encapsulated correctly in the Chinese expression of *da hui zhan*; the three Chinese characters together can be literally translated as "the big concentrated battle." The first time I visited Aohan in late March of 2003 coincided with the moment that the Aohan government was about to launch the spring mass mobilization campaign. In the few days that I stayed in the county seat, I heard *da hui zhan* repeatedly in various places—government offices, restaurants, and even in the hotel in which I lodged, a term not universally heard in China in 2003. However, it was still widely used in Aohan, in government reports and the local press alike. It was part of the daily vocabulary in village life of the residents in Ao Village, surfacing frequently in everyday conversations.

Certainly, the term was neither a static concept, nor an unchanged practice.

Tracing back its evolution in Aohan, I had been impressed by its continuities and discontinuities with the collective past. It seemed an all-embracing concept, and a broad range of activities was put under the rubric of *da hui zhan*, ranging in different periods from building bio-physical infrastructures such as dams, levees, roads, reservoirs, irrigation schemes, reforestation projects, terracing, and since the 1990s, to small watershed projects stressing the integrated management of hill, water, field, forest, and road simultaneously.

In Aohan, the county government was long a key actor in the campaign-style conservation practices. The mass environmental practices were promoted via powerful political and administrative mechanisms. The typical mass conservation campaign was always top-down with concentrated procedures and mass participation, pushing down to the grassroots from the county level in the name of development. *Da hui zhan* often involved practices both within and beyond the village boundaries, and through which the governments strengthened their presence in the countryside. Yet, as we shall see below, the conservation goals, content of activities, target population, frequency, and willingness to participate were constantly shifting.

During the collective era, *da hui zhan* constituted a local as well as a national pattern of combating nature. Mao Zedong (1966: 44) stated, "If people living in nature want to be free, they will have to use natural sciences to understand nature, to overcome nature and to change nature, only then will they obtain freedom from nature." In that period, "An entire discursive formation was built on the notion of the socialist transformation of nature in China" (Muldavin, 1998). Military metaphors such as to conquer, to fight, to battle against, and the like were widely used. Murphey rightly described Mao's view of nature as follows, "nature is explicitly seen as an enemy, against which man must fight an unending war, with more conviction and fervor and with a brighter vision of the ultimate results than even the Darwinian-Spencerian West held. Articles in the contemporary press glorified this campaign, with titles such as: 'the Desert Surrenders,' 'We Bend Nature to Our Will,' 'How We Defeated Nature's Worst,' 'Chairman Mao's Thoughts Are Our Guide to Scoring Victories in the Struggles Against Nature,' 'Hard Work Conquers Nature' and 'The

United Will of the People Can Transform Nature' "(Murphey, 1967:319).[1]

During the 1960s-70s, as elsewhere in rural China, water conservation works, especially reservoirs were prioritized by the central government. Nature was viewed as something that could be tamed by technological solutions and willpower. Ecological considerations usually overran those of economic production. The ideologically inspired campaigns sparked tremendous "revolutionary" zeal and active mass participation. When I was a primary school student in a county in Jiangxi province, we were occasionally required to take part in*dahuizhan* to plant trees and repair canals. I still remember the mass participation scene on this occasion. Hundreds and thousands of participants seemed in high spirits to keep themselves busy. The work sites were always "armed" with slogans, flags, high-volume speakers, music, and even gongs and drums, presenting a scene of noisy hilarity. It was indeed a familiar phenomenon for anyone who lived through that era. The degree to which mass labor stimulated zeal, of course, varied over time and space. Young men and women, particularly those who were militia members, played a key role in mass labor.

Then, what motivated people, particularly young men and women, to engage in this arduous work? In discussion of the motivation of *da hui zhan*, Murphey (1967: 328) notes, "There is no denying the truly awesome force generated and channeled by the war against nature, especially in its apparent success in converting individual interests into the sacrifices of an austere campaign whose rewards are predominantly ideological or even mystical." In opposition to his statement, I would argue at least in Ao Village, men's and women's enthusiasm in practice derived mainly from meager material incentives. Apart from the rewards of usual work points, additional money or grain, were frequently offered to participants by their teams. Young men from the poorest, grain-deficient team tended to compete with each other for the chance to work beyond the village for extended periods of time so that they did not need to worry about their food. Furthermore, some of them wished to take the opportunity to meet young people from other villages. Love occasionally arose

1 For fascinating accounts of attitudes towards nature and wars against nature and their environmental and social outcomes in the pre-reform period, see Murphey, Rhoads (1967) "Man and Nature in China," *Modern Asian Studies,* Vol.1, No.4; Shapiro, Judith (2001) *Mao's War Against Nature: Politics and the Environment in Revolutionary China,* Cambridge University Press.

out of such collective labor through the help and interactions with each other. A love song produced in Anhui province, recounting young people's involvement in building a reservoir during the Great Leap Forward (Kuo,1959:120, cited in Blake, 1979: 46), describes how young people of the opposite sex competed with each other in the mass labor of mixed groups in high spirits:

> Little sister carries mud, big brother digs the pond;
> Pearls of sweat mix with muddy water.
> Little Sister doesn't tire carrying ten-thousand catties;
> Elder brother doesn't shiver standing in the mire.
> We can't take freely working here in the crowd,
> (We are like) paper lanterns all aglow inside.
> Big brother and little sister want to be heroes;
> They dig until the stars set and the sun rises.

As elsewhere, in the wars against nature, the institution of "labor model" was widely employed in Aohan. Almost exclusively male "green heroes" were continually created in both the collective and reform periods by officials at different levels. There was no equivalent status bestowed by officials on rural women. The slogan of "the power of models is immeasurable" (*bang yang de li liang shi wu qiong de*) motivated the production of labor heroes. These masculined models were represented as having the spirit of sacrifice and devotion to "green causes." Their stories were scattered in the local archives, books and newspapers. An elder man in his seventies in Hamlet D once proudly showed me a wall clock given to him by the township government for his prominent work in conservation labor. A labor model from Hamlet B, who was praised as a "foolish old man who removed the mountains" (a familiar Chinese legend), was created. The story of his vigorous efforts in constructing a small reservoir through mobilization of his family members was circulated widely in Aohan. Unfortunately, such representations seldom touched on the sacrifices of their female family members.

During the Cultural Revolution in 1964, Mao called on people to "Learnfrom Dazhai in Agriculture." The Dazhai brigade in Shaanxi province became a model for overcoming poverty by embarking on natural resource conservation through mass labor, and as a result, its key male leader Chen Yonggui and female leader Guo

Fenglian became well-known national emulation models. The mass movement to learn from Dazhai developed rapidly throughout rural China. Analyzing the Dazhai model, Friedman (1978: 877) examined its gendered character, "It was a very labor-poor village. The imperative of production, as in a war economy in which the young men are in the military, required utilizing female labor. Few, if any places in China have made such maximal use of female labor as Tachai (*Dazhai*): Its party leader, Kuo Feng-lien (*Guo Fenglian*), rose in part from her leadership of a group of women workers who competed with the men. Tachai had been a backward place full of patriarchal ideals, a village where women received a fraction of the pay of men. It actually made extraordinary strides on issues of gender equality, as symbolized by the female members in leading positions in its militia and its Party."

At the level of Inner Mongolia Autonomous Region, a Mongolian woman was shaped into the major icon during the "Learn from Dazhai" campaign, in contrast to the Han Chinese models, who were mainly males. In 1965, Ulanhu, introduced in Chapter three, nominated Ushenju (*wu shen zhao*), a commune in Ordos, "the Pastoral Dazhai," as the pastoral equivalent of Mao's agrarian model village of Dazhai. A Mongolian woman, Broldai, who made great contributions in clearing poisonous weeds and planting bushes on the desert, was simultaneously created into the role of regional model (cf. Bulag, 1999). The construction of a regional female model might partly demonstrate women's remarkable contributions in the pastoral economy and environmental conservation. This model seemed to have produced little effect in Ao Village.

After decollectivization, the conditions that once motivated mass labor had been somewhat changed. The market-oriented economy loosened the centralized control of the national state, and gave local authorities more room to manipulate their own campaigns. In the post-reform period, the mass conservation campaigns in rural areas were primarily carriedout through "obligatory labor"(*yi wu gong*)and "accumulated labor" (*lao dong ji lei gong*) requirements as specified in the land contracts of individual households. Both were basically uncompensated work compared to those in the collective era. With the lifting of state ideological pressure, the collective spirit was diluted and even minimized throughout rural China. Honorable titles such as "the labor hero" or "the labor model" were frequently downplayed. Farmers saw no economic benefits to compulsory labor. Under these circumstances, it was not surprising that there was a corresponding wane of zeal for collective actions. In most cases, the governments were unable to launch the same kind of mobilization campaigns that they had in the past.

In contrast to the general trend in China as a whole, a centralized regime with coercive labor control was re-invented in Aohan and became institutionalized. The county authorities established a green goal responsibility system among key state-party leaders at various levels. The county governor or vice-governors were made responsible for *da hui zhan* in person. Their performance in this field was judged as one of their key work achievements. The cadres who made extraordinary contributions in environmental initiatives had the chance to be promoted to higher-level leadership posts. Initially, the participants had broader sectoral representations, but the Qi Forestry Bureau had assumed the major responsibilities. In the 1990s, more sections of the government were involved in *da hui zhan*. An institutionalized mechanism functioned as a means of social control to mobilize the rural population. Each year several townships were to be identified as project areas, which would be implemented in the form of pooling and exchanging labor among farmers in neighboring villages and even adjacent townships. This was locally called "large formation warfare" (*da bing tuan zuo zhan*). The county authorities handed down the tasks, which the township and village cadres were obliged to carry out. Before 2000, this was often repeated several times a year, extending to 2-3 months of work overall.

After the return of household farming, the nature of labor requirements as well as labor control changed over time. Labor imposition went from mustering primarily able-bodied men and women during the collective era, to imposing forced labor demands on individual households on a per capita basis through 2002. For all its continuities with the collective past, the implementation process became more coercive in character in the post-reform period. By coercion, I mean not only compulsory labor levies, but also disciplinary labor impositions. Moral and material incentives gave way to the threat of economic penalties for noncompliance. Before 2000, whether farmers accepted it or not, they had to comply with their mandated labor assignments, otherwise they could be fined. If they did not pay the fines in time, their domestic holdings might be confiscated. As a resident complained, "Even the dead could not be immune as long as their share of land was still kept."

The coercive labor imposition was relaxed after 2002. The labor requirement shifted from a per capita basis to that of labor power. Males aged 18-55 and females aged 18-50 were treated as labor power, and were required to take part in *da hui zhan*. In 2003, the village committee in Ao Village organized three campaign-style conservation practices. The first project formed part of the state-sponsored cropland conversion campaign. This time, only project households were involved in it (see the discussion below).

For the second project, each labor power was required to dig 40 tree pits of 0.7 meter in width by 1.5 in length by 0.5 in depth for the small watershed project. If they finished all 40 pits, they would be paid 32RMB (0.80RMB each), or they were also allowed to pay the same amount of money (32RMB) to the team leaders to demand exemption. In 2003, villagers were paid for the first time for their mass labor. This was also the first year that they were permitted to pay the money instead of participating in it themselves.

For the third project, each labor power was requested to build the ridge of 40 meter long at the base of the large gully under the small watershed project. As with the second case, they could either complete their paid labor requirement or deliver 40 RMB to team leaders to be exempt. A township cadre told me 15 days of uncompensated labor per labor power were required in 2003, which would be reduced to 10 days in 2004 and 5 in 2005. Labor imposition seemed to become increasingly lighter.

In the section that follows, I contextualize *da hui zhan* in a specific rural setting of Ao Village. I examine the conservation practices and policies without paying focal attention to the differences between men and women, as well as the environmental consequences and particular implications for women's lives from the perspective of villagers in Ao Village. In so doing, I hope to shed light on broader conservation and development issues at the local scale.

The History of Mass Conservation Practices in a Peasant Village

The long history of mass conservation in Ao Village over the past 50 years, as an integral part of regional practices as well as a larger Chinese pattern, had been shaped and continued to be heavily shaped by extra-village state power, showing great continuities and discontinuities. For all its professed success at the county level in Aohan, as the following testimonies show, the successive and frequently overlapping programs launched within the boundary of Ao Village had many disappointing failures interwoven with a few impressive gains. That was at least what most residents, men and women, old and young, believed, which was also woven into the accounts of local environmental actions. Ethnographically based research delving into *da hui zhan* allowed me to cast doubt on the alleged universal successes and to shed light on the conservation dilemmas in the contemporary rural scene. In addition, what I record here are the invisible stories of local men and women as well as their agency and sufferings beneath the official discourses. In this sense, this ethnographic description is an effort to rewrite the history of *da hui zhan* from a grassroots perspective. Rather than offering a comprehensive picture, I will instead focus on select moments or episodes in the village setting.

Early Years after Liberation: Incipient Efforts

The history of *da hui zhan* in Ao Village couldbe traced back to the first few years immediately following local Liberation. After the first bumper harvest in Aohan in 1950, the township to which Ao Village belonged declared war against nature in the year that followed. Both male and female residents were called upon to take part in planting trees on barren lands, reclaiming wasteland, and building irrigation works so as to reforest denuded hillsides, improve flood control, and build agricultural and conservation infrastructures. In those years, drought and flood disasters were quite common, and the priority was to control water resources. According to elder residents, no large-scale mass labor was deployed within the boundary of Ao Village, yet some men in the households with rich male workers were transferred to certain waterworks projects beyond the village for prolonged periods of time.

Since that time, a long war against nature seemed to have been waged non-stop in the village. As evidenced in the historical records of the township, the local campaign to conquer nature was replete with heroic accounts of turning barren hills green, and converting wastelands into productive croplands. This campaign was strengthened by a belief in the material benefits of shaping nature and the ability and sacrifices of "our diligent, hardworking people" to transform the physical world (see LTPC, 1960).

As elsewhere, the Great Leap Forward (1958-60) marked a tide of conquering nature and transforming nature in the village.[1]After the local people's commune was established, some men and women in the village were sent out to "conquer" nature, which continued to focus predominantly on some big waterworks projects. Inside the village, men and women were mobilized to build a small reservoir to the west of

1 For an excellent account of labor exploitation during the Great Leap Forward, see Chapter nine "Life and Death Struggle" in Edward Friedman, Paul G. Pickowicz and Mark Selden (1991) *Chinese Village, Socialist State,* New Haven & London: Yale University Press. For the impact of the Great Leap Forward and the People's Commune on the environment see Chapter four of the book.

the settlement. Since all the cropland then was located on the northern and eastern sections, it turned out to be of no use. The reservoir was abandoned after many failed attempts to cultivate fish.

"To Learn From Dazhai in Agriculture": A Radical Thrust

The Cultural Revolution (1966-76) marked another radical phase of the mass conservation practices for village men and women. The most important campaign during this period was"Learn from Dazhai in Agriculture." As stated above, one of the major reasons that Dazhai gained its fame was that the residents in the Dazhai Brigade had changed nature by engaging in water and soil conservation through intensive mass labor.

Following Dazhai's paradigm, the environmental efforts in Greater Ao Village took a combination of three forms: the small-scale "shock brigade" *(tu ji dui)*, large-scale mass labor and protracted specialized teams (*zhuan ye dui*). Aside from taking part in the mass labor of their own village, both unmarried men and women were often dispatched to far away places to work for other collectives. The construction of infrastructures such as roads, dams, and canals were launched by different levels of officials throughout the county. As across rural China, some of that infrastructure continued to serve local agriculture through 2005.

Under the shadow of Dazhai, not only was the battle against nature intensified, "iron girls" or "*tie gu niang*"—labeled with a masculinized image—were created and celebrated as a sign of gender equality across rural China. "The iron girls—strong, robust women capable of performing jobs more traditionally done by men, such as repairing high-voltage electric wires—symbolized the Maoist slogan that 'whatever men comrades can accomplish, women comrades can do too" (Honig, 2000). It was an era of deliberately erasing gender differences. Most mass conservation efforts were physically demanding and definitely "heavy physical work", yet these arduous assigned jobs were socially constructed as women's labor by official discourses. As evidenced in county archival materials, "iron girl" teams were formed across rural Aohan.

In Ao Village, each team once had an "iron girl team" consisting almost entirely of young single women. Most women of the generation of "iron girls", who were in their fifties in 2003, experienced extremely hard physical work in their youth. The hardships that mass labor imposed on them when they were "iron girls" punctuated their recollections of that period. There is reason to believe it was not peculiar to the community under study. As we shall see soon, the Dazahi campaign and the official stereotypes of young women's roles in physical work had profound implications for gender-environment interactions in Ao Village.

In the history of Greater Ao Village, a total of four reservoirs were constructed, three of which were built during the collective period. However by 2003, not one reservoir was still serving irrigation purposes.

In the slack season of 1972, villagers were not allowed to sit idly. Two irrigation works were launched successively in that harsh winter, with one located in Ao Village and the other in Hamlet D. The irrigation works built in Ao Village were then called "*er ji ti shui*", which literally means to raise water through two stages. The main task then was to build a kind of diversion structure so that the elevated water could flood the surrounding fields by gravity. Participants, regardless of sex, were granted 10-12 work points, plus 2-3 catties of coarse grains each day. Not all residents were forced to participate in the project, yet the need to earn extra work points, and above all, the highly needed subsidy grains became overwhelming motivations. Even on the eve of 1972 lunar New Year, people were forced to work as usual in the appallingly cold wind and continued their work during the New Year Holiday.

An overwhelming majority of both men and women transported earth by hand. Only a few elite men in power were able to rely on animal power to perform the hard work assigned to them. Zhang Guisheng, mentioned in the last chapter, was long an accountant in the biggest team in the village. He proudly told me of his masculine pride when residents built the works of *er ji ti shui*. When working on that project, he often drove a big cart drawn by four animals to transport earth mostly loaded and unloaded by women. He stated, "Men in those days took pride in driving this kind of big cart and the feeling was no less than to drive a car today." When they carried earth by using a shoulder pole, men and women were strongly encouraged to work cooperatively with each other, with women walking in the front while men walked behind to hold the relatively heavy load. But several women mentioned to me, since their work could not be finished in a day or two, no men other than their own family members would volunteer to work with them continually. Sometimes men helped them to put baskets as heavy as 70-80 *catties* of clay on their backs. As an elder woman expressed when she described *da hui zhan* under the collective regime, "We ate 'pig feed', and worked like animals."

Relentless poverty forced some women to undertake such arduous work well into their pregnancies, and even in the advanced stages. Two women, both in their fifties in 2003, recalled that in those days, women did not take pregnancy seriously and they often disguised signs of pregnancy by wearing big jackets. Both of their husbands, one was a cart driver and the other a carpenter-were often sent away for other team works. In building the works of *er ji ti shui,* the two pregnant women had to cooperate with each other to carry soil in the absence of their husbands. One of them was eight months pregnant and the other 4-5 months. Since toiling in the wet mud made it difficult to walk, they even took off their shoes in the bone-chilling winter of 1972. Each day, they came back home exhausted. A few women noted that when they were working outside they felt like they had lost their ears to the biting northwest wind. Many more men and women recalled that they were often worn out after a whole day's work. Like the first reservoir, the irrigation work of *er ji ti shui* was abandoned not too long after completion because of expensive costs and poor functioning.

Mass labor was also devoted to building the reservoir in Hamlet D in the two consecutive years of 1972-73 during the slack season. Toavoid disrupting agricultural activities, a specialized team consisting of over 20 persons (3-4 persons from each team) was formed in Greater Ao Village to continue the remaining work. The team included a large proportion of young women, some young men, and a few old men. They worked almost year-round for three years (1974-76) and only stopped working when the soil was completely frozen. As part of the collective agricultural activities, they were awarded work points at a rate of 3600 per year, which were much higher than what they could earn in their regular team activities.

For example, *da sao* Song Ling spent three years working on the reservoir and was put in charge of a female group for one and a half years. As a female leader, she always took the lead in the labor process. While I was living at her home, she told her life story repeatedly. Like many of her peers in their fifties, she was deprived of literacy when she as a child. Since she married within the village, she took part in numerous *da hui zhan* since she was young, which became one of her most bitter memories. The following narratives by her mirrored many widespread phenomena experienced by women of her generation, particularly those who grew up and married inside Ao Village. Her narrative also allows us to glimpse the arduous labor process, bitter experiences, and hard life under the collective regimes.

> I am the first of five siblings and the only daughter. My mother came from a landlord family. Both of my parents had some school before

Liberation. My mother was neither good at farm work nor needlework, so she wanted to keep me close at hand. My parents chose your *da ge (elder brother)* for me on the grounds he was so honest and kind, and thus I would not be mistreated in the future. Before marriage, your *dage* and me belonged to two neighboring teams, yet we did not meet very often. After I was engaged at nineteen years old, we both felt embarrassed to speak directly to each other. In those days, youngsters were ashamed to be seen with their mates in public. When I saw him from afar, I always took another path immediately. Youngsters in my generation mostly behaved like this.

Three days after our wedding ceremony in 1977, your *da ge* went back to a construction site to open up rice fields in another village about 20 kilometers away from ours, where he had already been working for several months. Not until their team finished their tasks and returned home to celebrate the lunar New Year two months later did we meet again. In our youth, this kind of separation was common and I had no complaints at all. It was said that our generation grew up to be nurtured by socialist ideals and our labor would make contributions to the country's development.

I took part in numerous *da hui zhan* myself prior to marriage and was always full of energy and fervor. I participated in the mass labor of building the reservoir in Hamlet D when I was 15. Despite being young, I worked vigorously like an able-bodied adult. After I was engaged at 19, I was sent to work in the specialized team. The participants from this village commuted daily on foot to Hamlet D, 3 kilometers away. We stayed working until the soil was totally frozen. During the winter, we ate two meals here. After eating breakfast, I headed to the site, and ate the second meal after returning home at 4 or 5 o'clock in the afternoon. For the rest of the year, I carried my lunch with me. We did not have good food to eat then, and I did not even have a lunch box. I always carried a cloth bag and used tree leaves to wrap my food. While we were working, we did not feel cold in the chilling wind. We worked the same way as men did—carrying soil, pushing carts, and shouldering baskets of clay. Due to working long hours in the brutal cold, many of us suffered from frostbite. During the lunch break, young women always sat together to make shoes or do other needle work. I did not feel tired when I was young. Village women of my generation only

> knew how to intensify our own labor.
>
> How foolish were the young people of my cohort! We only knew to work and work. When I was young, I endured extreme hardship in my natal family. Like most women of my age, I am illiterate. I only attended school for a few days. Since my mother was not a good worker, I shouldered ceaseless domestic work within the household and beyond since I was quite young: hauling water, fetching firewood and fodder grass, collecting wild plants, grinding grains. During the winter, I made shoes for the whole family under the kerosene lamps. Even now, your *da ge* often says that I was living and working like a donkey before marriage. After decollectivization, I continued to be involved in various tough *dahuizhan*. But right now, I don't have so much strength and often feel aches all over.

Indeed, women of the generation of "iron girl" experienced numerous arduous physical work when they were young and they continued to assume a bulk of the mass labor after the advent of household farming when the assigned tasks were allocated to individual households. In the post-reform period, Ao Village was punctuated by *da hui zhan* imposed by senior officials. As noted previously, the mass labor was assigned on a per capital basis. Government officials at all levels used the "household" as a universal unit of planning and assessment without looking inside of it, which imposed extremely negative impacts on women. Apart from the outside-imposed mass labor, there were also some local initiatives. Successive waves of intensified conservation practices started in the late 1980s and persisted through 2000. In the pages that follow, I outline some of the conservation practices that occurred within the boundary of Ao Village.

Building a Reservoir and Remaking the Landscape

In the summer of 1989, villagers started the grandiose project of building their third reservoir. Since it was driven by their own initiative, this work strictly did not belong to the category of *da hui zhan* in the eyes of inhabitants. By any measure, it was a huge scheme with enormous labor investments and great sacrifices on the part of residents. No inhabitant could tell me the exact storage capacity of the reservoir, but it required a total of 370 cubic meters of earth from each of about 500 residents living in about 130 households. Adding the earthwork of opening irrigated fields simultaneously, a total of 500 cubic meters of earth was required from each resident.

At first, fifty cubic meters of earth was assigned to each person for the first session in 1989, followed by about 20 cubic meters each successive session. The construction was organized four times each year, and lasted for three consecutive years from 1989 to 1991. The main dam was constantly reinforced year by year in both height and width until it approached around 22 meters in height. After its completion, small repairs continued. No fatalities happened, but the building process was accompanied by numerous small accidents.

Most men and women who lived through it had bitter memories of the huge labor burdens. The monetary labor value of one cubic meter of earth was set at one *yuan* by the village government. More specifically, if any household owed one cubic meter of earth, it would be fined one *yuan RMB*. For a big household, with many children or elders, the task was overwhelming. One man in his sixties told me, "I remember the scene as if it happened yesterday. When we built the reservoir, like all other households, all my family members worked from dawn to dusk. We were always streaming with sweat. We were exposed to the hot sun in the summer, while working under the chilly wind in the winter. At that time, we owned a kind of small animal-drawn cart, 4-5 loads could merely transport one cubic meter of earth. Quite often, we dug the earth at night and carried it to specific sites during the day. The excavation of earth was indeed backbreaking work." It can be safely assumed that without the labor inputs of the whole family—men and women, even old and young—there was no way for residents to complete such a tough job. Within a space of 7-8 years after its completion, the economic benefits brought about by irrigated agriculture led to a short "honeymoon" period in the history of Ao Village.

However, before villagers had the opportunity to enjoy the long-term fruits of their relentless efforts, the reservoir began to dry up in 1996 and was never been used for irrigation after 1998. A combination of reasons, water seepage, evaporation, drought, and above all, the direct impact of digging pits for tree-planting over large areas, were responsible for this unfortunate outcome. The source of reservoir water came from an area of about 10 km^2. After the reservoir was built, more intensified conservation campaigns to dig tree pits were continually imposed. A pit of 0.7 meter in width by 1.5 in length by 0.5 in depth can absorb over 0.5 cubic meters of rainfall. After the pits were widely scattered over large areas, they inevitably influenced the hydrologic properties of the surroundings. The small watershed project launched in 2003 further jeopardized the reservoir. In 2003, most residents had a dim view of its prospects. A middle-aged man commented to me several times, "All our blood and sweat have been spent in vain. As you know, the value of the reservoir definitely outweighs the state fund of 400000 RMB for the small watershed project. With more pits being dug, it will completely destroy the reservoir!"

"The Death Pits"

For village women, the most frustrating conservation labor was probably digging tree pits. Given the ecological importance of trees in water and soil conservation, tree-planting was always identified by the county government as a key means to reverse degradation and control desertification and wind erosion. Consequently, afforestation campaigns were carried out annually in the county. People were instructed to dig pits to retain water so that the earth inside the pit would be moist enough to support saplings. This was thus promoted by various levels of government in the county as one of many anti-drought measures in the region.

Instead of turning bare land green, the successive drives of afforestation and reforestation in the village not only injured nature in significant ways, but also brought much suffering to locals, particularly to women. In this sense, it can be treated as are presentative example of conservation malpractice. I heard so many stories of women's sufferings related with painstaking pit-digging, which helped to explain why women talked about it more negatively than men. On several occasions when describing pit digging, women dubbed them "the pits for the dead", a metaphor that fully captured their complaints and anger.

Local men and women frequently complained, "It was this way for a while, and then that way for a while." They were first required to dig a small-size pit in the shape of a fish scale, followed by a medium-size pit, and then to the large-size pit. A woman remarked angrily, "It wasn't easy even for a man to shovel out sand and remove stones inside the pit in localities full of stones, let alone women. It is fair to say that tree planting launched through *da hui zhan* was a waste of money and manpower. If we are required to dig the pit again, the next target should be nowhere but our courtyard and village street!"

I was told again and again that the hill slopes within the boundary of Ao Village had been dug all over several times. However, only a small proportion of trees were still alive in 2003. Strange as it might seem, no effort was made to rectify this problem. The most intriguing puzzle for an outside observer was perhaps the fact that most saplings planted in the tree-planting campaigns actually died before reaching maturity. As a former cadre explained, "However ridiculous, the higher-ups did not allow us to abandon the practice. In this area, the pits dug on sandy slopes could be filled overnight after a heavy flood or even a strong wind. Herding is another major reason that explains the failure of afforestation." An old man repeatedly said to me, "Weather is partly to be blamed for the failure. I believe, the key lies in the fact that too much priority has always been placed on the quantity of newly planted trees, whereas too little attention was placed on the quality of planting, and subsequent management. Following the completion each time, no follow-up action was taken."

Contradictory Terracing

In this hilly semi-arid region, terracing had the potential advantage of improving farmlands on the slope and increasing the yield if properly constructed. In Ao Village, a total of 1300 *mu* of less steep fields covered by irrigation water were first terraced when they were opened up by individual households, followed by over 400 *mu* on the hill X by a county governor project in 1998. In 1999, a large patch of dry land was terraced through *da hui zhan*. Unlike the first two projects, the terracing of dry land turned out to be problematic. The terracing campaign launched in the autumn of 1999 coincided with severe droughts so the soil was exceptionally dry. A considerable number of male and female farmers from the whole township were sent to participate in it. Without strict monitoring, most participants built terraces at random. As with the tree-planting campaigns, control over the labor quality on this occasion was almost impossible.

Contrary to official expectations, this mass project designed to serve agriculture, ironically, jeopardized agricultural production itself. Many ridges collapsed quickly after their completion, and the loose soil was washed away in a heavy rain in the summer of 2003. When being terraced, the fertile topsoil was turned upside down. With the sub-soil brought to the surface, yield fell in the first few years. In addition, the structures in the fields occupied 15 percent of the surface area. As a result, 0.5 *mu* land per person was withdrawn from their ration land. As Zhang Huamin commented, "It is a good thing if terraced fields of high quality are built, otherwise a tragedy for ordinary people. Since the project failed to pay attention to concrete contexts, it served no purpose at all."

"The Qi Governor Project"

In the eyes of villagers, both men and women, a typical scenario of improper *da hui zhan* was a project locally called "The Qi Governor Project". The project—

guided directly by the county governor—was launched in the summer of 1998. The project site was located on part of a flat-topped hill (thereafter hill X) on the eastern side of the national highway, a potentially excellent showcase. The hill X was shared by three administrative villages, with the west slope of approximately 1300 *mu* under the jurisdiction of Greater Ao Village facing the highway.

Historically, this vast patch of land belonged to Team Three and Four. During the collective period, it was left uncultivated most of the time and served primarily as a public grazing land. Only occasionally, millet or sorghum was planted. After decollectivization in the period from 1981 to1984, whoever rushed to open up the wasteland harvested the benefits from it. In response to a call of the regional campaign of the "Three-Norths" Shelterbelt Scheme, a total of 900 *mu* of land was allocated to individual farmers in Team Three and Team Four as privately owned woodlots in 1986. Team members were charged 1.5RMB per *mu* of land, plus 2 cents per poplar sapling and 0.9 cents per elm sapling. Almost all households planted the elm with the exception of a few who planted some poplars. Before the trees grew up, alfalfa was grown in between them.

Before being chopped down, the diameters of trees averaged 4-6 centimeters. They were not of good quality and only a few grew into useful timber. Yet the elm leaves were a most palatable feed for animals when they were tender. By late the 1980s, almost all households in Ao Village had livestock, large or small. After the reservoir was completed, animals were allowed to graze among the groves of elm and poplar so as to protect the irrigated fields. After hill X was chosen as a project site, the woodlot owners were ordered to chop down all their trees. For those who refused to obey, the village committee hired others to do it. Their private property was endangered without any compensation being offered. As usual, villagers had no way to resist a project led by the county head.

The project was carried out in July 1998, lasting a total of 28 days. Over 1000 participants from seven administrative villages (including Greater Ao Village) participated in the project. Among them, there were a few cadres from the county level, a dozen from the township government and about 30 outside village leaders. The outside village cadres were housed among households in Ao Village, while ordinary peasants either lived with local people or in the tent camps that were erected. Around 400 *mu* of land was terraced, 100 *mu* jujube and 300 *mu* poplar were planted. More than 300000RMB, funded by the county government, was spent on the saplings as well as a set of sprinkling irrigation equipment (it was able to cover 270 *mu* of terraced fields if water was readily available). The project cost Greater Ao Village a large sum as well—approximately 50000-60000RMB—to provide outside cadres with food, transportation and lodging. As a knowledgeable ex-cadre put it, "Such a scenario can apply to many other similar projects in the county. Whichever village is targeted as a site of *da hui zhan*, it is inevitable that the village will pay for it." This "showcase" project was then arbitrarily hailed as a success in local newspapers.

In the wake of the state-sponsored project, this tract of land was expropriated as collective property. The terraced land, along with other plots was contracted out to some prosperous households inside and outside the village. Afterwards, almost all the trees—jujube and poplar—planted during the project disappeared. The failed projects have always resonated strongly with villages. On a summer day of 2003, I went with Song Ling and others to collect firewood on hill X. On the way to the top of the hill, I discovered the remains of a broken memorial tablet erected during the county governor project, which was formerly inscribed with the name of the governor. At the end of 2002, 400 *mu* of terraced land was contracted out to a former accountant for 80000RMB on a ten-year contract. This became a major source of complaint among residents.

Like many other ill-conceived projects, the above-mentioned efforts ultimately yielded disastrous ramifications for the natural environment as well as for local people, particularly for women. As many women frequently complained, when a considerable amount of land was converted to farmland, many medical herbs such as licorice, large-flowered skullcap and milkwort on the X hill disappeared. They thereby were deprived of an important source of income, upon which many relied to pay school tuition fees or even to sustain their daily lives.

Latest Chapters of Conservation Drama

During my fieldwork in 2003, I witnessed in person some of the latest chapters of mass conservation practices. The first event occurred on April 12th, three days after I settled in the village. That morning when I reached the site with three male officials from the township government, the saplings had not yet been transported to the site. Many male and female residents, mostly wearing cotton-padded clothes, were waiting in the chilly wind. As soon as a tricycle carrying seedlings driven by the husband of Ding Hangmen (the village women's director) arrived, a group of residents immediately gathered around it. Ding Hangmen was in charge of distributing the bundles of seedlings to them. I noticed a few men and women took the bundles away themselves before she took note of it. Under the guidance of the present township cadres, villagers started to dig pits before putting in the seedlings. This work was obviously nothing new to villagers. As usual, my host and hostess cooperated with Liu Xing and his wife. The four of them worked together. I observed that two men dug the pits, while two women put in the seedlings and covered them with soil. In the afternoon, Liu Xing drove his tricycle to transport water in big plastic bags to the field and Hong Xiang and Liu Xing worked together to water the saplings planted in 12 *mu* of the woodland (6 *mu* per household).

On the first morning of the second *da hui zhan* that occurred in August 2003, I noticed many residents from different hamlets walking with shovels or driving their animal carts to their designated fields. The head and several vice-heads of the township government showed up on the scene. During the course of the watershed project, the officials from county and township levels paid frequent visits to the field to oversee and show on the scene what to do and how to do it. I was told that most cadres in the township were expected to work in project fields for about three months each year. Since the work sites were scattered on numerous hills, I could not determine how many residents took part in the work that morning. A small proportion of men and women continued to work on the project later to earn extra money after they had finished their own compulsory tasks.

The third *da hui zhan* that I witnessed occurred in October. Team leaders informed their teammates of the schedule and the sites proposed ahead of time. In the morning of the designated day, residents, male and female, gathered at a place near the site. About twenty women finally clustered near a wall to escape the cold wind. Some of them waited a long time before township and team leaders showed up. I went with a township official to a site at the base of the large gully to the eastern side of the reservoir, whereas members of the east team went to a site on the opposite side of the reservoir. I went down a sloping path to the base of the large gully with a group of women from the west team. A township cadre gave a brief introduction to the project before they started to draw their lots. When the township official was speaking, residents kept silent. Perhaps this was because the procedure has been too familiar for them to raise any questions. On this occasion, the physical presence of township cadres in the field seemed welcomed by participants. The township leader launched the first effort, and patiently showed the residents how to do it. I found there were more women than men on both sites. One of the main reasons was that some men were recruited to replant trees along a highway that morning. I observed that Cao Yun, introduced in Chapter four, worked with her daughter-in-law, with her small grandson of four years old staying nearby. The work schedule was flexible as long as people met the deadline. Because some people came later, and some left after drawing their lots, I could not tell exactly how many men and women participated in the field labor that morning.

Gendered Experiences of Frustration and Bitter Memories

Almost all the above-mentioned projects launched via *da hui zhan* had gendered implications for local people. That was, the consequences for women had been significantly different and severe for women, even though both men and women of the village experienced them in the form of hardships and disappointments. Therefore, *da hui zhan* became a regular source of discontent and resistance. And both discontent and resistance turned out to be different for men and women. In describing *da hui zhan*, such sentiments were particularly strong among women. Yet as will be illustrated in next chapter, this by no means implied that local residents were totally passive. By piecing togethertheir testimonies, I can provide the following vignettes that offer fruitful insights into gendered conservation experiences and reveal the accompanying frustrations woven into the fabric of their accounts.

Physical Sufferings and Property Costs

Many residents described to me tragic accidents caused by *da hui zhan*, which included personal injures or detriments to health, especially women's health. The persistent heavy physical labor demands took a long-term toll on women's health. A woman in her early fifties explained to me, "*da hui zhan* sometimes lasted for 15-20 days for one session, and happened several times a year. When men were away for wage work, women were left to finish their quotas themselves. It was unlikely for women to loaf on the job, and most of them worked wholeheartedly. Most women my age ache all over." Indeed, during the household visits, a handful of women showed me the bottle of pain relievers that they relied on regularly.

Many men's and women's narratives were fraught with wounded feelings of injustice and unfair workloads. In almost all descriptions of *da hui zhan*, both local men and women criticized the use of uncompensated labor. They often complained that *da hui zhan* was all unpaid. On the contrary, they had to purchase their own picks, shovels and other tools. Many pointed out that they were obliged to borrow money to buy stronger livestock or new carts, which consequently created considerable family hardship. A few mentioned the deaths of their livestock due to accidents. Many noted that the occasionally promised compensation never materialized. As an impoverished old man stated, "We can't make ends meet, how can we be willing to give free labor?"

In official documents, labor control was rarely identified as problematic; at the village level, however, *da hui zhan* violated the principle of voluntarism and gave rise to numerous conflicts between agricultural and domestic work routines, as well as subsistence and commercial activities. This created much suffering in the households with insufficient labor, especially female-headed households. In this circumstance, it was all too common for women to drive themselves to exhaustion. A middle-aged woman explained to me, "To avoid having our stuff confiscated, we often left any other work routines aside to be able to complete *da hui zhan*. Under the deadline pressure, the sooner we finished the task, the earlier we could do other things. Whenever we had enough workers available, we desperately tried to finish extra cubic meters of work so that we could do less next time. Sometimes I had to accept the fine when my husband worked far away." A few of them mentioned, even though there was no alternative way to make a living locally, men were discouraged from migration due to the impositions of *da hui zhan*.

Punishment and Its Aftermath

In Aohan, punishment was invented by local officials as part of an attempt to strengthen labor control, which was once a source of local anxiety. In the most intensive years of mass labor, no one could resist imposed *da hui zhan*. A refusal to perform *da hui zhan* or delay in their task could result in being punished with cash penalties, withdrawal of ration land or confiscation of property. An implementation group, locally called *dui xian zu*, consisting of policemen from the township police station, the hill keepers, and village cadres, confiscated whatever valuable items they could find in residents' home and sometimes sold the items of monetary value at a low price to cadres. A few inhabitants described them "acting as if they were the bandits." This practice was utilized to "to kill a chicken to scare the monkeys," as a traditional Chinese saying demonstrated. Powerless people had little means to protest these manipulations. A former village leader explained to me, "The confiscation of private property as a fine was stipulated by the county government. How could ordinary people afford to engage in a lawsuit with the county government? "

When discussing *da hui zhan*, a sobering story surfaced repeatedly involving one of the most impoverished households that was once punished very severely. This was an extreme case, but by no means an isolated one; I heard at least 6-7 similar cases. I first met 43-year-old Sun Yan, the wife of Dong Fu, this particular household head, on the very day that I took up residence with my host couple in April 2003. She came to borrow 10RMB to pay for tractor-plowing services. After being refused by Song Ling, I gave her 10RMB, although I did not know then who she was. She mistook me as the daughter-in-law of my hostess, saying she would soon return the money to "my mother". Hong Xiang immediately corrected her by saying that this was teacher Hu from Beijing. She thanked me and soon left. I later learned more stories about the couple trapped in a sizeable debt. As with many other households in heavy debt, what they earned each year was not enough to pay the interest. The reason why Song Ling refused her request was that Sun Yan already owed them some money, but "never thinks of giving back the money with no interest."

I soon met the couple in their home. Both of them were Mongols. The woman was Sun Yan. Sun Yan came from a village in the same township. I found that Sun Yan's anger and feeling of utter frustration woven into the fabric of her narratives had not been softened through time. One day, she angrily recounted the disastrous story of punishment:

> When the reservoir construction began in 1989, my two sons were still small, the elder son was seven and the younger one only five. My father-in-law was then ill and needed me to take care of him. Only Dong Fu worked on it himself. We were so poor and could not afford to buy a mule or horse. The donkey that we had was not strong enough to transport earth on steep slopes. Due to unfinished earthwork, the bandit-like cadres from the village and township levels came to take all those valuable belongings we purchased before our marriage: a sewing machine, three chests, a wall clock, a radio and the like. In addition, we were compelled to pay about 400RMB, plus 6 *mu* ration land being withdrawn for two years. I was filled with deep sorrow when I discovered nothing valuable was left. After being heavily penalized and fined, our life became really hard. Out of hopelessness, Dong Fu had to migrate in search of an alternative livelihood

> in 1991, and he did not return until four years later. This was perhaps a wrong choice, as we lost the best time to cultivate crops. Really, nothing can compensate our losses.

It is worth noting that the punishment that they received had a tragic impact on this family. In the subsequent years after Dong Fu migrated out of the village, Sun Yan was left behind to deal with the sufferings, and struggled for daily existence. In the end, Dong Fu did not earn back much money in those years, yet they lost the "golden time" of crop production. One day, they showed me the two fine-paying receipts they still kept. One receiptsigned by a village accountant in January 1991 recorded the earthwork money 200RMB (It notes owing 200 cubic meters of earthwork); the other receipt of 213.80RMB was signed by a team leader in November 1992. As noted earlier, the monetary labor value of each cubic meter of earthwork equaled one *yuan*. According to their own estimates, the total value of the penalties approximated 1600RMB, a huge figure at that time. In 2003, they still lived in an almost empty mud house without a TV set or even a radio. A brick house framework was built in front of the mud house, which was initially constructed for the marriage of their elder son. Since he married into a family in a village within the township the year before, and went to live with his wife's parents, the house was left unfinished.

When we got familiar with each other, I learned more sad stories that had happened to this socially marginalized Mongol household. Dong Fu's grandfather was classified as a landlord during the land reform. He was previously a tax collector for a Mongol noble, owning merely a landholding of 40 *mu*, even less than a few middle peasants in the village (but according to the village rumor, he was an evil man). One of Dong Fu's uncles was persecuted to death in the political campaign of "*nei ren dang*". It was practically inevitable that Dong Fu experienced many hardships during the collective period. Although Dong Fu had a younger brother living next door, the two households did not get along very well with each other. That's why Sun Yan always said they had been at a disadvantage since they were a "*xiao hu ren jia*", meaning a small family. Indeed, they were one of the weakest surname groups in the village.

When I returned to Ao Village in 2004, I felt extremely uncomfortable to know that their elder son of twenty-three years old with a nine-month-old daughter had already divorced and they were then in the middle of a legal dispute to split the property. He was engaged at nineteen and got married at age of twenty-one in 2002. It was rumored that he migrated out to work in a city after marriage, but brought back no money to his wife. Some guessed that he might have sent money to his parents since they were trapped deeply in debt for his marriage. The Dong couple spent a total of 18000RMB for the marriage transaction, most of which was borrowed at high interests. According to the court decision, the baby girl would be kept by her mother and their son could only expect to claim back around 5000RMB, but he still was required to pay an allowance of 600RMB per year for the girl. I observed that the Dong couple was in a somber mood, and I did not know how to console them. This time, Sun Yan's hostility towards village cadres had shifted to the frustrations of going to court, betraying her deep feeling of hopelessness and powerlessness in carrying out a lawsuit. This scenario produced sympathetic reactions among villagers, and reinforced the idea that uxorilocal marriage was an unwise choice.

Cadres, Power and Da hui zhan

In the narratives of common villagers, images of inequality were strongly felt. Men and women alike were well aware of the power differentials and an unfair distribution of labor between themselves and the officials from the village and township levels. They constantly stressed that not only could village cadres have the privilege of avoiding physical labor themselves; they also extended that privilege to their family members and relatives. Since village cadres were made responsible for organizing and coordinating the process of mass labor, according to village regulations, a village cadre and two of his/her family members were exempt from *da hui zhan*, yet I was frequently told that their entire families tended to escape the drudgery of mass labor. A few even spared their relatives by helping able-bodied persons to get a Certificate of Disability.[1]

To ensure meeting designed criteria for success, cadres often supervised and monitored the labor on the scene. For instance, they stayed around to make sure that trees were planted at proper intervals and the pits were dug in the appropriate shape and size. For a long time, an iron frame was put inside the pit to check whether or

1 Those persons who had a certificate of disability or a certificate of one-child, the hill keepers and others were eligible to excuse themselves from *da hui zhan*.

not it met the size requirement. If the shape was irregular or the size a little bit small, it was actually impossible to put it in. Women were particularly conscious of this official scrutiny and forced compliance in the fields. One woman told me, "Unlike a small minority of men, we women normally have 'thin faces' (means to be unwilling to be blamed by others publicly) and thus we worked extremely hard so as to not to be blamed by cadres. To make the pits bigger so as to meet the criteria might not be a big problem for men, yet to move out even a few shovels of sand made a big difference for women."

One notable theme that stood out sharply in the testimonies was that *da hui zhan* benefited the powerful at the expense of the powerless. Talking about the outside assistance flowing into the village along with environmental conservation, people often complained that the project money got "lost" before reaching the hands of ordinary folk. Liu Xing remarked pointedly one day:

> The distribution of the project fund is just like the shape of a carrot plant. There is much foliage on the upper part of it, whereas there is merely an increasingly slender root underground. Our common people are just like the tip of the root, who can hardly reap any real benefits. Even if village cadres embezzle the money, we will never be informed of it. Whenever a key village leader comes to power, instead of helping the real poor to make their fortune, he knows nothing but to organize mass conservation labor constantly in the interests of himself and not in the interests and priories of *lao bai xing* (ordinary people). Quite often, he won't be able to get anything done. If cadres relied on a once-and-for-all solution, they would not win further funds. That's why projects were always incomplete and will never stop...

Liu Xing was apparently not alone in holding this perspective. According to knowledgeable residents, many local officials gained political capital for themselves through *da hui zhan*, a conclusion that was certainly not totally unfounded. I learned from a local newspaper that the very county head that initiated the qi governor project in Ao Village was later transferred to Chifeng City to serve as the head of the Forestry Bureau. To deal with the inspection from the higher-ups, local bureaucrats tended to purposely exaggerate their achievements and discount their failures to increase their likelihood of promotion. Residents constantly reminded me of the fact that the relevant numbers were always inflated, holding too much "water".

The genealogy of *da hui zhan* from a larger historical context demonstrated many intersecting topics. Over a long period of time, the vulnerable locals were made to participate in *da hui zhan* in the face of powerful state power. The top-down, coercive, externally imposed *da hui zhan* often operated to the detriment of individual peasants, most notably women on the one hand, and gave rise to the abuse of power among male cadres on the other. The militarized labor of *da hui zhan* seldom contributed to the improvement of the local environment, as was generally believed. On the contrary, some misguided and even ridiculous projects imposed negative impacts on local ecosystems. That's why the mass mobilization conservation campaign became a topic of constant resentment and a site of serious contestation. Although residents paid a terrible price, they were not silent victims.

Gender figured prominently in *da hui zhan*, which often involved heavy physical labor that demanded strength and stamina to shoulder, dig, and push heavy loads. Gender differentiation in strength made women particularly vulnerable to the endless processes of *da hui zhan*. Putting aside the differences between women and men in physical strength, the constraints of childbearing and domestic work borne by married women differentiated the perceptions of *da hui zhan* among residents along gender lines. This helped to explain why women tended to situate their vulnerability and the negative image of inflexible mass labor in their everyday lives and their reproductive roles.

It was widely acknowledged that women played an essential role in *da hui zhan*. During the collective period, young men and women took part in the mass conservation practices in almost the same way. As in the past, it was not uncommon when able-bodied men migrated somewhere else for wage labor inside or outside the village that it was women who were left to take the bulk of the tough *da hui zhan* labor. During my 2003 fieldtrip, I found that in a household of six adult persons, a Mongol woman in her fifties was obliged to complete all the assignments of six persons by herself alone, since all her three young sons and one daughter-in-law had migrated out of the village, and her husband was taken to work on highway construction. It was true adult women were most likely to be left behind to assume the burden of this arduously physical labor. After reconstructing a history of *da hui zhan* in Ao Village, I will proceed to describe the story of a Party secretary and the environmental and other developmental practices that he promoted when he was in power.

From Success to Tragedy: The Legacy of a Party Secretary

The idea of writing the story of Party secretary Wang Sheng in Greater Ao Village occurred to me afterwards while writing. I had no opportunity to talk with him face-to-face, nor were systematic interviews conducted. Looking through my field notes, there was a great deal of information regarding his work, life and his successes and failures. His story was so closely linked with the pros and cons of drastic environmental initiatives, and the ups and downs of local men and women's livelihoods. During my stay in Ao Village, the accounts of his legacies surfaced and resurfaced frequently among men and women. The years when Wang Sheng was in office seemed to have become an unforgettable part of the history of Ao Village.

As was well known, the Party secretary, the highest, ranking position in most villages in the late twentieth century rural China—was usually the de facto ruler. Ao Village was no exception. Wang Sheng was an authoritarian figure when he was in power from 1988-1996. Under his leadership, the configuration of village power changed; resource management and control were strengthened; environmental initiatives were launched; innovative economic ventures were pursued, and community cultural activities boomed.

The dramatic changes that occurred in Ao Village had tremendous impacts on households, which in turn, structured men's and women's division of labor and responsibility. Although all these male-run ventures in large part privileged men and marginalized women, most men and women shared a short period of prosperity. In addition, all of these pursuits overlapped with intensified *da hui zhan* flowering across Aohan. When more men were attracted to the brick factory or sent to dig wells outside the village, many women experienced terrible hardship and had to assume a larger share of *da hui zhan* labor. Most of these gendered projects not only won Wang Sheng prestige, but also sowed seeds of resentment among inhabitants. He migrated out of the community in 2001 and seldom returned. It was said that whenever he came back to visit his sisters in the community, he felt that he had no "face" to meet his fellow villagers. In 2003, villagers still recalled him with mixed feelings of respect, regret and resentment.

The Rise and Fall of Wang Sheng

Wang Sheng was widely acknowledged by village men and women as a man of courage, insight and innovation. He rose to the position of Party secretary in 1988 and fell from power in 1996. After graduating from a senior high school, he became a village teacher. In the early 1980s, he was removed from his teaching post for violating a family planning policy by having his second son before the required interval. After losing his job, he returned to his home team and soon became a team leader. In 1986, he obtained a post in the village government. Two years later when he was thirty-three years old, he rose to the top leadership post.

His story cannot be understood without looking at the perplexing economic and political factors within and outside the community. When he was the highest leader, he maximized the importance of the village collective as an institution, which was strengthened in significant ways under his leadership. The village party branch and the village committee including nine cadres were mostly controlled by Wang Sheng. Among them, only the women's director was a female. So overwhelming was his authority and power in his heyday that no one—not even his fellow cadres—challenged his status. In a sense, he became almost a "local emperor". The influences of the village authorities seemed to exceed all former collective structures in the history of Greater Ao Village. Strong village leadership, in turn, played a significant role in strengthening collective institutions that supported community-wide activities. Owing to unchallenged command without a strong financial and administrative monitoring system, Wang Sheng later arbitrarily made some poor decisions, which led to a split in the village government.

Wang Sheng's connections with a larger political world were still a source of pride among some residents. He was one of three renowned and powerful Party secretaries in the political network of the township, and had a reputation for his political and economic ambitions. It was uniformly acknowledged that no other leader was able to win as much outside funding for the village as he did by deploying his political connections and influences. There was no denying that there existed some transaction costs such as outright gifts or bribery, yet most informants claimed that it was done for the benefit of the village rather than for himself and his family. Additionally, he was a cadre who knew how to manipulate external authorities, and was capable of handling complicated administrative duties that were imposed by higher authorities.

Those years under the leadership of Wang Sheng were a relatively prosperous period in the village's history. The ambitious economic, conservation and infrastructure building practices that he vigorously pursued transformed the village scene with the availability of large tracts of shrub, planted grasses, cornfields, the kiln, and the reservoir, which somewhat improved the fortune of local people. Ironically, due to his major errors, the village debt left behind by him accumulated and still afflicted the village in 2003. However, his contributions to the village were remembered and highlighted by his fellow villagers, both males and females. A few people asserted that if he had remained in power, all might be different from the current situation.

A charge of embezzlement eventually put an end to his political career. To his own great astonishment, higher-up township authorities placed the blame on his corruption, which he denied and resisted for some time. Even the door of his house was sealed before he could remember certain sums of money spent without receipts. His wife died suddenly soon after he lost power, followed by his mother. In 2003, I found that a homeless old couple was using his house. After he was dismissed from his post, he refused to participate in *da hui zhan*, and thus he was fined as other ordinary people. He quit farming, since he had never had any experience in managing a farm. After the failure of a short second marriage, he was forced to leave the community of his birth, along with his two unmarried sons. It was a heartbreaking story, in the words of a resident, "The family was broken up and decimated (*jia po ren wang*)." This tragic personal story, in some sense, was also a tragedy of the community.

To Launch Environmental Initiatives of Its Own

The village committee under the leadership of Wang Sheng forged institutional arrangements to embark on some successful NRM and environmentally sound practices. A string of environment-related local efforts were frequently cited among residents, which were mostly credited to his remarkable contributions. For instance, the village committee met with great success by mobilizing individual households to grow large tracts of the shrub *ning tiao* in the most vulnerable land. Also, most of the over 3000 *mu* of alfalfa was planted during this period. A specialized work team (*zhuan ye dui*) was established to carry out reforestation projects throughout the year, which operated a tree nursery, producing the seedlings for use in the village. A Forest and Grass Protection Brigade (*hu lin hu cao da dui*)—led by a village cadre and staffed by 3-4 young men—was established to safeguard trees and grass reserves. The mechanism of forest and grass protection in place at the community level functioned satisfactorily. Villagers still somewhat benefited from the fruits of these community-level conservation endeavors, such as the planted grass and shrubs.

The hallmark of local environmental initiatives came with the reservoir construction. It was the most ambitious and arduous collective activity of all the projects launched. It was not until the reservoir was almost finished that the village government finally received some external assistance. Under considerable pressure from the higher-level governments to launch *da hui zhan*, shortly after he took office, Wang Sheng posed a suggestion to build a reservoir so as to seek a path to community prosperity. The practical reality at that time, as many claimed, was that if a village did not initiate its own *da hui zhan*, its villagers might be channeled to other projects beyond the village. In this sense, the reservoir building was used as a political strategy by the village authority to resist the external impositions handed down from higher governments. Yet even the reservoir building did not totally relieve Greater Ao Village from participating in *da hui zhan* inside and outside the village.

At the outset, the whole community was surprised at the idea of building a reservoir to the south of the settlement. A few residents refused the move on the grounds that it was against the folk belief in the system of winds and waters (*feng shui*). Frightened by huge labor requirements, coupled with failed attempts of reservoir building in the past, about 20 percent of residents publicly raised opposition to the project. Despite numerous obstacles from inside and outside the village, the male-dominated village authority took up the challenge to launch the project. The prospect of access to irrigated fields motivated some reluctant residents, while many others had little choice but to comply with it. The success of reservoir building was an unprecedented display of the administrative and political power of the village government, which consequently raised the prestige of Wang Sheng in Greater Ao Village and its vicinity. He later won two sets of irrigation equipment from the county government.

This was a notable achievement, representing a watershed in the change of physical and social landscape in the village. When the reservoir was still under construction, individual households were mobilized simultaneously to dig an irrigation ditch and reclaimed 1300 *mu* of wasteland. The abundant water supply created a new era of irrigated agriculture. In the very year of reservoir building in

1989, residents received 0.6 *mu* of irrigated fields per person, followed by another 0.9 *mu* in 1990, and a total of 2.3 *mu* was allocated on a per capita basis. The reservoir was once capable of providing an adequate volume of water twice a year for a total of 1300 *mu* of farmland. And its equipment was kept in good repair. Trees were planted in most of the newly opened terraced fields and both sides of the ditch. The reservoir provided an essential source of water for livestock as well.

Ao Village used to have poor access to drinking water and was notorious in neighboring villages for its scarce water resources. Before two wells were dug within the settlement by the county government in 1977, the community of over 400 inhabitants relied entirely on one well located outside the settlement, almost 0.5 kilometer away from some of the family houses. Every possible means of transportation was mobilized in those days. Most households carried water using the shoulder pole; only a few richer residents transported water with donkey carts.

In most households, women took the major responsibility of carrying water from the well. It took half an hour for a woman to make a round trip to shoulder large buckets of water from the well. Many women mentioned that they needed to take a rest several times during the return trip. It was quite common for many women to fetch water even in the advanced stages of pregnancy. I was told that one woman fell down the well when she drew a bucket of water from the well by herself a few days after delivering her child. Even with the availability of the two wells in the community, with one located in the east village and another in the west village, access to drinking water was still a severe problem. After decollectivization, as villagers raised an increasing number animals, the demand for water sources also increased.

Wang Sheng pioneered the drilling of a well in a pig factory in the community in 1992. The technology for digging wells in sandy soil was successfully tested there, and spread quickly to individual households. Many local people installed electric pump wells in their yards. Many male residents learned how to bore wells and became seasonal well diggers within and outside the community. Since the mid-1990s, Ao Village has witnessed a shift from large-bore wells to small-bore. The former draws shallow water from about 20-30 meters underground, while the latter pumps deep water from about 40-50 meters.

The availability of domestic wells greatly eased the labor burden on women. Giving credit to Wang Sheng, an older woman said to me, "To drink water we will never forget the well-digger" (a poplar Chinese saying). However, a few years ago, after a few relatively rich villagers no longer used the public well in the west village, they destroyed it by filling it with stones or other things. A poor woman complained to me, "Much of the village property created by Wang Sheng has been undermined. Nowadays, no one takes care of collective affairs. Even a well that once benefited so many people was destroyed. If Wang Sheng was still in office, he would not let this happen. Inhabitants took seriously what he said."

Diversifying into Nonagricultural Enterprises

The strengthening of the positions of the village authority paved the way for a re-structuring of the village economy. When Wang Sheng was in office, he set in motion two rural enterprises that never before existed in Ao Village. The mushrooming and miraculous growth of township and village enterprises from the 1980s to the mid-1990s was once a major motor of development in many parts of rural China. However, west China lagged far behind the wealthy coastal areas that had a relatively mature collective industrial sector. As was often the case in many localities in west China, the indigenously fueled industry in Ao Village relied mainly on locally available natural resources and labor.

The first enterprise was a pig-raising factory established jointly by the village committee and the Qi Materials Bureau in 1992. The original investment on the part of the village committee was 50000RMB, which was all borrowed from the bank. At its climax, around 90 pigs and 11 mother pigs were raised in the factory. Without appropriate managers, it turned out to be poorly managed and inefficient, creating only a few jobs for a small minority of young girls from the village. The enterprise was closed down in 1998, ultimately bringing little benefit to the village. The bank debt later reached around 100000RMB due to increasing interest. It was generally acknowledged as the biggest failure of all Wang Sheng's ventures.

A second joint venture was the brick factory set up in 1994. Most of the village's investment of over 300000RMB derived from a loan with an interest rate of 30 percent from some elite villagers, and the township government invested about 240000RMB. Villagers also contributed their compulsory labor in the building of a kiln. Technicians were hired from the outside, but four male managers were all village officials without prior experience. The advantage that Ao Village enjoyed was that the clay around the kiln was of good quality. Constrained by lack of experienced managers with both technical and administrative skills, it soon ran into difficulties. The township government withdrew from the money-losing pursuit after it had operated for less than one year. In this situation, the village committee could not maintain it any more by itself. In the following year, the newly created enterprise was quickly contracted out on a five-year basis to the village committee of a relatively richer village in the same township, which was under the leadership of an influential Party secretary. The outsider-run factory operated for another four years and then came to a halt in 2000 when it suffered from lower market demand. Because of the failures of the village enterprises, Wang Sheng got into serious trouble.

The labor-intensive brick factory employed about 70-80 full-time workers. Over half of them came from Ao Village and almost one third were women. It was true that women were assigned the most tedious, lowest paid work. In those years, many surplus village laborers in Ao Village were diverted away from agriculture and absorbed into the enterprise, which made it possible for some villagers "to leave the land but stay in the countryside", a phenomenon widely existed in many prosperous coastal areas. Ordinary workers earned on average 3000-4000RMB per year, which apparently brought an improved income to many households.

In addition to working in the factory, some men and women took the opportunity to sell their grain, vegetables and other produce to the factory, or engaged in supplying transportation and other services. The shutdown of the brick factory sent the workers back to the land. During my fieldwork in 2003, I observed that certain brick-making equipment was exposed to the weather and many residents expressed their strong wishes for the reopening of the factory. In the eyes of many villagers, in spite of its negative ramifications for the village collective, many residents benefited from the factory in significant ways.

The operation of the brick factory provoked several environmental concerns.[1] A house construction boom in the community accompanied the development of the brick factory. I observed in my 2004 revisit, with the reopening of the brick factory, there was an even deeper and bigger pit near the kiln due to unlimited excavation. As before, the clay was collected freely from 100 *mu* of land near the brick factory. When I put forward the question of clay waste to the village director, much to my surprise, I was told that it was not his business and the Qi Bureau of State Land Administration would take charge of the problem. I learned from one of the key factory managers in 2004 that the factory normally consumed 200 cubic meters of

1 I was uncertain about the sheer magnitude of the air pollution problem, which is beyond the scope of this study.

earth per day, producing 100000 bricks and using 20-30 tons of coal.[1] Many villagers predicted that after exhausting the clay supply, the factory contractor might close the factory again.

Both village-run pig and brick factories were short-lived. Their failure cost the village a great deal. To help to pay off the village's debts, 1.5 *mu* ration land was taken over from each person in Greater Ao Village and contracted out to earn the contracting fee. To make the collective venture profitable proved a challenge, which in practice went out of control even of Wang Sheng himself. As a township leader confided to me, industrial ventures owned and operated through collective management had seldom succeeded throughout the township, and more broadly in Aohan as a whole. In 2003, I visited a profitable privatized brick factory established one year later than the one in Ao Village in a neighboring village 4 kilometers away. There, I discovered that, despite the inferior quality of the clay used, there was a high local demand for its products.

The "Honeymoon" Years in Ao Village

Ao Village witnessed a brief "honeymoon" period in the early to mid-1990s. The availability of more cropland as well as corn cultivation in irrigated fields ushered in an agricultural boom. Within a space of about 7-8 years, corn cultivation brought significant wealth to Ao Village. With an adequate supply of water, the yield of corn amounted to around 1000-1200 catties per *mu* even in a bad year, from which many villagers earned a considerable income and carved out better living niches in livestock farming. Since then, corn provided a large quantity of stalk to be used as fodder and fuel, which greatly reduced not only the burden on other natural resources, but also on women who assumed the major responsibility for fuel collection.

During the boom years, Ao Village also witnessed thriving cultural activity. An amateur *ping* opera (a popular opera in north China) troupe was re-created under the auspices of each production team in 1977. For a couple of years when Wang Sheng was in office, actors and actresses in the troupe enjoyed the privilege of being allocated an extra 2 *mu* of land. It consisted of over 30 male and female villagers, and once became a very famous grassroots drama troupe in the area around Ao Village. The rehearsal and performance were conducted in the slack season. For

1 They mixed much of the coal into clay so as to raise the heating when the bricks were fired.

almost one month near the lunar New Year, apart from offering performances on the makeshift stage inside the community, they were also dispatched to the surrounding villages. After Wang Sheng fell from power, no one paid serious attention to the opera troupe. As some young women married out, the once flourishing cultural performance team was finally disbanded. As of 2003, the costume and props were still preserved in the village office. Prior to the droughts, Ao Village always held an annual parade of *yang ge* dance, a kind of folk dance popular in rural north China, which was performed in a large group of around 100 people during the lunar New Year. The dance team visited and danced in the courtyard of each household that was willing to receive them and offer them candies, sunflower seeds or cigarettes. After 1999, almost all collective activities disappeared, mirroring the weakening of community-level solidarity.

In those years, Ao Village gained a good reputation in the surrounding areas. It was said that the number of "bare sticks", or bachelors, was reduced, and young women in adjacent villages were willing to marry into the village. Due to the political connections of Wang Sheng, he won some extra money for the village; a new school building and a new village headquarters were built. By the time I settled in the village, the village headquarters had been sold off to an elite villager in 2002, while the school building was converted into the village office building. The boom that began suddenly in the early 1990s collapsed suddenly around 1996 when the reservoir started to go dry before villagers had reaped adequate returns, which coincided with the fall of Wang Sheng.

The Tale of Wang Sheng's Wife

Wang Sheng's wife—locally termed *xi fu*—whose name had never been mentioned to me by anybody,[1] was universally acknowledged as a very capable and hardworking woman. There was no denying that Wang Sheng's political career was based upon the economic contributions of his wife. It was reported that Wang Sheng was seldom involved in work inside the household, productive or reproductive alike. She married into the village from a neighboring township in 1980, being three years older than her husband. She learned a complete range of farming skills and was one of the few women in the village who could plow as well as men did.

When Wang Sheng worked in the village committee, she took on the full

1 See the gendered naming practices in Chapter two.

responsibility of agricultural activities and contributed greatly to the household wealth. She also coped with all the domestic matters by herself without any complaints. In spite of her husband's prestigious position, she had never showed off. I was told that she was the rare family member of village cadres who participated in *da hui zhan*. After her husband lost his power, she died of a cerebral hemorrhage suddenly at the age of fifty-five in 1997 when she was working in the courtyard. Her death must have shocked Wang Sheng, who held a large memorial service for her. One woman commented to me with great emotion, "When she was alive, she worked so hard and always had two rough hands. She became somewhat relaxed after her husband rose to power. A group of village women often voluntarily came to help her with fieldwork, she, in turn, always kindly entertained them. If Wang Sheng did not feel pity for the death of his wife, he should be regretful for the loss of her excellent work."

A Political Myth

I was puzzled by various versions about Wang Sheng's failures. The reason why Wang Sheng was expelled from the office remained somewhat a mystery to many villagers as well. He suddenly fell from the power as a "corrupt official," though no one could tell exactly how much truth there was in this label. Several men assured me that he embezzled only a bit over a 1000RMB (about 120 US$) without receipt. Compared to the rampant corruption that had swept the surrounding areas and the Chinese countryside as a whole in 2003, this was too small a sum. During my stay in Ao Village, the accusation of graft was always directed to other cadres, seldom did I hear anybody blame Wang Sheng for embezzling money. On the contrary, many claimed although he might appropriate the public fund to pay monetary gifts, he did so neither for himself nor his family, but for the sake of the village collective. Although his household was relatively prosperous, it primarily relied upon his wives. However, a few asserted that he did set a bad example for the corrupt among village cadres in later years.

Many maintained that his personal behavior eventually brought about his failure. Some attributed it to his abuses of power when he handled village affairs. He later had little tolerance for disagreement and did not share decisions with most other members in the village government. When he was in power, the overwhelming majority, if not all, of his fellow villagers acknowledged his authority. During the lunar New Year, many residents queued up to invite him for banquets, but he showed favoritism towards a small number of them, which alienated him from the rest of the villagers. Others stressed, as a man of power, his most serious weakness was that he was notorious for his illicit affairs with several village women and he even offered them benefits publicly. Zhang Huamin explained to me, "like almost every other male cadre, when he was in liquor, he could not distinguish East from West, North from South! As a result, he sometimes signed or agreed to something wrong at random."[1] Apparently, a host of reasons converged to contribute to his falling out of power. A younger sister of Wang Sheng commented about it by borrowing a famous Chinese saying, "When a wall is falling, everyone might have pushed it!" (*qiang dao zhong ren tui*), but she did not specify how and why.

Despite all his flaws and failures, many villagers still praised Wang Sheng from time to time. A former female teacher noted, "I once worked with him and admired him. When the wild gooses pass by, they leave behind the sound. He was just a man of this kind, who left so much to the village." Many claimed that if he had remained in power, the village would have a much brighter prospect. Some inhabitants still respectfully called him secretary Wang. Some mentioned that he cared about the real poor and intentionally found some work for them and then offered them compensation. In Ao Village, there were at least 12 Party secretaries since Liberation, rarely did I hear anyone refer to other Party secretaries this way. It was quite possible that frustrated local people perceived and praised him in retrospect after comparing him with other Party secretaries before and after him.

Since the dismissal of Wang Sheng, an outside man was appointed by the township government to succeed him as the Party secretary of Greater Ao Village, who partly reversed some of his former measures. This man was not in the village long enough (only one and a half years) to ensure the continuity of his own policies. By 2004, there had been four male Party secretaries after Wang Sheng. Villagers complained that, apart from several sets of irrigation facilities funded by the higher-level governments, no other impressive infrastructure was ever constructed. On the contrary, the village debt had soared dramatically. With the weakening ability and will of the village authority to promote cohesion among residents, the community had become fragmented.

What emerges from an account of Wang Sheng is that a united village authority

1 As is well known, Mongol men are often heavy alcohol drinkers. In this part of rural China, many men and even some women drank a large quantity of low-quality wine on an almost day-to-day basis.

under the leadership of an influential figure could be a key element in launching economic and environmental initiatives, which led to village prosperity. However, the ambitious pursuits pursued by Wang Sheng developed in ways that compelled men and women to fulfill different responsibilities to carry them. The result was that his projects imposed divergent impacts on local men and women, negative and positive. The masculinized attitudes and practices of Wang Sheng being taken for granted by villagers—mirrored in the deep-rooted male bias in the Chinese countryside—were also responsible for his downfall. Wang Sheng was 48 years old in 2003, and I asked on various occasions, if there was any possibility that he would assume power again. And why didn't you unite together to encourage him back? Only a few villagers said they did not rule out the possibility. Most of them did not respond positively. They cited some political obstacles rising from Wang Sheng himself, from township leaders, and from other hamlets in Greater Ao Village.

In the Shadow of a New Round of "Development"[1]

Since the launch of the West China campaign in 2000, the impoverished "others" in Ao Village, as elsewhere in rural west China (Liu, 2000; Williams, 2002), were constantly placed in the shadows of "development" by extra-village forces, in the name of modernity and progress. This, in turn, had shaped their perspectives on and understandings of "development" in their daily lives at the local level. My encounter with a small group of Ao Village residents one day in July 2003 illustrated this point clearly. I was struck by a folktale that was told and the political sentiments surrounding it in a conversation, which I jotted down from my memory as best I could. I record it here, as this episode often provoked me to ponder the new round of gendered "development" unfolding in the landscape of Ao Village in 2003.

The participants included myself, the Zhang Guisheng couple, introduced in Chapter five, and their daughter Zhang Huamin (a former women's director), an elderly man who had served as a team leader for about 30 years, and a middle-aged ex-solider handicapped from a motorcycle accident. In the middle of our conversation of "*ren jian di bo*" (meaning people become crafty and land quality declined), the ex-solider complained, "What's development in West China?

1 Following Ferguson (1994), I utilized the term of "development" in quotation marks, since "development" was often deployed by local officials to represent their own political priorities and interests without bringing any real change for the target population.

Development nowadays can do nothing to improve the predicament of the poor, even distributing the old relief clothes, village cadres always pick out first, reserving the good for themselves and they give us the bad." The elder team leader followed with anger, "Even the worn-out clothes will not be extended to the powerless like me!" Before I realized it, he had shifted to telling the following story:

> When an official-like male traveler from a faraway place was passing through an isolated village, he saw a village woman holding a baby in her arms with a diaper. He approached the woman and asked to purchase the diaper from her. Since it would take a few more days for a louse hiding in the diaper to get mature, the male traveler thus told the woman that he would return to buy it a few days later, and pay whatever money the woman requested. The poor woman was too excited to believe it. As soon as she returned home, the kind woman washed the diaper in hot water repeatedly. When the outside man returned to buy it, the louse certainly had already died. As a matter of fact, the louse was a key to a mountain full of treasures in the village.

After hearing the story, the group responded quickly. The ex-solider commented first, "How could the woman be so stupid and not ask the guy why he wanted the diaper!" The mother of Zhang Huamin refuted, "How could she know what was inside the diaper? What could a village woman know!" The elder team leader cut in, "The woman would otherwise get rich. Why did the man not inform her in detail." At this point, Zhang Huamin remarked, "She was fated to remain in poverty. How could an ordinary woman make a fortune! To this day, can I get rich or can you become wealthy?"

For a long time, the tale and their comments regarding it leaped into my mind frequently: How did our discussion of "*ren jian di bo*" provoke such a tale? What did the narrator want to convey? How was the story associated with their everyday existence? Why was the marginalized linked always to the female gender? It seemed to me that many cross-cutting political themes related to developmental projects were captured nicely in this conversation: gendered traveling and male travelers, a marginalized community and an uninformed woman, the intrusion of outside forces, and the lost fortune. All these may be understood as an evidence of intractable development problems confronting local people, and particularly women.

Ever since the West China Campaign was launched in 2000, this region was increasingly constructed as a region lacking "development." The environmental rehabilitations were identified as one of the key priorities and environmental conservation practices pushed to a new height. In Aohan, the new round of "development" had triggered large-scale infrastructure projects under mobilization schemes. The fame of Aohan in environmental conservation perhaps played a significant part in attracting more international and government investments from the outside than many other localities.

As elsewhere in the county, Ao Village witnessed an influx of "development" projects focusing predominantly on environmental conservation. In 2003, there were at least five projects, foreign or indigenous, government or non-governmental, operating at the community level. Three of the ongoing projects were associated with environmental conservation practices. As in the past, all the projects but one were channeled through the village government, which implemented the projects under the guidance of higher-level governments. In what follows, I will briefly outline four on-going projects in 2003, evaluating their implications for the local economy and the environment, especially for the livelihood of residents, male and female.

Stall-feeding and Zero Grazing

The concepts of stall-feeding and zero grazing were not totally foreign terms for local inhabitants. The county government had implemented similar policies on and off since the 1990s. Yet not until 2003 did it begin to be implemented more strictly, after Aohan won the UNEP'S "Global 500 Roll of Honor Award". In July 2003 when I returned to Ao Village, I discovered a proclamation regarding stall-feeding and zero grazing—locally called "*she shi jin mu*"—on the outside wall of the grocery store. It had faded from exposure to the weather, with some sentences becoming blurred and unrecognizable. The storekeeper told me that it had been there for almost half a year. I later found Chifeng Daily—an Aohan Version featured the project announcement in the form of a letter on 16th June 2003.

The policy released by the county government was entitled *An Open Letter to Peasant and Pastoralist Friends All Over the Qi from Aohan People's Government.* Superficially, it was a letter, yet the policy was put into effect beginning in 2003. The letter began by expounding the policy and its justifications in a friendly tone. It specified sheep periodic stall-feeding from April 1 to July 1 each year and zero grazing of large livestock all year round. Its discursive construction highlighted the necessity of a shift from free grazing to an intensive regime of stall-feeding so as to realize "a shift from traditional livestock husbandry to a modern industry, protecting the fruits of ecological construction and attaining sustainable development in the county."

The overarching objective of the policy, apparently, derived from the purpose of conserving the environment. Its underlying assumption was that free grazing was the only major threat to local environment. It suggested that the confinement of sheep in the most vulnerable period of the vegetation growth cycle as well as zero grazing of large livestock could fundamentally realize the switch of livestock farming from an extensive to intensive method, and thereby attain "sustainable development." Obviously, "sustainable development" as a trope had entered the official thinking at the county level, however, there was an apparently simplistic explanation of the conservation-with-development problems.

This naïve and superficial understanding was, obviously, far from enough to deal with the daily socio-economic realities in different localities. In Ao Village, after the three-month confinement was over, livestock, large and small, continued to graze the village "commons". In opposition to the intention of the ban, the period of confinement proved to be followed by the same, and even more exploitative and predatory grazing practices. As a result, the policy in practice had done little to improve the environmental conditions. In 2004, the grazing restrictions seemed somewhat loosened.

The policy made no mention of the disadvantages confronting herding households. With the imposition of the policy, local people were left behind to adapt to the challenges themselves. Despite the government's commitments, to the best of my knowledge, herding households in Ao Village were accorded neither technical, financial nor organizational support services before or during the confinement. From the very outset, not all residents were informed of the policy. A few residents mentioned that not until they grazed their stock out and were warned by hill keepers, did they know about the new move. Others noted that they got the information from TV or their peers. I heard some villagers complain about the extreme contradictions between sudden forage demand and availability.

This policy, undoubtedly, imposed unexpected implications for many women who were the main fodder collectors and animal raisers, especially for those who lived in sheep-owning households. Many women were obliged to devote more time and energy not only to collecting and storing fodder, but also to looking after stall-fed sheep.

The policy also denied the social reality that local people virtually lacked techniques and the capital to deal with some of the problems themselves. One of the key troubles related to stall-feeding was the detrimental impact of it on the health of sheep. One experienced herdsman told me that during the three-month confinement, he lost eight large sheep, averaging 300RMB per head, as well as three small sheep. He claimed that as of 2003, he had been a shepherd for over 20 years, never before did he experience such a big loss. When I posed the problem of confinement-induced loss to the township head, he merely perceived it as an unavoidable "natural" death.

In addition, nowhere did the letter acknowledge the divergent and even conflicting interests inherent in the government's objectives of grazing control and local people's livelihoods. On the contrary, the letter presented the government as a protector of the interests of peasants; and arbitrarily stating, "The government and the masses of peasants and herdsmen essentially share a common interest."

In practice, the statement was only true in a limited sense. The locals retained a strong preference for free range grazing, which was a belief and practice that was firmly entrenched. It was impossible to change it by a simplistic policy. When the daily use of previously accessible environmental resources was threatened, especially as the policing in the communal land was strengthened in coercive ways, aggravated conflicts and resistances occurred frequently. The policy intended to be beneficial to local people was, ironically, rejected by them. The implementation of any policy in rural China must filter through local cultural attitudes and social realities. Without paying sufficient attention to them, no policy can be implemented in a sustainable fashion.

The Cropland Conversion Project

The national Cropland Conversion Project or *"tui geng huan lin"*, was an afforestation effort initiated in selected Chinese provinces. The project was implemented gradually in some localities from 2000 onward. Its avowed purposes were to halt water and soil erosion, increase income and reduce poverty. Afforestation was mainly undertaken on marginal cropland on the slopes exceeding 25 degrees so as to rehabilitate damaged ecosystems. The use of arable land for afforestation purposes was a major departure from previous policies.

The economic incentives provided by the Central Government to the participants who had met designated success criteria included: 200 catties of unhusked grain and a subsidy of 20RMB cash per *mu* per annum of the cropland converted. The compensation also included seed and seedlings worth 50RMB per *mu*. The land use rights would be unchanged for thirty years, while the subsidy would be maintained for eight successive years. The agricultural tax was still collected from the conversion cropland. According to a local policy of Inner Mongolia, apart from planting trees on the converted cropland, participant farmers also faced a mandatory requirement to afforest two *mu* of wasteland for one *mu* of cropland converted.

My field observation and interviews suggest there were far more complex scenariosthan might be imagined from the information of some aggregate studies at the county level across the nation. In 2003, Greater Ao Village participated in the campaign for the first time. As usual, the implementation of state policy at the village level virtually left larger maneuvering spaces for the practices of local cadres. First, part of the conversion lands used was the contracting land rather than farmers' ration land. Second, according to a village policy, each registered member was entitled to two *mu* of conversion land, yet the village committee collected 200RMB cash for one *mu* of it, which consequently deprived many poor people of the rare opportunity to access the promised material benefits. Third, the seedling subsidy was not provided to the households in cash. Instead, local governments opted to provide farmers with the seedlings decided by the higher-level governments. Fourth, not only was the distribution of the conversion land sharply uneven among inhabitants, two township cadres as non-locals without cropland in the community gained access to a very large tract of the conversion land. All these aspects obviously deviated from the objectives of the Central Government.

According to my own survey, there was a total of 1040 *mu* of the conversion land among residents,[1] with the west village owning 707 *mu*, or 68 percent, and the east village 333 *mu*. The figure did not encompass the conversion land owned by those villagers who lived outside the community as well as those owned by the township cadres. That's why it was lower than the official figure of 1300 *mu*. Not all villagers were the equal beneficiaries of the state policy. My survey indicated that 48 households, or about 33 percent, did not participate in the project at all, whereas

1 A few residents gave their own ration to relatives outside the community, which were still registered under their names.

some households only requested part of their ration. The holding size among project households varied sharply, from 2 to 110 *mu*.

The reasons for not participation proved to be surprisingly complex. Closer examination revealed a very complicated story. To repay the village debt, the village committee imposed 200RMB mandatory fee for being eligible for one *mu* of the conversion land, which discouraged the real poor from enjoying their rations. In the view of village cadres, the conversion land did not use the ration land owned by residents, so it was legitimate to charge the money. Most informants who did not take part in or only requested part of their ration mentioned that they could not afford to pay so much money.

Another main reason cited by some informants was that they were worried about policy changes and the insecurity of the promised benefits. One man told me, "Even if I have sufficient money, I do not dare invest too much money on it. As you know, policies always change so quickly and we all have had many such social experiences." Indeed, given recent and past experience, inhabitants had every reason to fear and mistrust this kind of activity and promise.

A small minority of them noted that they were not well informed of the contents of the policy when they made their decisions. There was clearly ambiguous and even contradictory knowledge of the policy among villagers. A few people who already owned some private woodlots did not require it. A handful of female-headed households with their husbands being absent emphasized that they lacked domestic labor to plant and water tree seedlings, and thus they chose not to join the project.

Since the compensation in the form of grain and cash per *mu* almost equaled or even exceeded farmers' rewards from the land, the concentration of the conversion land, as a consequence, widened the already pronounced wealth gap among villagers. For instance, Zhang Xuejun had 110 *mu*, or 10.6 percent of the total conversion land in the village, and most of it was secured from the rations of over a dozen other households. It should be noted that to hide the fact of land concentration, the ration land of the others was still registered in their names. In other words, the personal holdings of Zhang Xuejun were much smaller on formal papers than in reality. He invested over 22000RMB for the project, including the hire of others to plant and water the seedlings; yet in 2003 alone, he harvested about 4400RMB from the sale of rapeseed intercropped among the trees. In early 2004, he obtained the promised cash payment of 2200RMB (20RMB per *mu*) and 22000 catties of grain subsidies,[1] which brought him a net income of at least 13000RMB. This meant in less than two years, he would recover all of his investment and still reap a substantial long-term benefit. On the contrary, the poor non-participants not only lost the chance, since two contiguous plots of land were targeted as the conversion land, some of them were also dispossessed of their former well-manured plots and granted instead poor quality land in other sites. Apparently, the implementation of the project did not represent a policy favoring the poor, nor did it promote equity within in community.

As of 2003, it was still too early to determine the environmental implications of the project. From the very beginning, the choice of tree species was widely identified as being problematic among residents. In Ao Village, the project required farmers to plant three rows of poplar and one row of a kind of shrub in the conversion land. This rule was decided by the higher-level government officials without any flexibility. Many villagers complained that the project trees did not necessarily adapt to the yellow soil in the conversion land. As before, they might be destined to become "small and old trees" some years later, whereas the shrubs were bound to die if the poplar grew big. Although the survival rate of the trees was estimated over 90 percent this time, the sustainability of project was still uncertain, especially after the end of the compensation period. The National Farmland Conversion Project was later incorporated into the Source of the Sandy Wind Management Project around Beijing and Tianjin that I will trace in the following section.

The Small Watershed Project

The small watershed project, locally called the economic gully or *jing ji gou*, was launched in Ao Village in 2003. It was part of the Source of Sandy Wind Management Project around Beijing and Tianjin initiated in 2000 as a regional campaign against desertification. The direct distance between Chifeng City and Beijing is less than 300 kilometers. According to some reports, 12 severe incidents of sand storms occurred in Chifeng in 2000, and 18 in 2001. Two major desertified zones in Chifeng City Prefecture were source areas responsible for the sand storms in north China. The sand storms posed serious threats to Beijing, other places in north China and even the Far East regions. Due to its strategically significant location and severe problems of degradation, Aohan was incorporated into the project.

1 In early 2004, participant villagers were offered 100 catties of unhusked rice and 100 catties of corn.

Since the mid-1990s, the small watershed management was increasingly identified as the most effective way of controlling soil and water erosion and desertification, which relied upon a combination of various measures of biological, engineering, agricultural techniques, and even socio-economic inducements, and focused on control over the mountain, water, field, forest, and road simultaneously. When I first visited Ao Village in April 2003, ordinary villagers had no idea of the upcoming project targeting the large gully. Under the leadership of the Qi Water Affairs Bureau, the township and village governments were put in charge of the planning and construction. It was the external agencies that decided what to do, how to organize the project, and how to use the workers. The total financial aid from the Central Government was 400000RMB.

The small watershed targeted by the project extended 6 kilometers along the large gully spanning Ao Village and Hamlet B. Its width covered 240 meters including the large gully and the slopes on both sides of it. The project area totaled 1.44km^2. As outlined in the preceding section about the second *da hui zhan*, through a hasty mobilization, villagers in Greater Ao Village were mobilized to dig tree pits in August 2003. The precise number of the workers involved was unknown. According to an internal report of the township government, a total of 25000 people from six administrative villages were mobilized to take part in it based upon the accumulated labor plus subsidy. The project lasted from August to November in 2003. Two bulldozers were used day and night. In late 2003, I found tree pits were scattered all over the surrounding slopes. After the pits were finished, various trees and shrubs were planted. It did not diverge sharply from the past schemes, since the environmental project was largely reduced to a series of technocratically determined practices. In the report, it was hailed as an example of successful planning and construction. The focus on technical input benefited the outside bulldozer owners, who were paid 70RMB per machine hour.

Again, the project was still in its infancy; it was too soon to predict its environmental implications. The project did not provoke a uniform reaction among residents. Generally, villagers expressed a widely shared skepticism and concern about its future development. Even in the process of construction, many residents complained that village cadres were more interested in showing their superiors "quantity rather than quality" and they instructed villagers to make the work look beautiful before the inspection of higher-up officials. This did not strike me as surprising after living in the village for some time. As usual, it finally passed the inspection of the higher-ups with flying colors. It was reported that due to two heavy rains in the summer of 2004, many newly planted trees on the slopes were washed out and some tress at the base of the gully were inundated by the floods. Some of the construction works were damaged as well. In addition, the project virtually countered the previous environmental efforts in multiple ways. For example, with the digging of tree pits all around, it was widely acknowledged that the reservoir was destroyed permanently. Numerous pits dug before as well as local's labor contributions were wasted as well.

The potential benefits were captured only by a small fraction of residents. Since the 1990s, half a dozen households gradually put the low-lying base of the large gully in the section within the boundary of Ao Village under cultivation from the "wasteland". A few men took advantage of the low-lying position to turn them into relatively high-yield farmland. After experiencing many negotiations and even lawsuits and considering their former inputs, all the former contractors continued to be granted the use rights of the land at a low price on a thirty year contract, and the trees would belong to them permanently. One household paid a total of 1500RMB for 11 *mu* of the land, equaling 50RMB for one year. Another household was granted more than 40 *mu*, and a total of 3700RMB was paid. A few large landholders subcontracted part of their holdings to their kin or friends. The overwhelming majority of the remaining residents were prevented from participating in the re-distributive process.

The radical reduction of natural resource bases available for grazing caused by the project imposed profound consequences for many livestock-owning households. As one herdsman commented, "We can't tell if it's going to be a good or bad thing. If the project succeeds, the base of the gully may become a 'green corridor'; if it collapses, many residents are going to face an even bleaker economic prospect. As you know, in response to the sudden shrinking of pastures, many people were obliged to dispose of their animals this year." In addition, to guard against livestock incursions on such a large patch of land did not prove easy, which further created tensions between hill keepers and herders.

The Sheep-raising Project under a World Bank Loan

In late 2002, Ao Village was granted an opportunity to gain access to a World Bank loan for raising sheep. According to the initial project document, the donor-financed scheme aimed to alleviate poverty by facilitating sheep production among the poorest households. The donors' objectives of "openness, equity and justice" bore a striking resemblance to many other projects. Given the relatively low interest rate and a long period of repayment requirement, many competed for it. Village officials were charged with identifying the target households in need. As usual, cadres and their relatives in the end received preferential treatment in access to the project resources. The seven project households included the less poor villagers like the women's director. Among them, three households belonged to the most populous lineage in the village. Strangely enough, all seven beneficiaries were concentrated in the former Team Two. A poor woman once angrily approached the village cadres to initiate complaints and finally got the chance through her connections with a county official. Although these households were all "average", they were by no means the genuinely most impoverished cases.

The World Bank project was filtered through the state apparatus and its agents. The government agencies at various levels were supposed to offer practical training and marketing services. However, little more than lip service was served. Almost all participating households complained about the extremely high price of the sheep supplied by the county project office. The sheep-raising venture itself virtually did not prove as profitable as was anticipated among almost all project households.

The "development" experiences sketched out above suggested that although the ecologically motivated environmental initiatives launched in 2003 showed multiple departures from earlier practices, whether they would be sustainable in the future was far from clear. The evidence accumulated had demonstrated that project objectives often ran counter to local interests or were inconsistent with local realities. Even if these projects were dressed up as "green" or economically beneficial for the rural poor, in practice neither the entire village nor its poorer households benefited from them. On the contrary, these initiatives strengthened pre-existing disparities. As a result, only a few elites benefited from the fruits of "development."

Concluding Observations

My first-hand accounts filled in the pictures obscured by official discourses and exposed many crosscutting themes. The experiences of Ao Village in the twin campaigns of "war against nature" and "rebuilding beautiful landscapes", more broadly, rural development, epitomized many dimensions of a multilayered bureaucratic control, combined with cadres' malpractice, and thereby challenged the state's way of seeing the world (Scott, 1998). The simultaneously "gender-blind" and male biased *da hui zhan,* which was based upon false notions of femininity and masculinity, as a consequence, had extremely negative impacts on women.

First, even if the government-initiated campaigns appeared to be pro-development and pro-conservation, it was apparent that the somewhat paradoxical efforts brought little tangible benefit to the majority of Ao Village population. Obviously, it was not a matter of lack of "development", but the politics of "development" was not designed in the interests of the poor majority, especially poor women. Instead, the officials sometimes imposed an unintended and inevitable price on this segment of the local population. The expansion of top-down bureaucratic power often led to negative results; ranging from disappointing to disastrous. Female villagers were particularly vulnerable to these arbitrary plans and projects.

Second, the evidence drawn from Ao Village indicated that the top-down nature of project implementation was reflected in various aspects of local practices. As a powerful force in shaping local ecology, *da hui zhan* always manufactured an organizational nightmare. Under the guise of economic "development" and environmental conservation, these campaigns were quite often carried out without the necessary consultation with the villagers per se. The community was marginalized and local men and women were frequently compelled to accept policies and projects against their interests. Seldom was indigenous knowledge incorporated into the projects. As a result, local interests were often sacrificed, with people bearing the consequences such as increased labor burdens, reduced pasturelands and the loss of Chinese herbs.

Third, nature was manipulated for short-term advantage rather than long-term use. Consequently, most projects were short-lived. Successive interventions attempted to "conserve" a broad spectrum of natural resources, however, they did not simultaneously incorporate the use and management of natural resources in their strategies. It was not surprising that the prioritization of conservation without paying attention to comprehensive management led to contradictory outcomes. In addition, these projects seldom integrated ecological objectives with other long-term communal development goals. None of them fundamentally dealt with the underlying structural factors—poverty, gender inequity, and the lack of viable livelihood strategies—in a holistic manner. Viewed from a grassroots perspective-through the eyes of those who lived through and participated in environmental campaigns in a village setting—it was clear that irrational organization of labor—socially unacceptable—was won at great cost to the locals, while putting the natural environment at risk, which in turn, threatened local men's and women's long term livelihoods. The above analysis allows us to draw a conclusion: the abuse of men and women and the abuse of nature were closely connected within the context of these state policies and programs.

da hui zhan had a gendered history, with crucial inputs of female labor as well as divergent implications for women of different age groups. The experiences of *da hui zhan* differed greatly between men and women along diverse axes of age, wealth, ethnicity, and political status. During the collective period, more young men and women were involved in the war against nature. In most cases, able-bodied males undertook the lion's share of the mass conservation labor. With the return of household farming, the task of *da hui zhan* was shared by household members. By 2003, some young women had never experienced *da hui zhan* personally. Women of the middle-aged generation experienced *da hui zhan* as teenagers or young adults, they continued to supply the bulk of the local labor when their children or husbands migrated out of the village. Some women took the demands more seriously, while others found ways to avoid them. Their differential participation largely explained the different responses to *da hui zhan* among them.

My study exposes the invisible stories and silent voices of women as well as their sufferings and agency. As elsewhere, economic re-structuring led to a pattern of labor re-gendering in the village, however, the state and its local agents always treated the "household" as a unit of measure and of policy assessment without looking at the differentiated relations between men and women, boys and girls inside a household. Even within a particular household, husbands, wives, sons and daughters normally did not share the same experiences. If we treat women and men within a household as working together as equals, it disguises the reality that men had more opportunity to move out of the village or engage in off-farm work locally and left the conservation labor to women. On several occasions, women told me that no matter how pretty they were when they married into the village, they became old quickly, because they were burdened with too much work—productive, reproductive and mass conservation campaigns. This alerts us to the fact that any community environmental conservation projects must take women more seriously, particularly their multiple roles, responsibilities, needs and interests.

Chapter Six

The State, Community-based Natural Resource Management and Resistance Politics

Diverse institutions, both formal and informal, often act in combination, shaping the ways in which differentiated actors access, use and derive well-being from environmental resources and services, and in so doing, influence the course of ecological changes (Leach et al., 1999). To unravel the puzzles of sustainable and unsustainable environmental practices illustrated in the preceding chapters, it is essential to examine multiple interrelated institutional processes within which natural resource use, management and conservation are embedded. For the purpose of this dissertation, the following three chapters will explore the significance of interacting institutions: the state and community, marriage and household, as well as the market. Through this examination, I will identify institutional shortcomings embedded in economic, social and political life at the grassroots level. In this chapter, I will address the significance of politics in community-based natural resource use and management. Rather than focusing merely on formal politics, I will also stress everyday micro-politics outside formal power structures.

The State at the Grassroots Level

As elsewhere in rural China, the state entered into the private life of villagers in Ao Village after Liberation. It was true, as Pasternak and Salaff (1993: 5) describe, there was no time "in Chinese history has the government so controlled where people lived, where they worked, what they might grow, what they could eat or buy, when they could marry, and even when and how many children they could have."[1] As illustrated in the preceding chapters, environmental and social changes at the village level were closely interconnected through these policies and practices. Indeed, environmental practices and management at the local level were always in the shadow of the state, because as an environmental and political authority, the Chinese state lived in the careers of its cadres. To trace the institution of the state in NRM, it is worthwhile to examine the local agency of the state—the predominant political force in the village world. We cannot deal with NRM and environmental changes without a good understanding of the state, which in turn, relies on a sufficient understanding of gendered local politics.

In the pages that follow, I will first deal with the formal political structure at the village level, followed by an outline of land and land-based NRM playing out "on the ground." I will then proceed to the topic of local politics—particularly resistance politics—in a broader context of bureaucratic power and local corruption.

The Formal Political Structure at the Local Level

In the Chinese countryside, the village-level party-state administrative agency has long been the lowest level of state bureaucracy in the political system,[2] a crucial conduit between the higher-level government structures and local people. Many Chinese and Western scholars have provided a clear picture of the origins and development of local bureaucracy after Liberation. Huang Shu-min (1998: 5), succinctly summarizes it as follows, "A new and more penetrating administrative system was established to promote development. Not only was the formal administrative system extended to the countryside, the Party itself also established a parallel network to ensure that party decisions were faithfully executed at the grass-roots level. The establishment of the communes in 1958, further integrated all peasants into a comprehensive organization that was at once administrative,

1 Many feminist scholars have explored the penetration of the Chinese state in rural society and its impacts on women in areas of rural kinship (Croll, 1981), marriage law (Johnson, 1983), household registration (Judd, 1994), family planning programs (Wolf, 1985) and so forth.

2 There is a multiple-layered state in China. Throughout this text, the government is broken up into six levels: central, provincial/autonomous region/city, prefecture, county, township and administrative village. The term 'local state' mainly refers to the levels of county, township and administrative village.

economical, education and medical." Likewise, Yan (1996:152) argues cogently that, "After the 1949 Revolution, especially during the collective era (1956-1982), a new social hierarchy was established that quickly replaced the dominant role of kinship in social life. Through its agents at the grassroots level, the power of the party-state penetrated every corner of village society and turned the previous social order upside down." Soon after I resided in Ao Village, it became clear to me that the Chinese State was by no means monolithic, and there was much to learn about the role of the state and its local agents—village cadres—in environmental resource use and management.

As elsewhere in rural China, a three-tier collective system of the people's commune, production brigade and production team was established during the Great Leap Forward drive in 1958, which persisted until the early 1980s. Each level of this structure was organized hierarchically. The people's commune served as a grassroots government body. As noted in Chapter four, the production team, the lowest tier in the commune system, owned lands, draft animals, tools and other economic resources and was put in charge of daily productive practices. There existed patron-client relationships between cadres and peasants (Oi, 1990; Ruf, 1998; Siu, 1989). For example, Siu (1989) argues that the legitimacy of rural cadres was based solely on their affiliations with the Communist party-state. During the commune period, the brigade committee was usually composed of a Party secretary, a deputy Party secretary, an accountant, a brigade militia head (*min bing lian zhang*), a women's director, and for some time a family planning worker. Most brigade cadres were released from agricultural production and won the average work points of all its constituent production teams, which equaled approximately 0.40-50RMB per day and 3600 work points per year. At the team level, the team committee was often made up of seven persons: a team leader, a vice-team leader, a female team leader, an accountant, a cashier, and sometimes a team militia head (*min bing pai zhang*). Being tightly tied to land under the collective regimes, villagers' access to key resources such as jobs, income, grain, health, and education was intimately related to their membership in these different collectives through the party-state administrative agencies.

Team leaders were chosen by their own teammates and most of them were usually long-serving cadres. Many residents complained that team leaders in those days enjoyed an overwhelming authority, keeping the best paid, least tiring, and most secure jobs for their own family members, relatives or friends. To defy them could bring on trouble and invite vengeance afterwards, which was locally referred to as "making you to wear small shoes." Those residents with "bad class background" were especially marginalized. On the contrary, almost all former cadres unanimously made the point that cadres in the Maoist era seldom abused power for private interests. Instead, they showed sincere attitudes toward their job and provided honest services to their fellow villagers. Corruption was eliminated by repeated political campaigns[1] launched nationally through frequent criticism/self-criticism at mass meetings. As illustrated in Chapter four, the social organization of collective production dampened enthusiasm and bred cynicism among residents, which in turn, hurt agricultural production and local ecology.

The workings of party-state power at the village level were reconfigured in the post-reform era. In 1983, the township, administrative village and villagers' small groups, respectively, displaced the people's commune, brigade, and production team throughout Aohan. Greater Ao Village was put under the jurisdiction of Lan Township, which was, in turn, politically subordinate to the Aohan Qi Government. Following the collapse of the collective regime, no radical changes in local political structures occurred. All these layers remained hierarchically structured and interacted closely in everyday political processes. In 2003, the highly visible presence of cadres from higher levels of administration could be seen in the frequent parking of cars, motorcycles and jeeps in front of the village headquarters. The village cadres rode motorcycles to and from work on motorable village roads. The township officials normally came to the village by jeep or motorcycle, while those from the county level often traveled by car.

In Ao Village, the power of the agents of village party-state structure shifted after decollectivization. Nationally, it was widely believed that the disbanding of collectives in post-reform China gave rise to the weakening of state control, and thus led to an erosion of the power and authority of local cadres at the grassroots level. Yet since village cadres retained control over a major collective asset—the land, they thereby still held the power to shape local economic activities. As illustrated

1 Successive national mass campaigns, such as the "Three-anti and Five-anti campaigns" and "the Four-Clean-ups Campaign" launched in the 1950s and 1960s, primarily involved an attack against corrupt cadres.

in Chapter five, when Wang Sheng was in power, Ao Village experienced a period of strong village administration. The village leaders—made up of nine members—monopolized both economic and political power and launched a series of impressive environmental initiatives in Ao Village. In addition, the then village leadership could somewhat balance the interests of township officials and other higher authorities with those of their constituents, completing upper-level policy directives, while launching local initiatives.

In sharp contrast, decollectivization greatly weakened the power and supervisory functions of team leaders. The ownership rights of land were initially vested in villagers' small groups. When Wang Sheng served as Party secretary, the village authority took control of the allocation and management of ration land and other natural resources. As of 2003, team leaders were relegated to very limited administrative functions such as collecting agricultural taxes or various fees, communicating some information from higher-level administration to their teammates, and organizing irrigation. A few residents even portrayed team leaders as "lackeys". There was little incentive for residents to become team leaders. It was said they took home tiny salaries that often went unpaid. Unlike during the collective era under which some residents served as cadres for a long time, cadres changed more frequently after decollectivization. To reduce administration costs, four official small villagers' groups were amalgamated into two in 2000. There were thus only two team leaders in Ao Village by 2003.

The villagers' committee was staffed by five persons when I first visited the village in April 2003, which included a director, a vice-director, an accountant from the township, a treasurer, and a women's director (see table 6.1). After the 2003 election in July, the village committee was made up of three elected officials, which included a director, a vice-director and a women's director. The former accountant was sent back to the township and the post of treasurer was cancelled. A new policy by the county government specified that a small administrative village under 1200 persons no longer kept the position of accountant, but rather should render accounts to township accountants.

Paralleling the administrative structure, there was a village Party branch. In theory, the elected director of the villagers' committee was supposed to have more authority than that of the Party secretary. But in practice, the Party secretary as a rule was the most powerful cadre—the so-called "first-hand" in the village. As noted in

Chapter two, the village Party secretary was appointed by the Township Communist Party Committee. He was an ex-soldier and his deceased father was long a Party secretary in Greater Ao Village. After the 2003 election, all village cadres were immersed in the small watershed project. It was rumored that the Party secretary controlled the allocation of most project funds. He returned to his former position in the township government after the project was basically finished.

In 2003, the village party branch was made up of three members: the Party secretary, a former Party secretary and the former women's director. When I returned to the village in 2004, I found that the three elected members of the villagers' committee all served as the members of the Party branch simultaneously. The villagers' committee director concurrently acted as the Party secretary, which was widely called "holding twin roles on one shoulder" or "*yi jian tiao*". This meant power was more heavily concentrated in the hands of a few elites. There were a total of 25 party members in Greater Ao Village, eleven of whom were residents of Ao Village and three of whom were women. Although party membership remained a key variable in political participation, it was not necessarily a marker of one's relative power. In 2003, the Party member meeting was only held once in a while and no mass meeting was convened. As some party members and non-members asserted, there was no use for the party member meetings, because most decisions were made ahead of time.

As can be seen from table 6.1, these two gendered political institutions had overlapping membership. The party branch members before the election were almost all long-serving village cadres. After the election, the average age of village and team leaders was 38.6 years old, having 7.9 years of formal education, and serving for 7.25 years. There were no Mongol members and only one woman sat on the villagers' committee and the Party branch. As was common, the bureaucratic power was occupied by a few male elites.

The genealogy of power in Greater Ao Village indicated that a few Han Chinese men had long held a monopoly on the positions of power. In the memories of villagers, there were at least fourteen persons who served as Party secretaries between 1947 and 2004. Only two women ever held this position. One Han woman occupied the post for avery short period of time during the Cultural Revolution. Another Mongolian woman from Hamlet B held the position of authority for two years from 1973-1975. Soon after graduating from senior high school—the highest educational level among her peers–she assumed the leadership role in Greater Yangzi Village when she was only eighteen years old. In spite of the prevailing androcentric culture, she claimed that nobody discriminated against her because of her sex.[1]

Table 6.1 Greater Ao Village Leaders (2003)

Position	Age	Sex	Ethnicity	Education	Years of Service	Location
Village committee before election						
Director	47	M	Han	8	16	Hamlet C
Vice-director	36	M	Han	10	8	Hamlet B
Accountant	23	M	Han	11	2	Township
Treasurer	26	M	Han	8	8	Ao Village
Women's director	36	F	Han	8	3	Ao Village
Village committee after election						
Director	47	M	Han	8	16	Hamlet C
Vice-director	36	M	Han	10	8	Hamlet B
Women's Director	36	F	Han	8	3	Ao Village
Party Branch in 2003						
Party secretary	46	M	Mongol	8	24	Township
Organization member	58	M	Han	10	30	Ao Village
Propaganda member	45	F	Han	8	29	Hamlet D
Party Branch in 2004						
Party secretary	47	M	Han	8	16	Hamlet C
Organization member	36	F	Han	8	3	Hamlet B
Propaganda member	36	M	Han	10	8	Ao Village
Team Leaders						
West Team	32	M	Han	8	4	Ao Village
East Team	34	M	Mongol	8	11	Ao Village
Team Three	34	M	Mongol	8	3	Hamlet B
Team Four	47	M	Han	5	7	Hamlet D
Team Five	43	M	Han	8	6	Hamlet C

Source: interviews in 2003 and 2004.

In 1975, she was recruited as a state cadre by an ethnic minority project of the county government. Her appointment derived in part from the ethnic discourses and

1 I happened to meet her in the Qi Archive Bureau, where she serves as a deputy director.

policies at that time as well as her own higher education and resulting capabilities. Ostensibly, the social acceptability of female leaders was long an established fact.

Under certain ethnic minority quotas, ethnic-minority officials were sometimes guaranteed in the earliest years of Liberation and over much of the collective period. Two of the three Mongolian men who held the position of Party secretaries during the collective period worked for a relatively long time. The first village Party secretary of Greater Yangzi Village was a Mongol man from Hamlet B. During the Cultural Revolution, political struggles were often closely related with ethnic struggles. A few Mongolian cadres at the brigade level experienced several ups and downs. After decollectivization, Han Chinese dominated the constituency of village leaders and Mongols were politically marginalized. From the mid-1980s through 2003, four Han Chinese male Party secretaries of Ao Village controlled village affairs, which probably partly encouraged corruption to blossom. As scattered throughout this dissertation, there was a remarkable relationship between village power structures and the distribution of natural resources.

After Wang Sheng fell out of power in 1996, one Party secretary succeeded another. The power struggles within male-dominated village leadership were mirrored in the constant changes of village Party secretaries. Two out of five, who served for a relatively short time, were sent from the outside, and another two left their positions ahead of time due to internal confrontations.[1] During my fieldwork, frequent rumors circulated about the quarrels and conflicts among male village cadres. It was reported that they even fought among themselves about what kind of wine and staple food was supplied, since male cadres usually ate free meals at noon in the village headquarters.[2] The quick turnover in leadership made it difficult for cadres to carry out coherent policies and practices concerning natural resource use, and sometimes they even reversed the policies of their predecessors. Local political succession clearly had profound impacts on local ecology.

The following episode about the village election offers a glimpse of complex relations between village cadres and ordinary people, as well as the persistent hard-to-change gender and ethnic asymmetry.

1 I was told that a few young Party members were actively involved in removing them from their posts on charges of mismanagement.

2 The women's director lived in Ao Village and thus she seldom ate in the village headquarters.

A Political Myth: The Villagers' Committee Election from Within

The villager' committee elections heralding rural democracy were launched in 1988 in the Chinese countryside. From that point on, villagers were able to elect their own leaders of villagers' committees every three years outside the framework of the Party system. The Central Government issued the Organic Law of Villagers' Committees in 1998, which guaranteed the right of all villages to hold directly competitive elections, often called the "sea election" or "*hai xuan*". Greater Ao Village held its first election in 1991, yet in the first three elections, the nomination of candidates was largely controlled by the township government, and inhabitants could only vote for the nominated persons "circled" by township leaders.

While I was staying in the village in 2003, I witnessed the process of the fifth election in Ao Village. Before the election day, a list of eligible voters was put on a courtyard wall standing at the crossroads near the village headquarters. People over eighteen, excluding migrants absent from the village, were eligible to cast their ballots. On an early July morning of the primary election day, I met a female township cadre in the village headquarters, who told me nine cadres had been sent down from the township level to monitor the election process[1] held simultaneously in four hamlets.

Voters were supposed to go to the polling station set in the village headquarters to cast their votes. Realizing that the turnout rate would be surprisingly low, township and village cadres had already started to go house to house early that morning to collect votes. A ballot printed with the name of the village was given to each voter, who was supposed to write down the name of one candidate for the village director and two candidates for the committee members. One present household member could fill in votes for the other two members, theoretically, with the consent of the latter. If they were illiterate, they could also require present cadres to fill out the ballot for them. By the time I returned to the village headquarters again at noon with my host couple and Liu Xing couple, I learned that only an old man living nearby showed up to cast his vote. Late that afternoon, the names of two candidates for the director and three candidates for members were posted on the wall of the grocery

1 To strengthen the legitimacy of the election process, the county government sent cadres to guide the election at the township level, which in turn, sent their cadres to monitor the election in villages.

store without revealing the actual number of ballots won by each of them.

On July 20, a formal election was held. As with the primary election, cadres had to pay household visits one by one to collect votes. This time, the voters just needed to circle the candidates of her/his choice: one director candidate out of two and two member candidates out of three. I remember one woman once mentioned to me that she was "deprived" of the right to vote when she was away and her husband filled out the ballot on her behalf without her knowledge. This might be true for a large percentage of village women, absent or present, since most middle-aged women were illiterate. If there were male family members at home, I believe few of them would volunteer to circle their own ballots, especially in front of cadres.

This undoubtedly cast doubt on the effectiveness of the village election. It was said that the ballots were counted publicly. The names of winning candidates were put on the outside wall of the grocery store the same day, and no actual number of ballot results was publicized. All three of the elected cadres were Han Chinese and one of the three was a woman. The women's director won election again as a committee member.

During the election, village rumors spread that several cadres had attempted to muster support from their relative and friends. A few of them were suspected of treating their supporters with favoritism.[1] Despite a severe conflict between Zhang Hualan and her elder sister, who had not spoken to each other for a long time, Liu Xing couple actively supported their brother-in-law—a former Party secretary—to run for office again. As a vet, Liu Xing was considered to be more familiar with inhabitants in other three hamlets. I was told he went to one hamlet or two to campaign for his brother-in-law. An anonymous township official once confidentially remarked to me (interviewed by author in 2003), "There is now still a severe competition for the administrative posts at the village level. However, if there will be no tangible material benefit to secure in the future, I believe, the administrative structure at the village level is bound to become 'an empty shell'."

The direct election made it possible for the participation of villagers, male and female, in political affairs, which also provided a channel for villagers to vent their

1 This phenomenon was not confined to Ao Village alone. It was rumored that in a few villages in Lan township, some cadres ran for office by "buying" votes through offering about 5-50RMB per vote to their supporters.

dissatisfactions. Surprisingly enough, as evidenced by the low turnout rate in the 2003 election, most villagers seemed to be politically apathetic about the election, just as they were indifferent to other local public affairs beyond their immediate households. When asked why they did not unite to elect the persons that they trust most to the village committees, the most common responses were: "There is no one in the village with both ability and honesty;" "Whoever is in power will do the same thing; they think only of themselves and their relatives;" "Why should I bother to vote for the corrupt cadres?" It appeared a paradox, on the one hand, they complained severely about village cadres for their lack of commitment and capacity to deal with community-wide issues, on the other hand, they had lost enthusiasm to change the reality. However, the obvious electoral defeats of a couple of former cadres indeed indicated some acts of resistance among residents.

Village Women's Directors, Gender and "Public Patriarchy"

In the pages that follow, I will contextualize the topic of how power structure at the village level was organized around patriarchal assumptions to strengthen men's monopoly over power, privilege and wealth. The position of the village women's directors seemed to function as a point of contact in mediating the relations between village women and women's federations at the township and county levels. According to elder residents, ever since Liberation, there has always been a women's director in the village leadership. The continuing guarantee of at least a seat for women in the village leadership suggested that women were not entirely excluded from local political participation and public space. In spite of marginal positions in village politics, women's long physical visibility in local political life marked, symbolically and practically, women's improved status at the grassroots level.[1]However politically active they were, female leaders always worked in the shadow of men in the bureaucratic hierarchy. As I found in Yunnan and Sichuan provinces, as a rule, women's directors were seldom involved in the key processes of decision-making under the androcentric political structure. The story of Zhang Huamin, who worked as a village women's director for almost 28 years spanning

1 In 2003, among 12 administrative villages in Lan Township, as was the case of Ao Village, eight villages had independent women's directors. In one village, a man held the position concurrently, and in another two, women's directors were only compensated for their loss of working time.

both the collective and post-reform period tells us a lot about gendered political participation in Greater Ao Village.

Zhang Huamin, aged 45 in 2003, was serving as the village women's director from 1972 until 2000. Immediately after graduating from the junior high school in the village, she was appointed to do "women's work" or "*fu nv gong zuo*" as a teenager. There is no denying that it had something to do with her kinship network in Ao Village. Her natal family belonged to the biggest Han lineage in the community. However, her own unique capabilities and achievements helped to explain how she could maintain the leadership position in local society for such a long time. She was a dedicated woman. Since she married into Hamlet D in 1979, she commuted almost everyday by foot between the two hamlets. As a result of years of walking, she even trampled a shortcut. Occasionally, she headed home very late at night; she said she was so familiar with the path that she did not even use a flashlight to avoid being a target of possible attack. In a summer afternoon, I walked the path of 3 kilometers long with her to her married village.

Zhang Huamin was a vocal and politically ambitious woman. After she took the position, the priority of women's work was then the family planning program. Over a long time, the two jobs of women's work and family planning overlapped at the village level, and which one became a priority depended upon local and national policies. In the late 1990s, she even assumed the position of the director of family planning affairs when the family planning program was strengthened. Apart from these two responsibilities, she was also burdened with other duties in the village. Quite often, her major work was merged with the function of the village authority and she often had no time in her schedule to engage specifically in women's work.

One example was that she was often put in charge of supervising *da hui zhan* in the field. The first time that I met her was one afternoon when I sat on the ground with a group of women to tidy up beans while talking about village changes. A middle-aged woman came over to issue a greeting and left early. Her clothes and way of speaking indicated she was not identical to other village women of her age. After she turned away, a woman in the group pointed to her back and said sarcastically, "go ask her, the former women's director, how she drove us to work so hard in *da hui zhan* in the past." Later that day, I met her in her parent's home. I met her the second time when she came back to Ao Village to finish the share of *da hui zhan* assigned to her household by herself. She admitted to me, "I was previously a supervisor myself, now people all look at me, I can now only do better rather than worse."

Zhang Huamin admitted that she did little to mobilize village women to participate in economic activities advocated by Women's Federations, as confirmed by many women, who claimed that the influences of women's work had been very limited. For example, since the late 1980s, Women's Federations at various levels had launched a "Two-Learnings, Two-Competings" (*shuang xue shuang bi)* campaign among rural women, which aimed to deploywomen's labor to develop the "courtyard" economy or other off-farm work as a way out of poverty.[1] As elsewhere, Women's Federations at the county and township levels in Aohan carried out some sporadic education or skill training sessions and offered training sessions in certain practical skills regarding crop and livestock production. Yet, Zhang Huamin frankly acknowledged that she once attended some training sessions in person. Even she could not put what she had learned into practice herself, let alone average women. Her long-term concern was to mobilize women to engage in handcrafts to help women to get rich, but in this part of rural China, she had never found any viable ways to do so.

Zhang Huamin acquired intimate knowledge of many village affairs over the course of her long career; yet as many villagers told me, key male cadres often made decisions without her knowledge. She claimed that when she was working in the village government, she was not overwhelmed by male power in the men's world. Although she took orders from other key leaders, she made decisions for her own work by herself. But as a female leader, she had no intention of involving herself in power struggles among male cadres. She told me, in the 2001 election of a village party branch among all party members, she won the same amount of votes as a man running for the position of Party secretary. The man was ultimately appointed by the Township Party Committee to assume the post on the grounds that a woman was not competent enough for the post.

As a female leader, the conflicts of her official work and domestic work figured prominently in her narratives. She reported that when her two children were small, her life was quite hard. With no parents-in-law available to help with childcare,

1 For a detailed analysis of the "Two Learning and Two Competing" campaign, see Shirin M. Rai and Zhang Junzuo (1994) "Competing and Learning": Women and the State in Contemporary Rural Mainland China," *Issues and Studies*, Vol. 30, No. 3.

she was often obliged to leave her children to her own mother in Ao Village, and quite often she carried one child in her arm, with another one on her back to shuttle back and forth between Ao Village and Hamlet D. Whenever mentioning these experiences, she always said it was extremely hard for a woman with "family encumbrances" to do administrative work. Working as a cadre since a young age, Zhang Huamin did not learn many farming techniques until retirement. Since her husband had worked in a nearby mine since 1990 because of her connections, for a long time nobody in her family actually worked the field. By 2003, she had been the sole village cadre in Hamlet D with only 19 households. In 1985, three village cadres jointly contracted the reservoir located in Hamlet D for fish-raising and later only Zhang Huamin herself contracted it for a long period of time at a low price. After the reservoir dried in 2003, she subcontracted most of the reservoir bottomland, around 100 *mu*, to others for crop cultivation and tilled the rest of it by herself.

The current women's director, Ding Hongmei, aged 36, married into the village in 1988. She was not very articulate, yet was widely acknowledged to be one of the most industrious women in the village. Her deceased father-in-law was once a Party secretary and her husband's family belonged to one of the most powerful surnames in the community, with kin scattered in other hamlets. This somewhat mirrored the persistence of long-established lines of power.

As I found in almost all the villages studied in Yunnan and Sichuan provinces, as a women's director, her major work focused on family planning matters. When asking other women about "women's work" in the village, many of them anonymously told me that there was nothing at all, and the women's director was merely in charge of filling the monthly family planning forms. The women's director herself largely confirmed this fact. Yet as the only village cadre in Ao Village, she did have a say in deciding many things by herself. Ding Hongmei confided to me frankly that in her capacity as a village women's director, she was able to obtain low-interest loans from the bank, and she was also one of the beneficiaries of the World Bank-sponsored sheep project. As with Zhang Huamin, Ding Hongmei had neither authority over elite men nor control over many village resources. Unlike the former, she did not even know about many village matters when I inquired about them.

There was no telephone line in the community. The first time that I met some village cadres, male cadres all had cell phones of their own except her. After the watershed project was launched, she often needed to go to the field to monitor the project. At the beginning, she sometimes sat on the back seat of the Party secretary's motorcycle. It caused some speculation among some inhabitants and rumor had it that she had had an affair with the male leader. Later, she had to purchase an old motorcycle and rode it herself on business.[1] The husband of Ding Hongmei benefited a lot from her position as a village cadre, but he was unhappy with her going on business beyond the community. I was told that she was often called back from the outside by her husband even during meetings.

It was clear from the above account that political participation of women's directors could not guarantee their full participation in decision-making, nor village decisions that reflected women's interests. On the contrary, they sometimes perpetuated women's disadvantages. For instance, the implementation of coercive *da hui zhan* long depended upon the complicity of women's directors. As local leaders, they enjoyed some privileges not extended to other women. Compared with male elites, who often drew on their family members or hired labor for productive and reproductive work, helping only in the peak times, the work of female leaders in the public sphere was severely limited by their responsibilities and power in the domestic sphere. With the return to household farming, gender relations within the household were significantly altered (see Chapter seven), yet they remained largely unchanged in the public arena.

As we will see soon, not only were there distinctive gendered men's and women's space, there also existed a gendered pattern of women's exclusion from "public" work opportunities. The male-dominated political structure and male privilege in the public sphere helped to shape these practices. The village headquarters, situated on the main street, was almost at the center of the neighborhood. This gendered public space first caught my attention soon after I settled into the village. On the very day of the launch of the cropland conversion campaign, I headed to the village headquarters at about 8 o'clock. By that time, a group of men had already gathered inside the office building. Three male officials from the township government came down to

1 This reminded me of what I found in Yunnan province. In an administrative village, a young man was put in charge of women's work and family planning affairs. When asked about the reasons, the Party secretary of the village told us that it was inconvenient and somewhat dangerous for a woman to travel alone to all the constituent villages scattered on the tops of many hills. If male cadres always went with her, there might be rumors going around about it. That's why they were unwilling to recruit any female cadre in the village government.

guide the afforestation initiative. Before my departure, at least two dozen men had drifted in and out of the building. Some came to inquire about the specific activities that day or to negotiate their own issues, while others just came to wait. Strangely enough, not a single woman except me showed up in this 'world of men' during my observations there for almost an hour.

Throughout my stay in the village, no community-level meeting was ever held. The cook's room in the village headquarters often functioned as a meeting place for some men to exchange information, have a chat, or to watch TV. The village headquarters was an almost exclusively men's world where few women except for the women's director and a female teacher taking care of pre-school kids often showed up in this space. There was a well inside the compound. Whenever there was no cadre there, a tiny fraction of villagers, who lived nearby without a well of their own at home, came to "steal" water. I often saw an old widow living just across from the village headquarters engaging in the onerous task of hauling water from various neighbors or from the public well with no pump. I never met her fetching water from the village well. A few men who cultivated good relations with the cook were able to gain access to certain benefits such as helping to cook the meal to earn a wage, eat a meal or two, or to get some leftovers when village cadres entertained a large group of outside officials there.

As noted before, another male world was the grocery store, which consisted of three rooms: a big room displayed with a broad selection of goods, a kitchen, and a bedroom with *kang*. Every night, even during the day, especially during the winter months, males—old and young—always gathered together to drink, smoke, relax, play cards, and catch up on local news. For a few of them who seldom did household chores at home, visiting the store became part of their everyday existence. Just like the local ritualized behavior of village men entertaining guests on the *kang* while their wives kept busy in the kitchen, this phenomenon was widespread in the rural landscape. As illustrated by the sentiments offered by Zhang Huamin in the next chapter, due to the workings of localized femininities and masculinities, local people took for granted the practice of men strolling in the neighborhood while women worked at home.

Gendered assumptions about masculinities and femininities were also maintained in community life through gossip and labeling in public and private spheres. A middle-aged woman living nearby occasionally intruded on the men's world to play poker. Since she reputedly had affairs with a few village men before, she was branded as a "broken shoe", meaning a "loose woman". I was told only a "woman like her" would behave like that—entering into this exclusively men's space of recreational activities.

During my fieldwork, I was continuously reminded of village cadres' usual bias toward assigning paid jobs to men and the consequent pattern of gendered opportunities for wage labor. One afternoon when I returned to my host's home, Song Ling immediately complained about the absence of Hong Xiang. Song Ling told me with regret that the women's director just came over to require Hong Xiang to show an outside driver the way to Hamlet B. "You are so familiar with the village path, why didn't you take the initiative to do it yourself?" I suggested. Song Ling responded quickly, "She came over to search for your *da ge*. It is too embarrassing for a *niang men* who stays at home (a term with negative connotations, which literally means an adult married woman at home) to move close to village cadres to say I can do it. It would be ridiculed by others." She added, "What an embarrassment!"

Song Ling's statement demonstrated the long ingrained sense of inferiority among some village women in the androcentric social structure of the community. This stood in sharp contrast to Song Ling's extensive daily ties to her husband's kin and the kin of her natal family. I was initially struck by her usage of the derogatory local idiom—"stay-at-home *niang men*"—to describe herself. In various contexts later, I heard many men label women as such, especially when they devalued women's roles in some areas such as economic decisions. Such androcentric prejudice institutionalized women's subordinate position in local society. Song Ling was not alone among women accepting this unfair treatment, but I am not arguing that all women responded in the same way. I did hear many examples of assertive women who contested the stereotypes of women and asymmetric gender arrangements.

Many women expressed their frustration about the refusal of being hired in paid community work. On one autumn morning, I encountered a small group of four women standing on a roadside not far away from the village headquarters. They were waiting for a large group of men to go to fix positions (this means to locate the place, measure the distance, and put up the signs) for the upcoming small watershed project. The daily wage rate was 20RMB per day. Since adult men in their households could not make themselves available that day, these women would temporarily fill the posts. One woman was there to take her father-in-law's job and the other three were there to substitute for their husbands. In comparison to their male counterparts, women might be less familiar with such a job, yet some men confessed that women were generally more careful and responsible for the jobs assigned to them, and they could do a better job than men at certain tasks.

Under the shadow of household heads, village cadres always assigned similar work to men under the assumption that adult men were the family breadwinners. Even if workers were recruited on a one-per-household basis, very few opportunities were open to women. This illustrated that gender differences were both reinforced and created by state policies and practices. This did not rule out the possibility that one or several households jointly took up a specific job, with both male and female family members involved together. With the launch of the small watershed project, there suddenly emerged numerous wage jobs in the village. I often heard about men winning various contracts from village cadres, although women sometimes took part as coworkers.

In one such example, an elderly man contracted the job of building a stone bridge over a deep gully in the fields, mentioned in Chapter three. He organized another six men to work together, who earned, on average, 30RMB per day. After "triumphantly" completing their task, they celebrated at the home of one of the group members. It seemed quite common among village men to get together for a meal either in the restaurant or at home after completing their joint work.

Men's claim to a larger share of paid work and economic benefits was systematically maintained since the collective period. As analyzed in Chapter four, well-paid skilled work was masculinized during the collective period, which perpetuated patriarchal inequalities between men and women. The masculinization of paid community work helped to maintain the patriarchal ideas of "masculinity" and "femininity". Such male-oriented gendered exclusion was clearly still an established pattern in the public space of the community in 2003, and was not considered particularly problematic in daily administrative practices. Power was apparently at work. Men had more opportunities to earn and accumulate money. In Ao Village, the watchman/cook, veterinarian, doctor, hill keepers, and those in charge of irrigation equipment or providing transportation services were all men, illustrating the prevalence of male domination in public employment.

Village women tended to form friendships with each other. This was reflected in intensive interactions among them at home, in the marketplace, in wage labor groups and group migration. However, as in rural China as a whole, there were very few documented examples of village women's organizing, although various women's organizations have boomed in post-reform China in urban areas. Due to this lack of formal organization, local women lacked bargaining power to redress gender asymmetries in public spheres. It should be noted that gaining access to such opportunities was also differentiated by wealth and social networks, both of which were deeply embedded in the unequal distribution of power and authority in the community. As many inhabitants harshly criticized, village cadres only favored their own relatives or friends.

The next section of the chapter is mainly concerned with community-based natural resource management and the negative impacts of men's exclusive role in patrolling forage crop and tree reserves.

Community-based Natural Resource Management and Its Dilemmas

The role of village authority in NRM was subject to the influence of larger historical and political forces. From the early 1980s, the Central Government increasingly relinquished land use and environmental management decisions to the market and local governments (Huang, 1990). In spite of macro-level laws regarding NRM and conservation, as outlined in Chapter one, there was no denying that there were often large discrepancies between state policies and local practices.

My point is that the multi-layered state was not a monolithic entity. Although the village leaders often faced strong pressure from the higher levels of government to enforce laws and regulations, there was still much room for village cadres to maneuver. In Ao Village, ordinary people were hardly conscious of these laws, although they knew something about relevant local agencies implementing these laws at the township level, which included the forest station, grassland station, water management station, livestock station and so on. As representatives of the owner of collective land and the local agents of state authority, village cadres sometimes took advantage of poorly defined and implemented laws and local people's ignorance of them to pursue their own personal gains. As was typical with other Chinese laws, environmental laws were open to local interpretations and the "unruly" practices of local actors (Fraser, 1989).

In Greater Ao Village, the village organs regulating natural resource access and management encompassed two gendered organizations: the village authority and a team of hill keepers. The village authority, the most influential institutional actor at the grassroots level, apparently still played a significant role in the implementation of NRM and environmental conservation practices: allocating and redistributing land or other natural resources; crafting rules and regulations governing natural resource access and use; mediating environmental disputes among villagers, coordinating the services of agricultural production such as watering, electricity supply, or other public infrastructure; and maintaining communal capital assets such as irrigation equipment, forest and grassland reserves, windbreaks, and wasteland. As we will see below, the problems of natural resource use, management and conservation that vexed Ao Village during the collective era continued well into 2003.

In a rural community like Ao Village, divergent social actors have long relied overwhelmingly upon different natural resources, to various degrees, for their agrarian livelihoods, ranging from crop and livestock production, to the collection of medicinal plants, tree crops, fodder, fuelwood, and to game hunting. NRM was neither homogenous nor static, but varied over time and space in the village landscapes, as did the environmental experiences of men and women, and the environmental outcomes.

Satellite images taken in 1972 showed a total of 67000 *mu* or around 4467 hectares of land under the jurisdiction of Greater Ao Village, with about one third being controlled by Ao Village (approximately 22333 *mu* or approximately 1489 hectares). As noted in Chapter three, the scenario of shifting land use was most clearly reflected in an increasing amount of land being converted to perennial plants such as alfalfa, ning tiao, and trees through various environmental initiatives. The multiple land use patterns (see table 6.2) signified a departure from the vegetation cover in the collective past.

Local people's interests in land-based natural resources—which played a key role in local livelihood strategies—changed over time with their shifting value in meeting subsistence and commercial needs.[1] Women in general drew more heavily than men on the natural resource base. This difference reflected gender-based responsibilities as well as women's limited opportunities for paid off-farm employment. Some

1 Hunting was an age-old masculinized practice in local society. According to elderly informants, many wild animals have disappeared from the surrounding hills in their lifetime. In 2003, the main game included hare and birds. To my knowledge, many men, but not a single woman were involved in hunting each winter. During the winter season, Hong Xiang always got up very early in the morning to go to the sites where he had already laid iron wire traps the day before. He usually spent more than three hours walking to these sites.

consistent dilemmas in NRM persisted. Subsistence crises and commercial forces both increased the pressures on natural resources. In the next section, I will elaborate on these points with reference to the use and management of land and land-based natural resources: croplands, trees, shrubs, grass, green crop and water resources.

Table 6.2 Acreage of Major Land Uses at Village Level (2003)[1]

Land Type	Area (*mu*)	Percentage (%)
Cropland	3761	16.8
Woodland	4500	20.1
Pasturlard	3100	13.9
Shrub tracts	1100	4.9
Industrial lands	140	0.6
Residential lands	750	3.4
Others[2]	8982	40.3
Total	22333	100.0

Source: 2003 household survey and interview.

Notes:

[1] The first six categories accounted for about 59.7 percent of the total land. The actual area was much larger than this figure. The cropland figure derived from my own survey, excluded those fields tilled by villagers who lived outside the village. In the eyes of local residents, woodland only meant a large tract of trees, which did not include the land with only a few scattered trees. With the inroads of the small watershed project, a considerable amount of the land at the base of the large gully and around it had been converted into woodland.

[2] Others included graveyards, village road, reservoir, wasteland, slopes, gullies, and part of the hills without vegetation. In Ao Village, large tracts of wasteland have been cleared, but small ones exist among the woodland. Previously, the ancestral graves dotted many fields; they were later removed to specific areas in the hills.

Shifting Land Use after Decollectivization

In October of 1980 when the decollectivization drive swept Aohan, individual teams in Ao Village divided up its land and allocated it to smaller production units, small groups, which were locally called "*fen zu*". When dividing land and other collective assets, a small minority of influential males—team and brigade leaders, a few senior males and mass representatives—formed an assessment group to oversee the process. In later stages, the representatives of each household—mostly male household heads—took part in drawing the lots of land parcels. On a voluntary basis, 2-4 households formed a small group so as to share insufficient draught animals. Land distribution was carried out in a roughly egalitarian fashion, with each person being allocated an equal share of ration land of about 7 *mu*. Their landholdings were also relatively equitable in terms of the quality of land parcels.[1] In the spring of 1981, group members planted crops together. By the spring of 1982, almost all small groups subdivided their land again on a per capita basis. Individual households started to till their own land from that time.

Beginning with the land reform, each team gained access to the cropland within its boundary. In the early 1990s when Wang Sheng was in power, almost all natural resources previously owned by individual teams were gradually placed at the disposal of the village government. As an increasing amount of reclaimed land was put into cultivation, a two-land system—ration land (*kou lian tian*) and contracted land (*chen bao di)*—was implemented in Ao Village. Rationland was used to meet basic livelihood needs of farm households, which was subjected to agricultural taxes, even the fees of township and village levies and collective public benefit.[2] By contrast, contract land was awarded by village cadres through an intricate web of connections in the community. The contract fee, ranging from 25-40RMB for rain fed fields to 100RMB for paddy fields, was required, and the contract duration varied. By 2003, even some marginal land unsuitable for agriculture—the plots on slopes or at the base of the large gully—had been put under cultivation and converted into contracted land.[3]

Three large-scale land redistributions have occurred since 1990.[4] The first redistribution came with the availability of irrigated land. By 1992, there was a total of 1300 *mu* of irrigated fields covered by reservoir water, with each resident gaining access to 2.3 *mu*. The community—level allocation of irrigated land led to a significant adjustment in rainfed fields as well. A second large-scale redistribution

1 During decollectivization, rain fed land was originally classified into three classes to maintain fairness among all team households. With the availability of irrigated land, the patch of land was categorized into four classes. Households in Ao Village had, on average, 5-6 discrete parcels of land.

2 Since the advent of the drought, only agricultural taxes were collected.

3 In China as a whole, there was a trend of dwindling farmland after decollectivization, which was caused by soil erosion, drought, and expansion of land set aside for industrial development, housing, highways and the like. Yet Ao Village witnessed an expansion of its cropland with the advent of household farming.

4 The Central Government at first allowed farm households a contract duration of five years for ration land, which was extended to 15 years in 1984, and lengthened to 30 years in 1993 during the second round of land contracting for the purpose of long-term management and investment.

coincided with the second round of land contracting launched in Aohan in 1998. To pay the village debt left over by Wang Sheng (see Chapter five for a detailed discussion), a total of 1.5 *mu* of ration land was taken off from each villager in Greater Ao Village. A third adjustment was implemented in 1999 when much of the rain fed fields were terraced. Since 15 percent of land was wasted after terracing, when the terraced fields were allocated to residents, their ration land was reduced to 5 *mu* per person. In 2004, each individual was granted an extra 0.5 *mu* of cropland. Apart from the large-scale adjustments, the first five-year interval minor adjustment was carried out at the end of 2002. My survey illustrated that due to recurrent reallocations, no household still kept the land allocated to them from the original land distribution in 1980.

Land Access and Control: Winners and Losers

In spite of a relatively equal distribution of ration land, the allocation, access, and control over a spectrum of other land or land-based resources among differentially situated residents, along lines of gender, wealth, political status, and social relations, were far from equal in Ao Village. Command over and access to communal land has often been mediated by and through market channels, as well as social and political relations, especially kinship networks, which were all gendered in local and specific ways. Invariably, male elites took advantage of their economic or political positions to get the "lion's share".

It has been almost a quarter century since Ao Village embarked on household farming. Land has long been something that local people valued, although land-based livelihoods were relatively less important in 2003 than in the earliest reform years. As in most less developed inland provinces, most farmers in Ao Village still lacked livelihood opportunities outside the agricultural sector. In the local context, land guaranteed a relatively secure source of at least a minimum level of income to village households, and therefore served as a social safety net in the absence of other collectives or state support. Indeed, if residents failed in shifting to non-agricultural sectors or if dire conditions in the city proved insufferable, they were able to resume farming practices in the community.

The more or less universal access of ration land tended to disguise the huge discrepancies in access to other kinds of land (in the case of Ao Village, the contracted land, woodland, pastureland) and therefore hide the skewed distribution of wealth. In the post-reform period, actual land utilization was more complex than it sounded. The complexity stemmed from multiple factors: market stimulation, commercialization, livelihood diversification, lack of economic alternatives beyond agriculture, political maneuvering, and owning plentiful low quality land. In the context of changing livelihood strategies, the profiles of land use and access varied greatly among households. As of 2003, it was up to individual households to decide to cultivate land themselves or to subcontract part or all of their land to others, continuously or temporarily, within the contract period.

In 2003, only 13 out of 146 resident households, or 11.2 percent did not farm. They included: two households that engaged in off-farm enterprises: a grocery store and a drugstore. One household had non-agricultural registration and gained no access to village land. One migrant household returned to the village too late to plant crops. The remaining nine were elderly households (three couples, one single woman, and five bachelors). Some of them had lost the capacity for physical labor, and most of them gave their ration land to their children or relatives in exchange for ration grains. Half a dozen households who lacked sufficient laborers also contracted out part of their land to others. According to my own survey, the actual cultivated area among residents amounted to 3761 *mu*, and at least one third belonged to contracted land.

Table 6.3 Cropland Access among Resident Households (2003)

Area of acreage (*mu*)	No. of Households	Percentage(%)
Not engaged in farming	13	11.2
Under 9	4	2.7
10-19	30	20.5
20-29	58	39.7
30-39	24	16.4
40-49	9	6.2
50 and above	8	5.5
Total	146	100.0

Source: 2003 household survey

As the competition for cultivated land intensified, a powerful minority—the richer, current or former cadres and their relatives, and those favored by cadres—gained land disproportionately, above all, typically more productive plots. This made it possible for them to increase income, and to diversify their livelihood strategies. As a result, there was a sharply skewed distribution of cropland access among resident households. Among crop production households, the smallest land holding was only 2 *mu* of corn planted by an older couple, and the largest was 178 *mu* tilled by a former village accountant, almost 12 times the average for his household of three persons. To pay village debt, the village committee granted 400 *mu* of terraced fields on hill X to the accountant for 80000RMB on a ten-year contract in late 2002. He in turn subcontracted over half of it to his relatives.

As shown in table 6.3, the percent of households living on a landholding of less than 20 *mu* was 34, or 23 percent of all households. The parcels, farmed by over half of the households (56 percent), ranged from 20-39 *mu* of land. Three households grew over 100 *mu* of cropland. Almost all households holding more than 50 *mu* of farmland were relatively wealthy.

As we will see below, the privatization of farmland under the HRS was also applied to pastureland, woodland and other natural resources. Gaining access to land beyond ration land and land-based resources was not merely mediated through their membership in certain social institutions, households or villages, nor was it distributed on an egalitarian basis. On the contrary, distribution of the land was embedded in market transactions and competition as well as personal networks of power.

Observations in Ao Village suggested an imbalance in access to and control over scarce natural resources between the poor and the rich. A minority of elite men made unfair claims on village resources in the keen competition. For example, a small number of aggressive men secured large tracts of land at the base of the large gully for a thirty-year use right at a low price and half a dozen households contracted certain sections of hillsides as their private pastureland. These natural resources were de facto privatized in different ways, being translated into difference in family wealth and perpetuating the pre-existing differences among residents on the village scene.

Social differentiation was also complicated by the claim of wider social interests. Under some state policies, village land was also allowed to pass into the hands of "external" forces and actors such as town people, and township officials. This in practice ran counter to the original objectives of poverty alleviation as well as soil and water conservation. Due to the continuing process of de facto privatization of land resources, built on a trickle-down policy, gaining access to common property resources among the village poor—and consequently their incomes from the natural world—were increasingly threatened. This widened the gap that already had potentially serious implications.

The prosperous household headed by Zhang Xuejun represented one example of this phenomenon. This family created remarkable family wealth through heavy use of multiple natural resources. Albeit illiterate, Zhang Xuejun was a very entrepreneurial farmer. He and his wife were proud that he had "enough brains" to make shrewd decisions. The household enjoyed a head start in natural resource use and control since Zhang Xuejun's current wife married him in 1988, with a daughter and son from a village in the same township. Two daughters of his own and two children of his wife ranged from 13-16 years old that year. From the next year onwards, the household cultivated over 100 *mu* of cropland each year and pursued multiple ventures, which brought them an average yearly income of approximately 20000RMB. As he claimed, "In those years when farming was relatively profitable, we always contracted a large amount of land. Unlike others, all our children worked together in the field without migrating out of the village. We got rich through our own hard work." Even in 1999 when residents were hard hit by the drought, this family obtained a considerable sum of income of about 9000RMB from the sale of *ning tiao* seed. He was one of the few elite men who contracted a patch of hill from village cadres to graze their sheep.

In 2003, the household planted a total of 50 *mu* of cropland. Compared with what they cultivated before, this was a relatively small amount. In 2003, the household raised a maximum of 60 head of sheep. Zhang Xuejun's wife and daughter-in-law secured the highest income in the community of 2400RMB from the *ningtiao* seed sales. The household also secured 110 *mu* of cropland conversion fields (see a detailed analysis in Chapter five). As a result, they reaped tremendous profits from the project. Zhang Xuejun belonged to the dominant surname group in the community and his social networks played a part in facilitating his economic success. In 2003, he contracted 25 *mu* of land situated at the fertile bottom of the reservoir in Hamlet D from his patrilineal cousin (*tang mei*), the former women's director. Among them, 20 *mu* was devoted to sunflower cultivation, and the remaining 5 *mu* was for corn cultivation. The sunflower seed alone brought them a net income of about 11000RMB. Zhang Xuejun differed from his poor neighbors in that he had the inclination and resources to take risks. Needless to say, larger-scale land operations tended to bring considerable wealth to the household.

Land Registration and Women's Land Rights

The gendered nature of land tenure was reflected clearly in the issuing of land titles as well as women's land rights. I found two versions of land contract booklets: "the Agricultural Production Responsibility Contract Agreement" issued by the Bureau of Agriculture in Aohan Qi and "the Land Contract Management Rights Certificate" issued by Inner Mongolia People's Government. Both are standardizedly printed documents that describe in detail the contents, rights, and obligations associated with land contracts. In these two documents, land titles were issued in the name of male household heads only, which undoubtedly helped to reinforce women's institutionalized subordination to men. Only in a small minority of cases, such as widows, and a few teacher households with their husbands having nonagricultural registration, were the wives treated as official heads of household.

The rural land and residency policies in China have long locked natural resources into each hamlet, which has had profound impacts on women's access to these resources. As members of their parental families, unmarried women were entitled to a share of land in their natal villages. But widespread patrilocal residence meant women were supposed to leave their natal home upon marriage and the land originally allocated to them would be re-allocated to others. Theoretically, a newly wed woman was entitled to a share of land in her husband's village, however, the village only redistributed its land periodically. When moving from one village to another, the newly married woman might experience a period of actual landlessness. Such institutional constraints were widely reported across rural China (Bossen, 2002; Li, 1999; Ruf, 1998) and applied to Ao Village as well.

Women in Ao Village were rarely equal to men in their access to land. As elsewhere, village land tenure policies discriminated against women in adverse situations such as divorce, separation, or widowhood. In one instance, a woman was forced to flee out of the village ten years ago to escape her husband's bad temper and frequent violence, leaving behind a son of nine years old. She never returned. Since she did not formally divorce her husband, her allotment of the village land was still kept by her husband. In another case, a young woman married into the community years ago and did not live with her parents-in-law happily. She returned to her parents' household in a nearby village for a prolonged period of time without formal divorce. Her husband's family cultivated her per capita allocation. In this case, the land became the household property of her husband's family. There was little possibility for divorced women to gain land again in their natal villages. These two women actually lost access to land in both their marriage and natal villages. That was one of the reasons why divorced women in Ao Village and the surrounding area often remarried quickly.

A remarried woman's right to a share of collective property was another example of such discrimination. Two remarried widows did not register their marriage legally nor did they transfer their registration to Ao Village, they were thereby issued no share of the community land. One of the former widows aged 68 from a neighboring province had resided with an elder bachelor for six years in a customary marriage. She enjoyed no land rights of any kind and the elderly couple relied merely on the man's allocation of 5 *mu* of land for a living. Although she held land rights in her former marital community, to my knowledge, she left behind her ration land to her youngest son. She had four adult sons, but none of them were willing to offer support to her in her old age. The old couple thus faced an uncertain future, and her poor health imposed a huge burden on her husband's already poor household.

Since the inauguration of the rural reforms in 1980, the infringement on women's right to land[1] widely reported in other rural areas happened to the daughters in Ao Village as well. For instance, a young woman lost her land when she got married in 2000 and moved to her husband's village in a relatively prosperous village near Chifeng City. The land policy at work in her marital village would be unchanged for 30 years. As a result, a sizeable percent of women and their children, like her, were deprived of their shares of land. As other young households with the burden of another mouth (or two) to feed, her family of three persons owned a total of 4 *mu* of land. I first met her in 2003 when she returned to Ao Village to collect the *ning tiao* seed to sell. During my 2004 revisit trip, I found her working in the brick factory. She had left behind her small son in the care of her husband. One day, she came to ask me how to deal with her land problem.

1 *The Law on the Protection of Women's Rights and Benefits* states that women enjoy equal rights in contracted land, and their legal rights must not be infringed upon. Women's Federations at various levels have made great efforts to protect the rights of women. Many female farmers also actively defended their rights to land.

I did not encounter any evidence of public discrimination against women in allocation of less ration land or land of poorer quality as observed in other regions (Judd, 1994). However, women's land rights to woodland, pastureland or other forms of land resources were, undoubtedly, constrained. For example, according to local policy, the housing land was allocated to sons only, who were eligible for a site of 0.8 *mu* for house building. In addition, a married-out village man in Ao Village could retain his ration land before gaining his share in his marital community, but his female counterparts were not always so lucky. As far as I know, only a few married-out daughters, who had not yet transferred their registration, continued to keep their land in Ao Village. All these land-related policies clearly perpetuated the ideology of patrilocal residence patterns, and to some extent, strengthened the patrilineal inheritance system.

Tree-Crops and Tree Management in Perspective

In 2003, some perennial trees were interspersed in the landscape of Ao Village. The most popular tree species was poplar (native and exotic), apricot, and elm. According to elder residents, there were only a few elms in the settlement before Liberation. Yet a kind of indigenous wild elm was then scattered all over the hills and slopes. Since the earliest years of Liberation, successive tree-planting campaigns were launched locally. For example, before collectivization, local men and women were mobilized to plant large patches of apricot on each of the four hills to the north of the settlement. In the 1970s, the brigade set up a forest specialist team consisted of about ten men. The team maintained a tree nursery and engaged in tree-planting on a regular basis. In 2003, the only visible legacy of their work was a patch of poplar near the village entrance, which was the private property of two former Party secretaries.

Successive afforestation campaigns were launched after decollectivization. Large stretches of wasteland were allocated to individual households to plant trees. According to my own survey, there was a total of 598 *mu* of private woodland, excluding the trees in individual homesteads.[1] In spite of the general trend of tree tenure devolution, the village committee itself still owned some patches of trees, particularly the shelterbelt. The forests in Ao Village were thus under both individual

1 The actual acreage should be much larger than this figure, as some residents did not count their woodland short of trees as such. Many villagers mentioned that they did not care about their "useless woodland" and had not harvested branches for many years.

and communal tenure. Generally, the trees on private or communal woodland were of poor quality with relatively low economic returns. Villagers were seldom able to use trees as commercial resources and the tree income merely constituted a tiny part of the village economy. In addition, few trees except for those in the courtyard were managed properly.

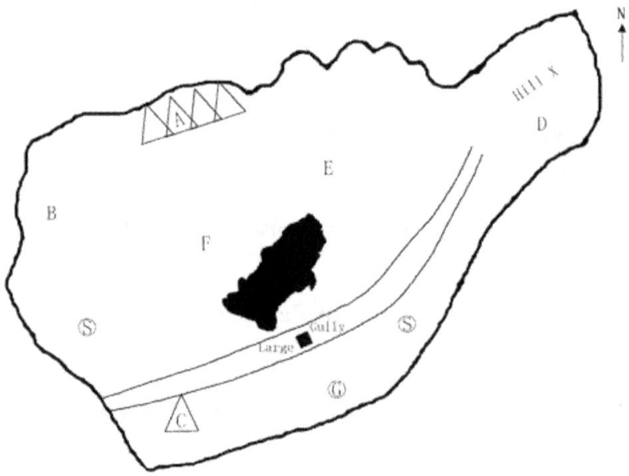

Figure 6.1 Distribution of the Main Woodlands in Ao Village (2003)

Note: Ⓢ shrub Ⓖ pastureland ■ Reservior

Table 6.4 Distribution and Area of the Woodlands at Village Level (2003)

Planting year	location	Tree species	Acreage (mu) [1]
1953-54	A	apricot	1000
1986	B	poplar and elm	750
1996	C	apricot	350
2000	D	mulberry	100
1998 and 2000	E	poplar	450
2003	F	poplar	1300
Total			3950[2]

Source: 2003 Interviews.

Note:

[1] The acreage was estimated by villagers and therefore was only an approximation.

[2] Taken together, there were approximately 4000 *mu* of the woodlands. But it was by no means densely or well forested. To the best of my knowledge, most tracts of woodlands were only dotted by trees. Only some poplar inside the courtyard or in a few private woodlands could be used as timber.

Woodland A: A monocropped cash crop of apricot scattered on the four hills (see Fig. 6.1). One elder man recalled when he served as the head of a militia brigade after he returned to the village as a demobilized soldier, he led villagers to initially plant apricot trees on the four hills in 1953-54. In the 1960s, the four teams replanted some sections of the hills under their own jurisdiction. During decollectivization in 1980, the trees on the hills in the east village were contracted out to a few elite households, while in the west village the woodland was divided up into small parcels to be allocated to each household. When the village committee imposed a kind of fee for hill keeping, many households quit their allocation. The sporadic trees on the hills planted almost half a century age were too old to bear fruit. There was obviously a need to renew them, but no owner took any action.

Woodland B: In the drive of "whoever afforests will get the benefit" in the early 1980s, when a large stretch of land in hill X was allocated to households in Team Three and Four, analyzed in Chapter five, a large patch of wasteland located to the west of the settlement was allocated to individual households in Team One and Two to plant trees. The patch of privately owned woodland covered a total of about 700-800 *mu.* Most households grew elm or the shrub *ningtiao,* except for a small minority of the richer households from Team One who bought and grew poplar seedlings. Some trees grew into mature wood, producing timber, and firewood. When the village committee imposed a hill keeping fee on the woodland, most households except some households that owned poplar quit their woodland. Due to the severe drought over the prior few years, it was said that many trees were dead.

Woodland C: was situated on a hill not far away from the settlement. In successive mass conservation campaigns, residents were mobilized to "green" the denuded hillsides full of stones in 1996. The apricot was planted through extremely strenuous work. In 1998, part of the hill was contracted out to the two households of Hui ethnicity by the village leaders as a private grazing land rather than for management. Many residents complained bitterly about it since the tree pits that they laboriously dug were worth much more than the contract fee.

Woodland D: An abortive state-sponsored project to build a mulberry garden on a small section of hill X was imposed in 2000. About 100 *mu* of mulberry was planted by about 20 participating households, which cost the village committee approximately 50000RMB. The raising of silkworms in this part of the county proved inappropriate. Since the mulberry leaves were of no use, the project ended up a total failure. Many trees there were dead.

Woodland E: was a large patch of shelterbelt located to the north of the settlement, locally called the forest network or *lin wang.* The monocropped poplar aimed to function as a physical wind-break for the farmland. According to a few former village leaders, the total area of tree cover was less than 500 *mu,* but they stretched out over about 2000 *mu* of cropland. Counting the cropland conversion fields planted in 2003, the shelterbelt area added up to over 3300 *mu* in Ao Village. In 1994-95, over 100 *mu* poplar of a 400 *mu* tract each with 6-8 rows on its four sides was planted on the rainfed land. Almost all trees had been contracted out to individual residents for 4RMB per *mu.* The land was held in common, but the trees belonged to individual contractors forever. In 1999-2000, a further 300 *mu* poplar of a tract of 200 by 200 meters with 4 rows of trees was built through mass conservation labor. Some parts of the tree plots were contracted out for 30RMB per *mu,* and the contractors were granted fifteen-year use rights to the plots and the trees that stood on them. Before the trees were mature, the contractors could plant crops among tree stands. As of 2003, about a dozen or so households had contracted a small proportion of the land, but only a few villagers succeeded in crop cultivation. Branches were thus the most important product being harvested.

Theoretically, the shelter should lead to positive changes in environmental conditions such as slowing the speed of wind, inhibiting land degradation and erosion, enhancing environmental conservation functions, and improving land productivity. However, the potential effects of on-farm trees along field boundaries were perceived by farmers as a greater hindrance for crop growth and thus crop productivity. To prevent trees from developing a large shade canopy to block the sunlight needed for crop growth, some farmers with their plots in the immediate vicinity of the poplar secretly cut and uprooted newly planted trees. For lack of long-term land and tree tenure, contractors were discouraged from active investment and sustainable management of the trees. Livestock were always tethered at the edge of the fields while residents were working their land. On the route to and from the fields, animals ate poplar leaves. In the spring before new grass germinated, livestock tended to strip off the bark of trees. As a consequence, the trees on the fields were often damaged by livestock before they matured. I observed that few of the poplar around farm sites had reached maturity and no tree was large enough for timber. A male contractor put it, "I have contracted the woodland confusedly. The only benefit is to collect some branches and twigs as firewood. Since trees will be transferred back to the village after they mature, who would care whether they are alive or dead? If we are granted trees as private property for ever, I believe the trees will all grow large."

Woodland F: About 1300 *mu* offarmland were converted into woodland under a national environmental initiative in 2003 (see Chapter five for a detailed analysis). Project participants would be entitled to the trees forever, a radical re-structuring of tree tenure. A few villagers treated it as a capital investment, they were not interested in the tree per se.

The newly introduced poplar favored by the local government was a fast-growing, drought-resistant species. In spite of anti-drought technology such as deep plowing and digging tree pits to keep soil moisture, the land in drought-stricken areas like Ao Village remained unfavorable for the growth of trees. The climate was far too dry to support the tree to take root. A lack of proper management was indeed complicated by the drought, which caused the death of many trees. Even where the initial planting succeeded, trees were still vulnerable to severe droughts as they matured.

In the view of most locals, planting green crop and shrubs was far more effective, which was also confirmed by many professionals. According an internal report, after an inspection in Aohan, a professor from Beijing warned against the technical bias that favored tree planting over the planting of other types of vegetation. In his view, shrubs and green crop were much easier to grow than trees in water poor regions like Aohan. Some experts also pointed out that the tree's capacity for soil fixation was much less than that of the land protected by shrubs. However, in Ao Village, as in Aohan as a whole, the tree bias had long been an impediment to promoting more flexible conservation in terms of vegetation cover.

A Valuable Yet Ignored Shrub

Ao Village was densely vegetated with a kind of perennial peashrub, locally called *ningtiao*, in certain parts of its landscape. There was a total of about 1100 *mu* of the shrub within its boundary.[1]It is drought resistant and well adapted to semiarid and arid environments in north China. The shrub has a large root system, which sometimes penetrates to a depth of two meters underground. Whenever residents mentioned the reduced sand-bearing wind in the village, they always cited the growth of the shrub as the major determinant. The shrub was initially planted and

1 There were over 10000 *mu* of the shrub in Greater Ao Village, with Hamlet B owning 2000 *mu*, Hamlet C 5800 *mu*, and Hamlet D 300 *mu*.

owned by individual households after the launch of the reform. All households quit them later when the village committee imposed an annual fee for hill keeping.

When free access was permitted 5-6 years earlier, the subsistence and commercial uses were quite common among local people in their everyday lives. Its stalks were utilized to make roofing material, fences or baskets. The plant burnt exceptionally hot and thus it was an ideal domestic cooking and heating fuel. Despite the cutting restrictions, illegal cutting remained rather common, providing an alternative source of firewood. It somewhat reduced the pressure on existing sources of energy. When I revisited Ao Village in 2004, the ban was lifted temporarily, many residents and non-residents rushed to cut and transport back carts of the shrub without any limit. Its leaves as a fodder source provided a good forage for livestock, especially sheep.

Although it was a valuable multi-purpose plant, the shrub was basically devalued by locals, ordinary folks and officials alike, for its environmental conservation or economic values. They often cleared the shrub to make space for other uses. After the shrub seed was ripe, I witnessed a constant influx of outsiders harvesting the cash-earning seed by picking the seed or cutting the plant. Most gatherers wore gloves to tear down the peas mixing with the leaves from the prickly branch stems. This way was faster than picking off the ripening peas one by one. Even before the seeds grew to maturity, many people rushed to collect them. I once confronted the Party secretary and asked, "Why not impose a ban to forbid the gathering before its full maturity and guard against the incursions of non-locals at the entrance of the village?" He justified himself defensively, "We have a myriad of administrative responsibilities. Whoever has the time to deal with such a minor thing?"

The commercial gathering of the shrub seed began about ten years earlier. In the beginning, the price was exceptionally low. With the launch of the West China Campaign, the seed increasingly enjoyed a high demand and the prices soared. The highest price reached approximately 6RMB per catty in 2003. According to my survey, the seed income amounted to 40275RMB in the whole village in 2003. The income distribution was, however, far from uniform. During the period of seed collection, many men were preoccupied with the newly emerged wage labor of a road construction project. Women, particularly those from some prosperous households grabbed the opportunity to earn considerable cash. The wife and daughter-in-law of Zhang Xuejun, mentioned above, earned the highest income in the community of 2400RMB, a figure almost equivalent to the income from farming over 10 *mu* of crops. They both spent six days to harvest about 360 catties of the seed. Their daily income of about 200RMB per person was almost ten days of peak season wage labor. A teacher's wife earned an income of 1600RMB in multiple trips. A group of elderly people, who were least occupied with farm work, also gained valuable earnings from the seed sales. The Zhang Guisheng couple, for instance, earned 1300RMB, a huge income in the budget of a household of poor elders.

Apparently, both the poorest and the richest segments in the community were involved in the seed collection, contradicting the conventional wisdom that commercial gathering of tree crop was an exclusive activity of the poorest households. For the rich, the income from the shrub seed was a welcome source of additional income, whereas for the poor—especially poor elders—the "appreciable" earnings from the seed sales greatly improved their well-being. With the seed income, the Zhang Guisheng couple was able to repay their long overdue loans, as well as to attend to some necessities of life—an electric cooker, two sacks of white flour and some medicine. But during the 2004 harvest period, no middlemen wanted to purchase the seed. Not until the seed fell down to the ground did a little demand emerge. Yet the price dropped significantly to an unexpected low of about 1-1.2 yuan per catty. Even so, some residents—especially elderly women—hurried to collect the seeds from the ground. The Zhang Guisheng couple ultimately earned an income of about 200RMB. The collapse of the market had greater implications for elder people, especially elder women, since this was a rare and valuable source of income for them.

The seed collection was differentiated in significant ways along lines of gender, age and other markers. Women-old and young-were heavily involved in it. In contrast to women, only a small minority of elder men took part in this activity. It was perhaps not a coincidence that all three anecdotes of death incidents associated with seed collection in Greater Ao Village involved older women outside the community—one became sick and died while she was working under the full sun. She fell down under the shrub grove and was discovered by others the following day; another aged mother was killed accidentally by her son, who wanted to seize by force the money derived from his mother's seed sales; the last one was killed in a tricycle accident on a harvesting trip.

One afternoon, a young woman drove a donkey cart taking a group of us—me, her mother-in-law, and two elder couples in their sixties and seventies—to a shrub land.

An elder woman whom I met for the first time spoke to me immediately, "How miserable we women are, we are approaching seventy and still have to collect the seed to earn a little money." Without an animal or cart of their own, they otherwise could not walk long distances to the denser sites and carry back the harvested products. As soon as we arrived at the shrub site, they scattered to search for the groves with denser peas. An elderly man aged 75 was too old to move constantly. He continually sat down on the ground and picked the peas one by one. Elder people tended to access the shrub around the settlement, while others drove their animal carts or tricycles to the denser areas over greater distances. Several married-out women came back from far away to take part in the collection. Many villagers who lived beyond the community returned for the harvest. The gendered interests in the shrub product illustrated women's greater dependence on natural resources.

The collection required no capital input, and the daily income serendipitously far exceeded the earnings from the field. In retrospect, many women expressed their regrets of "losing too much money." Their "economic loss" needed to be scrutinized in the local contexts. Many able-bodied men—young men in particular—were reluctant to collect it, because they did not treat it as "a proper business." The harvest lasted half a month in early-to-mid July, which coincided with the busiest weeding season in 2003. Most adult women were then busy with weeding either in their own fields or in the fields of others, fetching ready cash of 20RMB after a day's weeding. Many mentioned they did not realize the price would soar. Many women put the neglect of the collection of *ning tiao* seedin the context of cultural explanations. In their eyes, "The poorly weeded field is a sign of laziness, which will be ridiculed by their fellow villagers." This demonstrated the cultural significance of maintaining proper farming.

Pastureland at a Crossroad Under the "United Plan" (*tong yi gui hua*)

The pastureland in Ao Village referred to the land where a kind of purple—flower alfalfa or *zi hua mu xv*—a superior class of forage-was cultivated. Even before decollectivization, the drought-resistant forage crop was planted in the village. Since 1983, a contract system was initiated in Aohan to encourage alfalfa cultivation. The township government was put in charge of the "united plan", but management was carried on a household basis. When Wang Sheng worked as Party secretary, a large patchwork of 1700 *mu* of the former pastureland was allocated to individual households to grow alfalfa in 1988. Another large expanse of 1400 *mu* of land was planted in 1993 as well. The planted crop, totaling around 3100 *mu*, was not allocated to residents on a per capita basis. The household holdings of the pastureland resources varied greatly from nothing to a maximum of 60 *mu*. Many households had no pastureland at all. The village committee itself owned 150 *mu* of the grassland. The fresh alfalfa matured the following year after being planted. As a feed, it could be mowed twice even thrice per year when there was abundant rainfall. In Ao Village, alfalfa production focused predominantly on harvesting the alfalfa seed, and it was mowed only one time per year. After the seed was collected, its stalks and leaves were either chaffed as feedstuff for pig, sheep or poultry, or fed to animals directly.

The high-quality pastureland species not only had the potential to control land erosion, but also to generate extra income. For many years, the economic benefits of harvesting the seed were greater than they would have been if the land had been put into crop cultivation or used to harvest the green crop. In the worst crop year of 1999, the seed was sold at about 8-9RMB per catty. As of 2003, these two tracts of pastureland were too old to produce sufficient seeds. The life cycle of the alfalfa was approximately 8-10 years, yet both these tracts of pastureland had exceeded ten years. Coupled with the successive drought, the quality and quantity of the seed and alfalfa declined greatly. The price turned down significantly in 2003 and 2004, as alfalfa seed sold at about 2-3RMB per catty. In 2003, less than 10 catties of the seed were harvested per *mu*. The obvious deterioration of its productive capacity indicated that the alfalfa seed had become an increasingly unreliable source of income.

Pastureland management was subject to heavy bureaucratic scrutiny and monitoring. The concentrated control imposed by the township government via "the united plan" prohibited villagers from making any disposition of the pastureland themselves. Keeping the pastureland pure was required, and land use of any other kind would be fined. According to my household survey, only 1159 *mu* of the pastureland was reported, a surprisingly huge discrepancy from the official figure of 3100 *mu*. In retrospect, I realized that residents seldom treated their pastureland without crop as such. I remembered, after reporting their holdings of the pastureland, informants always emphasized the bad conditions of it. Ordinary people could not afford to waste their share of the holding. Despite the fact that few seedlings could survive due to the drought and the replanting of the same crop species in the same field,[1] constant attempts were made by villagers to replant the crop. Due to its

1 The alfalfa plant prevents its young plant from surviving if replanted in the same field.

nitrogen-fixation property, intercropping with grain crops could greatly increase pastureland and grain production. Under the watchful eyes of local officials, a young man intercropped soybean in his 16 *mu* of pastureland and he was fined 400RMB in 2002. In the same year, a young man plowed and replanted his share of 15 *mu* of pastureland without permission, and he was ultimately obliged to pay a fine of 800 RMB imposed by the township grassland station. To my knowledge, a few others secretly intercropped crops in far away sites without being "caught".

Under this management regime, villagers had no incentive to develop their own initiatives. The most efficient use of the pastureland resource required a continuous stream of inputs such as fertilizer, labor, and irrigation. Yet no resident paid attention to such pastureland improvement. When the seed was lucrative, residents did not allow livestock to graze the pastureland even after the harvest. During my 2004 revisit, I found that the pastureland tracts were open to free grazing after the harvest with the approval of the township government. During the day, livestock, large and small, scattered over the pastureland. It was widely recognized that large animals sometimes uprooted the crop. However, nobody really cared about it, since its economic value had declined greatly. Meanwhile, almost all households kept livestock, and few complained about the practice.

Regeneration held a great potential to increase income, improve low productivity and promote equity. However, to relocate the pastureland to farmland or to replant it was, undoubtedly, a politically charged issue. First, it was subject to the approval by the township government. To ensure a fixed amount of the pastureland in the whole township, each administrative village was not allowed to make any changes to its pastureland without prior approval. It was said that Ao Village was still standing on a waiting list, while the approval was a very bureaucratic procedure. Second, the redistribution might affect large holders or those households with good sites. Many villagers feared they might not have the use of the same land after reallocation. They also felt confused about whether or not they needed to pay extra money for redistribution. As a man complained to me, "The village leaders always betrays you, you just do not know what they will do next." Third, confronting so many intractable issues, village cadres seemed willing to maintain the status quo. They had not fashioned a workable response to pastureland readjustment. Indeed, it took great political sensitivity to carry out the work involving village households with such divergent interests.

The Scenarios of Water Resource Development

Situated in a semi-arid region, Ao Village faced chronic and often severe water shortages, either for farming or drinking, which constituted severe constraints on its development. During the collective era, whenever there was a drought crisis, residents even shouldered or transported buckets of water by animals to the fields. Irrigation experiments were tried several times in the history of the village. A small reservoir was first established to the west of the settlement in 1961, followed by a two-stage pumping facility in 1972. Both irrigation infrastructure projects were actually short-lived.

After decollectivization, a large reservoir was completed in 1991. The reservoir was initially capable of producing an adequate volume of water to irrigate 1300 *mu* of land. Double pumping equipment was used, which took only about 20 days at a time to deliver enough water to farmers' fields in the quantity that they needed. The availability of enough irrigation water in Ao Village signified a great shift from entirely rain fed agriculture, which brought a short honeymoon period to the village. The drying of the reservoir predated the arrival of the succeeding droughts starting in 1999. Not all irrigated land could be covered by reservoir water in 1997. A combination of factors such as reduced precipitation, evaporation, seepage, and particularly the ubiquitous tree pits dug all around, contributed to the result. The reservoir was no longer deployed for irrigation from 1998 through 2004.

To combat the drought, "development" projects to tap new sources of water were developed. The first set of pipe irrigation relying on surface water was installed by a government-funded project in 2000 and another set in 2001. In the spring of 2003, they had the capacity to irrigate about 630 *mu* of land, but by the summer, only 300 *mu* fields were irrigated, reflecting insufficient and unreliable surface water supplies.[1] Since the 1990s, one of the investment priorities in Aohan had shifted to pumping groundwater resources as a way of drought relief.[2] In Ao Village, the first "mechanical" well was drilled in 2002 and was put into use in the

1 Most figures in this section represent local residents' assessments.

2 The electricity-powered "mechanical" wells, locally called *ji jin*, have proliferated in Aohan since the 1990s. There were a total of 3591 such wells throughout the county in 2003, with 3054 of them having a complete pumpset. The irrigation acreage was approximating 0.414 million *mu*. The corresponding figures in Lan township were 60 wells, with 35 having a complete pumpset, and irrigating 7800 *mu* of fields (ASB, 2004).

spring of 2003. The county government sent in a well-drilling team to build it. The potential command area was expected to be approximately 190 *mu*, but it actually only irrigated about 120-130 *mu*. Installing such a well with a complete pumpset would cost at least 100000RMB. Unlike reservoir or tube irrigation, water flowed slowly from the well. Residents complained bitterly about the site selection. It almost collapsed after a heavy rain in 2003. The second "mechanical" well without a complete pumpset was installed more closely to the east village. If put into use, they believed, it would affect the use of domestic water resources, as many households ran out of water in their wells after the first well was utilized. In 2003, a maximum of 760 *mu* (at least watering once) of land was under irrigation through both "mechanical" well and tube irrigation, accounting for only one fifth of the total cultivated area of 3761 *mu* in the village.

There clearly existed a paradox in the temporary drought relief and long-term sustainable water resource development. It was widely believed that over-extraction of groundwater for irrigation purposes had led to an alarming sinking in the underground water table in the North China plain. However, from the points of view of local officials, "The present situation is far more important and urgent than that of the future development." As the Party secretary put it, "Since excessive exploitation of underground water occurs widely in the county, if we do not use the water resource, we will certainly become poorer than others." Irrigation water was free of charge in the village. The payment that team leaders collected from residents was the electricity fee and the wage of equipment operators. The local electricity fee was 0.68RMB per kilowatt hour for irrigation use. In 2003, villagers spent about 40RMB for watering one *mu* of land. This practice did not provide any incentive for the efficient use of water resources among local people, officials and ordinary people alike. If watered four times a year, one *mu* of field could consume about 200 cubic meters of water.

Such irrational water extraction, irrespective of long-term sustainability, placed a tremendous pressure on the scarce groundwater resource. These short-sighted practices of withdrawal had already caused obvious problems in water use within the residential area. In Ao Village, 114 out of 146 households installed wells in their courtyard. Seven households reported that they had wells that ran out of water in 2003 and many more residents complained that their wells had limited water with the operation of the "mechanical" well. It was predicted that if the second "mechanical" well was put into use, all shallow wells in the east village would dry up. They were initially bored to a depth of about 20 meters. Inhabitants had to deepen existing wells and use more powerful pumping systems in response to the falling groundwater table. The deepest wells in the north village penetrated about 50 meters underground, which cost approximately 3000RMB, a significant major burden for the village poor.

In Ao Village, the troubled management of water resources also manifested itself in the arrangement of irrigation scheduling. It was the individual decisions of cadres, especially those of team leaders, that in large part determined the water delivery service. At the time of irrigation, team leaders were in charge of counting the time spent for watering the fields of each household. The amount of electricity fee was calculated indirectly by recording the time elapsed. During the irrigation period, two men were usually hired to operate the equipment. They took turns working day and night for a daily wage of 20RMB each. I witnessed the rainfall deficit in the summer of 2003. When the sun scorched the fields, villagers anxiously waited for irrigation. However, two events led to delayed irrigation delivery, which seriously affected corn production. First, village cadres did not allow water supply equipment to be installed before residents finished their *da hui zhan* quotas for the small watershed project. Second, a former team leader, who had just lost in his team leader re-election, refused to purchase electric power from the local power supply bureau by using the money he had collected from his team members. Again in the summer of 2004, due to the conflicts between village and team leaders, neither of the team leaders took care of the irrigation matter at the expense of the residents.

The poor maintenance of existing irrigation infrastructure constituted another notable problem. Even if there was enough water in the reservoir, the water deliveries were threatened by deteriorating infrastructure. The channels suffered from serious seepage loss and damages. The communally owned irrigation infrastructure was not in good repair. For instance, a set of sprinkler irrigation systems were introduced to the village to irrigate about 400 *mu* of terraced fields on hill X by a government-sponsored project (see Chapter five). The irrigation equipment was worth at least 100000RMB. During my 2004 revisit, it was stolen and the tube irrigation equipment was partly damaged, which placed Ao Village's already threatened water supply under further stress for the following years. This loss further exposed its problematic water resource management.

The distribution of irrigation water resources was uneven among residents, which resulted from a variety of factors, the site's accessibility to irrigation water, whether or not the field was flat, soil moisture, the timing of irrigation and the affordability of the delivery service. Deteriorating infrastructure, coupled with the reduced availability of irrigation water, aggravated distribution inequities, which in turn, resulted in inter-household competitions and conflicts among different users. The conflicts surrounding irrigation were sometimes closely linked with land conflicts on the village scene (see Chapter seven). The possibilities of developing reliable water supplies were limited. In the foreseeable future, the conflict of increasing demand for water availability and unreliable supplies would continue to plague Ao Village. It is reasonable to expect that water shortage would become a bottleneck harming Ao Village's future agricultural development. Ostensibly, there was much room to improve water resource use and management[1]as well as the management of land and land-based natural resources in the community.

"The Wolf is Coming"

In Greater Ao Village, a key organization responsible for natural resource conservation was a team of hill keepers that consisted of four men in 2003. Local residents referred to them as "*kan shan de*".They were employed by the village committee to enforce the rules and regulations by higher-level administration as well as the village committee itself. This village-level organ had long been a male domain, especially of young men. Guo Fa, aged 32, was put in charge of the team as well as the conservation matters in the whole Greater Ao Village. He came from Ao Village and had been a hill keeper at either village or township levels for about ten years. In principle, each hamlet should have had its own resident being responsible for the patrolling duties within its boundaries. Since Hamlet D was small in size and adjacent to Hamlet B, the person from Hamlet B took the responsibility of policing both hamlets.

The patrolling of forest and green crop reserves was severely weakened by the poor performance of management institutions at both village and township levels.

1 One of the measures widely recommended to promote water conservation and efficient use in rural China was water pricing, namely, to charge fees for the water used by the farmers. Yet in a poverty-ridden community like Ao Village, to raise water charges might become a socially and politically difficult challenge, as it could counteract the development goals of maintaining food self-sufficiency and improving well-being among villagers. In particular, it might further deprive the poorer users. In this context, it would probably be more fruitful to turn to water-saving crops or irrigation methods to raise water use efficiency.

Theoretically, there was a profit sharing from fines between the village committee and hill keepers, with half of it going to the village committee and the remaining 50 percent being retained as the team bonus. From the perspective of hill keepers, village cadres provided no strong incentives to them. The team head Guo Fa received a fixed payment of 2400RMB per year, and the remaining members received 1600RMB per annum. They complained that the wage they received was not enough for the gasoline budget of their motorcycles. Furthermore, delayed payment was not unusual. In 2003, the team members were exempt from mass conservation labor, yet they were not allowed to engage in extra income-generating work inside and outside the community.

Although hill keepers imposed cash penalties on rule breakers as part of their regular duties, to collect fines from inhabitants was offensive. Guo Fa described his dilemma to me one day, "If you fail to guard the resources owned by inhabitants, they will curse you, on the one hand; if you fail to do your duty, the village cadres will deduct your salaries, on the other. We now work almost for free for village cadres, which often holds up our own farm work." Another hill keeper from the community echoed a similar sentiment, "This is a job of offending people, from the very day you start the job, people will unavoidably complain about you, and whatever good or bad you have done." He continued, "That's why I often turn a blind eye toward illegal infringements, and have not yet started a feud." Under such a low fixed-wage contract, the hill keepers did not have a strong incentive to enforce the rules. In most cases, they were reluctant to press village violators themselves, but rather called upon township-level keepers to enforce fines against village violators.

The patrolling practice at the village level was subject to that of the township level. According to the directives of higher-level administration, there was supposed to be a three-tier forest and green crop conservation organization at the levels of township, administrative village and villagers' small group. In Lan Township, a township forest and grass conservation brigade was established in 2001, which was initially made up of 12 member, one each from its 12 constituent administrative villages. The brigade originally functioned as part of the township livestock station, which was later incorporated into the grassland station in 2002. Armed with modern communication facilities such as mobile phones and motorcycles, the staff member could arrive at the spot quickly. The brigade was short lived. During my stay in Ao Village in 2003, there were only 3-4 members left. Guo Fa, once one of the 12 staff members, had been sent back to serve at the village level.

The village team was supposed to assume broadly defined obligations to patrol the vast tracts of common and private property resources to ward off livestock and people, residents and outsiders alike, from illegal grazing, shrub and tree cutting, and other prohibited uses of croplands or other protected sites. It is easy to imagine that to strictly patrol such a large area was a time-intensive job, and was in fact beyond their reach. Field observations showed that the enforcement of community rules and regulations crafted by the village committee was sporadic and arbitrary. For instance, the restrictions on grazing the pastureland after alfalfa had been harvested was relaxed in 2004, and the ban on the cutting of the shrub *ning tiao*, which has been carried out every now and then, was temporarily lifted as well.

Even the severity of sanctions did little to deter residents from grazing their livestock on protected sites. According to "*The Pact of Forest and Pastureland Protection and Fire Prevention*" formulated by the township government in January, 2002, a fine of 10-20RMB on small livestock and 100-200RMB on large livestock would be levied upon the persons caught for grazing animals on the pastureland and woodland. As with the township regulations, the village bylaw had a similar fine for animal encroachment. While I was in the village, animal incursion occurred quite often. Although stockowners seldom paid a large fine, they were always resentful of forced compliance, angrily stating that "They led away our sheep and I had to pay fines to get them back." On several occasions, I heard sheepherders refer to the field patrol of hill keepers as "the wolf is coming." In spite of fines and policing, herders often adopted opportunistic strategies. Trees and green crops were often lost to animals, tree pits vanished due to grazing. A few young men resisted by resorting to late night herding, demonstrating the resistance among residents as well as the weakness of the village institutions. The hill keepers tended to place the blame on stockowners, "They have little understanding of conservation and only care for their own gains or losses."

By contrast, in the eyes of many residents, the hill keepers were to blame. *"The Responsibilities of the Hill Keepers"* set down by the township brigade stipulates that, "The hill keeper in each administrative village is obliged to consistently patrol the woodland and forestland." However, I always heard residents' complain about hill keepers, "When livestock damages happened, hill keepers were sleeping at home;" "Guo Fa turned a blind eye to his own relatives; his neighbor, who helps to herd his sheep, is allowed to graze the forbidden areas." Guo Fa was always wearing a green "army" suit; well known locally for his ruthlessness. He was often treated as "a hired roughneck." According to village rumors, he met his wife when he migrated out to work in a city. When they decided to get married, his father-in-law refused him, since his parental household was then so poor, with three unmarried sons. He came to the home of his prospective wife and threatened his father-in-law with a knife. On my return trip in 2004, I learned that he had been recruited again as a sole staff member by the township tree and green crop conservation brigade, receiving 400RMB per month. Probably in the eyes of local officials, only a man like Guo Fa could enforce conservation rules against local offenders.

Under such a scenario, there developed very complicated triangular conflicts among village cadres, hill keepers, and residents, particularly herdsmen. Herding violations became a major source of social conflict. The persistent contradictions essentially arose from the clash between local needs and long-term conservation interests. The following narrative offered by Guo Fa vividly captured the dilemmas and frustrations confronting a hill keeper:

> I have done this job for a long time. Some people really hate me, and perhaps hate me in their hearts. It goes without saying, as a hill keeper, I have offended dozens of inhabitants and made a lot of enemies. Even if I merely warn them, some residents bear grudges. Taking Yang Baosheng for example (see in Chapter eight), he has been keeping a large sheep herd without stopping since the advent of household farming. Not long ago, they were obliged to sell all their sheep after being caught and fined constantly. When they sold their sheep, the market price was not so favorable. I guess they must curse me since the price has been pushed high now. This year, somebody took "revenge" against me by uprooting my mung bean crop. If I died today, I am sure that somebody would organize a shadow play to celebrate it tomorrow. Each night, I have to carefully lock my door and close my windows even if it is very hot during the summer. Whenever I am going away from the village for some time, I will not let anybody know about it.

Each time I approached his house, I felt frightened by a small barking dog tied in their courtyard near the gate. Inside the main room, I noticed that a sharp, shining knife with a long stick was leaning against one wall. When I asked, "Since the job offends your fellow villagers, is your wife content with your work?" He replied, "She has no way of interfering in my own business, I don't need her interference!" Guo Fa behaved as he liked and often ignored his wife's ideas.

The above analysis problematizes the implementation capacity of the village authority and its conservation practices, an imperfectly functioning gendered organization combined with inefficient implementation on the part of the male hill keepers. The problematic relationships, distrust and conflicts among village officials, hill keepers and residents in everyday interactions helped to explain the disappointing outcomes.[1] Indeed, it was naïve to rely on the patrol of a small all-male team rather than the active participation and cooperation of the whole community, men and women, old and young, to implement community environmental conservation.

In a Yunnan village, I learned that half a dozen female Party members, mostly middle-aged women, successfully took charge of the conservation efforts under a state-sponsored project of natural forest conservation, protecting the trees on the surrounding mountains within the boundary of the village. This was because females seldom migrated out of the village. They also took the task more seriously and pursued it with patience and determination. Furthermore, they were less likely to have violent conflicts with violators. This was not an easy enterprise at the start, since the community had long depended on trees as a major source of energy. The story hinted that to strengthen the community institutions was urgently needed. It also suggested that villagers, particularly women, must be empowered to possess the knowledge, information and incentives to manage and conserve natural resources upon which they depended.

The Powerless Fight Back: Resistance Politics in the Village

As noted earlier, as soon as I settled in the village, I was amazed by widespread complaints and even indignation among local men and women towards mass

1 Talking about policing, some residents always compared the practices of the current hill keepers with those of a retired person, who long assumed a similar responsibility for over ten years before and after decollectivization. I was told that this man handled complex relations quite well and thus residents understood his work. They said that, "He ate that bowl of rice, how could we smash his rice bowl—the job."

mobilization conservation campaigns and cadre corruption,[1] which were so closely interrelated in their everyday discourses. I originally thought my initial impression of cadre-people relations might be biased by the fact that most villagers probably treated me as a "big official" from Beijing and thereby they were eager to tell me about the "dark sides" or "*yin an mian*" of the village out of divergent purposes. But throughout my fieldwork, I found that however divided the community was, both male and female residents seemed unanimous in challenging the authority of village cadres and lodging complaints against them from time to time. In the pages that follow, I will first turn to the topic of village cadres and wealth.

Village Cadres, Corruption and Wealth

Throughout my stay in Ao Village, I heard numerous charges of corruption among village cadres. The frequently cited corrupt practices included: drinking and eating at restaurants, taking taxies, "selling" land resources at the expense of villagers, and pursuing material advantage for themselves and their relatives. All these phenomena were actually rampant in many rural areas across rural China. It was no secret that as of 2003, the village debt, real or alleged, had reached an "astronomical figure", which became a constant source of complaint among residents. In Aohan, the presence of "development" programs, particularly the intrusion of the mass conservation campaigns, were filtered through the village government. This actually enabled village cadres to strengthen their power through control over funding. I observed that when coordinating the watershed project, village cadres seemed to concern themselves more with pleasing their superiors at higher levels rather than with representing the interests of locals.

As noted above, as of 2003, village cadres had less authority than they did during the collective period or in those years when Wang Sheng was in power. Yet in the pursuit of prosperity, current and former cadres, regardless of sex, were apparently in a better position than ordinary farmers to take advantage of the opportunities offered by the growth of markets and commercial activities. This was a historical and contemporary phenomenon that existed across rural China, as captured correctly by a traditional saying, "To be promoted in political rank is to become richer and richer." On the surface, this did not seem to fit the case of Ao Village.

At first glance, cadres seemed indistinguishable from common folk. For

1 For a detailed discussion on the problem of corruption, see Oi (1990).

example, the women's director could not afford a principal house and was still living in a small brick wing house. There was also nothing special about the houses or lives of the households headed by two recently retired Party secretaries. Whenever I mentioned this point, some residents admitted that the women's director had merely benefited marginally from her position. She dressed better than before, which probably derived from the relief goods channeled to the village. They responded, it might be true that the two Party secretaries were not of notable prosperity, but "look at their children, you will change your idea."

For example, one Party secretary invested in the education of his son, who finally won an "iron rice bowl", a state-payroll job, in the township government. When he hosted a wedding ceremony for his son in 2003, the monetary gifts that he received from guests amounted to about 13000RMB in cash, much more than an ordinary resident could expect. In 2004, he started to run a new grocery store. The other Party secretary had two sons, with one owning a small tractor worth around 20000RMB and another son owning a nice brick house. He once held big wedding celebrations for two of his sons, inviting almost the entire village to participate. After the daughter-in-law of their youngest son "threw them out" in 2003, they were soon able to build a simple house themselves, which cost them at least 4000RMB. He still benefited from his prior experience as a village cadre and was hired to take care of the equipment of the closed brick factory at night, earning 200RMB per month in 2003.

On several occasions, I heard village men and women of their same age commented, "We know how much land they farm and how their land is cultivated. We have been working strenuously decades without staying idle. Why do we still have nothing and they become relatively richer than us?" I was told that when they were in power, they persistently accepted small gifts or even dinners from inhabitants. It was also alleged that they funneled the money from certain projects into their own pockets.

The fact that male village elites were well placed to take advantage of new economic opportunities through their political and social connections was mirrored more clearly in the following case. This former village cadre headed the most prosperous household in the village. He was once the head of the village tree and green crop conservation brigade under the leadership of Wang Sheng. He later worked as a vice-director and retired in 2000. His household had been keeping a large sheep herd and slaughtered one sheep or two each year. In 2002, he owned as many as 150 head of sheep. He knew how to tether sheep on grassy spots without being fined and how to deal with powerful officials within and outside the community. He sent one of his two daughters to college without getting into any debt. He was very reluctant to talk about his wealth, yet it was generally admitted that he was a principal moneylender in the village and received a significant amount of money from the interest rates.

Many of their neighbors remarked that the household's wealth could be largely attributed to his own boldness and creativity, his wife's industriousness as well as no domestic burden. This last factor meant that they had no elders to support and did not need to pay a large sum of money for the marriage of their son(s). Villagers always mentioned, "Why don't they kill sheep for their own consumption, since they had no sons."[1] His wife was a capable and hardworking woman and well known for her skills in taking care of lambs. Like most women of her age, she was illiterate. I was astounded when I inquired about their household income, she told me she knew nothing about it and I should ask her husband. When I talked with her husband after he returned, she sat far away and was totally silent. As in the collective period, it seemed quite common in male cadre's households, although wives might share their husband's privilege, they were more marginalized in their own households than other women.

Rumors abounded that the relatives of village cadres received much preferential treatment and shared the privileges of cadres. Among them, a few had made a good fortune out of natural resources in the village. One of the most telling examples frequently cited by residents was that a former team leader—the youngest brother of one of the retired Party secretaries, introduced above, won a long-term contract from another Party secretary to use the reservoir—initially for fish cultivation-at a very low price. This young man also bought the former village headquarters built in 1994 when Wang Sheng was in office—costing around 100000RMB then—at a low price of 30000RMB from the village committee when his brother served as Party secretary. As the reservoir became dry in 1998, the young man turned a large tract of land surrounding the reservoir into crop fields and earned a substantial amount of income by sub-contracting them out.

This was not an isolated case. The son of Liu Xing was sent out to learn some veterinary skills by the village leaders when Liu Xing's brother-in-law was in power

1 Villagers in Ao Village seldom killed sheep for their own consumption. For a detailed discussion about the sex of children and wealth and poverty, see Chapter eight.

as Party secretary. After his son migrated out of the village, Liu Xing was appointed as a veterinarian to take charge of stock immunization in Greater Ao Village. I heard many residents continually complain about his poor performance. All this indicated that non-market mechanisms such as gendered social and political connections played a significant part in the construction of social and economic inequalities. These kinds of inequities "manufactured dissent" (Carney and Watts, 1990) and jealousy among ordinary women and men. My ethnographic study indicated the conflict between village cadres and ordinary villagers became a notable character of village life, which framed the general milieu within which the politics of resistance developed.[1]

Everyday Forms of Resistance

Feminist theorizing about "the personal is political" as well as studies of "the processes by which struggles over resources and labor are simultaneously struggles and bargains over socially-constructed meanings, definitions, and identities" (Hart, 1991:95) have made visible the rich reality of everyday politics. This was largely left unexamined until the 1980s. Feminist formulations have allowed us to challenge common assumptions about resistance and struggles of the "weak". This has also found strong resonance in mainstream scholarship. The study of Kerkvliet, for example, indicates that politics was part of daily life in a Philippine village, which "consists of the debates, conflicts, decisions, and cooperation among individuals, groups, and organizations regarding the control, allocation, and use of resources and the values and ideas underlying those activities" (1990: 11).

Much recent scholarship on the resistance of the less powerful has derived from the stimulating and influential writings of James Scott (1985, 1990). In *Weapons of the Weak* (1985), Scott theorizes "everyday forms of peasant resistance" grounded in class-based economic differentiation and social stratification in a Malaysian rice-planting village. In his view, indirect resistance was the principal manner by which the weak articulated their relations to the powerful. He distinguished "public" and "private" transcripts in response to dominant discourses. The "hidden transcript" was articulated in private spaces. And he argues that most of time the weak did not express explicit opposition to the prevailing social order because the power of the

1 This section is not intended to exhaust all everyday politics in Ao Village, but to focus on the conflicts between cadres and common villagers. For a discussion of inter-household conflicts, see Chapter eight.

elite made this too dangerous. As a result, this engendered a forced acquiescence on the part of the former. When it came to the nature of resistance, he notes that, "the struggle between rich and poor is not merely a struggle over work, property rights, grain and cash, it is also a struggle over appropriation of symbols, a struggle over how the past and present shall be understood and labeled, a struggle to identify causes and assess blame, a contentious effort to give partisan meaning to local history" (Scott, 1985).

Struggles under the Collective Regimes

In the context of rural Chinese society, with the state's long involvement in and control over community affairs, the relationship between the state (and its agents) and the peasantry has been rather complicated. As noted before, over most of the collective period, in the face of hegemonic political discourses and practices of the state and those of their agents, village people did not show an open demonstration of resistance to power and authority of brigade and team cadres. Most of them, particularly those with "bad class background", typically swallowed their grievances over the bureaucratic allocation of labor, opportunities or other resources, and avoided overt conflicts. They resisted in a somewhat less confrontational manner, most notably, through a minimal degree of effort toward collective labor. This manifested mostly clearly in the poor performance of Team Three. For instance, its team members never worked with enthusiasm in the late years of collectivization. Generally, they waged silent struggles in their daily lives.

As in many other places, the "struggle of the harvest" was the main issue that pitted the national government, local governments and farmers against each other (Oi, 1990). Strategic team cadres secretly traded livestock for cash on the free markets. Team leaders also underreported harvest or reported poor crop yields to higher-up cadres. For instance, when the latter came to check, they put the shriveled grains on the top of sacks so as to keep them for their teams. A topic that frequently surfaced in their recollections was that when grain supplies totally ran out within the household, both men and women managed to negotiate with team leaders for their ration grains. In a clandestine manner, team members also intentionally did not cut grains completely, so that they could glean the remaining grains from the fields later. Although "class enemies" were often blamed for carrying out thievery or pilfering collective grains, some audacious persons with good class labels virtually engaged in the petty thievery of the collective grain harvest and even buried grains underground. In the context of widespread poverty and starvation, a small minority of residents tended to secretly pilfer grains and stalk unheeded by team leaders as long as they could. At first, thieves were forced to parade what they had stolen in the street. In the last year of collectivization, the collective system had almost crumbled. Although team members were still forced to work during the day, petty theft from the collective fields had become ubiquitous "public robbery".

Many recalled that at harvest time when cartloads of grains were loaded and transported to the threshing ground, people chased after them. As they claimed, it was "no different from snatching and robbing publicly." One woman recalled, like other male teammates, her husband went to the team headquarters almost every night in those days. She left her baby son alone on the *kang* and headed to collective fields to cut soybean plants. One night, when she returned home, she found her baby was sleeping soundly on the ground. After nursing the child, she went out again to cut soybeans. In the last year of collectivism, residents were also allowed to reclaim the so-called "pickaxe land" to grow crops when brigade cadres lost almost all control.

New Forms of Struggle

After decollectivization, the government and Party's legitimacy in the countryside was weakened. O'Brien and Li (1995), for instance, explore uprisings among the peasantry by relating them to the outcomes of a series of rural reforms, more specifically, the HRS, decollectivisation, commercialization, migration, and the political reforms. O'Brien and Li (1995: 756–783) argue that peasants are very conscious about their rights and are willing to protect their rights through "rightful resistance." They start to lodge complaints with higher authorities (O'brien and Li, 1995). The tax burden was often cited as the key determinant that prompted mass demonstrations or riots among peasants who were forced to pay taxes. To "lighten the peasants' burden," therefore, has become one of the most important strategies enforced by the Central Government.[1]

1 Large-scale protest movements by peasants have been intermittently reported in the Chinese countryside since the 1990s. Peasant violent and non-violent collective actions included group visits to higher authorities beyond the township level, evasion of taxes or fees, demonstrations, sit-ins and blockades of roads and railroads, sacking of party-government compounds, and beating and killing of local cadres. As a result, the tax-for-fee *(fei gai shui)* reform was partly carried out in many rural areas. It abolished all of the previous fees and taxes and instead levied only two taxes on peasants: a reformulated agricultural tax and a surcharge on the new agricultural tax. With the implementation of this new policy, peasant's burdens were reported to have reduced by two thirds in Aohan.

After the implementation of the Household Contract Responsibility System, farmers in this part of China defended their rights to resources more consciously. From the 1990s, the struggles were increasingly directed towards the corrupt practices of village cadres. In a few localities throughout Lan Township, more severe struggles were waged by local residents.[1]It was widely reported in one village, females were more heavily involved in high-risk rebel activities against corrupt officials since they faced little danger of being arrested due to their gender. In this context, the nature of women's political acts did not relate specifically to their own gender interests, but more to overall peasant concerns. It was also frequently mentioned by residents that the herding ban was met more severe resistance in Hamlet B and Hamlet C, where residents' livelihoods relied more heavily on livestock. Even teenage girls rebelled by deflating the motorcycle tires of hill keepers. In addition, the decisions by the village committee often could not be implemented successfully in these two hamlets due to residents' boycotts.

In Ao Village, as in most other places throughout the global "South" (Scott, 1985), large-scale mass protests were extremely rare. However, when seen from within, everyday politics constituted an indispensable part of village life. The forms of struggle have mainly fallen into the two categories identified by Scott (1985)—discursive contestation and physical action. In the specific context of Ao Village, intra-village politics has predominantly revolved around the politically charged conflicts over natural resource use and environmental conservation among various social actors with different resource interests. The practices of natural resource use, management and conservation were inherently political, which constituted an area of conflict (Leach et al., 1999). In this sense, Ao Village can serve as an example to indicate "everyday forms of resistance" could be and situation-based and gender differentiated in everyday use and control over local natural resources. By making explicit the conflict and struggle—an inseparable reality on the rural scene—this study aims to stress the agency of individuals and groups at the

1 The reason cited by villagers why resistance in Ao Village was not as radical as in other surrounding communities included: Mongols have long been known for their honesty; residents in this village lived under the eyes of local officials; individual villagers avoided running the risks of offending local officials at the expense of their own interests; and villagers in the community were divided. There was no evidence of membership in any formal or informal associations based on neighborhood, kin networks or common pursuits.

grassroots level.

To explore local resistance, we must first look at the legacy of complaints—a site of "discursive contestation." Everyday village discourse itself constituted an inseparable part of daily resistance. As of 2003, the political climate no longer posed such a hazard for locals to challenge the authority of village cadres. Men and women dared to answer back to and even criticize village cadres not only in their absence but also sometimes in their presence. However disunited the villagers were, they seemed unanimous in their complaints of corruption and corrupt officials—specific or general—at the local level. Villagers maintained their faith in the Party and the Central Government. In the eyes of local people, "the Party is a good Party, and the scripture (meaning the Party's policy) is good scripture, but it is crookedly recited by local cadres." Many residents believed that the welfare they enjoyed after decollectivization was granted by the Party rather than by village cadres. Following the first visit of the then vice-premier Wen Jiabao in 1997, particularly with the arrival of the drought, the overall tax burden had dropped sharply throughout Aohan. During my fieldwork, I heard villagers commonly express their gratitude and admiration towards premier Wen Jiabao.

Local people's views of politics and political actors became an integral part of local culture. Generally, villagers took a hostile view of village cadres. As have seen in Chapter five, almost no mass mobilization conservation campaigns, including the ongoing projects launched in 2003, ever went uncontested or unchallenged. In the eyes of most villagers, village cadres responsible for the implementation of "development" projects tended to scratch the surface. As one man argued, "If cadres get something done once and forever, they can't continue to receive funds; if construction work is constantly repaired and rebuilt, the cadres could harvest extra benefits." In their descriptions, "The project serves as a springboard for the promotion of cadres and achieving their own goals."

If we look at the discursive politics through women's eyes, we find women's versions highlighted some gender specific aspects. For example, they complained about male cadres to "drink too much so that they cannot distinguish East from West, North from South!" Women also tended to emphasize the negative impact of mass labor on their daily lives and livelihood strategies. Some women interpreted their attitudes towards malpractice by using terms with more negative connotations. For instance, they dub the tree pits as "the death pits".

In this part of China, local men and women experienced state power and the power of its agents through unpredictable and sometimes coercive *da hui zhan*, which fundamentally influenced how villagers respond to and voice it. As evidenced in Chapter five, villagers' memories of *da hui zhan* were always imbued with complaints. *Da hui zhan* was long a major source of considerable conflicts. In this aspect, people waged silent struggles for the most part, although there was no dearth of public confrontations. Residents often resisted by carrying out sabotage such as planting or watering trees in improper ways, burying tree saplings, or throwing them away. The remarkably low survival rate of trees mirrored the resistance acts among residents. This helped to explain why reforestation was carried out year after year, but little forest existed. Local officials' explanations often cited residents' attitudes and actions as showing no concerns about local environmental conditions but only their own interests.

The list of complaints beyond *da hui zhan* was long. The issues of building a proper road, bridge or other infrastructure often sparked a great deal of concern and resentment among residents, as illustrated by the most popular complaints. For example, in 2002, residents in Greater Ao Village were mobilized to repair a village road connecting Ao Village and Hamlet B along the large gully, and an outside state funding of 100000RMB was spent. By the time I stayed in Ao Village, the land had already eroded considerably. The condition of the road was so bad that people would rather continue to travel on the base of the gully. The newly built stone bridge that I searched for, introduced in Chapter three, was ultimately used only by a few residents due to the inappropriate site selection. Prior to the autumn harvest in 2003, I witnessed the women's director arrange for a tractor operator to bulldoze a temporary road again. All these cases highlighted the failure and inability of village cadres in reconciling state assistance and local interests in the implementation of practical projects.

In Ao village, the most radical source of tension revolved around certain natural resources. Among them, land and its use was the focal point of community politics, an issue that frequently emerged in the context of the complaints about corruption. The typically cited examples included the fact that cadres and their relatives were prioritized in the allocation of natural resources or cadres "sold off" (virtually leased out) cropland, woodland or other land and land-based resources to village elites or outsiders. In Greater Ao Village, land control was key to the power of village cadres, which became the target of maneuvers and manipulations. As a consequence, a considerable level of discontent had to do with the performance of the village cadres in its land policies and practices. As confirmed by county officials, the conflicts over land tenure and land use had become a number one issue in rural Aohan.

The Newest Chapters of Fighting Back

During my fieldwork in 2003, I heard and even witnessed a series of conflicting events between cadres and ordinary villagers. Here are some examples. The following two cases against road construction managers sparked by crop pollution were closely linked to the struggle against local cadres. The first case took place in the autumn of 2003. On one mid-August day, Song Ling told me when I was away for household visits, a man approached her house, hoping to seek help from me for his damaged cornfield. A project to broaden a nearby section of the highway began in June, which was finally completed in late September. A project manager had contracted a parcel of 20 *mu* of land for 500RMB per *mu* on a one-year contract from the village committee to use it as a construction site to store machines or other construction materials.

On the next morning, when I went with my host couple to irrigate their cornfields, I happened to meet the man, who was in his early forties. He told me that the nearby cornfields were negatively affected by the dust flying from the operation of the on-going constructing project, and his plot was hardest hit among 15 affected households. I was told, "Covered with heavy dust, even animals don't want to eat the corn stalk and the yield is bound to be reduced."[1] Some men and women with affected corn plants had gone to the village headquarters to seek assistance from village cadres. Since their complaints went unheard, they decided to turn it over to the township government. That's why he hoped I would take some pictures for them as "evidence". I did as he requested. I observed that the dust covered some neighboring fields bordering the construction site, which apparently turned the leaves of corn plants yellow. A few days later, I heard a group of 11 people—including seven women—hire a tricycle to go to the township seat. A former Party secretary, whose field was slightly affected, was encouraged to go with them. He was credited with special knowledge of dealing with superior officers. He discouraged a few of the most radical residents from stopping or smashing the machines. Ultimately, they

1 An alternative explanation among residents was that a big rain could wash all the dust away, and therefore its impact on the plant was limited.

won a token compensation fee of 800RMB, which was divided among the affected households according to the amount and severity of damages to their fields.

The second case happened soon after the first one was settled. Inspired by the success of the cornfield struggle, Xiao Yang, introduced in Chapter four, decided to seek a pollution compensation for her paddy field lying on the east side of the highway. The patty fields of Xiao Yang, her younger sister's and several other households were affected to different degrees by the dust from the construction project. Her husband was then away as a migrant worker. She and her younger sister's husband, who had just returned home from migration, first approached village official to initiate their complaints. Frustrated with the slow response, they decided to turn over the case to the township government. One day, I happened to meet them inside the township government compound. She told me that the staff member there refused to take it into account. They decided to go to the county seat.

Two of them traveled to the county town several times. The county officers took their case more seriously. When higher-up officials came down to investigate it, she was accused by village cadres as a "troublemaker". She finally won the case and specifically requested me to keep the outcome to myself because she was not willing to share the small amount of compensation fee with those residents who were not involved in the effort. She said her time and transportation fees spent must be compensated if others wanted to share the money. At first glance, these two cases had remarkable parallels. Yet in the latter case, a woman—a female de facto household head—took the initiative. Her defiance involved more complex negotiations. She also carried the matter to higher authorities at the county level.

A third event occurred immediately following the 2003 harvest.With the launch of the small watershed project, the contracted land lying at the base of the large gully was about to be withdrawn and converted into woodland. Bai Ru of Hui ethnicity, who owned the largest patch of land there, approached me one day, thinking that I might be able to help him to deal with the loss. He cleared the fields on his own initiative, which had brought a tangible income to his family in the previous years. Following him, half a dozen elite men had put the rest of the land at the base of the large gully under crop cultivation. The conversion would hurt their chances of long-term prosperity. As Bai Ru claimed, "The rest of my life will depend upon it. How can I afford to lose it?" He showed me the contract document that he had signed with the village government. In the face of a fading dream of fortune, all those who owned land there were worried about the transfer.

Ultimately, they succumbed to power and huge pressures from township leaders, who threatened them that no one could stop a state-sponsored environmental project. Under these circumstances, they had no choice but to yield. Their fields were leveled off by using bulldozers without their knowledge, let alone securing any consent from them. By that time I had lived in the village long enough to understand such ridiculous things. I suggested they go to the "letters and visits office" (*xin fang ban*) in the county town to seek help. By the time I was about to leave the village in December 2003, nothing had been settled regarding the compensation. Nine months later when I returned to the village, I learned that they used the law as a weapon against village officials. Their rights to their former plots were given some recognition and all of them were able to keep their former cropland as their own woodland on a thirty-year contract at a very low price. This case made it clear that the struggles waged by a few elite men ultimately won them favorable outcomes (see Chapter five for a detailed discussion).

The fourth case can illuminates the complexity of resistance and struggle in a village setting. The conflicts of multiple interests were encapsulated in the episode that occurred in the spring of 2004. The contract for a large patch of land from the village committee in 1998 expired in late 2003. With an agreement from village cadres to pay the construction fee of the stone bridge, the team leader in the west village contracted out part of the land at 25RMB per *mu* on a four-year basis to some of his relatives and friends. Village officials contracted out the remainder of the land at 30RMB per *mu*. The land allocation sparked a great deal of anger and vigorous opposition among ordinary people.

In the end, the village committee decided to take back all the land to re-allocate it to residents. Being unhappy with the decision, the team leader and his family members started to "make trouble" in the village headquarters. Village officials were blockaded inside their offices. For several days, the dispute drew a large crowed of inhabitants to the village headquarters. At the beginning, most onlookers kept silent. Local gossip held that the whole family of the team leader was united to defend their private interests. Their aggression gave rise to intense oppositions among many residents. It was finally turned into a face-to-face large-scale collective conflict. An outspoken woman, who was not at all politically active in a formal way, took the chance to express her dissatisfaction towards the team leader as a "little person".

Her bold move was even admired by many men on the scene, and several other men and women immediately reacted to what she complained about. It was reported that the State Land Administration Bureau of the county government later took part in mediating the dispute. The village leaders eventually won the land and contracted it out to all registered villagers at 20RMB per *mu* on a per capita basis, which was warmly welcomed by residents. The results of this episode further splintered the village.

Shortly afterwards, the defeated team leader organized a group of inhabitants to carry out a lawsuit against village officials for corruption in the cropland conversion project (see Chapter five). The rumor spread that he later abandoned his action as he finally got certain benefits through maneuvering. He himself once told me with pride that he did not lose a lot in the transaction. It was reported that after that encounter, the team leaders did not cooperate with village cadres and even made trouble in many village matters. This case was complicated by the involvement of multiple and conflicting interests, including ordinary villagers, the team leader and his family members, village cadres, township and county officials.

The immediate causes of all these cases were closely associated with the material benefits of the participants. The first two examples involved small-scale collective bargaining, while the last one encompassed more complicated political conflicts. All in all, the villagers employed informal, and even organized forms to carry out resistance so as to protect their economic interests. The following story involved villagers' resistance against a township official. In Ao Village, inhabitants were well acquainted with some township officials, since they were often assigned to oversee mass conservation campaigns on the scene. The township official spent 4000RMB to contract 60 *mu* of wasteland bordering Hamlet C from the village committee to plant green crop in 2002.

On a summer afternoon in 2003, I went with a group of women hired by the township official to harvest the green crop in his field. When we arrived at the site, all of them agreed that it was too early to harvest. When I brought it to the owner's attention, he admitted this was a fact, but he said he had to cut ahead of time to avoid unexpected loss. A total of 15 persons were hired that day, 12 of them were women. I witnessed that most of them slowed down in their work when the owner was not present, while they sped up their pace in his presence. During the break, with the permission of the owner, most of them started to chop wild grasses. They cut so vigorously, which stood in sharp contrast to what they did for the township official behind his back. A few women from the east village worked as slowly as possible. I remembered Zhang Hualan later grumbled, "Women in the east village loaf on the job. I have never done such easy wage work." She continued, "Half a dozen people could have finished it within a shorter time. The town people knew nothing about it!" When I revisited Ao Village in 2004, I learned that inhabitants from Hamlet C had depleted his immature green crop by grazing their animals. This was an outstanding example of local resistance to outside officials.

Although these examples were not based on formal politics, and might not usually be perceived as resistance by conventional standards, the picture that I presented here was by no means a passive populace in rural China. I was very impressed by the fact that both adult men and women were brave enough to talk about politics frequently and publicly, not only in the absence of power holders but also in their presence. Resistance occurred at both individual and collective levels. Individual resistance happened on a day-to-day basis, whereas once in a while, group visits to higher-level authorities occurred.

My observations in Ao Village support Kerkvliet's (1990:114) findings in a Philippine village, "The spectrum of resistance is broad from organized and confrontational forms to subtle, indirect, nonconfrontational ones." This series of events demonstrated the power of ordinary people or "the weak" in Scott's terminology (1985). The findings also indicated gender-specific forms of resistance, and thereby contradicted the prevailing stereotypes about the political inactivity of women. Although women were disadvantaged political actors, they were absolutely not silent about political issues. They complained and confronted as bravely as men, and sometimes complained more radically than the latter.

Corruption, interwoven with other intra-village social relations and conflicts that plagued the community, split the village. As popularly acknowledged by residents, "The community is not of one mind;" "We are currently a plate of sand;" "There is no respectable leader of our own;" and "No one shows real interest in community affairs." As conflicts sharpened, deep social mistrust permeated village life, which intensified community fragmentation. For example, when there was a drought in the past, elder women often conducted "rituals" to pray to the heavens for rains as a last resort, but no one was willing to organize such an event in 2003. As described in Chapter five, even *niu yang ge*, a traditional dance mirroring internal cohesion among residents, had disappeared. The changed community spirit, as a result, had profound implications for both locals' interactions with nature and with each other. In this context, local people resorted to opportunistic action rather than taking the initiative to protect their surrounding environment on a voluntary basis.

Concluding Remarks

As elsewhere in rural west China, natural resources were instrumental to the well-being of residents, particularly women. However, the determinants of land and land-based natural resources have been firmly embedded in the larger political economy. They were not only shaped by the development policies and practices imposed by bureaucratic state powers at various levels, but also by the daily practices of multiple resource users, male and female. Social dynamics were key elements in understanding the dynamics of gendered rights in land use, access and control. The repeatedly shifting policies of private and collective management policies, which were rife with uncertainty and subject to changes, have significantly influenced the legacy of land cover and vegetation. Apparently, environmental practices and landscape changes in this part of China epitomized Berry's (1989) phrase, "no condition is permanent."

Since the advent of the rural reform, the integration of tree, shrub, and green crop for the concurrent development of agriculture, forestry, and animal husbandry have been promoted, yet no mechanism was instituted which accommodated proper management strategies. Despite the fact that privatization might not always offer the best solution to addressing certain efficiency, equity or resource sustainability objectives in either the short- or long-term, the rural development policies since decollectivization have promoted the privatization of natural resources. Privatization in and of itself generated many other problems. Contrary to Hardin's 'tragedy of the commons' thesis, privatization could lead to increased environmental damages as well. The increasingly unequal distribution of resources and thus the resultant conflicts between the more and less powerful actors was just one such example. Obviously, commercialization and privatization on the one hand and natural resource degradation on the other have intensified the pressures on local natural resources and the environment

This chapter sheds light on the continuing power of the party-state, the uneven relations of power of local people vis-à-vis the state and state policies, and resistance politics in village life. Village women were marginalized in the wider world beyond their immediate domestic world. They had far less opportunity to gain access to formal political structures or even paid jobs offered by the village government. The gendered organizations of NRM at both township and village levels that relied on only a few male actors were ineffective and problematic. All these gendered power structures and spaces were common to the familiar rural scenes in the Chinese countryside. Challenging the common assumptions about politics and resistance, this study demonstrates that although women were not the principal political actors in the village landscapes, the everyday politics of resistance was not an exclusively male domain.

Chapter Seven

Intra-household Dynamics and Inter-household Interactions

As shown in the previous chapters, the mutually reinforcing social relations in village life governed access to and control over natural resources, and thereby shaped the working and living conditions of villagers. Among them, men's and women's roles in use and management of environmental resources were refashioned into the local environment through gendered divisions of labor, responsibilities, rights and spaces. Both Chinese and Western observers of rural China widely recognize the rural household as a social institution governing the organization of agricultural production and natural resource use. As Croll argues, "What characterizes the period of reform in the past decades has been the identification of development with the domestic sphere; it is the site where development is produced and reenacted so that domestic organization and activity are the center piece of the rural development plan" (1995: x).

Indeed, state policies continued to reinforce patriarchal family structure through land allocation, loans or other programs. For instance, the social and political construction of the administrative household, or *hu,* made the household—the "black box" with mysterious nature—even more complicated than it superficially appeared to be. One of the most adverse consequences was the household was identified continually in all public events by the name of male household head as an everyday practice. For example, almost all certificates were issued in the names of men.[1] Men's involvement in the outside world was often regarded as masculine, "natural" and inevitable, and few perceived it as problematic. Since social and physical

1 This included, for example, the land contract agreements, the certificate of house ownership, the bills of agricultural taxes, and other formal documents.

landscapes interacted closely with each other in the fabric of rural society. What concerns me in this chapter are newly invented or modified gendered social relations within the household and outside, and their implications for environmental practices. This chapter begins with the workings of gender and power within the household, followed by an outline of gendered intra-household interactions in practice.

A Shift of Gender and Power in Intra-household Dynamics

My ethnographic evidence indicates that gender roles and conjugal relations were constantly changing in response to new social realities in the local circumstances. This change was accompanied by a re-structuring of gender and power within the household and beyond it. Seen from a historical perspective, gender relations became more malleable, fluid and subject to constant negotiation after the advent of household farming. Some public and private patriarchal practices remained in the practice of daily life, yet patriarchal authority and power were increasingly negotiated and challenged on multiple fronts inside the household, albeit not in the public sphere. As we shall see below, women's roles in the household economy, and their increased economic autonomy and decision-making within conjugal households, coupled with the breakdown of the traditional authority structures, helped re-shape women's status vis-à-vis men's.

In the next section, I will trace some aspects of the political economy of gender—men and women in the marriage market, household budgetary negotiations, household division, and old age support—that influenced natural resource use and environmental changes in significant ways.

Gender and the Marriage Market

In Ao Village, as elsewhere, young women, compared to young men, long enjoyed a relatively favorable bargaining position in the marriage market, which had, in large part, increased their bargaining power within the household and beyond. According to my 2003 survey, village men married for the first time at a mean age of 23.6, as opposed to a mean age of 20.7 among women. The oldest age for the first marriage was 53 among men and 29 among women. The rate of nonmarriage among men was relatively higher. As of 2003, there were at least 24 adult bachelors (over twenty-five years old), who were either divorcees (3), widowers (7), or those never married (14). In contrast, all marriageable women except one were married. The only young single woman aged 26 was a migrant worker working in a city in 2003. The remaining half dozen single women were all over sixty. As we shall see below, the skewed sex ratios in the marriageable cohorts stemmed not from the genuine scarcities of brides, but rather from the outflow of women.

By 2003, most boys and girls quit school at the age of about 15-16. They were usually engaged as early as 18-19 years old and got married when they reached their early twenties. Children from richer households tended to get married even younger. If a young man was engaged late, people would question his "masculinity" and his overall fitness as a marriage prospect. If he remained single in his mid-twenties, it would become too late for him to find a desirable partner. A man's status as a bachelor, locally called *guang gun*, or "bare stick", was a shame for any parent in their lifetime. As we shall see in Chapter nine, however impoverished parents often struggled to have their sons engaged and married in good time, and often borrowed a large sum of money with high interest to finance the marriage agreement.

As we shall see below, some young women manipulated this source of female power to their advantage in areas of partner selection, marriage payment requirement,[1] divorce, and so forth. Previously, a young woman had little voice in the decision of her own marriage partner, nor did a young man. When asked about their marriage choice, those who married before decollectivization unanimously remarked, "The parents had the final say in marital matters." As of 2003, this was no longer entirely true in Ao Village, although the powerful tradition of arranging marriage by parents through introductions or go-betweens continued to play a major part. Migration had greatly increased marriage chances among young men and women.

In Ao Village, women's remarriage, locally called *gai jia,* was long socially acceptable and widely practiced without stigma. Widows normally sought remarriage quickly, which often came out of some very practical considerations. For example, the status of widowhood could interrupt their normal lives. As a popular expression put it, "Slanders cluster around a widow's door." One frequently cited case was that of a deceased woman, who had remarried three times within the village apart from her first marriage in another village, leaving behind her children, respectively, in three different families. Only in rare instances would women refuse to do so and try to tide through hard times with the help of their children. During the collective era,

1 For young women's maneuverability in marriage negotiations, see Chapter nine.

to break a marriage contract was quite difficult.

Yet by 2003, marriage had become fragile, and the divorcee suffered little stigma. There were approximately six divorces in Ao Village, formal or informal, since the mid-1990s. As elsewhere, in most cases, women initiated divorces. During my stay in the village, two daughters of the residents returned to their parents' homes after a formal divorce and remarried very soon afterwards. By contrast, a second marriage for males was rare, especially for those with son(s) by their former wives. All these phenomena helped to change son preference among residents.

For most people, to bear sons became less important than before. Jiang Mei had practiced midwifery more than a decade about 20-30 years earlier. She explained to me that previously, whoever gave birth to a son, she always shared the happiness with them, whereas if they were "displeased to bear a daughter," she felt sad as well. She always offered sympathy by comforting them that "a flower blossoms before bearing its seed" (the flower means daughter, and the seed means son. The pronunciation of seed in Chinese sounds like that of son).

However, the reversal was true for her later, as for most other residents.As of 2003, young girls were mostly born, educated, viewed, and even spoiled in almost the same way as young boys. However, in a rural society without a guarantee of social security, the son biases remained strong in the minds of a small minority of people, who were still under the shadow of the traditional Confucian cultural belief of "more sons, more prosperity." As an old woman remarked, "A son bears the surname of his father and thus is a "real" offspring. A daughter is often unable to kindle incense when she sweeps their parents' tombs. When she burns the paper money to her parents in the other world, the money flows to her husband's household rather than to her own natal family." Overall, women's favorable positions in the marriage market and the reduced biases towards baby girls contributed to women's improved status within the household.

"Temporary Wealth God": Household Budgetary Negotiations

In Ao Village, one of the newly emerged on-going renegotiation processes of "conjugal contract"[1]was reflected in domestic budget management. As is well known, the household in most villages is still a corporate property-holding unit in

1 Following Ann Whitehead (1981: 88), in this dissertation, the conjugal contract is defined as "the terms on which husbands and wives exchange goods, incomes and services, including labor within the household."

the early twentieth-first century, and the household economy is characterized by a strict pooling of income. During the collective period, the invisibility of women's economic contributions gave rise to little or no domestic power for women in both their natal and married households. Control over the household budget was almost exclusively the privilege of male household heads. After the onset of decollectivization, the balance of power in intra-household financial issues was negotiated in complicated ways. Men's and women's control of financial resources depended upon the conjugal contract negotiated between husbands and wives on a day-to-day basis. After the implementation of the Household Contract Responsibility System, an increasing number of village women won the struggle for control over household finances.

During my stay in the village, residents, particularly men, commonly claimed that women were the "family managers" (*dang jia*). The family manager traditionally meant s/he ran the practical affairs of a family—organizing production tasks, directing errands, handling finances, and making most everyday decisions about consumption, investments and expenditures (Ruf, 1998:34). However, closer investigation showed it to be otherwise. It was ostensibly not true for most women, or not for everything cited above.

In the case of Ao Village, women's *dang jia* mainly meant that women kept household money in their hands rather than really control the family wealth. Although husbands asked for money from their wives in most households, it was men who mostly deployed household resources in the name of household interests, exerting more control over economic affairs, investments, and expenditures than women did. In addition, it was widely acknowledged that men spent more money on their personal consumption for tobacco, tea and wine. There was no denying that the traditional view of "men govern the affairs outside the household, while women govern the affairs inside" remained prevalent in the community. No wonder, women often put it in a local idiom, they were merely "the temporary wealth god" or "*guo lu cai sheng*".

The problem of budgetary arrangement was far more complicated than it appeared on the surface. As both income and expenditure were pooled, it was difficult to determine exactly how much money was under the control of women. Although their husbands might turn over almost all cash income to them, many women probably had decision-making power over only a very limited portion of the family budget, with which they could buy their personal and family daily items, such as shoes and clothing without the knowledge and agreement of their husbands. The control was also differentiated depending on the wealth of households. There were clearly considerable variations in managerial competence among women. In some households, only when men migrated out of the village did women take full control over household budgets. A small minority of women, as the case of Yang Baoqin, had been the de facto *dan jia* ever since their marriage, and possessed considerable discretion over domestic income and other matters. To my knowledge, apart from keeping the family assets, a few young women retained their own separate accounts-mostly the bride payment that they brought with them to the marriage, as their own personal funds, known in standard Mandarin as *si fang qian* (Zhang, 2000: 65).

However, much to my surprise, when I asked women about the annual household income, a small minority of women had no idea at all and told me to ask their husband about it, even though they were the "*dang jia*". Indeed, women's *dang jia* role was often constrained by their illiteracy. I was told a small minority of women could not count money, nor could they distinguish a paper note of 5RMB from 50RMB.

Keeping the family purse in a conjugal family provided a space for women to assert their agency. They saved as much money as possible by carefully budgeting family expenditures. Women sometimes could refuse to give the money, that they kept, to their husbands for an expenditure on which they disagreed. From this perspective, even this "nominal" control represented a partial reversal of patriarchal authority within the household, signaling a symbolic, if not real, economic power for women. This was paralleled by women's increased economic autonomy vis-à-vis their husband. Many women wielded a significant amount of power over domestic affairs. This was evidenced in the fact that they had a great deal of input into agricultural production and its decision-making processes at the household level. On numerous occasions, women told me that in spite of their husband's objections to watering cornfields, they insisted on doing it since no irrigation meant poorer harvest, and hence miserable earnings.

When I asked the major reasons for women's increased role in household budgetary arrangements, many informants attributed it to the visible value of women's labor and their earning power, the absence of men, and the nature of women's management of money. Men were often perceived to have no concern for saving money. For instance, a young male trader drove his truck to do some small trading beyond the village most of the year. To prevent him from squandering money freely, his wife always went to "help" him as much as possible.

Dividing the Household (*fen jia*)

Household division was also an important factor that shaped natural resource use. Before Liberation, landlord families normally kept extended patrilineal families. Brothers in poor households did not often live separately after they got married. It was not until the land reform when villagers were granted land of their own that things began to change. During the long collective period, the male household head maintained considerable power and authority over the members of his family, trying to keep a large household. The elder sons often split off from their parents' household after their younger brothers took in wives. The household head benefited from co-inhabitation, and thus the family's primary resource—the young couple's labor and their income from collective labor. Normally, at least one son's family, usually that of the youngest son, remained in the parents' house. Not until the last few years of collectivization, when a few young women rebelled against elder male authority, did this pattern begin to shift. From that time on, Ao Village was split into increasingly smaller households. As of 2003, it was fashionable for young people to leave parental households as early as possible and set up their own nuclear conjugal families.

As elsewhere in the Chinese countryside, women in Ao Village historically took up post-marital residence with their parents-in-law. The timing of separation varied over time in the period of 1980-2003. The generation that got married around decollectivization tended to move out of their parental households a few years after marriage. Young people who married in the 1990s tended to live separately at, or shortly after the marriage. Even in those households with only one son, or merely the youngest son, newly married couples left parental households and lived separately.

In 2003, there were around 14 households that remained undivided.[1] These households maintained decent, if not harmonious, intergenerational interactions and cooperation. In such households, either the older or younger generation managed household finances, which often excluded the other generation from having an independent income of their own. Only in rare cases was what young couples earned kept for their own consumption. The existing extended families fell into the following categories. In the first case, the parental households were relatively prosperous and thus the younger generation was unwilling to leave. In

1 Field data from various locations throughout rural China demonstrate that early separation was a fairly common pattern in rural society.

the second case, two generations temporarily lived together before a new house was completed. In this circumstance, co-habitation tended to diminish the enthusiasm of young people to work hard for the household. In the third instance, the children of the younger generation were very young or the husband migrated out of the village for wage labor. In the last category, the daughters-in-law were "obedient women." Generally, most extended households could still manage domestic relations satisfactorily.

Generational conflicts among family members figured prominently in village discourse. Older people complained that young women were too greedy and domineering, and consequently, their married sons did not listen to them but instead to their wives. Elder women at the margins always stressed how they respected the authority of their parents-in-law and sincerely took care of them in the earlier times. Numerous anecdotes were heard about young women's conflicts with their in-laws. In most cases, it was young women who initiated early family division, reflecting their aspirations for independence. It was reported that some of them intentionally made trouble to pressure for separation, pushing their husband behind the scene, while others employed more subtle strategies.

The threat of divorce or departure was sometimes used as a strategy or a signal to force or speed up a family division. Some married women stayed in their natal families for a prolonged period of time. In autumn of 2003, the daughter-in-law from one of the most impoverished households disappeared suddenly after she visited her relatives one day, leaving behind a son of four years old. Before departure, she had already expressed her wishes to live separately, but the household was too poor to afford another house.

One day, I went with other women to console the family members of the household at their house. The whole family regretted deeply they had not taken her threat more seriously. They spent quite some time searching for her everywhere, without any result. It seemed to come as no surprise to many residents. The village conversation was then focused predominantly on two topics: first, she must have fled out of the household intentionally to escape impoverishment; second, if she was "sold" by others, she wouldn't be able to return home because she knew no Chinese characters.

There were unavoidable disputes in the process of household division, which sometimes further deepened the split between the older and younger generations.

Some households divided up the household property on a per capita basis, while in others, the older generation was "driven out of the house with little assets." After division, some households maintained close economic and social ties with one another, and even lived in peace under one roof. While in others, there were weak, and even hostile relations and constant frictions. A few residents even openly spoke against each other. Especially when they shared the same courtyard, livestock sometimes "created" troubles between them. This helped to explain why most divided households preferred to live separately in different courtyards.

The following case illustrated some of the problems mentioned above quite clearly. Zhang Guisheng, mentioned in Chapter four and six, was sixty-nine years old in 2003. He asserted himself to be once "a team leader-like person." He came from the largest lineage in the community, and enjoyed the seniority in his kinship group. He was formerly one of the most influential ceremony managers in the community. The Zhang couple had three daughters and two sons. All but the eldest daughter—the former women's director—married and lived in the village. The Zhang couple lived with the family of their youngest son for less than one year. Initially, the older and younger generations were merely unhappy with each other. After the Zhang couple was "driven out" by their daughter-in-law "with nothing", they had to search for a shelter. Originally, they borrowed an abandoned house to live in and were later granted a small piece of a house site of 0.5 *mu* to build a tiny mud house themselves.

In an angry mood, he recalled that he was then feeling extremely frustrated because the separation so shamed him. He felt that he had lost face in the village society and became silent for several years afterwards. During my stay in Ao Village in 2003, a township housing staff member came down to solicit the housing fee from those households that lived separately without approval. Zhang Guisheng complained to me one day, "Who does not wish to live with his children and enjoy a happy old age? But looking around you, it is totally no good to live together with the younger generation. In my heart, I treated my sons and daughters the same, but my daughter-in-law blamed us for having partiality for our daughters. We have sacrificed everything for them, including my daughters' marriage payments. How could she (his daughter-in-law) be so conscienceless! Even our grandchildren do not greet us properly. I just can't understand how things could have turned downward that way in these days. Now we have lost the capacity to work and become valueless to them, we would rather pay the extra housing fee than to live with them again!"

The growing popularity of household division between older and younger generations contributed partly to the enhancement of young women's status within their conjugal households at the expense of senior people. Without the help of their parents, young men could not create new families by themselves. Parents in Ao Village sacrificed a lot for their sons in the intergenerational property transmission, rendering themselves into unfavorable circumstances (for more discussion see Chapter nine). Not surprisingly, not only was the authority of senior people eroded, they were sometimes discarded by their own grown and married children. As in the case of the Zhang couple, they could not even claim the share of family wealth that they had accumulated in their lifetime. As we shall see below, some young women selflessly made sacrifices for their own juniors, yet they sometimes mistreated their elders. When household division reduced the size of household, it also stimulated house building as well as further land fragmentation. Household division, as a result, seriously threatened elder care and financial security among the senior generation.

Economic Security and Inheritance Patterns

The post-reform period witnessed a reversal of the status of the senior generation, especially that of senior men, in Ao Village and its vicinity. They had lived through those years of hard times under the collective regimes, and were still the most vulnerable segment in the community. Female elders always stressed, they ate "much bitterness" throughout their lives, whereas male elders strongly felt that they were marginal to the authority and power within the household and beyond, especially for those who were once authority figures, long-serving team or brigade leaders. Most elders complained bitterly there were no filial sons and few had great respect for "worthless" old persons. "You are lucky if your daughters-in-law do not find fault with you," an elder woman said bitterly. Most senior people felt lonely, that's why in the west village, a cluster of elder people often gathered together to chat with each other under the shadow of trees and houses.[1]Even in this marginalized segment, men sometimes still held certain authority over their wives. In the case of Zhang Guisheng, he enjoyed a prerogative of eating better and working less than his wife. Elder women were thus in the weakest position. The disadvantages of senior

1 I do not imply all sons treated their parents badly. In reality, some sons and their wives addressed their parents with respect and a few older men still wielded undisputable authority within their households.

people grew out of their lack of economic security, which in turn, exaggerated their vulnerability.[1]

In the absence of social support, villagers in Ao Village like the overwhelming majority of rural people in China, depended predominantly upon their sons as a major form of social security in old age. Sons were bound, by law and custom, to guarantee the financial well being of their aged parents. Despite the legal recognition of equal rights between women and men in property inheritance, and thus parental support, the local practice of property inheritance[2] at play was that sons—especially the youngest son who lived with their parents—bore the primary responsibility of supporting their parents in their old age. He also enjoyed the rights to the family estate, which were little more than a house of residence, a garden and some furnishings. Under customary law, women, married or unmarried, were not entitled to inherit family property.

Only occasionally did the obligation of taking care of older parents fall on the daughter, especially if the aged parents had no sons or had bad relations with their sons. For example, after the husband of Jiang Mei died, she brought her youngest daughter with her to remarry a village man against the will of her sons. For some time, her three sons refused to accept her. In 2003, she lived alone in a small clay house not far away from her married daughter's. The family of her daughter treated her quite well. They tilled her share of ration land and provided her with grain, fuel and other necessities. Her three sons were each supposed to provide her 60RMB per year. She had intensive interactions with her daughter and her family, while having weak relationships with two of her three sons. Her youngest son, who headed one of the most prosperous households in the village, once, tore a note of 50RMB in her face in a dispute to show their unwillingness to support her. Jiang Mei fainted suddenly during the insult. After she recovered, she sought the help of township officials to seek medical compensation and "old age" support. As of 2003, she and her youngest son were still not speaking with each other.

Abandoned mud houses were readily available in the neighborhood, which made it possible for elder residents to live apart from their married children. To the best of

1 I discovered that a social hierarchy based on generation (*bei fen*) was more or less weakened, even though the custom of forehead-to the-floor kowtowing (locally called *ke tou*) to the senior generation was still maintained among some households during the lunar New Year.

2 For a discussion of patrilineal inheritance and property management in China, see Cohen (1993).

my knowledge, in 2003, a total of four single people and approximately 13 couples lived separately from their married sons or daughters. Most of them were poverty-stricken, residing in one-room dwellings conspicuously bare of possessions. Their shares of ration land were mostly tilled by their sons, who in turn, provided them with grain, fuels or other services for exchange, either individually or in rotation. Only a small minority of elders livingly separately planted the fields themselves. I was struck to know a few of them were badly treated by their children.

For example, an aged father of seventy-three years old in 2003, had four married children in the community—two sons and two daughters. All his children were living in less poor households and enjoyed relatively comfortable lives, yet neither of his sons wanted to assume the burden of supporting the elder father. In 2003, I saw the little house where the father lived by himself. He shared a courtyard with the family of his eldest son. While I was staying there in 2003, I heard the aged father was still busy with gathering fuel for the forthcoming winter. By the time of my return visit in 2004, he had already passed away.

Another example resembled this case. A Mongol elder couple had three grown sons and two daughters. All of their sons and one daughter married and lived in Ao Village. Like their Han peers, they were living in a separate mud house not far away from those of their married sons. Initially, they lived with the family of the youngest son for a few years after the latter married. Their daughter-in-law insisted on splitting the household and threatened divorce otherwise. After the couple resided and ate separately, none of their sons initially wanted to provide them with financial support. One of their sons requested that the old couple parcel out their woodlot to three of them in exchange for their support. Village officials were later called in to decide the responsibilities of each son. The couple allocated equal shares of about 3 *mu* of woodlot holding and their ration land to the three sons (daughters had no share of it), who in turn, each guaranteed the following annual support for the couple: 100 catties of flour; 50 catties of rice; 10 catties of soybean; some millet, and 360 RMB of cash. However, the promised supply seldom materialized in time or in sufficient amount. Fortunately, the couple still had grain stocks and their married daughter residing not far away often offered some help. Their third son's marriage did not last very long, and he was living with his ten years old daughter in 2003.

Many seniors referred to "begging" for money from their sons as very difficult, exposing a striking sense of frustration and hopelessness among them. Constrained by their cash-earning capacities in the labor market, the only way to supplement the meager cash provided by their children was to resort to certain communal resources to harvest a little money—collecting Chinese herbs or whatever could be sold at the market. Elder women seemed to be more actively involved in these kind of cash-earning activities, since they had relatively good health (perhaps it was because they were often a few years younger than their husbands). Physical disability and disease further increased their vulnerability. This somewhat supported the views of "the demise of social mores" in this community, and more broadly in larger society. I heard about many similar and even dismal stories in Ao Village's vicinity. The plight of senior people often received publicity in the region, as illustrated by the frequent reports featured in local newspapers.

Domestic Politics

The Chinese family was long officially constructed as cooperative, harmonious and egalitarian. However, as in other rural societies in the global "South", although not always conflicting, household relations were always negotiated along gender, generation, and age lines (Agarwal, 1994; Carney and Watts, 1990; Hart, 1991; Schroeder, 1999). Historically, the strife between mother-in-law and daughter-in-law was constructed as a key domestic conflict. With the advent of household farming, domestic politics were characterized increasingly by generation and gender-based conflicts. As noted above, women in Ao Village challenged the authority and power not only of their in-laws, but also that of their husbands on a daily basis.

Conjugal friction and even struggles proliferated and figured prominently since the 1990s. Given limited household resources, almost all social and economic decisions made at the household level usually involved careful negotiations between husband and wife, which produced various conflicts. In Ao Village, the tensions between husband and wife frequently revolved around expenditure disposition, labor and resource allocation, gambling,[1] and alcoholism. Rural Chinese women were historically glorified for their self-sacrificing spirit. Yet a phenomenon that warrants mention was that compared to the past, many women might be willing to make self-sacrifices for their own children, but not their husbands.

1 Gambling was rife in a few Yunnan villages that I visited and there were even public casinos in the community. But in Ao Village, only a small minority of men squandered money in poker games, especially during the period of the lunar New Year.

One morning shortly after I settled into the village, I witnessed a fierce conjugal quarrel that erupted on the village street not far from my host's home. A Mongol couple scolded each other face to face in public. The man drank alcohol not only at home, but also in the grocery store on an almost daily basis. His wife was a *"dang jia"* at home, yet according to the village gossips, the man could always "cheat" money out of her. His wife had no way to prevent him from spending money on liquor, which often sparked off many family quarrels. That morning, before going to work in the field, the man drank a bottle of beer in the grocery store. His wife could not stand it any more and picked a fight with him. During my stay in Ao Village, I observed several similar conjugal confrontations. Compared to the past, women no longer hesitated to challenge their husbands for their unwise practices, privately and even publicly.

Although wife beating could not be said to be a common practice in the village, it occurred occasionally. Du Fang, thirty-six years old with a son aged 19, was one of the rare victims of wife beating. She and her husband were both born and grew up in Ao Village. They fell in love, independently of family arrangements, and got married when Du Fang was seventeen years old. Her husband had a bad temper and did not hesitate to resort to physical violence once they were married. Occasionally, she was beaten black and blue. The family of three workers was not prosperous. In 2002, Du Fang ran away from the village after being beaten and found a job in a restaurant in the county town. With the help of Qi Women's Federation, she later traveled to Beijing to work as a domestic servant in 2003.

At the request of her husband, she returned to Ao Village for her son's engagement in late 2003 after working in Beijing for half a year. I met her several times, and she impressed me as a capable and articulate woman. She was empowered by broadened horizons through her experiences of working in the city for half a year. When Du Fang was at home, she assumed most of the household chores. Her husband was known to be quite lazy. When she was absent, he leased out four of their six *mu* of paddy fields and hired others to graze their small sheep herd.

While I was staying in the village one day, Du Fang quarreled with her husband, and an open confrontation ensued. She accused him of being lazy. Her husband scolded her for earning "dirty" money outside. He shouted at her and furiously scratched some hairs from her head. She angrily fled to the home of her natal brother in the community. A week later, the Party secretary as well as some of her kin went to persuade her to return home. This episode further poisoned their conjugal relationships. True to her word, she left for Beijing again after the lunar New Year. Some residents predicted that Du Fang's husband would ultimately share the lot of Wu Yin—another abusive husband who had been left behind without a wife for over a decade.

This was by no means an exception in Ao Village and its vicinity, where a small minority of men took advantage of women's smaller stature or differences in physical strength to express their power. In the case of Du Fang, her husband's use of violence exposed his sense of powerlessness and frustration over her migration. As one of Du Fang's relatives pointed out, "married male migrants are essentially 'rotten' persons (low quality men) and it was impossible for them to flee away with other women. As opposed to men, female married migrants who could find a job in the city were normally capable women. Husbands were always unwilling to let their wives migrate alone." Unlike in the collective past, there were more complicated conjugal negotiations and confrontations in day-to-day lives within the household. But sometimes, women intentionally exhibited submissive behavior to their husbands to avoid unnecessary or direct confrontations between husband and wife.

Gender and Education among Villagers

Education was a remarkable example of women's disadvantages in their daily lives, which affected their capabilities in natural resource use and management. Shortly after my arrival in Ao Village, I learned from the women's director over a chat that her elder sister had never had any opportunity to attend school. However, when I checked the village record, I discovered the status of her elder sister's education was recorded as junior high school.[1] The same was true of many others. Hong Xiang finished his fourth grade, but his education was recorded as junior high school, whereas illiterate Song Ling was recorded as having completed primary education. Disturbed by the great discrepancy in actual and recorded educational

1 In the village record, the education status of residents was recorded as illiterate, primary school, junior high school or senior high school. For the students studying at school, it was recorded as primary school, junior or senior high school. In this context, it was impossible to identify which grade they completed. Compared with my own survey on education, I found the recorded educational status was artificially raised. A former cadre confessed to me, the higher-level governments constantly imposed the task of eliminating illiteracy. If the educational levels were recorded too low, the village committee would be burdened with the task of combating illiteracy. While I was staying in the village, I heard two high school graduates—a man and a woman—were paid by village cadres to attend a literacy examination to cope with the high-up requirements.

status, I decided to investigate it more thoroughly myself. Table 7.1 summarizes the education status among adult villagers by my own survey in 2003.

Table 7.1 shows an upward trajectory of educational status among residents, males and females, indicating tremendous progress in rural education. There were 374 people of 20 and above among 146 resident households. The average schooling among female residents of 20 and above was three years, as against 4.4 years among their male counterparts. As of 2003, residents valued the education of both sons and daughters more than ever before. Children of either sex enjoyed universal primary school education with little discrimination against women. No matter how hard it was, parents voluntarily sacrificed themselves to struggle hard to put their children through school. Of 84 teenagers aged 10-19, the average schooling was 6.6 years for girls and 6.7 for boys.

Young unmarried women were the most educated group, yet an overwhelming majority of them withdrew from junior high school before they completed this level of education. In 2003, only eight teenagers-four boys and four girls-continued to study beyond the level of junior high school. The frequently cited reasons for quitting school include: insufficient economic support, poor school performance, and little motivation or interest in school. Since the rural reform, six young men, as opposed to three young women, attended college. Children of teachers, officials, or rich residents had more opportunities to move on to higher levels of education, and thereby leave the fields.

Table 7.1 Education among Adult Residents by Gender and Age Cohorts

Age Cohorts	Females		Males	
	No. of persons	Years of educations	No. of persons	Years of education
20-29	46	6.0	44	6.2
30-39	42	6.0	55	6.0
40-49	40	3.1	38	6.1
50-59	25	1.2	37	4.1
60-69	13	1.5	15	3.4
70+	9	0.3	10	0.3
	175	3.0	199	4.4

Source: 2003 household survey.

The educational level of women of different age cohorts varied sharply. School attendance for the age cohort under 40 was similar between men and women. A disproportionately larger number of middle-aged women, either married-in or native women, who grew up in the 1950s were entirely illiterate. A total of 71 residents had never attended school, with 51 persons, or 71 percent are females and 34 of them belong to the 40-59 age group. The mean number of years at school for 65 women aged 40-59 (who were born in the years from 1944-63) was 2.2. When they were girls, their parents did not perceive the importance of educating a daughter who would marry out and leave the family. A popular Chinese proverb vividly captured the idea, "A married out daughter is like split water."

It was, therefore, popularly believed that there was no use taking a girl to school. Additionally, their labor was highly needed at the home and in collective labor to sustain families. Many women of that generation mentioned they failed to attend school due to family difficulties, nevertheless, however hard it was, their male counterparts in the same age cohort completed more or less schooling. By 2003, middle-aged women were the major workers in the village and household economy, yet their mobility and income-earning potential were severely hampered by their lack of education. While I was staying in the village, I heard numerous stories regarding the embarrassing illiteracy among them; they frequently remarked, "We grew up before the kitchen range, and will die behind it. Even when we wander in the county town, we may not know how to get back." This ignorance due to immobility and spatial constraint was quite remarkable in women's narratives.

Married women were always overwhelmed by heavy work burdens upon marriage, and never had any opportunity to study in their daily practice. That's why many women who had already attended school for a few years before marriage frequently noted, "What we learned have been eaten up with the meal!" This phenomenon was probably quite common among rural women in the Chinese countryside. In a few initial focus group discussions administered in Yunnan and Sichuan provinces in my 2002 fieldtrips, we required villagers to answer some questions in a written form. In spite of wrong characters throughout their statements, most men could express their basic ideas. By contrast, women were totally "frightened" by the requirement, and most middle-aged women could not even write their own names (Hu, 2002). In daily practice, it was male household heads who utilized their names when they dealt with village cadres or outsiders. Women's names were always "useless" and not counted even on the ritual occasions.[1]

The testimonies offered by Zhang Huamin, an outspoken woman boasting herself of knowing village women quite well after serving as a women's director for 28 years in Greater Ao Village, illustrated many topics around gender relations in the village, the political economy of gender, intergenerational conflicts, and the rather androcentric village life:

> Nowadays, the price of women's improved status is that they work harder and harder, and thus endure more hardships than men do. Married women are destined to live a slave-like life of hard toil. For example, women work alongside their male counterparts, doing the same kinds of field labor, and even learning how to plow, but their domestic responsibilities remain basically unchanged. After husband and wife return home from the field, women had to prepare the meal, while men might lie down on the *kang,* or sit to smoke. If there is a reversal, women might be overwhelmed by village gossip, being blamed to be unable to live industriously and frugally. I am sure in nine out of ten households women are more tired than men. Fortunately, thanks to the family planning programs to control the family size, women's physical and financial burdens of childrearing have been lessened. Married women had little experience outside agriculture, or more broadly, beyond the village. If they move out, they might become homesick. The prevalent attitudes still prevent them from moving out. Males refuse it out of the fear that they run the risk of losing their wives. That's why there are always village discourses that labeled what married women earn beyond the village as "unclean" money.
>
> Women now play a pivotal role in determining the prospects of a household. It is widely acknowledged that a home is not like a home without a married woman. As a common expression puts it, "the bad or good fortunes of a household are all up to a capable woman." Indeed, most women take the major responsibility for many practical affairs in daily life.

---

1 Men's names were recorded in the list of guests and gift presenters in the ritual context such as weddings and funerals, even in a woman's natal family.

> However, some "big matters"[1] such as financial transactions have been conventionally perceived as men's responsibility. Consistent with this view and even under this name, it's all right for men to stroll in the neighborhood without being questioned. Although most men now hand over income to their wives and request money from the latter, it is quite common that men have a final say in how money is spent. I believe nine tenths of women are the typical "money keepers." Even if they are real *dang jia*, the money that they actually control is quite limited. Many of them manage household resources carefully, but they are begrudged every penny to spend for themselves, even if money is in their own hands. There is no denying that men spend more money for themselves on alcohol, cigarettes or tea.
>
> If you have son(s), you must think of accumulating wealth before he comes of age. Since a daughter-in-law marries into the household, multiple frictions may otherwise have arisen if the parents-in-law do not comply with her ideas. This generation of young women is so aggressive, they want to have a final say in family affairs and never feel satisfied. The breakup of a marriage will render parents-in-law at risk for losing not only the bride, but also all the hard-won money spent. No one wants his/her son to be a "bare stick." For this reason, parents-in-law are obliged to bear all her greedy requirements. The world has been totally changed today!

After Liberation, China introduced extensive legislation to promote equality between men and women; however, there has always existed a divergence between official ideology and actual practices. As illustrated by the above testimonies, the traditional notions of masculinity/femininity still played a part in naturalizing gender inequality. Conventional gender stereotypes, albeit being weakened, died hard in real life. The view of "men superior, women inferior" was absorbed into everyday practices and internalized among some women. I was so struck by the following remarks of a former female teacher, who noted that, "males are the household heads, they are supposed to be in charge of 'big businesses' in the extra-familial sphere, whereas women should act as storekeepers. Women's physical mobility is

1 Unlike in many other rural areas, in Ao Village and its vicinity, a matchmaker was most often an elderly or senior man.

confined to home and even the neighborhood, how can they know everything? If a man cannot control his wife, how could he establish his authority before others in the village?" The traditional stereotype like "women have long hair but short intelligence" also was prevalent. As of 2003, men were still occasionally identified as the "lord" or "master" (*dong jia,* which refers to former landlords in the pre-Liberation period by laborers) by their wives or perceived as the pillar of a house (*ding liang zhu*). No wonder, when we talked about women's improved status, a retired male village cadre commented with frustration, "The household head now should be switched to women."

These findings resonated with what I found in south China as well as coinciding with what other scholars have described across rural China (Jacka, 1997; Judd, 1994). This reminded me of a point made by Davin (1995: 29), who argued that, "The inequality of women is rooted in family structures, and that as these structures have been reinforced by recent economic policy, it is unrealistic to think that such inequality will be eliminated in the near future."

Inter-household Relationships in Practice

In the following section, I will analyze inter-village interactions, more specifically, agricultural cooperation and daily conflicts in natural resource use and management in the social landscape of the community. With regard to social networks in China, Fei Xiaotong's insight on the "differentiated mode of association" (*cha xu ge ju*) ([1947] 1992: 25-33) is very useful. His argument made over half a century ago-Chinese society was organized by concentrical *guan xi* circles, extending from the family (the core), to relatives, friends, and so on—seemed still applicable to the rural community like Ao Village. Before dealing with household interactions, I briefly examine the changing institutions of marriage and kinship system,[1]which were essential in access and control over labor and physical resources in the social networks of Ao Village.

Physical Environments and the Bride Recruitment

In Ao Village, all postmarital residence, with only one exception, was virilocal or patrilocal. Upon marriage, it was the bride who left her own natal family and community, and came to live in her husband's. In the only uxorilocal marriage,

1 Only in rare cases did villagers view those who shared a common surname as kin.

locally called *dao cha men,*[1] a Han man married into a Mongolian household eight years ago from Lan Village. His mother-in-law died during childbirth in 1974 and his father-in-law had no son but two daughters. After he took up residence with his wife's family, he did not get along very well with his father-in-law. In the summer of 2003, the married-in man moved back to Lan Village with his wife and daughter, while his father-in-law was left behind to live by himself. The old man explained to me that he had totally failed in arranging his daughter's marriage.

His departure reinforced the idea in the community that uxorilocal marriage was not a solution to sonlessness. Many residents did not consider uxorilocal marriage a preferred form of marriage. They insisted that only those men of low quality or without means of selecting proper spouses would be willing to accept this kind of arrangement. Between 1999 and 2004, at least 7 young men, as was the case of my host's eldest son Hong Jun, married into other communities.

As elsewhere, a groom's family or village was expected to be of somewhat higher status than that of the bride's. In this part of rural China, the marriage strategies were not only socially and economically determined, but also shaped by physical conditions. Given the universal impoverishment in the region, physical environments had long played an important role in local marriage exchange. Many residents maintained that in a place with only dry land, men could not easily secure their wives outside the village. A woman once told me, "Not until the availability of irrigated fields, especially domestic wells, did Ao Village begin to gain a reputation in the surrounding areas. Word spread quickly that the residents in Ao Village were improving their harsh lives. Since then, it has become relatively easy for Ao Village to import daughters from neighboring villages into the community, and bachelors have been correspondingly reduced. And even the daughters of village leaders got married within the community. At one time, Ao Village almost became an "affinal village" with affinal teams. Huang (1989) described a similar situation in a village in Fujian province.

Altogether, there were 176 married women including widows in Ao Village in 2003. Bride recruitment by natal origin indicated that slightly more than one fourth of married women, 47 of them, to be exact, belonged to endogamous marriage, accounting for 26.7%. Among intra-village marriages, 10 women (21%) were in the

1 The term "*dao cha men*" carried derogatory connotations. For a description of the negative connotations of the practice, see Bossen (2002).

20-29 age group; 11 (23%) in the 30-39 age group, 12 (26%) in 40-49 age group; 6 (13%) in 50-59 age group; 5 (11%) in 60-69 age group and 3 (6%) in the 70-81 age group. Endogamy was practiced consistently for several generations without stopping, and a significant increase in village endogamy occurred in the post-reform period.

The local pattern of marriage flow indicated that marriages in Ao Village mostly occurred within the village and its vicinity. Among all married women, 34 or 19.3 percent came from Lan Village. 47.7 percent or almost half of village women came from Greater Village and Lan Village—4 kilometers north. Strangely enough, other hamlets in Greater Ao Village supplied few brides to Ao Village, which in turn, provided few for them. To my knowledge, only two married-in women came from Hamlet B and one from Hamlet C. Altogether, a total 139 women, nearly 80 percent, came from different villages within a 20-kilometer radius under the administration of Lan Township. The remaining 20 percent came from some adjoining townships, and only five women came from other provinces. Among women with "distant" marriages, two fled to the village in the pre-Liberation period. Women who married within their home village had the advantages of networking (*guan xi*) and having local knowledge of surrounding natural resources. For in-married women, moving into Ao Village might dilute their relations with their natal kin or communities. However, since these women did not relocate too far away, they still could retain close connections with their natal families.

In this part of China, people drew heavily upon their own resources to get through the hard period during the collective period. Given the near universal poverty among the rural populations, an abundance of natural resources in a community such as sufficient availability of firewood or water, could become a crucial, if not the only factor, in determining bride recruitment. A large percentage of women married into Ao Village from Lan Village (consisting of two natural villages) were intimately related to this factor. Ao Village was endowed with plentiful resources and flat land. By contrast, Lan Village lacked adequate natural resources for its residents' subsistence. During the collective period, Hamlet B tended to secure brides from more remote, impoverished communities in its neighboring areas, while Hamlet C mainly attracted brides from an adjoining village that severely lacked firewood. During the reform period, Lan Village became more prosperous than Ao Village, but it was characterized by more remarkable economic differentiation. The administrative village had a population of over 2,000, yet only owned about two thirds of the surface land of Greater Ao Village. By 2003, some Lan Village residents still relied on Ao Village to get firewood and Chinese herbs. The village statistical records did not show where women who married out of the village went. I guess more daughters of Ao Village should have married into Lan Village since the advent of the reform. The intermarriages between these two villages allowed the brides to marry out without moving to a totally strange locality. Instead, the bride exchange and affinal ties promoted intensive social interactions and economic cooperation among numerous households in Ao Village and Lan Village.

Kinship Networks as a Resource

In Ao Village, most residents were enmeshed in an intimate web of kin relations—patrilineal kin, affines, matrilateral relatives and so forth. Following Bourdieu (1977), and many other scholars (Judd, 1994; Liu, 2000; Yan, 1996), I use the concept of "practical kinship" to indicate how kinship was in practice operated and manipulated in the changing setting of the rural community. As in most other rural communities, kinship-based interactions and practices in Ao Village were highly significant in everyday life and at times of crisis. During the household visits, I always met residents other than the members of specific households, and most of them were their kin in one way or another. I was always confused by the kinship terms used frequently and the crosscutting kin networks among the dwellers, especially those who were distantly related. The frequently happened *chuan men* (means to drop by somebody's home) of men and women in the neighborhood within their respective kinship group mirrored the intensive kinship interactions.

Villagers in Ao Village tapped into their intra-village social network to access and control a variety of natural resources. What Ruf (1998:120) observed in a Sichuan village could apply to Ao Village as well, "kinship, affinity, friendship, and other forms of social organization continued to provide the basis for interfamily associations and alliances, and were of great importance to the structuring of power and status among local families." No wonder, the wife of Dong Fu always highlighted there were only two Mongol households of its surname, and this helped to explain why they were disadvantaged in access to village resources. For those residents whose patrilineal network was small, they actively invested in maintaining ritual kinship. It was quite common for many villagers to be godparents (*yang fu mu*) to each other's children.

As is well known, the lineage system was a distinctive and prominent feature of Chinese rural societies in the pre-Liberation period. As elsewhere, the economic foundation and organizational structure of lineage networks were systematically dismantled and replaced with collective farming and village administration. In some rural localities in south China, the implementation of the HRS ensured a return to the patrilineal extended family as the basic economic and social unit (see Potter and Potter, 1990). In Ao Village, although patrilineal groups survived into the post-reform era, they were not as strong as they had been prior to or during the collective period.

Ao Village was a multi-surname community. Out of 161 households in 2003, there were a total of 41 agnate groups, belonging to 27 surnames.[1]Among them, six dominant agnate groups consisting of over seven households, amounted to 63 households, or 39 percent of all the households in the village. A total of 25 agnate groups had only two households or less. The two largest patrilineal groups, respectively, consisted of 14 households. The Zhang agnate group with 48 persons was the largest Han descent grouping, whereas the Zhao agnate group with 47 people was the largest Mongolian grouping. These two surname groups represented at least 17.4 percent of all village households. In the Zhang agnate group concentrated in the west village, three out of its four daughters in two generations married men from other large Han surname groups. Among them, one daughter's husband long served as a village cadre and even a Party secretary.

The Zhang agnate group therefore long enjoyed an advantageous kinship and social ties. As in the cases of Liu Xing, analyzed in Chapter four and Zhang Xuejun, mentioned in Chapter six kin-based power and support played a key part in their economic success and prosperity. I was told on many occasions, when any of the households in this numerically largest surname group hosted a family ceremony, at least one third of the village population would take part in the ritual. In late 2003, one household held a betrothal ritual for their son. It was true, on my arrival at their house that morning, a chaotic crowd was already gathering inside and outside the host's house. I discovered most of them were the agnate kinsmen of the host family. When a big bus carrying a large team of bride senders arrived, approximately 200-

1 The amount of agnate and surname groups in the village were counted according to the surnames of the household heads.

300 people stood outside to watch it.

By contrast, in the Zhao agnate group living in the east village, two of its daughters married men from less influential surname groups. In spite of the historical prominence of the Zhao groupings before Liberation, in 2003, their descendents were economically and socially marginalized in the community. Since decollectivization, four out of five Han agnate groups in the community produced a Party secretary. These few elite males once dominated village economic and political life. They allegedly manipulated kin relations to their advantage and brought tangible benefits to the members of their own groupings. In spite of potential conflicts and complex mediation among them, it was reported that the members of a few dominant agnate groups always stuck together to further their common interests.

As in many multi-surname villages, marriage was the main means of strengthening social and economic ties among villagers. Affines, or *qin qi,* as opposed to agnates, or *fu xi qin shu* were created through wives and daughters' marriages.[1] The centrality of affinal ties was pronounced among some men. Given relatively common endogamy, a large percentage of men like Liu Xing maintained strong ties with their wives' agnate kin. Many women like Yang Baoqin also kept close relationships with her matri-kin in day-to-day life.[2] The outflow of males from the village greatly strengthened women's informal networks—the ties of mother-daughter, sister-sister, daughter-in-law and mother-in-law, and distantly related women outside kinship circles such as neighbor and friend.

Household Interactions: Cooperation and Conflicts

As anywhere in rural China, farm households in Ao Village were embedded in a wider network of the extended family, kin, neighbor, friend, and even patron–client relationships. In the indigenous context, not only were kinship interactions essential for local life, access to resources—labor, land, other agricultural capital, and broadly speaking, economic opportunities—were shaped by other social networks as well. In spite of a notable shortage of cooperation at the village level as a whole, residents actively built social networks among households as a form of safety net, activating

1 William L. Parish and Martin K. Whyte (1978) *Family and Village in Contemporary China,* Chicago: University of Chicago Press; Elisabeth Croll (1981) *The Politics of Marriage in Contemporary China,* Cambridge: Cambridge University Press.

2 For a detailed description of women's relations with their natal families, see Judd (1989).

a variety of flexible social ties, and simultaneously utilizing a variety of boundary-maintaining mechanisms to distinguish themselves from others (Judd, 1994). As a result, local social networks built on the principle of reciprocity were flexible, selective and loosely connected. Here, I will offer a brief look at two opposite interactions, cooperation and conflicts, among differentially positioned villagers.

After the advent of the rural reforms, farm households enjoyed relative autonomy to manage their own ration land and other natural resources. However, most households were two-generation conjugal families. Massive migration of young adults, coupled with economic diversification, further reduced the size of households. Household supportive networks developed out of a great deal of cooperation, interdependencies and even competition. Residents manipulated various economic ties in their own favor. The changing character of inter-household relations illustrated the adaptation of locals to new circumstances.

Agricultural labor, including familial labor and extra-household labor, were often mobilized via the social relations of agricultural production. The former involved household members working individually or collectively on their own plots. The latter referred to both horizontal labor exchanges among households and hired wage labor. Local wage labor was always characterized by group labor. The hosts might be the village government, individual farm households, township officials, townspeople and others. As far as Ao Village was concerned, the rise of patron-client ties among residents was a fairly rare and new phenomenon, which was quite likely to develop further in the social landscape of the village. The labor processes of all these forms were often arranged along gender lines.

As noted in Chapter four, from the very beginning of household farming, residents maintained labor exchanges among the households with similar socio-economic standing. It was locally known as "*cha huo*", which literally means to enter the partnership, a popular practice in Ao Village and its surrounding areas. Theoretically, it referred to small-scale reciprocal exchanges of labor in spring planting when a series of urgent tasks were performed one after another, farm households took turns helping out one another to save time and improve productivity. According to inhabitants, two or three days' delay in planting might make a big difference, which could even jeopardize the harvest. Work-exchange cooperation made it possible for households, especially those lacking workers to plant rapidly enough to take full advantage of the rainfall. In practice, such cooperation with a great deal of flexibility often extended beyond spring planting to the whole crop growth cycle, and from the farming process to many other spheres. Many households maintained such balanced reciprocal relations for long time.

The composition of the work-exchange groups was highly dynamic. Conflicts of interest or changed conditions among households might lead to disruption and consequently joined or formed other groups of their own choosing. For instance, my host family engaged in labor exchange with the natal family of Song Ling—more specifically, her youngest brother—since decollectivization before a severe quarrel between Song Ling and her brother in 2001. The household of Liu Xing exchanged labor with different households after the advent of household farming: first with a group of four households, then three households, later with the household of the elder sister of Zhang Hualan, and with my host's family since 2002.

The scope of partnership was relatively small. On average, two households and at most four households formed an exchange group. The partnership took into account relationships, laborers and their abilities, landholding, availability of animals and other factors in specific households, although strict reciprocity was sometimes impossible. Smaller groups made it easier to reach consensus in decision-making and be more efficient. In 2004, there was one rare case that four households exchanged work in spring planting. All the four households had paddy fields, and they were obliged to transplant rice almost simultaneously with planting other crops. Households without paddy fields were unwilling to work with them. Furthermore, each household had one to two workers, if they did not cooperate with each other, it would have been difficult for them to plant the crops in time.

Table 7.2 summarizes the types of partnership arrangements in spring planting among 30 sample households in 2004. Over 70 percent of the sample households were involved in labor exchange with their extended family members, kin or neighbors in crop planting. Over half of the remaining households working alone were those households with a big farm. There was a similar percentage of labor exchange among patrilineal and affinal kin. As introduced in Chapter three, a north-south road cut the settlement in half. This geographic division seemed to create two neighborhoods in the community. Few work-exchange groups cut across ethnic boundaries, and even fewer crossed this geographic boundary. The possible explanation was that their land might not be adjacent.

Table 7.2 Inter-household Labor Cooperation in Crop Cultivation (2003) (n=30)

Type of Labor Exchange	No of Household	Percentage(%)
Oneself Only	8	27
Patrilineal Kin	9 [brother (7); parents (2)]	30
Affine and Matrilateral Kin	8 [distant relative (2); affine (1); wife's natal kin (5)]	27
Neighbors	4	13
Others	1[1]	3
Total	30	100

Source: 2004 sample survey

Note: [1] This household cooperated with three other households, which included the household of one of their younger brothers, one daughter and the daughter's parents-in-law.

As elsewhere, increased agricultural production for the market gave rise to an increasing demand for farm labor within the community. In Ao Village, as elsewhere in the region, commercial wage employment developed since the late 1900s. The households with a labor shortfall began to hire field hands as needed during the busiest agricultural periods. The households with large farms increasingly relied upon labor hiring. Although the poor were generally unable to afford hired wage labor, they resorted to it in times of labor shortage as well. During my stay in the village, many residents, female groups in particular, were hired out intermittently in the fields of others inside and outside the village. As of 2003, local people saw no reason to do regular agricultural work free of charge. A household head, who even paid his daughter-in-law for her labor contribution of weeding, told me that there was no difference for him to pay his daughter-in-law living separately and to pay others. "Why not let money flow to the purse of others?" The hidden message was that it was no longer embarrassing to hire his family members to do wage labor.

When asked why market relations penetrated domestic relations, many respondents attributed to a shift in social mores in the region. In the words of villagers, "people are now increasingly lacking affection (*ren qing*)" in the context of the money economy. There are multiple meanings of *ren qing* in the context of rural China. In this case, it referred to "a set of social norms and moral obligations" (see Yan, 1996:123). It was widely assumed that if you asked a favor from helpers, you might feel yourself to be indebted to him/her of *ren qing* (*"qian ren qing"*), who could reclaim the personal debt any time later. In addition, if they asked for free help, the host was supposed to provide at least a free meal, or even a small lunch with beer, which might cost more time and money. The worst thing was that the helpers might have no incentive to speed up their pace if working for free.

With regard to hired laborers, farm owners made prior arrangements with them, who were supposed to work very early in the morning until the day was too dark to continue in the fields. The summer season required a greater time commitment, which lasted for about 11-12 hours, excluding a noon break for an hour or two. If working nearby, the workers returned home for lunch, while if at a distance, they carried food with them. Outside laborers did whatever they were asked to do and took a rest with the permission of the host, who worked alongside with them. As some hired laborers acknowledged, "If you take the money from others, you should work very hard, after all it is not easy for them to pay you the money. If you hold down the speed, the differences will stand out clearly between you and the host working nearby. In this case, you are pressured to work hard." From the perspectives of farm owners, this was a more productive way of mobilizing labor.

Social relations, thereby, began to take on a commercial quality in the village. The daily wage rate rose from 20RMB per day for weeding to 22-25RMB for autumn harvest in 2003. Due to lack of field hands, it rose to 25-28RMB per day during the weeding season in 2004. The opportunities of access to such wage work differed greatly among inhabitants, depending on gender, age, working reputation, interpersonal relations, and even living location in the neighborhood. Villagers from Hamlet B, who grew larger tracts of crop, tended to hire wage laborers from the west village. Those who occupied a central location in the settlement, like my host couple, were more likely to be hired. A small percentage of middle-aged women were quite active as field laborers in the nascent labor market.

However divided among residents, there existed a variety of mutual supports in community life, especially at the critical times. After a young man attempted suicide by drinking several mouthfuls of pesticide in late 2003, one of his neighbors discovered him in time and sent him immediately to a clinic in the township seat. Most male members in his team and other young men from other teams voluntarily took turns to accompany him in the township clinic day and night for almost ten days. Despite radical transformations, a complex system of reciprocal obligations, outside cash transactions, was still at play. Labor exchange in non-direct productive practices was still widely practiced, collectively or individually, among residents for a variety of purposes. Throughout the lean period, residents, male and female, felt obliged to offer free help to each other to build or repair houses or animal sheds, dig wells, or cut short dry fodder. Labor donations in the context of "big occasions" *(da shi)* such as cooking in ritual events or serving guests were commonplace. Female's reciprocal networks played an important part in strengthening household ties.

With regard to intra-household cooperation, there were no notable differences between Han Chinese and Mongols, but there existed pronounced differences between the two Hui households, introduced in Chapter three, and the remaining households. The Hui Muslims are a religious and ethnic minority in China. The fact that they reverted to certain traditional practices after decollectivization deserves special mention. Bai Rong's parents originated from a neighboring province and had retained a high level of ethnic identity since they settled into the community in the early 1950s. Although pork was forbidden to them, a special marker of Hui identity, they seemed adapted to the local context during the long collective period. When they worked and played with Han and Mongols, they accepted food or water from other people. As a big cart manager, when Bai Rong drove out on business, he lived in the inn, and ate whatever food was available. Sometimes, they suffered the misfortunes of a weak minority and a small agnate group within the community. Both Bai Rong and Bai Ru married Hui wives from the villages in the same township.

Since decollectivization, the socially constructed differences between Hui and other residents took on new meanings in response to new socio-economic changes. With the improvement of living standards, they intentionally maintained ethnic boundaries. As a result, the cultural differences between Hui and other residents loomed large. Food preferences overwhelmingly became a sign of their ethnic identity and an important boundary marker. Generally, the two Hui households maintained good relations with their neighbors. They continued to offer food to non-Muslims, but not the reverse, which made it difficult for Han Chinese to return reciprocal gifts to them. Many felt it was difficult to return "affection" to them, which, consequently, somewhat distanced them from the rest of the residents. To the astonishment of villagers, in late 2003, the Bai Rong couple took a Han daughter-in-law from the same community. Many residents marveled at this Hui-Han marriage. It was said that an agreement had been reached that the bride, including her prospective children, wouldn't be allowed to eat food in her native household upon marriage.

It was widely reported that the two Hui households were well known not only for their status as a "real" ethnic minority in the township, but also for their shrewd trading traditions. They had long cultivated good connections with cadres at various levels. It was said that they previously killed cattle every year to treat village cadres, from whom they secured many benefits, including large sums of low-interest state loans for their livestock development. In 1998, they first contracted a portion of the hillside from the village committee under favorable terms on a thirty-year basis to graze their livestock. While I was staying in the village, I heard many villagers lament that the two households enjoyed the fruits of residents' hard work and the portion of the hillside worth much more than the amount of the contracting fee because they once onerously dug tree pits and planted many apricots there. The two Hui households were also the first to clear large patches of land at the base of the large gully and put it under cultivation. Following in their footsteps, many others turned the unfit land for cultivation. In 2003, the household of Bai Rong tilled 50 *mu* of land, raised 34 cattle herded by a cowboy, and kept a large herd of sheep. The household of Bai Ru farmed 56 *mu* of land and hired an old bachelor to graze sheep for them. Some inhabitants also attributed the newly emerged hiring relationships in the community to an invention of these two Hui households.

The power of their wealth and prosperity provoked "red eyes" (jealousy) on the part of some residents. I heard a bitter quarrel between Bai Ru and Zhang Hualan. They lived opposite a village street. As with some other conflicts between Mongol and Han residents, ethnicity in this case was largely irrelevant. In 2002, Bai Ru piled a heap of manure along a street against the outside wall of their courtyard, which was quite common among residents. Zhang Hualan was extremely unhappy about it, although it did not block the way. There was first a bitter quarrel, followed by a severe physical battle between them. It was rumored, with the help of her son, Zhang Hualan hit Bai Ru hard on his head. She intentionally hit herself soon afterwards. Both of them were finally sent to the hospital for treatment. The village officials were called in to settle the conflict. The two parties were required to pay for each other's medical fee. In this case, ethnic difference was often cited as a key reason for the conflict itself, but as a knowledgeable villager confided to me, the real reason for Zhang Hualan to initiate the quarrel was that Bai Ru tilled more land than they could cultivate themselves and often hired others to work for him. Zhang Hualan wanted to be hired so as to earn some extra money herself, but Bai Ru ignored her. After all, she belonged to the most powerful kinship groups in the community. It went without saying that the unequal power, rather than ethnic differences per se was the underlying cause of the conflict. Indeed, privatization and wealth difference contributed to many conflicts like this.

Here, I will frame my discussion more narrowly on some resource conflicts among households. Natural resource use and management was a contested terrain, which was inextricably connected to the conflicts between village cadres and ordinary folks, and composed a major part of everyday politics in the village. With the advent of household farming, Ao Village witnessed a considerable explosion of resource-based conflicts and battles. Given the primacy of natural resources in village livelihoods, villagers found themselves pitted against one another in access and control over natural resources. Due to incomplete management at the village level, opportunistic behavior among local actors prevailed and inter-household conflicts abounded.

The underlying sources of strife were closely related to the uses and boundaries of cropland, pastureland, woodland, courtyard, and irrigation access. Males sometimes did not hesitate to use violence. While I was staying in the village, two men who were next-door neighbors fought over a shared courtyard wall and in the end both were seriously wounded and sent to the hospital. Reduced supply and unequal distribution of natural resources stemmed from privatization and environmental degradation created new sources of tension and jealousies among villagers. This sometimes heightened the gap between those who had such access and those who did not, as evidenced by the physical conflict between Zhang Hualan and Bai Ru.

In Ao Village, the irrigated field always became one of the major sites of constant village conflicts each year when villagers watered their fields. After 2000, water shortage exacerbated the competition for irrigation water among inhabitants. To my knowledge, some young residents whose fields were not covered by irrigation water bought the tube themselves to direct water into their own fields. In the summer of 2003, I witnessed a verbal battle among three persons near my host's irrigation fields. A man occupied a field edge beyond the boundaries of his own ration land to plant some corn. Whenever watering the cornfields, the households with the fields next to his had to negotiate with him to let water flow down into their fields. It was reported during the spring watering, there had already been a fight and a team leader later opened a water passage to solve the dispute. This time, the team leader seemed unwilling to intervene. One man and one woman with adjoining fields shouted and yelled loudly back and forth with the man for a long time. No one seemed to let the other get the upper hand. The woman impressed me as being a quiet person previously, she apparently lost her temper in the battle. I felt uncomfortable witnessing such a fierce quarrel among inhabitants.

Needless to say, such environmental conflicts interwoven with social conflicts, had in turn, aggravated social divisions at the community level. During my stay in the village, I witnessed several similar conflicts on the scene. I believe Ao Village was no exception.

Things were beginning to change, and as elsewhere, farmers in Ao Village increasingly resorted to the law and went to courts to protect their rights and interests to environmental resources. In early 2004, three men joined together to appeal to the court for their fields at the base of the large gully, and they ultimately won favorable terms to contract their former fields at low prices. One of the three men also registered a case against his patrilineal cousin (*tang ge*) for his woodland. In 1985, he planted 3 *mu* of poplar and secured a forest license from the then county forest department. Fortunately, he found a copy of the license in the Qi Archives Bureau. When I met him in 2004, he took pride in his triumph in the lawsuit. This was not an isolated case in the village. The conflicting voices allow us to better understand the nature and logic of natural resource use and management at the local level.

To summarize, as elsewhere in rural China, with decollectivization and other reform measures, the village household became a basic unit of agricultural production, which set the parameters within which everyday resource use and management were implemented, negotiated and struggled over in the context of a multiplicity of changing social relations, particularly gender relations. Village men and women adjusted their marital and familial strategies to the changing environments, physical and socio-cultural. As a result, the assumptions regarding femininity and masculinity were constructed, maintained, and negotiated at the micro level over time since decollectivization. The social institutions of marriage and households in village society that structured natural resource access and use were also increasingly colored by power differences and competition for environmental resources.

Chapter Eight

Market, Off-farm Work and Socio-economic Differentiation: Money Changes Everything

With the advent of the rural reforms, a growing cash economy emerged in the countryside across China. The revival of rural markets, the change of state purchasing of farm products, coupled with the decontrol of farm product pricing, further promoted a commodity economy in rural areas. Under these circumstances, "to get rich is glorious" (*zhi fu guang rong)* replaced "to serve the people" (*wei ren min fu wu)* as the new watchword in the post-reform period. The market thus increasingly mediated natural resource use and exploitation, leading to not only the diversification of gendered livelihood strategies, but also the polarization of rural society along lines of wealth, gender, age and generation. All of these effects were echoed in Ao Village.

The pursuit and valorization of money was historically a driving force for the exploitation of natural resources in China. In his essay "The Environmental Legacy of Imperial China," Mark Elvin (1998:745) invents a phrase "the cash-in imperative," by which he asserts that, "the intensification of a market-oriented economy creates pressures to cash in natural resources at a faster rate." This statement could still apply to the case of Ao Village, as exemplified by the "money first" attitudes quite common among residents. This eagerness to get rich, now endorsed by the Chinese state, led to "an unprecedented attack on the environment" (Hinton, 1990). Meanwhile, the rush to "get rich quick" drove rural folks in this part of China to turn increasingly to the natural world to generate cash income.

In the market-driven economy, the re-structuring of the local political economy significantly altered capital penetration. China's rural reforms fell into two distinct stages, with the incentive moves dominating the period from 1978-1984, followed by a period of gradual market liberalization from 1985 onwards when both commodity and labor markets gradually developed. In the process, globalization gradually found its local expression in the relationships among the state, market, and peasantry through commodity and labor markets, wage labor, migration of male family members, and even international assistance. Apparently, an exploration of the market, off-farm work and socioeconomic differentiation at the grassroots could shed light on the understanding of macro and micro processes of development and environmental sustainability "in an age of market triumphalism" (Peet and Watts, 1996). This chapter traces, respectively, three interconnected dimensions of the market-driven economy—market, off-farm work and socioeconomic differentiation, all of which were frequently, but not exclusively gendered, carrying policy implications for both gender and natural resource use, and thereby for environmental changes.

The Evolution of the Market as an Institutional Mechanism

The Market in Retrospect

Throughout the preceding chapters, I have intermittently touched on the effects of market forces on agricultural production and natural resource use. In the following section, I focus particularly on the commercialization of agriculture, market participation among villagers, and their marketing dilemmas. As noted in Chapter three, in the pre-Liberation era, most male farmers, Mongols and Han in Ao Village were forced to turn to the market to hire out their labor to earn grain, or to rent land and other farm inputs at exorbitant rates in order to make a living. The new wave of commercialization marginalized the overwhelming majority of farmers. The land reform launched in the late 1940s aimed to alleviate the twin problems of stagnant economic growth, on the one hand, and growing wealth inequalities, on the other hand, through reallocation of the land and other resources.

Local rural markets flourished for a few years after Liberation until 1953 when the market economy was replaced by the planned economy, more specifically, the compulsory procurement system. This represented a shift in which the state began to implement farmers' compulsory grain sales to the state, and thus established a state monopoly on the purchase and sale of grain, which was termed "*tong gou tong xiao*." A local anecdote serves as an illustration of local perceptions of the state's initial monopolization of grain trade. I heard the phrase repeatedly during my stay in Ao Village. A former poor man surnamed Wan, the fifth among his siblings, gradually grew prosperous after Liberation through hard work, and his household consequently accumulated a large acreage of fields and a great deal of grain. A work team from the higher-level government came down to require him to deliver a larger amount of grain to the state than he actually had. He got sick and died soon afterward from overwhelming worry and pressures. That's why there was a local saying, "The mandatory sales of grain led to the death of Wan the fifth." The system of mandatory sales of grain was maintained throughout the whole collective era.

Once collectivization was in full swing, most commerce was banned or heavily curtailed for over 20 years. The restriction of private market transactions of rural produce was strengthened every now and then from 1947 through1979. During the Cultural Revolution, especially for some time in the mid-1970s, as in Aohan as a whole, private plots, animals and trees were treated as an embodiment of villagers' taking the capitalist road (AQG, 1991). Some inhabitants recalled that they were almost totally forbidden to engage in any private economic activity, "even vegetables and trees in the courtyards were branded as capitalism and uprooted, which was termed to "cut the tail of capitalism" (*ge zi ben zhu yi wei ba*)." The government's overwhelming stresses on staple crop agriculture and the prolonged food shortage actually left little space for locals to develop private economic activities. Before decollectivization, most households had only a small patch of private plots and only relatively rich households owned a few sheep or a donkey.

Despite this restriction, small-scale marketing activities never died out entirely under the centralized economy. Production teams struggled to market their extra products after meeting the official targets. Individual households were too poor to raise livestock or engage in other home-based enterprises, however, they handled the hardships in locally specific ways in some more liberal periods, turning in desperation to the natural world to earn a little bit of much needed cash, selling forage grass to their teams, firewood to someone on the state payroll, medical herbs to a communal branch of the state-run supply and marketing cooperative (*gong xiao she*), and producing a few handicrafts at home—*kang* mats or even shoes.

Gearing Towards Market Production

As in other parts of rural China, decollectivization resulted in a structural shift from subsistence to commercial agricultural systems. After the nationwide relaxation of grain delivery quotas, respectively, in 1985 and 1993, a more market-oriented economy evolved locally. Household farming, the availability of irrigated land, the inroads of new seed varieties and the increasing use of chemical fertilizers substantially boosted crop production. Although moderately commercialized, Ao Village was clearly integrated into the cash economy. As we shall see below, almost all inputs and most outputs were closely linked with the outside world beyond the village boundary. From the 1980s onwards, the need for cash promoted increasingly commercial livelihood strategies, producing and marketing any type of crops and animals that were profitable in local markets. Apparently, the process of commercialization increased the role of the market as a key institution.

In the first few years immediately following the reform, some households still eked out a bare subsistence, selling little grain to the market. A few men mentioned that they remained so poor that they had to graze cows, sheep or goats for others in neighboring villages. In contrast, some women noted that they harvested rice in other villages to bring back food to meet subsistence needs. Others households with sufficient labor and animal power began to reclaim large tracts of wasteland. The earliest years of the reform ushered in a sharp crop increase among some households, yet the state's pricing system still kept grain prices very low, and the price on free markets was merely a little bit higher. It was reported that millet averaged 0.20RMB per catty in the mid-1980s. Farmers could earn only marginal benefits from crop cultivation.

Coincident with the revival of rural marketing, there were almost eight consecutive bumper harvests in Aohan spanning from 1991-1998. The growing crop yields resulted in an impressive surge of agricultural income among some households. Despite this, each household then kept plenty of marketable surpluses in the house except when they desperately needed cash, a phenomenon that stood in sharp contrast with the pattern that existed in 2003. After decades of severe food shortages, villagers had clear memories of the regional food deficit. Yet as of 2003, the enthusiasm for the security of stored grain waned and private grain reserves in many households were exhausted.

With the deepening commercialization, Ao Village witnessed a significant shift in marketing practices. By 2003, villagers sold as much of their harvest as possible in rural or urban markets or within the community so as to get much-needed cash. Despite the severe drought, the grain that they produced could still meet basic daily dietary needs, yet brought a limited source of cash income. While I was staying in Ao Village, I noticed that some residents sold millet immediately after harvest when the prices were lowest. The husked millet was sold at around 0.70RMB per catty during the peak sale season in 2003, which rose to over 1RMB per catty in 2004. Surplus millet was the first crop to be sold in the county town, followed by rice sold in a rice market town 16 kilometers away. Since loans were customarily due after annual harvest, many residents had a pressing need for cash at that point in the year, which in turn, lowered the price in local markets. Cash crops like the seeds of hitting melon, sunflower, sesame, or sorghum were mainly sold to middlemen in the village. There were few exceptions to these patterns.

The decisions of whether, which or how many crops were sold in the market or kept at home for subsistence needs depended on myriads of complex factors, including population and livestock composition, the amount of consumption within the household, the changing consumption patterns and dietary preferences, gender and age characteristics, crop yield and types cultivated, and the grain saved from previous years. Considering so many variations, I found it extremely difficult to identify the percentage of residents' sale of surplus grain. All too often, they used the cash derived from crop sales to purchase supplementary fine grains such as rice and flour, which became more readily available in local markets in 2003. Impoverished households clearly consumed much less fine grains than others. In 2003, a sack of flour of 50 catty was sold at about 35RMB and rice about 1RMB per catty in local markets. Many residents frequently mentioned as a sign of their improved life that even former landlords often could not afford fine grains.

In spite of increasing commercialization, some conventional subsistence attitudes and practices persisted. As a woman in her late forties explained to me:

> Unlike urban folks who rely on buying everything from the market. Common farmers here do not count on the readily available stuff. We sometimes live for a long time without buying anything. To go to the market is to throw away money and time, why should I go? In most households,

> a pig is killed for the lunar New Year, and the lard is used as cooking oil for the whole year. In the summer, we eat vegetables grown in our own gardens. Vegetables are often eaten uncooked, since this saves cooking oil. Fresh vegetables are stored and consumed as preserved vegetables in the off-season. Rarely do locals buy fresh vegetables in the winter. Homemade soybean sauce on the dining table is often consumed with Chinese onion throughout the year in most households. Many households can now afford a meal of mixing rice and millet (locally called "*er mi fan*") or sometimes purely eat rice and flour.

This was indeed the pattern that I observed in the village when I stayed there. As with crop cultivation, livestock production was also increasingly implicated in deepening commercialization. As noted in Chapter four, during the collective era, after finishing annual quotas of state procurement, a larger proportion of team animals were used for subsistence. Although I lacked systematic data, anecdotal evidence indicated that villagers ate more mutton in those days than they did after decollectivization. In the earliest reform period, most households owned a few sheep, and they slaughtered more for domestic consumption than they did in 2003. In response to the incentives of the expanding market for animals, livestock production was increasingly geared towards the market. To my knowledge, only a few villagers killed sheep for domestic use.

Local Markets and Market Participation

Before Liberation, there was only one market town in the vicinity, which was located about 25 kilometers' away. Without animals or money, no poor people went to the market on a regular basis. Jiang Mei recalled that her father became blind in an accident and her only brother could not spare himself from working for the landlord, and thus her mother used to go the market town occasionally to buy things. On one winter day, she was robbed on her way back home by a bandit who stole all of her belongings, including her cotton-padded clothes. When her mother finally returned home, she was almost frozen to death. This incident stood as a reminder to village women that to travel alone as a woman was quite dangerous. During the collective era, men, especially team leaders and big cart drivers, had many more opportunities than women to travel to the market. Female residents occasionally took the big carts of their teams or walked all the way to the county seat to sell or buy things.

Unlike the villages in some remote, mountainous regions with notable transportation barriers,[1] market access did not seem to be a problem for residents in Ao Village. After decollectivization, the market town that had existed since the pre-Liberation times was relocated to a town 16 kilometers away from Ao Village. A new fair was established in the township seat 9 years ago. Added to the market in the county seat, this made at least three accessible marketplaces for villagers.

They approached different marketplaces for divergent marketing activities. The fair in the township seat, attended by people from some nearby villages, was merely 4 kilometers away, which was within walking distance of Ao Village. Making a purchase and returning home could be done by bicycle, motorcycle, and animal cart, tricycle or even by foot, alone and in groups. Only occasionally did people drive to the market town to buy meat and vegetables for family banquets. I observed two or three households normally hired a tricycle to the county seat to sell their millet. Both men and women actively participated in this selling activity. After all, they just had "a single harvest in the whole year." Many women took the opportunity to make purchases of their own or for their family. With the availability of a minibus taxi in 2003, four or five persons occasionally shared the taxi to the county seat for 40-50RMB for a round trip. As the lunar New Year drew near, there was another wave of shopping in the county town by local residents.

The lively fair in the township seat was maintained by an increased consumption by residents living in clusters of villages around the marketplace. The market field occupied a square of roughly 40 by 40 meters. Many grocery stores, restaurants, barbershops, a post office, a credit cooperative, and a few private veterinary stations were located along both sides of a highway. Not far away from the marketplace, there was also a township clinic, a Mongol middle school and two primary schools. This fair was held on odd-numbered days, while the town market was held on even-

1 It reminded me of some villages in Yunnan Province that I visited in my 2002 fieldtrip. The villages were usually built on the top of a hill. Each hill usually supported a hamlet, where inhabitants planted crops on steep slopes. In one village that we visited, there was no accessible motor road, and it took approximately two hours by walking through hilly footpaths to get to a highway where they could take buses to the county town. If they held a large basket of produce on their back, it would take much time. The distance to the market, however, did not prevent women from market participation, nor did it cut the village off from the cash economy.

numbered days. It mainly sold agricultural produce such as grains, seeds, vegetables, meats, fruits as well as some tools, shoes and clothes. Meats, fruits, cloth and clothes were usually displayed in stalls, while vegetables were spread out on the ground. All prices were open to negotiation.

The village taxi driver, who worked there every other day, told me that on almost every market day, there were always people from Ao Village making a purchase, while some others just went around without doing any "real" matters. Several residents mentioned that, "The fair cannot be operated without the participation of Ao Village people." On the day before the Mid-autumn Festival in 2004, I recognized so many residents, old and young, men and women, among the crowd, many of them were carrying their purchases in fertilizer bags. I was told that each household would send at least one member on this occasion. The buying power of villagers was severely constrained by their financial situations, however, the availability of the local market greatly increased men's and women's mobility and their connections with the outside world.

Although the fair was within walking distance, strangely enough, no resident regularly sold anything there. To my knowledge, only one young man peddled vegetables for a short period of time in 2003. He drove his tricycle to buy and sell some vegetables and fruits in the market town one day, and sold them next day in the fair first and then door-to-door in the neighboring villages. The other two small traders of farm produce often purchased whatever crops were profitable from elsewhere and sometimes from their fellow villagers, and resold them in the marketplace, which enabled their families to live a relatively affluent life in comparison to others.

After decollectivization, many men were absorbed into the petty trade in local markets during the agricultural off-season. In the mid-1980s, two recently demobilized soldiers first embarked on the day-long bike trip to purchase chicken eggs door-to-door at a relatively low price from a place about 40 kilometers away and resold them at a marginal profit in the county seat, which later developed into an "egg troop", involving 40-50 village men and lasted for a couple of years. A bike could be loaded up with about 80-100 catties of eggs. Some men also did small business such as purchasing grains, wool, seed or sold cloth or clothing. Prior to the drought, some men dove their tricycles to purchase grains from farmers inside and outside the village and sold them outside the village to win a small profit of

2-8 cents per catty. According to a local newspaper, in Aohan, small brokers of agricultural products emerged like "bamboo shoots after a spring rain", which made it increasingly hard for poor farmers, especially poor women, to do small trading.

Marketing Dilemmas

In spite of readily available urban and rural market outlets, villagers preferred to purchase things in the fair and sell products to middlemen at home. As a man told me, "unlike the greedy traders in urban markets who treat us like we are fools, the peddlers in the fair are honest, you do not need to check the weight, and they won't cheat you. By contrast, the traders in the county seat get rich through manipulation and collusion; they take advantage of and even bully rural folks. They also intentionally drive down prices and play tricks with scales, you might waste more than you can sell at home." I did observe that villagers took no notice of the scale when meat sellers in the fair were weighing the meat. The fear of being cheated often prevented residents, particularly women, from accessing to the county market. Several times, my female friends in the village required me to go with them to buy clothes in the county seat, "you come from the big city, and they do not dare to cheat you."

As a result, villagers sold most of their grains and animals to traveling traders in the neighborhood. When I asked if they knew there was a livestock market in the county seat, very few of them knew about it, let alone had access to it. Residents certainly had their own economic calculus. A desire to avoid spending money on transportation and to keep from being cheated by urban folks drove their marketing strategies. Wandering traders frequently passed through the village, yelling loudly door to door along the village street, and sometimes using a loudspeaker. They exploited farmers by purchasing produce at relatively low prices and reselling it at high prices elsewhere. Their business activities catered to the demands of larger markets within Aohan and beyond. The fear of getting cheated, the discrimination encountered in the county seat, and the dependency on middlemen all trapped village men and women in a disadvantageous position in their marketing practices.

Unpredictable market prices represented another major threat to the commercial sale among residents. By 2003, more than 20 years had passed since the return to household farming in 1980, yet the workings of the market were still elusive. The fledgling market system was accompanied by the vicissitudes of market demand. As was true with most rural areas across China, the price of crop and animal products fluctuated unpredictably from year to year, even season to season. For instance, sesame was in short supply locally in 2003 and the highest price was sold at 7.4RMB per catty. A year earlier, it was commonly sold around 3.5RMB per catty. One man told me he sold it three times for 3.8, 4.8 and 5.4RMB per catty, respectively, within a period of two months. In 2004, I observed many households shift to sesame cultivation. Before my departure in late 2003, the market price of grain went up quickly, however, the booming price was largely offset by the soaring price of other commodities on the local markets.

The selling prices of livestock were unpredictable as well. Pigs were sold for 3RMB per catty when I first stayed in the village in April 2003, and the price increased to 4.5RMB per catty by the end of the year. The price for piglets soared from 4-5RMB per catty in 2003 to 10-11RMB per catty during my 2004 revisit. Local people were always poorly informed of the changing market prices. Under the highly competitive market environment, the selling/buying prices seemed well beyond the control of farmers. It was not so much whether or not farmers were familiar with the local markets. As a township official commented to me, "Even cadres are ignorant about the workings of the market, let alone ordinary farmers. There always exists a risk of oversupply or short supply, and therefore a fluctuation in market prices. There is no way for us to guide farmers about what to plant or raise."

I often heard residents complain about the huge costs of chemical fertilizers, an indispensable input to crop cultivation. Urea was sold about 70-80RMB per sack (100 catties) in 2003, which reached about 100RMB per sack in 2004. Amine was sold about 95-98RMB per sack in 2003 and ranged from 105-125RMB in 2004. I was often told that fertilizer accounted for around 50% of all the investment in crop cultivation among residents, constituting a large proportion of farming expenses. It was widely believed that approximately 70% of the households needed to borrow money to buy fertilizers before spring planting when local merchants pushed up the prices. But villagers had no choices since they had no money to purchase them ahead of time. They also blamed the merchants for selling bad varieties and fake fertilizers. One resident told me, "White grains of chemical fertilizer that he applied last year can still be recognized in the fields this year."

In Aohan, many urban folks and even some government officials were deeply involved in commercial activities. A male villager summarized the plight of unpredictable selling/buying that he and other peasants faced as follows: "When our yield is good, the selling price is bound to be bad; whereas when the price is good, we tend to have meager returns. When we desperately need chemical fertilizers, the prices are frighteningly high. Our peasants always experience great disadvantages in the market economy." It was true as Hartmann and Boyce observed in rural Bangladesh over 20 years ago, the rural poor were "receiving low prices for what they sell and often paying high prices for what they buy, the peasants tend to lose, whether they enter the market as producers or as consumers" (1983:185).

In Ao Village, men were mainly in charge of marketing practices of livestock and their products. As with crop production, livestock production was explicitly geared towards the market and sold at negotiated prices principally in the neighborhood. Male residents often got together to press for a higher price. Soon after I settled in my host's house, Hong Xiang sold one of their donkeys. On the day he sold it, a couple of men were invited to help bargain with the trader. Later that year, he sold another donkey in the community without the presence of Song Ling. It was not too surprising for me to find out during the interview that some women did not know the sale price of their animals. A few men occasionally engaged in livestock trading, which needed special skill, but they were often severely constrained by lack of capital.

Women sometimes performed some small transactions. Their marketing products included shrub seeds, Chinese herbs, vegetables or grains. Women were often involved in intra-village trade for small quantities of rice, vegetables, and livestock. They were indeed canny market participants and shrewd bargainers, who could always buy items cheaper than I did. I attended many fairs with women, witnessing such transactions and their careful bargaining in the marketplace. Village women seemed to be far more active agents in marketing activities than commonly assumed. I sometimes marveled at their skill and strategies.

On one summer morning in 2003, a village woman drove a donkey cart carrying men and three other women to the fair. Each of them brought one or two fertilizer sacks of collected apricot seeds with them. On our way to the fair, they inquired about the prices offered by some middlemen at the roadside. Immediately after our arrival at the purchasing stations and stalls in the fair, they were busy inquiring about prices and negotiating back and forth. In front of a stall, a trader picked up one apricot seed and smashed it to check the quality, before I realized the reason, there suddenly erupted a severe quarrel between Bao Mei, the most vocal woman among the group in her early thirties, and a male trader. The male yelled, "1.2RMB per catty is reasonable these days, how can you be so greedy?" He seemed furious about the exorbitant charge. "What are you saying? Who is greedy? " Bao Mei responded with anger. After several rounds of quarrels, Bao Mei cried out, "You must pay me for the one that you smashed!" The man replied, "Do you want to blackmail me?" In the end, the man returned a handful of seeds to Bao Mei, who took just one and threw back the rest of them to the trader. More negotiations between them and other traders at several stalls continued. Bao Mei later told me triumphantly, the reason why she quarreled with the man was because she did not like the way the male trader looked down upon women in barter. After they heard a better offer of 1.6RMB per catty in the county seat market, they decided to sell nothing that morning.

As with men's and women's differing involvement in marketing activities, women's off-farm practices differed from men as well. Declining agricultural income, exacerbated by drought-induced changes since 1999, increased the pressure for some household members to pursue off-farm and non-farm ventures, and therefore sources of cash income beyond farming. There were apparently significant differences in resource use practices among villagers pursuing different livelihood strategies. Increased access to off-farm opportunities inside and outside the village, as a consequence, have reduced residents' dependence on natural resources, with accompanying bearings on the environment. In the following section, I explore both gender and ecological implications of economic diversification, more specifically, how changing livelihood strategies and labor migration shifted pressure to natural resources.

The Rush to Off-farm Pursuits

A permanent household registration system or *hukou* system[1]was created in

1 The household registration system distinguished peasants from urban residents. It aimed to control the migration of peasants from the countryside to the cities. Urban residents were provided privileged access to certain commodities at subsidized prices, legitimate employment with retirement and medical benefits, and a series of other preferential treatments. By contrast, being a peasant was a disadvantage in many respects (see Cohen, 1993). For a comprehensive discussion of the origins and social implications of the distinction between peasants and urban residents, see Sulamith Heins Potter and Jack M. Potter (1990) *China's Peasants: The Anthropology of a Revolution*, Cambridge: Cambridge University Press.

China in1958, through which urban-rural segmentation and mobility restrictions were strengthened. This *hukou* status was inherited from one's mother (Judd, 1994; Johnson, 1983; Wolf, 1985). Over much of the period since the late 1950s, there existed a strict residency policy that kept the vast majority of rural population in their home villages. Potter and Potter (1990:196) argue that the dichotomy between rural and urban sectors of post-1949 Chinese society reflected a "caste-like system of socialist stratification." During the collective period, if villagers wanted to leave the village for whatever reasons, they had to get approval from their team and brigade leaders, who tightly controlled mobility. On the other hand, there were few places rural folks could survive beyond their home village.

Under these circumstances, an overwhelming majority of villagers, male and female, were tied to the land, working in collective fields with little choice. As across rural China, officials stressed grain production and suppressed off-farming or non-farm activities[1]during that period. Only when antimarket policies were relaxed did villagers take up some off-farm activities. Under these circumstances, upward mobility required inhabitants to become a team or brigade cadre or obtain a scarce technical position such as a carpenter or tractor driver (Cohen, 1993; Potter and Potter, 1990; Yan 1996). A couple of village men took up the craft of carpentry. Despite strict constraints, a few "talented" men successfully sought their fortunes beyond the village, working in state-owned forest farms or mines, or becoming soldiers through military recruitment. By contrast, social mobility was extremely difficult for women, and the only opportunity for them to leave the village was marriage. To my knowledge, there was only one exceptional example. The fourth elder sister of Hong Xiang, a junior high school graduate, was luckily selected to work in the commune post office, and later was married to a "sent-down youth" from Beijing.

Livelihood Diversification

Since the return to household farming, a sizeable proportion of residents, young people in particular, were released from the land. Agricultural stagnation and recurrent droughts made it increasingly difficult for residents to sustain themselves

1 At that time, local off-farm or non-farm production (excluding crop cultivation) encompassed hunting, collecting Chinese herbs, raising livestock, producing family handicrafts, as well as various kinds of transportation or other services.

solely from the land. Many of them started to take up various off-farm or non-farm activities inside and outside the community, occasionally or permanently. The heterogeneity and diversity in livelihood strategies was differentiated between men and women even within the household. Table 8.1 gives us an idea of who still worked the land and managed natural resources, and who left the land to pursue part or full time off-farm or non-farm practices, along gender lines.

In table 8.1, occupations are categorized as full-time crop production, part-time crop production and non-farm activities. Ninety-one out of 146 resident households, or 62.3 percent, were engaged in full-time crop production. These households depended predominantly on crop production as their principal means of livelihood, but this did not exclude their pursuit of petty livestock production and occasional wage labor on the farms of other households. In Ao Village, an overwhelming majority of households, if not all, were engaged in petty livestock production, raising and selling large animals such as mules, horses, donkeys as well as pigs. Only 21 households or 14.4 percent did not raise pigs, and only 13 households (8.9 percent) did not raise livestock, large or small. Part-time crop production refers to those who worked on farm and off farm at the same time on a regular basis or occasionally. Forty-two households, or 28.8 percent took up part-time crop production, which consisted primarily of sheep-raising households. Only two households worked off farm entirely and the remaining 11 households did not engage in farming at all. Obviously, most households lacked a livelihood base independent of the land, albeit the relative importance of crop production declined.

Viewed from the light of individual occupations, about 40, 13 and 16 percent of the residents, respectively, engaged in full-time crop production, part-time crop production and non-farm employment. The corresponding percentages of women were 63, 6.8 and 23.2. Clearly, the rise of local labor markets diverted a small minority of men, completely or partly, from farm work. As opposed to men, only a small fraction of women were exempt from farm work. Since 2000, Ao Village witnessed a notable increase in intermittent cash-earning opportunities in the fields of other households. It involved mostly women who worked as farm workers for weeding or harvesting. In the remainder of this chapter, I address the vicissitudes of off-farm pursuits and participation among men and women.

Table 8.1 Employment by Gender and Household in Ao Village (2003)

	Households	No	Male	No	Female	No
Full-time Crop production		91		77		130
Part-time Crop production		42		58		10
	Mill plant Laying chicken Meat chicken[2] Sheep raising[4]	1 1 6 34	Trader and transporter Transporter Tractor operator Hill keeper Grain/fodder processor Vet and transporter Electric welding Brick factory guard Mill plant owner Laying chicken raiser Meat chicken raiser Sheep herder Cowboy	3 2 2 2 3 1 1 1 1 1 6 34 1	Women's director Teacher[1] Cook[3] Laying chicken raiser Meat chicken raiser	1 1 1 1 6
Non-farm work		2	+ 50 migrants[5]	60	+19 migrants[5]	22
	Drug store Grocery store	1 1	Villager doctor/drug seller Store keeper Taxi driver Village cook Teacher Decorating worker Timber factory worker Brick factory workers	1 1 1 1 3 1 1 1	Micro-credit worker Brick factory workers	1 2
Household not engaged in farming		11[6]		12		6
			Hired sheep herder Sheep herder Older men and children	1 1 10	Older women	6
Individuals not engaged in farming [7]				64		74
Total		146		271		242

Source: 2003 household survey

Note:

[1] It refers to a pre-school class teacher hired by villagers.

[2] All Six households raised only 2-3 batches of chicken in 2003.

[3] The cook also rented out her house to the crew of road construction projects and cooked for them for over 4 months.

[4] Three out of 38 sheep-raising households hired others to graze sheep for them, and one household with non-agricultural registration did not plant crops. Not all male herders completely separated themselves from crop cultivation. In the few busiest days of crop production, they might confine their sheep for a few days.

[5] See the next section for the migrants, male and female.

[6] A total of 13 households did not engage in farming; with two of them engaged in non-farm work and one owning a sheep herd.

[7] It refers to older residents, students and children. I only counted all the working adults aged 15-64, namely the official economic activity population. In practice, some people under 15 and over 64 were deeply involved in crop production.

Tapping Niches in the Local Market

Constrained by limited capital, only a small proportion of households ran self-employed businesses and few had the financial means to start new ones. Apart from crops and animals, residents produced very few commodities for sale. In 2003, only a small minority of households farmed vegetables commercially, however, courtyard vegetable production was severely constrained by the source of water. In addition, when garden vegetables were readily available, the market tended to reach saturation level. The inroads of mass-produced clothes and shoes undermined female tailors, just as the readily available furniture on local markets made male carpenters eventually give up their traditional occupations. Only one male carpenter had shifted to the booming field of housing decorations. Two unmarried young women, respectively, ran a small hairdressing salon, in the marketplace of Lan Village.

In the village, only three households owned formally registered private businesses, which were often referred to as self-employed private enterprises, or "*ge ti hu*"[1] in Chinese. When the collectives broke up their assets, a small minority of elite families gained industrial and commercial assets. During the collective period, the grocery store was operated as an outlet (*dai xiao dian*) of the commune supply-and-marketing cooperatives located in Lan Village. The storekeeper was a handicapped man in his early forties, whose father was a powerful team leader under collectivism. Before he took it over in 1985, his elder sister ran the store for some years before she married out of the village. The store was privatized in 1993, and his father, and then his younger brother were in charge of purchasing stock. By 2003, the two unmarried brothers actually ran the thriving household enterprise. They were wholly alienated

1 Ao Village never had any specialized households (*zhuan ye hu),* which independently produced various specialized agricultural and non-agricultural commodities, as reported in more prosperous regions(cf. Judd, 1994).

from agricultural practices. The grocery store sold a variety of daily necessities at relatively high profit. Take matches for example, they bought them for 3 cents per box and sold them for 5 cents. In the 1990s, four other households attempted to run a similar store and none survived, primarily due to the practice of offering "white notes (*bai tiao*)," or informal credit (*she zhang*). In 2004, a former Party secretary opened a new small store a few steps away from it.

A male village doctor, Han Tie, ran a clinic with a drugstore, which was the only medical facility in Greater Ao Village. It was almost exclusively stocked with a broad selection of western medicine. Han Tie studied medical practices in a technical secondary school for two years. It was said that the very common treatment that they offered was an antibiotic injection. This was essentially a household operation with much input from Han Tie's wife, Xu Shu. She received paramedical training in a hospital in the county town for one year when she worked as a health care worker in charge of the health of women and children in Greater Ao Village. Xu Shu helped her husband a lot to mind the clinic. According to Han Tie, the medicine sold on credit totaled about 6000-7000RMB in 2002, indicating it was a profitable operation. In 2000, Xu Shu earned an enviable salaried job of delivering micro credit to women in Lan Village and Greater Ao Village under a UNDP project. She became a roving field worker. This rewarding job conferred notable economic advantage and social prestige. From 2000 onwards after Xu Shu took up the job, the household was totally separated from farming.

Few households in Ao Village ever diversified into entrepreneurial industry activities. Immediately following decollecitivization, a former village cadre purchased grinding equipment from the village. He operated the mill for a couple of years and provided a service that was in short supply locally in those years. He later sold them to another creative man, who later became relatively wealthy due to running the mill. The owner in 2003 was a former electrician, who bought the mill plant from his brother. The mill was the only such facility in Greater Ao Village and residents from other hamlets sometimes came here to seek services, yet it did not seem to be a profitable enterprise. His wife lacked familiarity with machines and never operated it. They both still worked the land. Obviously, only two of the three privately owned enterprises were relatively successful, which made it possible for them to shift out of farming work entirely.

By 2003, commercial small-scale chicken production (meat or egg) emerged as a household-based enterprise in a small number of households. During the collective period, most households reared a few chickens to produce eggs to barter for salt, matches or other daily items. As of 2003, residents continued to keep a small amount of chickens to earn "pin money" or for domestic uses. The household of a team leader in the west village ran a prosperous poultry enterprise, raising 500 heads of laying chicken. For many years, it was the only egg-based family enterprise in the village. The residents, including the village committee, often bought eggs directly from them. To run a commercial enterprise was no small undertaking. It required close cooperation among family members. The team leader's elder father was in charge of feeding, his mother kept accounts, and his wife hauled water from the outside since they had no well at home. The monthly net income averaged 600-700RMB from the egg sales. In the end they could also earn extra money by selling birds. It seemed a viable economic strategy. In late 2003, another rich household shifted to this profitable venture.

A well-known poultry agribusiness firm in Inner Mongolia extended its enterprises to Aohan in the mid-1990s under a system of "contract farming". In the name of alleviating poverty, the company initially encouraged poor farmers to take advantage of their wing houses to develop small-scale meat chicken farming. In 2001, a former Party secretary in Ao village pioneered the project of raising birds under contract with the company, followed by some other households. In 2002, over ten households were involved in the venture and most households ended up with a tiny return at best and some experienced serious loss. In one household, hundreds of chickens died in the summer. The value of the birds, plus the cost of fodder amounted to almost 8000RMB, which pushed the household to the brink of poverty.

During my fieldwork in 2003, six households continued with it and only two households achieved real success. If there was no unexpected loss, after the cost of chicks and feed was subtracted, the producers expected to earn a net profit of around 2RMB per bird. The feed ration was strictly set by the company, which was technologically sophisticated. It took about 50 days for birds to grow to a fixed size required and to sell back to the company. Poultry production was characterized by a time-consuming labor regime under "contracting farming", which put heavy work demands on all concerned, especially women. In all six households but one, women took the major responsibility of taking care of birds almost day and night.

The operation of agribusiness proceeded largely according to the capitalist logic. The nascent chicken raising among villagers was threatened by the incursion of large-scale commercial chicken operations favored by the company. In Aohan, green crop, meat chicken and sheep became three burgeoning dominant industries. The governments at the county and township levels focused on "paying special attention to big households and establishing specialized small districts (*zhua da hu, jian xiao qu*)." In 2003, a total of eight chicken-raising demonstration districts were "showcased" along the highway.

In Lan Township, apart from a small sheep district, a small chicken-raising district was established in Lan Village in 2003, which occupied 60 *mu* of land in a site bordering the east edge of Ao Village. Eight brick chicken houses were built, with two households sharing a building. Each building was expected to produce about 3000 birds at a time. If birds were raised in six cycles each year, the annual total output was expected to reach approximately 150000 birds. The Lan Township government offered 7000RMB free subsidized funding for each participating household. To my knowledge, there were merely three real peasant households among the 16 participating households, with one from Hamlet D. The remaining participants were mostly urban people.

A large amount of capital investment prevented ordinary farmers from participating in it. The district was strongly favored by the company, which supplied young birds to the district in time, while almost totally ignoring the small-scale household operation. The project was clearly based on a trickle-down policy, yet it was unable to provide prosperity to ordinary farmers. In 2004, all participating households in Ao Village were squeezed out of the chicken-raising industry when the company no longer provided expensive small birds to them on credit. This case exemplified the negative impact of the market forces on vulnerable small farmers.

Small-scale gendered pig raising was long one of the major home-based enterprises since decollectivization, although no household ever specialized in large-scale pig cultivation. Pig raising was mainly identified as women's work, which made a major contribution to the household economy. According to Xin Xing, there were at most 270 heads of pigs in the community in 2003. To my knowledge, a household raised as many as eight pigs, and heavily relied upon the manure of young chickens raised for the agribusiness company. According to my survey, 125 out of 146 households, or 85.6 percent raised pigs. Among them, 49 households raised at least one sow, accounting for 39.2 percent of the pig-raising households. A total of 113 households, or 77 percent of households raising pigs reported they would slaughter a pig for domestic consumption.[1]

The hybrid pigs took about 7-8 months to reach a slaughter weight of 100 kilograms. During the period of growing, a pig could consume 1000 catties feed grain, mostly corn (it was sold at 0.5RMB per catty in 2003, and 0.6RMB per catty in 2004), about 1000 catties of chaff (0.13RMB per catty), two bags of compounded feed (100 catties per bag, costing 35RMB and up) and other daily dietary needs. Many grain by-products such as sunflower heads, sorghum and corn straw could be ground into chaff for feeding pigs. The final selling prices might reach around 800-1100RMB, deducting the cost of about 600-700RMB, the net profit per animal might be equal or even lower than the cost in the context of shifting market prices. Discouraged by depressing market prices, like some others, Song Ling did not raise pigs in 2004.

While the market value of piglets was high, raising sows was favorable; they usually produced 2-3 litters per year, ranging from 5 to 14 piglets per litter. An old woman aged 66, well known for her pig-raising skills, told me that during the collective era, even people did not have enough to eat, few could afford to raise pigs. Since the very year of decollectivization, she began to raise sows without stopping. In 1995, she raised two sows, which gave birth to litters of a total of 40 piglets, which were sold 13RMB per catty. Plus an adult pig, the cash earnings from the sale of pigs totaled approximately 9000RMB. Using this money, they built a new house for their youngest son. The older couple lived separately in a mud house in 2003 and they continued to raise a sow. Pig-raising was a preferred strategy for women to make some money or save money from buying meat or lard for household consumption. It also contributed greatly to generating manure for crop cultivation.

As noted in Chapter five, when the brick factory closed, its workers were thrown back into the fields.An outside man from the county seat signed a fifteen-year contract with the village committee to reopen it in May 2004. All its managers with higher earnings were all male outsiders. It employed a total of 40-50 persons and three fifths of them were recruited from Ao Village. As before, it created many wage jobs for a large percentage of resident workers in their own home community. Four elderly men were in charge of sun-drying bricks in preparation of firing. Young men were mostly clay diggers or brick carriers. A few young women loaded newly

1 A live-to-carcass weight conversion of sheep was not as ideal as a pig and thus few villagers actually butchered sheep for their own uses.

made unburned bricks onto carts and young men pushed them to the drying ground, where eight young women performed one of the most onerous tasks of removing the bricks with both hands simultaneously from the cart and piling them up to be dried in the sun. Each wet brick weighed about 13 catties. This group of women normally worked for about 12 hours a day on a piecework basis and their daily wage rate averaged 20-25RMB. Despite being onerous and low in reward, young women seemed happy to take the rare wage jobs available locally.

Venturing into the Outside World

On the eve of decollectivization, as many as 800 million rural population were tightly tied to collective fields and their communities. With the advent of the rural reforms, labor migration became one of the most dramatic and significant manifestations of rural modernization and globalization in China. In Ao Village, there was a steady stream of migration with the relaxation of mobility restrictions. From 1999 onward, recurrent droughts and consequent crop failures impinged on crop productivity and income negatively, which put enormous pressure on residents to migrate out of the community or raise more livestock. Some residents perceived out-migration as a last resort to escape poverty and indebtedness. Under such circumstance, they were in a sense environmental refugees on the one hand, and their movement somewhat eased the pressure on the local environment, temporarily or permanently, on the other. The outflow of inhabitants not only provided an alternative livelihood for surplus rural labor, but also reconfigured domestic space. I produced a list of gender and age-specific migration in table 8.2 to demonstrate my points.

As seen in table 8.2, a total of 69 migrant workers living in 47 households out of 146 resident households were away from the village for at least four months.[1] Among them, 50 (72.5 percent) were men and 19 (27.5 percent) were women. Apparently, female migrants fell well behind the numbers of men, especially among

1 According to the Year-end Production Statistics Forms (GYV, 2003a), there were a total of 76 migrant laborers in Greater Ao Village, which clearly had severely underestimated the real situation in the administrative village. It was widely reported that there were 100 000 migrants in Aohan in 2003. This demonstrated the consistency of my data with that of the county-level statistics. The county and township governments, including Qi Women's Federation, put the export of labor service or "*lao wu shu chu*" as one of their priorities in combating the drought. Qi Women's Federation ran a program to recruit female migrants for the markets of some big cities such as Beijing and Dalian. Yet most villagers relied on their relatives and fellow villagers to find work.

married women, who had far fewer opportunities to migrate out of the village. In 2003, six women as in comparison to 18 men were married and four of them moved out on their own. The average age of male migrants was 25.5, as against 22.9 among their female counterparts. The smallest age among men was sixteen years old and the oldest was fifty-three, the corresponding figures for females were, respectively, fifteen and thirty-seven. Male and female migrants had a similar mean year of migration. Generally, migrants had a higher education than non-migrants, with both men and women enjoying similar education levels. Most young men and women did not have an interest in farming and they attempted to get rid of the land. After quitting school, most of them migrated out of the community for some time prior to their marriage.

Table 8.2 Profiles of Migrant Laborers in Ao Village (2003)[1]

Person	Age	Year of Migration	Education Level	Locality	Category of Work
				Male (N=50)	
# 1	16	1.0	8.0	Beijing	Security guard
# 2	17	1.0	8.0	Beijing	Security guard
# 3	17	2.0	8.0	Beijing	Security guard
# 4	18	0.9	7.0	Chifeng	Factory
# 5	18	0.4	6.0	Liaoning province	Factory
# 6	18	0.8	7.0	Chifeng	Hairdressing
# 7	18	1.0	9.0	Laoning province	Road construction
# 8	18	0.6	5.0	Hebei province	Brick factory
# 9	19	2.0	6.0	Shanghai	Hairdressing
#10	19	0.8	8.0	Heibei	Brick factory
#11	19	1.0	8.0	Beijing	Security guard
#12	19	0.6	8.0	Jilin province	Road construction
#13	20	1.0	6.0	Shanghai	Hairdressing
#14	20	0.8	6.0	Beijing	Restaurant
#15	20	1.0	8.0	Beijing	Security guard
#16	20	0.5	8.0	Chifeng	Hairdressing
#17	20	2.0	8.0	Beijing	Safety guard
#18	21	0.6	4.0	Hebei province	Brick factory
#19	21	2.0	6.0	Chifeng	Restaurant
#20	21	0.6	4.0	Chifeng	Factory
#21	21	1.0	8.0	Beijing suburb	Brick factory
#22	21	2.0	8.0	Beijing	Security guard

contd.

Person	Age	Year of Migration	Education Level	Locality	Category of Work
#23	21	2.0	7.0	Beijing	Security guard
#24	23	1.0	8.0	Chifeng	Factory
#25	23	2.0	0.7	Beijing	Security guard
#26	24	0.9	5.0	Hebei province	Brick factory
#27	24	2.0	8.0	Shandong province	Factory
#28	25	0.5	5.0	Hebei province	Brick factory
#29	25	1.0	8.0	Beijing	Driver
#30	26	0.6	5.0	Chifeng	Massage
#31	26	2.0	10.0	Chifeng	Agribusiness company
#32	26	0.9	2.0	Hebei	Construction
#33	26	2.0	12.0	Guangdong province	Insurance company
#34	28	0.5	5.0	Inner Mongolia	Road construction
#35	28	0.6	5.0	Liaoning province	House construction
#36	28	3.0	5.0	Inner Mongolia	Mason
#37	29	3.0	3.0	Liaoning province	Construction
#38	29	3.0	5.0	Liaoning province	Construction
#39	30	1.0	3.0	Henan province	Road construction
#40	32	0.6	8.0	Hebei province	Brick factory
#41	32	0.5	5.0	Liaoning province	Factory
#42	32	1.0	6.0	Inner Mongolia	House construction
#43	32	0.5	8.0	Inner Mongolia	Road construction
#44	34	1.0	8.0	Inner Mongolia	Mine worker
#45	35	4.0	6.0	Liaoning province	Construction
#46	36	0.9	5.0	Liaoning province	Construction
#47	38	0.8	5.0	Beijing suburb	Stevedore
#48	40	0.9	9.0	Liaoning province	Road construction
#49	51	2.0	4.0	Henan province	Road construction
#50	53	0.8	5.0	Tianjin suburb	Quarry stevedore
Average	25.5	1.25	6.4		
				Female (N=19)	
# 1	15	0.6	7.5	Chifeng	Restaurant
# 2	16	1.0	6.0	Chifeng	Domestic worker
# 3	17	0.6	7.5	Chifeng	Domestic worker
# 4	17	2.0	8.0	Lan Village[2]	Hairdressing
# 5	18	1.0	9.0	Beijing	Restaurant
# 6	18	2.0	8.0	Tianjin	Factory
# 7	18	3.0	7.5	Beijing	Domestic worker

contd.

Person	Age	Year of Migration	Education Level	Locality	Category of Work
# 8	20	3.0	5.0	Tianjin	Factory
# 9	20	1.0	5.0	Beijing	Domestic worker
#10	22	4.0	8.0	Liaoning Province	Clothing seller
#11	23	2.0	8.0	Lan Village	Hairdressing
#12	23	0.6	6.0	Inner Mongolia	Restaurant
#13	24	0.4	7.0	Inner Mongolia	Cook
#14	26	1.0	8.0	Chifeng	Restaurant
#15	27	1.0	6.0	Liaoning Province	Domestic worker
#16	29	1.0	8.0	Inner Mongolia	Cook
#17	30	2.0	8.0	Beijing	Domestic worker
#18	36	0.6	6.0	Beijing	D omestic worker
#19	37	0.4	6.0	Chifeng	Restaurant
Average	22.9	1.43	7.0		

Source: 2003 household survey.

Note:

[1] This list only covers the villagers in 146 resident households.

[2] They worked and lived in Lan Village and did not return home on a daily basis.

The contours of labor movement indicated that men scattered in ten provinces, cities and autonomous regions, as opposed to four for women. Most men traveled within Inner Mongolia (13), Beijing (13) or a few other neighboring provinces. In contrast, over half of the women (10) traveled within Inner Mongolia. Some big cities such as Beijing, Dalian, Shenyang and Chifeng became the major destinations of women and young men due to geographical proximity. The most likely destination for young unmarried men with relatively higher education was Beijing to serve as security guards. Men were primarily concentrated in industry (14), construction (14) and certain service sectors (16), while women were typically domestic servants or in other service sectors. Less-educated married male migrants often relied on highly irregular and ill-paid manual jobs in brick factories or road/house construction sites. Young men with higher education tended to translate their advantage into relatively well-paying employment in the urban markets.

As noted in Chapter three, about one quarter of the total population in Ao Village were away from the village for at least four months in 2003. As a large amount of villagers moved out of the village, their attention should have been diverted from natural resources, thus contributing to a release in the pressures on local ecology. However, unlike in many other places in rural China where only "the 386199 troupe" were still anchored in the village community, many migrants constantly shuttled back and forth to the village.

This stemmed from a variety of reasons. Married men were generally unwilling to migrate out for many pragmatic reasons. Most middle-aged residents had no urban experience and were not accustomed to living in "the harsh outside world." As other migrants from the rural hinterland, many of them lacked the much-needed technical skills and tended to wander from one place to another to do whatever job they could find. They were mainly channeled into low-paying manual work as casual or menial workers and their chances of earning high wages were slim. Meanwhile, to deduct or withhold their wage by employers was quite common. Many young men ended up with little money to send back home or returned with empty pockets. While I was staying in the village, I frequently heard residents complain about delayed or little payment among migrants. Throughout 2004, the national media attention turned to a policy of the Central Government to demand appropriate and timely payment for peasant workers, which signaled the severity and widespread presence of the problem across China.

The marginal existence, uncertainty and risk of migrant workers in the city, particularly a few failed migration attempts, served as a constant reminder to villagers that migrating had in no way changed the nature of the household economy, nor their lot. When one partner migrated out, the other half, particularly men, could not manage the household properly and till the land profitably on their own. The prolonged physical separation of family members led to other domestic problems as well. In addition, in this part of China, livestock farming at least was not a total dead-end road.

As noted above, off-farm opportunities were few and far between for village women, and most of them were bound more closely to the land. Some deeply ingrained socio-cultural beliefs still prevented married women from pursuing migrant work. Even under such circumstance, village women were by no means passive victims. The following exceptional story of Lin Hui was about women's agency and their copying strategies. Lin Hui, aged 37, came from a rural community in a neighboring province. Lin Hui married into Ao Village in 1985. To improve their lives, Lin Hui and her husband never stopped to diversify the household economy.

They ran a bean curd business for a couple of years and developed plastic-sheet greenhouses in their courtyard for some time. In 2000, she and three other married women went on expeditions to Beijing to work as domestic workers through the help of the Qi Women's Federation. She worked there for four months. Based upon her prior experience, she ventured into Chifeng City in 2003 and worked in a restaurant for four months. She believed that women were more likely to find stable work in the city and exhibited great courage and traveled outside the community.

Emerging Wealth and Poverty through Villagers' Eyes

China was one of the most egalitarian countries when the economic reforms were launched in 1978. But as of 1995, income inequality in China had become greater than that of most other developing countries in Asia (Khan and Ruskin, 2001). The impact of macroeconomic changes, of course, varied from place to place and from household to household. The introduction of the HRS and other reform measures engendered an economic boom and rising income among villagers. Meanwhile, the process of growing social stratification and economic differentiation was underway. This trend became increasingly prominent with the diversification of livelihood, and gender emerged as a significant variable that shaped the household survival and prosperity. In the following section, I will outline gendered dimensions of wealth and poverty in a village setting.

Collectivization as a Miserable History

Before going any further into intra-community differentiation, I will first turn to the collective past. The collective memories of that period were always imbued with a history of material deprivation. Most, if not all, women surviving the miserable existence delineated a common scenario of relentless poverty and painful workloads within the household and beyond. When men were socially constructed as the breadwinners, and thereby more closely tied to collective labor all the year round, it could safely be assumed that apart from participating in public production, women almost exclusively shouldered ceaseless undervalued household chores, and thereby "ate numerous bitterness" (*chi le hen duo ku*).

Their physical labor was always painstaking, intensive, repetitive, induding hauling water over long distances, fetching firewood and forage grass, collecting wild vegetables, processing and preparing food, washing clothes, rearing children, provisioning shoes and clothes, and so forth. As of 2003, the use of human pole carriers was rarely seen, but in the past residents predominantly relied upon the carrying pole to shoulder heavy loads.For much of these domestic chores, men virtually spent little time. Women handled domestic financial hardships in various ways. Some mentioned that they often exchanged cloth coupons for cash rather than renewing their own clothes. Few of the residents had anything good to wear and even girls were sometimes dressed in rags. In the winter, villagers wore cotton-padded suits, since few could afford underpants or shirts; they sometimes had to tightly tie a rope around their waist when working outside against the freezing wind. Most young girls were taken up with shoe making under kerosene lamps for the whole winter night with "their nose and face often getting dark." At a time of serious financial trouble, some women even made shoes for sale. Young married women never stopped being busy from juggling childcare with field or domestic work. If there were no elderly folks available to look after the kids, it was quite common for elder siblings of even four or five years old to assume the childcare responsibilities. Many women constantly noted when they were working in the field, they sometimes were obliged to have their babies wrapped on their back, or tied on the *kang* alone at home.

Daily life in Ao Village had undergone an impressive transformation in ways previously unimaginable since decollectivization. One exceptional example was the tough job of grinding grains—once the heaviest work burden for women. There were then four hand-powered grinding stones in the community. Throughout the period of collectivization, women were obliged to push the heavy grinding stones almost on a day-to-day basis, only a tiny fraction of households had donkeys to help them. Only after a day's work could they get some subsidy grain, for which the whole family often waited to "fill their empty bellies." Not only was the work labor intensive, it was also time-consuming. It normally took 3-4 hours to grind 20 catties of grain. Resident regularly stood in line for their turns day and night. I was often told, "If you got up very early in the morning, you would find someone else might have not yet gone to sleep." Not until electrification in 1979 did the community own its own laborsaving food processing machines. Only a few years later, all village women were liberated from the age-old household chore. As with the mechanization of grain processing, to have wells at home made similar impacts on women's lives.

There was little doubt that the material well-being and living standards among residents had dramatically improved, breaking sharply with the collective past. As of 2003, almost all villagers were better fed, clothed and sheltered than in the past. Residents almost could not afford to raise pigs and had no pigs to kill during the collective era. But in 2003, 125 resident households, or 85.6 percent reared pigs and 77.4 percent could slaughter a pig for the lunar New Year. It was widely recognized that there was nothing worthwhile in individual houses, by 2003, most households held more productive assets such as carts, and small or large animals. Some households invested in luxurious domestic property such as motor vehicles, brick houses, color TV sets with satellite broadcast receiver and cell phones. For most residents, their main concern seemed not for basic physical survival but rather for enough subsistence and even the pursuit of prosperity.

This provided a context of understanding the fact that I was always taken by surprise, even though some inhabitants were still living a miserable existence, with meager income, monotonous diet, and even depressed debt, a prominent subject in everyday discourses among inhabitant, particularly among older women, was to blame the failures of collectivization, while comment about their material improvement. Such sentiments surfaced and resurfaced in daily dialogues: "In the past, we worked like animals, but ate 'pig feed';" "The livestock today enjoy a happier life than we did in the past;" "I have eaten a lifetime of bitterness, and I am more than satisfied with my current life;" "I have never dreamed of a life like today, it is as if we are now living in the heaven;" "Our brick houses are better than those of former landlords, who only owned thatched roofs with a few tiles."

In contrast to what Croll (1994) asserts, "Everyone feels the burden of the present and thus the past is remembered as happy." Very few men and women were nostalgic about the past when they were tightly locked into collective farming.[1]In explaining why unfair treatment of women did not dampen their feelings of life satisfaction, Woon (1991:164-165) attributes it to their limited exposure of the outside world, "not having lived or worked outside of their rural community, their social horizon, which like those of village women in other parts of the world is normally confined to their domestic spheres." This point was far from true in Ao Village. Almost all households at least owned a small black and white TV set at home. Additionally, young men and women were on the move, and thus greatly increased villagers' contact with the outside world. All these factors subjected the village to outside influences in many tangible and intangible ways. Although they did not lack knowledge about the

1 Some villagers did express their nostalgia about the inexpensive health services provided via the cooperative medicine during certain periods of collectivization.

outside world, their frame of reference was ostensibly their own immediate living world, especially their own distant or immediate past. As experienced by the eldest generation of women, after all, life in 2003 was better than any other time in the history of the village.

Growing Stratification at the Local Level

Here as elsewhere in the Chinese countryside, the gap in household wealth and socio-economic differentiation during the collective period was relatively small, which was determined largely by the ratio of laborers and dependants within the household. After decollectivization, economic differentiation grew in myriad ways and village inequality became an integral part of local social landscape.

The gap between village elites and their less fortunate counterparts could be traced back to the advent of household farming. At the time of de-collectivization, a few elites gained privileged access to collective assets, and a few of them established household enterprises such as the drug store and the grocery store. Although farmers' living standards began to stagnate and even decline across rural China after the mid-1980s, in this part of China, the policy stimulus, the intensification of domestic labor, rampant reclamation, good weather, and many other factors triggered an unprecedented crop increase over much of the 1980s, many households started to get rid of the shortage of subsistence cereals, and a few rose from poverty to modest prosperity primarily through industriousness and thriftiness. Throughout the 1990s, the availability of irrigation farming, the proliferation of livestock production, coupled with the harvesting of the seed of green crop, boosted income substantially among some households. The short honeymoon period in the early-mid 1990s further widened the intra-household inequality. Since 1999, Ao Village has suffered from income setbacks due to 6 successive years of drought, which made it extremely hard for the poor to grow crops profitably and even less chance of clearing up their debts. These dreary economic conditions did not seem to have any prospect of a change for the better, at least not in the near future.

Taken as a whole, there was a lower degree of economic differentiation here than was observed in other rural communities in more prosperous coastal areas. Most residents toiled in the fields and eked out a meager living as farmers. As voiced by many residents, "Unlike urban folks who enjoy monthly salaries, 'old' peasants receive the rewards for their inputs only one time in a year." This was especially true for full-time crop farmers. To satisfy many cash-dependent basic needs, the richer segment of the population had the capital accumulated to break out of stagnation to diversify into livestock production or other profitable family enterprises. An increasing amount of adaptive farmers sought chances through livestock production or migration. As residents frequently complained, "The present money world renders the rich richer, while the poor get poorer." It is worth noting that differentiated access and use of natural resources played a significant role in shaping the loss and fortune among moneyless residents and their rich neighbors. Particularly, the state policies of privatization of natural resources favored the already affluent households, and thus exacerbated rather than reduced socio-economic differentiation among residents.

According to official estimation, the annual per capita net income of Ao Village was 1423RMB (about US$170) in 2003 (GYV, 2003a), as against the aggregate figure of Greater Ao Village of 1498,[1] less than the average income of 1541RMB in Aohan Qi, 2284RMB in Inner Mongolia and 2622RMB in China among peasants and pastoralists (ASB, 2004). In the 30 sample households, there were on average 3.5 persons per household and the average household income was 10153RMB in 2003.[2]The combined overall per capita income calculated in cash was 2744RMB, a figure even exceeding the national level and much higher than official figures. Several reasons could explain this short-lived extremely high figure in the year of 2003. Their income was boosted by the intrusion of several emerged economic opportunities—the highway construction, the small watershed project, the profitable sale of shrub seed as well as the large-scale disposal of sheep.[3]

It can be seen from table 8.3, approximately 38 percent of the total household income came from crop production and 31 percent from the sale of animals. The returns from cereal production per *mu* were virtually quite low, and the relatively

1 But according to the village director, the reported annual average income per person in Greater Ao Village was 1040RMB in 2003, which was set by the township government based upon calculation rather than the real survey.

2 The estimated income did not calculate the costs of daily subsistence items such as the consumed grain, vegetables and others items.

3 The seeds that villagers sold earned them at least 40000RMB. Two households also rented out their rooms to the outside managers of the road construction project. In addition, at least three sample households sold off their large sheep herd accumulated for a long time entirely in response to the confinement policy and the sudden shrinking of pastureland caused by a series of projects.

high percentage was mainly because many households in the village operated relatively larger farms. For instance, two households running big farms in the sample households obtained, respectively, 16000RMB (50 *mu)* and 12000RMB (53 *mu).* Most smallholders virtually had no way to merely make a living from crop cultivation. Livestock income surpassed that of crop income as the most important source of income among seven sample households. The income from migrant labor averaged 10.6 percent, compared with 7.9 percent from local wage labor.

Table 8.3 Sources of Household Income and Percentage among Residents in Ao Village (2003)

Sector	Percentage (%)
Crop	37.7
Livestock	31.0
Migrant work	10.6
Local wage labor[1]	7.9
Transportation	4.8
Forest, shrub and green crop	3.7
Local non-farm wage labor[2]	3.3
Commerce	0.8
Total	100.0

Source: 2004 sample survey.

Note:

[1] It included income from *dahuizhan*, road construction, and working on the farms of others.

[2] It refers to the income earned by the teacher, hill keeper, vet and village cadre.

In this poverty-stricken community, villagers' income was much lower than the above figures in a normal year, and many of them actually stagnated in poverty. It was widely reported that about 70 percent of households were differently indebted, and a large proportion of them needed to borrow money for fertilizers before spring planting. According to my own observations, the income that smallholders generated through agriculture only allowed the continuity of subsistence. Most, if not all households, faced an uncertain and precarious future, and even the relatively rich were full of a sense of vulnerability. There was no sign that they would be able to increase their income in the near future. A local expression vividly captured the ongoing struggle among villagers, "you can feed the family without any problem, but you have little money available to spend."

Status Positions and Household Characters

Unlike more commercialized regions in the Chinese countryside, Ao Village was not a highly stratified village society, with its households appearing more homogeneous in their socioeconomic status. At first glance, there seemed no startling contrast between the wealthy and poor villagers in the social society, but the reality was far more complicated than it appeared. Initially, it was extraordinarily difficult for me to find any clear criteria by which to judge wealth and poverty among residents. For example, although a good house symbolized one's economic status, some prosperous households did not have brick houses, nor did they have relatively higher consumption levels such as better food, clothes, furnishings or modern equipment items. Quite the contrary, some poor households built new houses from the borrowed money, primarily for the sake of their sons' marriage. Some persons from relatively rich households claimed themselves poor, whereas some really poor persons never spoke of their impoverishment.

Only after staying in the village for an extended period of time did many shades of poverty and wealth become clear to me. In the local world, to explain wealth and poverty and their reasons and outcomes was part of daily discourses, and thus of local politics. Villagers' perceptions of wealth and poverty somewhat contrasted with that of the official criteria, which was basically measured by a simplistic index of yearly income. According to locals, income distribution was sharply stratified by access to labor, non-farm work, land or livestock, it was similar to the general process of social stratification taking place elsewhere in rural China.

However, some localized factors such as the amount of unmarried children, especially their gender, played a significant part in shaping the status of poverty and wealth among villagers. When asked to rank the rich and the poor, local men and women often made judgments about the economic status not mainly by houses, clothes, or food, but rather by the status of debt among the poor or the ability to lend loans among the rich. This locally created criteria perhaps reflected the most revealing economic distinctions between the poor and the rich. On closer inspection, many reasons and outcomes of wealth and poverty were differentiated along gender and age lines.

The village poor varied in several important ways. The economically distressed households (*kun nan hu*) principally belonged to two extreme categories. At one end of the spectrum was a group of elders, while at the other were the heavy debtors. These "shades" of poverty helped my understanding of the workings of differentiated processes in local social structure. The least fortunate senior persons or couples, were mostly in their sixties and seventies. They often lived separately in old-fashioned clay houses with merely one room of about 10 square meters in size, and struggled to eke out a marginal existence. They lost cash-earning potential and lacked money, labor and even health and thus subsisted at the lowest standard of living. As elsewhere, there was a limited social safety net for elders. Except four male veterans who received a monthly stipend of about 100RMB for their former military service, the remaining elders, male and female, depended totally upon their sons to provide financial support. Their income was usually well below the village average. One of the rare sources of extra cash income for them was access to some communal resources. The least fortunate among them were those who suffered from a variety of health problems, and therefore were in desperate medical need. Old "bare stick" (bachelors) constituted a particularly disadvantaged group, facing an even bleaker old age.

The poor at the opposite end of the spectrum were a host of households trapped in a heavy debt of 10000-20000RMB or even more. It was impossible for me to systematically document the dynamic debt among residents, but anecdotal evidence indicated that there were at least 10 percent of such households. The key reasons for their financial troubles included the accident, marriage and house building debt, improper investment and so on. Most households that fell into this category were headed by middle-aged people, who were mired in debt due to the marriage of their sons, for which I will elaborate more fully below. A small minority of households of the younger generation impoverished themselves for irrational investments such as buying a tricycle.

Against the background of increasing per capita incomes, everything became very expensive. The annual income of some households was not enough to meet some key cash-dependent basic needs, let alone to cope with a variety of contingencies. As elsewhere in the global "South", the global economic re-structuring led to increased health and education fees. Meanwhile, the demise of collective institutions, which provided certain social services in the past, resulted in sharp deterioration in access to health care, education, and other welfare services. As with other hinterland poor, the Ao Village population had to cope with the disasters on their own, and thus became increasingly vulnerable to contingences such as sickness, accidents, bride wealth, and so forth. Many people, especially elders, always cited privatized health care as one of the major causes of their impoverishment. Indeed, many households spent a considerable share of their cash income on drugs, medical care or treatment. On many occasions, elder people hopelessly remarked to me, "If we were seriously ill, we could not afford to stay in the hospital, and thereby could only wait for my death at home."

Another reason for village impoverishment was the increased education expenditure. Like other farmers across rural China, villagers faced increasing pressures to put their children through primary and secondary school. Education costs became a principal daily expense, and thereby "heavy burdens" (*fu dan hen zhong*) was a phrase that most frequently came to residents' lips. The village school previously went through the fifth grade, offering primary school education. When children attended this school, they lived and ate at home. Beginning in 2002, the village school was cancelled. All kids commuted weekly to the primary schools stationed in the township seat. Schooling payments included tuition fees, books, meals, living costs, and transportation fees, which totaled about 1200RMB per year. According to residents' recollection, the school fee shoot up by at least 200-fold compared with that in the collective era (normally 5-6RMB yearly). If studying in junior high school in the township seat, it cost about 1500RMB, if attending senior high school in the county seat, it required about 3000-4000RMB per year. In 2003, five teenagers continued to study beyond junior high school. The high cost proved beyond the capacity of most average farming households.[1]If villagers were burdened with two children in school, they had to spend almost all of their annual income.

Chen Jie from former Team Three was a long-indebted household due primarily to the education of their two children. Chen Jie and his wife, Huang Zheng, respectively, were aged 48, and 50 in 2003. Chen Jie became a farmer when he was demobilized from the army in the late 1970s. He seemed never to benefit from his prior military experiences. Huang Zheng was a high school graduate, which was extremely rare among women in her generation. Before marriage, she was

1 The situation was even more dismal in the impoverished villages in Yunnan province, where limited off-farm opportunities kept the opportunity cost of labor quite low. To pay for school fees, many males had to work on state-funded road construction projects for 10RMB each day, while the primary school fee for one child studying in the county seat was roughly equivalent to half a year's work on the construction project.

a primary school teacher in her natal village. Since she married into Ao Village, she permanently lost her post as a teacher. Even before their daughter, Chen Min, attended a technical secondary school and continued later to go to college, the household always had bad fortune and was at the bottom of the economic ladder in the village. Their poverty struck me strongly. I observed that they lived in a small mud house. There was only a small black and white TV, and a few pieces of old-fashioned furniture in the room. According to a newspaper report, the household was one of the very targets of a county governor's poverty alleviation project. Residents admitted that they were both hardworking people and the only fault on the part of Chen Jie was probably that he squandered some money on eating and drinking. It was rumored that however impoverished, they both drank alcohol a lot, and even borrowed money to buy it. Like his father, Chen Jie always addressed me with warmth. Each time when I paid a household visit, he warmly invited me to eat at their home. One day, before I realized it he had ridden his bike to my host's house to inform Song Ling that I would eat at his home.

Their daughter, Chen Min, a motivated girl, was two years younger than her elder brother. The couple admitted whenever education resources were scarce, they preferred to educate their son rather than their daughter. In spite of better performance, Chen Min was kept at a lower grade to let her brother enter junior high school first. When both children studied, the couple often struggled by relying upon the digging up of Chinese herbs to pay for their education fees. In 1999, when Chen Min was accepted by a technical secondary school, all but Huang Zheng, including many relatives expressed their objection to sending a girl to the school on the grounds that the household was abjectly poor and her brother was in an age of being engaged. Their son's marriage was finally held up, which helped to support his sister in finishing her college education through migrant labor.

From 1999-2004, the Chen couple made a huge sacrifice of spending about 30000RMB for Chen Min's education. The cost of tuition fees were a constant source of anxiousness. To finance their daughter's education, they had to borrow some money each year. In 2001, Chen Jie went with his daughter to work as a construction worker in the city where she studied for 8 months, and left Huang Zheng to struggle by herself at home. During my 2004 revisit, Chen Jie so was excited to tell me that their daughter had graduated from college and found a secure job in a city. The couple took considerable pride in their daughter's performance.

Indeed, Chen Min attained the highest level of education ever reached by a woman in the history of the village.

The economic situation of individuals and households could change drastically over time. A former male team leader ate and dressed well when he was a bachelor during the collective period. He could afford trousers of corduroy, the best cloth in those days. Twenty-eight years ago he married a widow, Li Hua, with two young sons. The couple helped the two sons to secure wives. They lived with the family of the younger son. The family fortunes started to go down suddenly in 1998 when their son's wife died in a car accident, leaving behind a 5-year-old boy. Their son spent considerable sums of money to carry out a lawsuit, and consequently mired a sizable family indebtedness of over 20000RMB. From then on, their son lost willingness to work hard. In 2003, he migrated out of the village to work elsewhere, and thus the burden of the young boy's life fell on the shoulders of the older couple, who managed to till 10 *mu* of ration land to earn a bare subsistence, however, they had much trouble offering the school fee of about 1200RMB per year for their grandson—a huge sum in the budget of the poor household.

Since Li Hua was a natural mother of their son, she had to assume more pressures to sustain daily life and productive practices. Like other village poor, Li Hua often struggled to beg help from others, buying medicine on credit from the drug store, as she did from the grocery store. They seldom plowed and irrigated the field, and used little commercial fertilizer. With tears trickling down her face, she complained to me, "no one really cared about the real poor. When they were rich, they had many friends and now few stopped by." She asserted, she did not want to cry poverty a lot, since nobody showed real sympathy. In 2003, only about 400RMB was created from 10 *mu* of ration fields cultivated. The average per capita income in the household was 526RMB, more than ten times lower than that of the richest household of 5875RMB per person in my 30 sample households. This was not the only case in which an affluent family was reduced to poverty immediately by tragic accidents. I was always struck to know many similar unfortunate stories, which demonstrated the vulnerability of rural life. Very poor people, like this older couple, were often short of cash to buy sufficient fertilizers, let alone make any investment in agriculture.

Both men and women were acutely aware of the wealth gap. I got the impression that there were subtle social oppositions among differentially positioned social groups. The better off looked down on the poor, blaming them for their own impoverishment. For instance, the poor were most likely to be blamed as too lazy, "They are unable to farm it properly or timely; if a person works hard, the field will never be lazy." Most impoverished people experienced a strong sense of deprivation, frustration and stigmatization.

By contrast, the richer strata often felt intense jealousy from the poor, and they described the envy of the poor as having "an ill of red eyes" or "*hong yan bing*". From the perspective of the local poor, the well-to-do residents grabbed wealth at the expense of the poor. A tiny fraction of the richest segment (about 10 percent of all households) shared certain common characteristics. While none of the affluent households had pre-existing family wealth, they had changed their family's fortunes via multiple paths. They tended to have surpluses, other businesses beyond farming, and thus multiple sources of income. Some kept larger sheep herds, or held profitable non-farm enterprises. They had more chance to access to labor opportunities, land, capital and even state resources. The interest from loans was often a significant source of income for a few of them. A couple of them had only daughters without any sons or with only one son. For example, using the savings accumulated, the household running the sole grocery store purchased many luxurious consumer items by village standards, including a motorcycle, a cell phone, a colour TV set with a satellite broadcast receiver. In 2003, they bought a minibus taxi for about 30000RMB. This was in sharp contrast with the purchasing power of the overwhelming majority of residents.

According to indigenous criteria, Yang Baosheng headed a rich big household with a reversed fortune. He, aged 50 and his wife, Xue Hua aged 45 in 2003, lived a with the family of their younger son. Yang Baosheng attended school for two years, whereas his wife never went to school for a single day. She was a hardworking woman, yet seldom participated in household decision-making. Like others who had already been well off, they did well with multiple pursuits. Their elder son was a college graduate, who worked as an insurance salesman in a city in another province. The couple spent about 30000RMB for his four years of education without becoming trapped in any debt.

Yang Baosheng was still haunted by the painful, humiliating memories of the collective past. His parents came to the village in 1949, two years after local Liberation. As an "outsider", they at first lacked any kin support in the village. He was bullied constantly by others due to the rich-peasant status of his father. Yang

Baosheng began to work for the production team when he was thirteen years old. He was always assigned the dirty and most backbreaking jobs that nobody was willing to do, but earned lower work points than others. Even still, they were scared to speak their own minds or air their grievances publicly. Since they had the least chance of getting good opportunities from their team, his family exerted all their strength into making money from nature. When he was going to be engaged, he was looked down upon and even discriminated against by their teammates. A former team leader once remarked sarcastically, "You would never think over to change your lot even in your next life. I would rather have my daughter to bed down the livestock rather than to marry into a household like yours." His own industriousness and that of his family members impressed his prospective father-in-law, who he required a marriage payment of 400RMB from his parents, a figure higher than others. The young couple lived with his parents three years before dividing out in the very year of decollectivization and the couple rose out of exceptional poverty quickly.

A notable continuity with the past was that Yang Baosheng continued to rely on natural resources to sustain his family and make wealth. During the collective period, his parents and siblings were desperate to resort to the natural world for survival. Since he was 15-16 years old, he had gleaned and sold grasses as fuel during the winter when no work was assigned by their team. A 100-catty load of grasses was sold for cash of 1RMB in the then commune headquarters. On a good day, he could gather two loads per day. They also made *kang* mats for the market. After decollectivization, his household augmented their wealth little by little through sheep raising, frugality and industriousness. Initially, they had only one sheep and continued sheep raising without stopping from 1980 to 2003. At first, he himself was a shepherd and later his younger son. Since the mid-1990s, the household often harvested an annual income of about 10000RMB from the sale of sheep products. Their sheep herd once amounted to a maximum of 130 head. Yang Baosheng was one of the first who contracted a tract of hill to pasture their animals. In 1999 when their crops were hardest hit, they earned over 5000RMB from 36 *mu* of pastureland. The Yangs also expanded their fortune through tilling plenty of land. In 2003, the household tilled a total of 73 *mu* of cropland.

Due to the sudden shrinking of the pastureland and a series of projects, Yang Baosheng was forced to sell off all of their 104 sheep for a cash income of 21000RMB. The total household income in 2003 was 25720RMB, divided among

5 members in the household. The average per capita income was 5144RMB, almost 10 times that of the poorest household in my sample households. Using part of the money gained from the sheep sales as start-up capital, Yang Baosheng successfully made a quick switch to the relatively profitable venture of chicken raising. By the time of my 2004 fieldtrip, they kept another 1000 small birds, apart from 1000 mature chickens bought a year earlier that had already laid eggs. From purchasing small birds to the stage of laying eggs, 1000 chickens cost about 18000RMB, a substantial investment few could afford. The enterprise seemed to be worthy investment. Eggs sold brought them a profitable reward of about 80-100RMB cash income per day.

"Money with Legs": Financial Institutions at Play

Indebtedness was rather common among residents, albeit the size of debt varied greatly. It was widely believed that there was a proliferation of debt with the onset of the drought. One of the key reasons that the poor had no way to catch up with those who "got rich first" was that a few prosperous households accumulated capital through engaging in usurping, which was undoubtedly rooted in local financial institutions. The rural banking system in the Chinese countryside consisted primarily of local branches of the agriculture bank and the credit cooperative (*xin yong she*). As in other rural areas, ordinary villagers, especially the poorest, faced discrimination in accessing formal bank loans. Lacking confidence in the repay capacity of the poor prevented the bank staff member from extending cheap credit to them. As a result, only a relatively wealthy few were qualified to obtain loans from government-supplied credit. In Ao Village, about 8-9 households were once identified as the so-called households with good credit (*xin yong hu*). As a credit staff member confided to me, to guarantee repayment, most credit went to rural elites or the households who had relatives employed in local credit agencies.

Since the household responsibility system reform started in 1980, Ao Village had witnessed the revival of the practice of usury, which widely existed in the pre-Liberation period. During the collective period, the practice of lending money at interest, was stigmatized as "*fang gao li dai*" (an illegitimate act). In those days, residents tended to borrow a small amount of interest-free money from their neighbors or relatives. Due to the lack of access to credit and other formal financial services provided by the states, common villagers had to resort to high cost informal credit sources.It thrived and was widely practiced in the market environment, reflecting a larger Chinese pattern in the countryside. A distinction was made locally between the loans with interest and the interest-free loans. For the former, the moneylender and borrower required a go-between to write down a formal note. The moneylenders were a handful of village elites, including a few "state" teachers and richer outsiders. A couple of prosperous villagers told me that the money received as their daughter's bride wealth was loaned out to others at usurious interest rates and later was given back to their daughters after gaining great returns.

Access to informal credit was nearly universal among the poor villagers. Exorbitant interest rates could rapidly force those households to slip into huge debt. I knew in some Yunnan villages that the rich offered private loans at usurious rates up to 50 percent annually. In Ao Village and its vicinity, the value of interest was calculated at 20-30 percent for 10 months in 2003. This meant within three years, the accumulated interest would equal the value of the money originally borrowed. In this context, poverty and debt became intertwined, forcing the poor household into a spiral of ever-increasing debt. What smallholders earned usually was less than the interest they were supposed to pay. In this scenario, it was extremely hard for the borrower to break debt cycles. This, therefore, became the major reason that led to an exacerbation of socio-economic differences among residents.

Notably, women were more marginalized in access to official credit. Even if the credit was originally geared towards them, ironically, it fell in the hands of a few elite men. The UNDP micro credit project operating in the village was just such an example. The project was launched in Aohan in 1998 based upon the model of the Gremeen Bank in Bangladesh. It was originally intended to benefit poor women through the granting of small loans. In Lan Township, an office staffed by four village women was set up in the township headquarters. One of the women, Xu Shu, was a resident of Ao Village.

Despite much official rhetoric about its success, it was widely believed among residents that only a few elite men gained and used the credit. To my knowledge, in 2003, only one of the team leaders borrowed a sum of 2000RMB for its chicken raising enterprise in the name of his wife even without the knowledge of the latter. Another man from Lan Village borrowed a sum of loans under the names of several of his female relatives in Ao Village. Since it was launched in the village in 2000, only a small minority of households ever utilized the source of the loan, mostly for men's enterprises. It was no secret that the really poor women were never eligible for the low-interest loans and many women actually had no idea at all about the project. Although the interest rate of the loan was far lower than that from private moneylenders, many villagers noted that it was too troublesome to repay the money every half a month. In addition, the total loan of 1000-2000RMB was almost no use for launching a profitable project and thus "hardly worth their time to use it." As a former cadre commented, the project became something that the staff member "made a gift" to her friends or relatives.

"Two Sons Equal Two Bombs, Three Sons Eat You Up"

The increased bride-price payment played an important part in local stratification. Most households trapped in severe financial troubles said it stemmed from marriage debts. In this part of China, the escalating marriage expenses often encompassed engagement payment (*ding hun fei*), house building costs, the wedding ceremony and other minor expenditures. As we shall see below, the bride wealth became one of the greatest contingent expenditures and a key economic burden for the groom's household. In the eyes of villagers, the huge cost of marriage payment meant having two or three young adult sons was "disastrous," which was vividly captured by a marital metaphor expressed typically by locals, "two sons equal two bombs, three sons eat you up." A few residents with engaged sons also experienced a great loss due to their failure of getting back the entire marriage payment from a broken engagement. The investment that parents made for the marriage of their son(s) was often far above the ability of ordinary people and their lifelong accumulation was often far from enough to pay for it. What interests me here is how marriage costs in the form of bride wealth and dowry affected local stratification and how gendered inter-generational wealth transmission was operated.

The "bride-price," known as *cai li,* was the marriage payment given from the groom's side to the bride's side, which was commonly practiced in rural China. After decollectivization, escalated and extravagant marital payments were widely reported across rural China, the case of Ao Village fit into the general picture in poor rural areas quite well. Ao Village households with son(s) had to accumulate funds before their children approached the marriageable age. As of 2003, they spent at least 20000RMB for the marriage of a son. However poor they were, parents struggled to arrange their son's marriage in a timely fashion, otherwise, it would be a "debt" to their offspring for their entire lives.

The bride price was always under negotiation between parents of both parties. The bride's family attempted to negotiate a better price in the name of ensuring a daughters' well being.[1]Sometimes, the brides themselves were involved in the economic transactions. A young man with better qualities might obtain a wife without paying a high cost. The poorer the household, the higher the bride prices were. An articulate young man told me, he and his wife fell in love themselves, because his own parents were so poor, his prospective parents-in-law from the same village did not agree with the free-choice marriage, and therefore negotiated a higher marital payment by local standards. When he was engaged, the betrothal gift offered was worth 6200RMB in 1994. Another 2500RMB was given when they got married in 1997. This marriage payment of 8700RMB was then good money. His parents also spent some money to buy a TV set and some furniture, and a total of 15000RMB was spent for his marriage on the part of his parents. The natal family of her wife only gave them a washing machine as dowry. Using part of the daughter's marriage payments, his parents-in-law built a new house and took in a daughter-in-law. The young man claimed, "People here always used their daughter's money this way!" Towards the end of 2003, a couple of young women were going to get married, a frequently heard topic was that the young girls competed to seek the highest bride price.

More recently, as in many other regions, to provide a new house for the new couple at or after the marriage gained some currency, and became a key component of marriage transactions (Potter and Potter, 1990: 209). The boom of house building could perhaps be attributed to the surge in income and the operation of the brick factory.[2]The house as an indicator of economic success or failure was increasingly valued by young women, who were no longer contented with living with their parents-in-law under one roof and desired a new living space of their own. This was probably one of the key driving forces behind a veritable explosion of housing building and interior decorations in Ao Village. Some young women delayed

1 The size of the bride price was always negotiated through matchmakers, mostly males in Ao Village and surrounding villages, only a small part of it was usually returned in the form of a dowry.

2 After the brick factory was established in the village, bricks houses sprang up in the neighborhood. Sometimes the factory paid them in bricks rather than in wages. A vast majority of villagers built their brick houses one after another.

marriage or resisted household division before a new house was built. The brand new houses tended to have ceramic tiles and aluminium-framed plate glass windows. A few prosperous households lavishly furnished their houses. House building and decoration became one of the largest expenses for most households.

Although a woman with a substantial dowry might improve her status over the other women who did not have (Watson and Ebrey, 1991), a dowry[1]was not identified as a necessary component of the marriage transaction in this part of China. For a long time after Liberation, the practice of providing bride-price payment was denounced as "purchase and sell marriage," by and large, the practice of giving a dowry to a daughter at her marriage was widely practiced. However, compared with the bride price, the dowry was quite low. For example, similar to other women in her age category, Song Ling's parents requested a relatively high engagement payment of 360RMB at her engagement in 1974—an amount that was quite common at that time. Song Ling told me that she was more than happy to keep 18RMB that she earned from her ceremony service on the day of engagement as her pocket money. When they got married three years later, she received four sets of clothing from her parents-in-law, and her own parents only offered her some small items. Her parents retained almost all the bride price to build a mud house, where her mother and youngest brother still lived during my fieldwork.

Of particular interest, this marriage payment was often and continued to be accumulated partly at the expenses of daughters, not only through their hard labor before marriage, but also through their own bride prices. Most residents merely returned a small proportion of the bride price as dowry. Several old men confided to me, they "sold" their daughters for a high price, daughters therefore had few duties to support them in their old age. The households with daughters but without sons could therefore save the wealth they accumulated in their lifetime, and sometimes kept the

1 The dowry analysis can also be seen in the writings of William L. Parish and Martin K. Whyte (1978) *Village and Family in Contemporary China*, University of Chicago Press; Chan et al (1992) *Chen Village under Mao and Deng,* Berkeley: University of California Press; Margery Wolf (1985) *Revolution Postponed: Women in Contemporary China,* Stanford, California: Stanford University Press; Johnson (1983*) Women, the Family and Peasant Revolution in China,* Chicago: University of Chicago Press; Elizabeth Croll (1981) *The Politics of Marriage in Contemporary China,* Cambridge University Press; Yan Yunxiang (1996) *The Flow of Gifts: Reciprocity and Social Networks in a Chinese Village*, Stanford, CA: Stanford University Press.

bride price as an "old-age fund".

By 2003, young women had some agency in their marriage decisions and I never heard of young women being married against their will. There were indeed some exceptions that parents did not receive marriage payments. For example, the daughter of Yang Baoqin was engaged at 19 and got married at the age of 21 in 2001. The value of her *cai li* totaled approximately 8000RMB in cash. Yang Baoqin loaned out all the money at a 30 percent interest rate. By the time of the daughter's marriage, it had increased to almost 20000RMB. She gave all the money back to her daughter and spent "lavishly" on a dowry. Yang Baoqin gave another 4000RMB collected from gifts to her daughter, plus a washing machine, gas stove, electric cooker and so forth. Her daughter kept much of the money as her personal money. As Siu (1993) rightly points out, marital payments "involve not so much the exchange of material goods and prestige between the families of bride and groom as the intense and rapid devolution of property to the conjugal couple at the time of marriage itself." Indeed, in this part of rural China, a significant amount of family wealth was transferred to male offspring at the expense of their parents.

To summarize, in this part of China, most men and women still relied heavily upon agriculture as their main livelihood and alternative opportunities were rare. The economic re-structuring had gendered impacts on NRM regimes and thus environmental practices via men's and women's interactions with the market, commodity or labor. As Ao Village was increasingly absorbed into the market economy, the vie for cash income and the demand of money had significant implications for natural resources exploitation, and thus shaped and continued to shape local environments through maximizing resources use. Labor market liberalization had a gendered impact. Men and women's differentiation in off-farm employment in the past persisted through 2003.

It is worth noting that only a small minority of men could maintain sustainable income streams from off-farm work in the community and beyond, yet there was a lack of occupation diversification among women in the gendered household economy. In the face of economic and environmental crises, a large proportion of villagers abandoned the land to join the internal migration to the city, and thereby tied Ao Village more closely to the world outside beyond its borders. Although migration somewhat alleviated the pressures on the land and other natural resources, the uncertainty and unpredictability of this global trend was still problematic in

China. This helped to explain why villagers were constantly on the move.

Local processes of globalization, as experienced by village men and women—fluctuating, unstable prices of crop and livestock products, migration of family members, increases in wage labor, rising aspirations for cash incomes and uneven wealth—had gender-specific ramifications. This was, I believe, not an exclusive story in Ao Village, but rather mirrored a larger scenario of globalization. Like anywhere else in the countryside of west China, many crosscutting factors of wealth, age and gender figured prominently in local differentiation. Most villagers faced the frustration of dwindling income and mounting debts. Their vulnerabilities derived from accidents, increased bride prices, lacking access to official credit and old age support as well as the reduction in state-provided services and benefits such as health care and education. The principal reasons were beyond the immediate control of villagers. It was reasonable to assume that improvement in life chances in the near future was unlikely for most men and women.

Chapter Nine

Gender, Conservation, Development: Sustainability Dilemmas

China's rural development over the past half-century was punctuated by an ambitious attempt to transform the natural environment. "Wars against nature" were long a nationwide characteristic in the Chinese countryside during the collective period. After decollectivization, rather than being reversed, overexploitation of nature was intensified by rapid economic development and increased inequality. The persistence and transformation of the interplay of gender-environment relations in the twin campaigns was shifting. The environment differed dramatically in time and space in the village scene, and this temporal and spatial variability added complexity to social relations in general, and gender relations in particular in a context of intra-community dynamics. The Ao Village case sheds light on a complex and fluid village landscape of environmental degradation, conservation and development enmeshed in the larger political economy.

This politically informed feminist study demonstrates the inextricably interconnected processes of ecological and social dynamics of natural resource use, environmental change, and the institutional mechanisms behind them in a village setting over the past five decades. The daily experiences of men and women in natural resource use, agricultural development and environmental conservation in the village, as an integral part of regional practices and a larger Chinese pattern, were heavily shaped by multiple extra-village forces that differentiated men's and women's lives and environmental experiences. Gendered political and economic power, as a result, loomed particularly large in the political ecology of natural resource use, management and conservation within the household and outside. This study highlights the significance of gender to local men's and women's lives and to environmental sustainability. In this final chapter, I return briefly to some of the key issues raised in the preceding chapters.

Engendering Everyday Natural Resources Use and Environmental Changes

To explore the current environmental challenges, one must look to the legacies of the past. A chronological discussion of the gender-environment nexus in a Chinese village over the past half-century demonstrates that the fate of natural resources and that of local men and women relying upon them was always enmeshed in shifting "development" strategies.

Natural resources use and management has never been gender neutral. Instead, it is embedded in asymmetrical power relationships among men and women. From grassroots perspectives, land use and land cover change showed a complex trajectory of both improvement and degradation in the village landscape over different historical periods. Ao Village was initially characterized by large expanses of pastureland, much of it was gradually put into cultivation after the Han migrants moved in. Environmental components in the village were not homogenous, neither were the lived environmental experiences of men and women. In this part of China, women's productive and reproductive work linked more closed with natural resource use, and thus they were more vulnerable to ecological changes.

In the pre-Liberation period, when poor men worked outside as day laborers or sharecroppers, poor women, Han or Mongol, unmarried or married, performed a variety of reproductive work, much of which was directly connected with natural resource access and use: collecting firewood, fetching water, and gathering wild plants to supplement the meager grains won by their male family members on an almost day-to-day basis. Over much of the time under the collective regime, the social organization of collective production dampened enthusiasm and bred cynicism among residents, which in turn, hurt agricultural production and local ecology. The poor performances of crop and livestock production, relentless poverty, and desperate food shortage gave rise to devastating environmental practices. When daily survival was at issue, the removal of natural vegetation proliferated among residents, particularly among women, and livelihood practices themselves became environmentally damaging. While men were socially constructed as the breadwinners, and thus more closely tied to collective activities, aside from participating in collective agricultural production, women almost exclusively shouldered ceaseless undervalued household chores linked closely with natural resource use. From this perspective, local men and women were crucial agents of environmental change, exemplified by the linkage of their lived experiences of work, both productive and reproductive, to the natural world.

In the post-1980 period, local economic and political re-structuring continued to shape men's and women's lived experiences and their interplay with the natural environment. After the decollectivization of agriculture, Ao Village was caught up in a whirlwind of changes. Although there was no lack of environment-friendly farm practices in the ration land at the household level, the accelerating pace of agricultural commercialization and intensification gave rise to less environmentally sound agricultural practices at village and regional level. The unequal access and distribution of natural resources along axes of wealth, gender, age and livelihood encouraged growing disparities in wealth among the least and most powerful village actors. As elsewhere, Ao Village witnessed a most significant pattern of labor re-gendering in the agricultural labor force. Under these circumstances, changing patterns of gendered agricultural practices, including shifting sites and spaces of women and men's work, responsibilities, rights, access to and control over natural resources, in turn, have complex implications for overall land use patterns and hence on the environment.

In the studied community as elsewhere in rural China, during a quarter century of collectivism, nature was treated as an enemy and the wars against it persisted. The legacy of mass conservation campaigns was perpetuated in Aohan with the advent of household farming, which stemmed from localized historical particularities of the county not widely found elsewhere. Despite national and international fame for its conservation work, the stories drawn from the grassroots shed light on the mystifications of contradictory interests of development and conservation. Environmental interventions were often based on flawed "scientific" apolitical assumptions in the name of "development" and progress, which often suffered from a naïve belief in the fruits of technology-driven projects. The experiences of villagers in Ao Village in the twin campaigns of "war against nature" and "rebuilding beautiful landscapes", more broadly, rural development, demonstrates many dimensions of multilayered bureaucratic control, combined with cadres' malpractice, and thereby betrayed the limitations of the environmental initiatives at the local level.

Not only has environmental conservation not been politically neutral, it has not been gender neutral either. Most notably, local residents, particularly women, were left with no consultation or choice, but to contribute their labor in the top-down campaigns, whether they liked it or not. The simultaneously "gender-blind" and male biased "*da hui zhan*", based upon false notions of femininity and masculinity, never took women's needs or interests seriously into account, and as a consequence, had extremely negative impacts on women. The waxing and waning of various shortsighted programs left behind painful experiences among local women found in each woman's accounts of mass labor. Most women of the generation of "iron girls", who were in their fifties in 2003, experienced extremely arduous physical work when they were young. In the post-reform period, the mass labor demands were allocated to the household on a per capita basis. Women of the "iron girls" generation continued to assume the bulk of mass labor.

Leach et al (1999: 226) cogently summarizes the determinants of failure in the practical implementation of community-based natural resource management initiatives. They include a tendency for the "intended beneficiaries" to be treated as passive recipients of project activities; a tendency for projects to be too short-term in nature and overreliant on expatriate outsider expertise; a lack of clear criteria by which to judge sustainability or success in meeting conservation or development goals; and systematic neglect of the interests of certain social groups that have been consistently marginalized. Indeed, all these pitfalls identified above could find strong echoes in Ao Village. They were related to institutional factors—the market, household, community and state, exposing some inherent dilemmas associated with contemporary rural modernization in the Chinese countryside.

Institutional Landscapes

In Ao Village, natural resource management and agricultural development has been embedded in a complex matrix of social institutions, macro and micro. To comprehend the institutional obstacles to achieving sustainability, this study explores the institutions of the household, community, market, and state in shaping sustainable and unsustainable environmental practices. The persistent problems trapping many villagers in a vicious spiral also faced male and female farmers throughout west China: fluctuating market prices, unfavorable price ratios between needed agricultural inputs and what they produced and sold, lack of official credit and high interest rates of private loans, little off-farm work opportunities, heavy indebtedness, as outlined below, all of which can be traced to institutional factors.

Paralleling decollectivization and other reform measures, the household once again became a basic unit of agricultural production, which set the parameters within which everyday resource use and management were implemented, negotiated and struggled over in the context of a multiplicity of changing social relations, particularly gender relations. However, the Chinese State and its local agents from Liberation through 2005 always treated the "household" as a unit of measure and of policy assessment without looking at the differentiated relations between men and women, boys and girls inside a household. Treating women and men within a household as working together as equals disguised the reality that men had more opportunity to move out of the village or engage in off-farm work locally and to leave the agricultural and conservation labor to adult women. On several occasions, women told me no matter how pretty and healthy they were when they married into the village, they became old quickly, because they were burdened with too much work—productive, reproductive and mass conservation campaigns.

As elsewhere in rural west China, natural resources were instrumental to the well-being of local residents, particularly women. However, the determinants of natural resource use were firmly embedded in larger political economy. They were not only shaped by the development policies and practices imposed by bureaucratic state power at various levels, but also by complex social dynamics. The repeatedly shifting policies of private and collective management policies, which were rife with uncertainty and subjected to changes, significantly shaped environmental practices. Meanwhile, the mutually reinforcing social relations in village life governed access and control over natural resources, and thereby shaped the working and living conditions of villagers. Among them, men's and women's roles in use and management of environmental resources were refashioned into the local environment through gendered divisions of labor, responsibilities, rights and spaces.

Village women were marginalized in the wider world beyond their immediate domestic world. As in other rural communities in West China, Ao Village was increasingly embedded in complex capital, labor and produce markets. As in most other agrarian societies, a majority of villagers, particularly women, still made their living from the land in 2003. There was little opportunity for women to pursued off-farm work locally. Married women seldom ventured outside the village. The gendered nature of occupations tied women more closely to the natural world. Women also had far less opportunity to gain access to formal political structures or even paid jobs offered by the village government. The gendered organizations of village leadership as well as NRM organs at both township and village levels relied upon only a few male actors. Institutional supports beyond the household for female farmers in the form of extension services, training, information and input supply were still elusive or even worked to their disadvantage. Even in the female-oriented UNDP projects, micro-credit loans ultimately fell into the hands of a few male elites rather than the intended beneficiaries. However, many stories presented in the preceding chapters challenge the characterization of women as passive victims. In daily village life, power between men and women were negotiated and challenged particularly in the intimate world of household.

Rural development in general, and environmental conservation in particular, were politically charged issues. Throughout the period addressed by this study, social inequities were interwoven with growing poverty, declining natural resources, degraded environments and unsustainable development. Conservation and development seldom fully integrated the ecological objectives with other long-term goals of community development. Nor did they fundamentally deal with the underlying structural factors—poverty, astonishing social inequalities, particularly gender inequalities and the lack of viable livelihood strategies—in a holistic manner. Without paying attention to all these political charged issues, far from rebuilding "beautiful landscapes" across the county, the crusade for nature was based on flawed technology-driven apolitical assumptions in the name of "development" and progress. It did not take into account men's and women's needs or interests, and ultimately functioned as an "anti-politics machine" (Ferguson, 1994), a kind of diversion from serious political issues of privatization and inequality.

The study raises many questions of welfare, equity, empowerment, especially with respect to environmental sustainability. From a policy perspective, only people-centered development can build effective and equitable community-based management of resources in the medium to long-term at low transaction costs. In the case of Ao Village, it is obviously urgent to build village institutional capability, and more explicitly, to strengthen the capacities of village men and women as well as community institutions to address their environmental and social challenges in a comprehensive manner. More specifically, it is crucial to empower local men and women to utilize environmental resources sustainably so as to shape a more secure future for the community and themselves in the long run. This will require involving them in the decision-making and implementation process, and incorporating indigenous knowledge, skills and opinions. Indeed, equity objectives, and gender equity in particular, must be incorporated into development policies (Agarwal, 1997b; Jacobson 1992). As Jacobson (1992) argues, without addressing the issues of equity and justice, the development goals that are ostensibly universal, such as the alleviation of poverty, the protection of ecosystems, and the creation of a balance between human activities and environmental resources, simply cannot be achieved. Practitioners and policy makers must take seriously the local actors' perspectives and interests if they wish to enable sustainable development.

The Numbers Game

The research findings persuasively disclose that social and economic development at the grassroots level was open to local interpretation. Official data at the village level was not always accurate, and was even artificially underreported or inflated for various purposes. At the outset of my fieldwork, I was originally surprised to find that the recorded educational status among residents was artificially raised. This suspect data alerted me to other official figures throughout my fieldwork. This study throws light on many unreliable and even conflicting data concerning education status, household composition, livestock size, land use area, migrant workers and the like. Having concluded this study, I believed that this is by no means a localized problem.

These discrepancies mirrored serious problems in the statistical reporting system at village level, and more broadly, in rural areas. If the statistics at the village level were not accurate, then, we could not guarantee the accuracy of data quality at the township level derived from it, which in turn could not guarantee data quality at the county level, and even at the national level. This serves as a reminder that we cannot accept many official figures simply at face value.

Such faulty figures were misleading for decision-making. This was indeed a dangerous game. This revelation not only has profound policy implications, but also warns us of the hazards of some scholarly research relying only upon available official data. Accurate observations and descriptions can better capture the trajectories of rural development, and thus contribute to formulating or reorienting appropriate public policy. It is clearly urgent to improve the rural reporting system so as to make sense of statistics about local men's and women's everyday lives.

The Significance of a Gender Perspective

In this dissertation, I treat gender that is the contested meanings assigned by local and external actors to being male and being female, as a power process interacting with other power hierarchies to structure complementarities, cooperation as well as negotiation and contestation among various social actors. These power hierarchies interact in multiple political sites, from the household, to the community, market and state. Each is a site shaped by, and also producing ideas about "masculinity" and "femininity" where competing and conflicting interests and struggles were waged over resources, labor, power and authority.

Indeed, gender is a mediating force. To take gender seriously makes it possible to shed light on more nuanced understandings of women's lives, agencies and copying strategies, to contribute to an exploration of various axes of power that are thickly intertwined in rural men and women's daily lives, and to give visibility to a variety of heterogeneous experiences among women so as to challenge the homogenous category of rural Chinese women. The significance of gender analysis is also that it allows us to look inside the household so as to see different consequences of policies and programs for men and women, boys and girls and thereby make deeper sense of women's lives.

In China, the Chinese State and its local agents still treat the "household" as a unit of measure and policy assessment without looking at the differentiated relations between men and women inside a household. Despite the everyday essential roles of female farmers in managing natural resources, producing food, and sustaining livelihoods, state policies have not addressed women as a group and gender as a category of social relations. As Judd (1994: 2) points out, agrarian reform and its policy changes "have had wide ramifications throughout rural society, and none can be viewed as gender-neutral. Each of the policy changes and the program as a whole has been officially presented as changes in political economy without reference to gender or to the specific interests of women." In Ao Village as elsewhere, women were more than "half of the sky", and constituted a key part of the labor force in the countryside. Gender, therefore, figured prominently into the well-known "three agrarian questions" or "*san nong wen ti*"—the three interconnected dimensions of farmers, agriculture and rural areas. As of 2005, these three linked topics are top priorities of academic research and policy interventions in China, and each is profoundly entangled in gender relations and power inequalities between men and women.

The concept of "gender" was first introduced to China in the preparation of the 4th World Conference on Women around 1995, yet it still has not enjoyed great popularity with researchers, let alone practitioners. Gender and power shaping rural men's and women's lives is a worthy subject of investigation in many scholarly spheres within and beyond China. This discussion of the intersections of gender, class, ethnicity and other social identities in a Chinese rural setting also has broader relevance, since privatization, commercialization, massive migration, and feminization of agriculture are widespread phenomena throughout the global "South."

Literature Cited

Agarwal, Bina (1992) "The Gender and Environment Debate: Lessons from India," *Feminist Studies*, Vol.18, No.1.

——(1994) *A Field of One's Own: Gender and Land Rights in South Asia*, Cambridge, Cambridge University Press.

——(1997a) "Gender, Environment and Poverty Interlinks: Regional Variations and Temporal Shifts in Rural India, 1971-91," *World Development* Vol.25, No.1.

——(1997b) "Gender Perspectives on Environmental Action: Issues of Equity, Agency and Participation," Joan Scott (ed.) *Transitions, Environments, Translations: Feminism in International Politics*, New York and London: Routledge.

Agrawal, Arun and Clark C. Gibson (2001) *Communities and the Environment: Ethnicity, Gender and the State in Community-based Conservation,* New Jersey, Rutgers University Press.

Alvarez, Sonia (1990) *Engendering Democracy in Brazil,* Princeton, New Jersey: Princeton University Press.

Andors, Phyllis (1983) *The Unfinished Liberation of Chinese Women, 1949-1980*, Bloomington: Indiana University press.

Aohan Qi People's Government (AQPG) (2003) (Aohan Qi Ecological Construction Plan 2001-2010)(*Ao han qi sheng tai jian she gui hua* 2001-2010) .

Aohan Qi People's Government (AQPG) (1987) (Aohan Qi Placename Records) (*Ao han qi di ming zhi).*

Aohan Qi Gazette Editorial Committee (AQG) (1991) (Aohan Qi Gazette)(*Ao han qi zhi)*, Hohhot: Inner Mongolia People's Press.

Aohan Statistics Bureau (ASB) (2003) (Aohan Statistics Yearbook)(*Ao han tong ji nian jian).*

Aohan Statistics Bureau (ASB) (2004) (Aohan Statistics Yearbook)(*Ao han tong ji nian jian)*.

Aohan Qi People's Government (AQPG) (2003) (An Open Letter to Peasant and Pastoralist Friends all over the Qi From Aohan People's Government)*(Ao han qi ren min zheng fu gei quan qi nong mu min pen you de yi feng gong kai xin)*, *Chifeng Daily-An Aohan Version,* June 16.

Banister, Judith (1987) *China's Changing Population,* Stanford, California: Stanford University Press.

Berry, Sara (1989) "Social Institutions and Access to Resources," *Africa*, Vol.59, No.1.

Becker, Jasper (1996) *Hungry Ghosts: Mao's Secret Famine,* New York: Free Press.

Blake, Fred (1979) "Love Songs and the Great Leap: The Role of a Youth Culture in the Revolutionary Phase of China's Economic Development," *American Ethnologist,* Vol.6, No.1.

Bryant, Raymond L., Sinead Bailey (1997) *Third World Political Ecology*, London and New York: Routledge.

Bulag, Uradyn E. (1999) "Models and Moralities: The Parable of the Two 'Heroic Little Sisters of the Grassland'," *The China Journal*, No.42.

Bossen, Laurel (2002) *Chinese Women and Rural Development: Sixty Years of Change in Lu Village Yunnan*, Lanham, Boulder, New York and Oxford: Rowman &Littlefield Publishers, INC.

Boserup (1965) *The Conditions of Agricultural Growth: The Economics of Agarian Change under Population Pressure*, Chicago, Aldine.

Bourdieu, Pierre (1977) *Outline of a Theory of Practice*, Cambridge: Cambridge University Prerss.

Brosius Peter (1997) "Endangered Forest, Endangered People: Environmentalist Representations of Indigenous Knowledge," *Human Ecology*, Vol.25, No.1.

Burton Pasternak and Janet Salaff (1993) *Cowboys and Cultivators: The Chinese of Inner Mongolia,* Boulder, Westview Press.

Chan, Anita, Richard Madsen and Jonathan Unger (1992) *Chen Village Under Mao and Deng*, expanded and updated edition (second edition), Berkeley: University of California Press.

Carney, Judith (1988) "Struggles over Crop Rights and Labor within Contract Farming Households in a Gambian Irrigated Rice Project," *Journal of Peasant*

Studies, Vol.15, No.3.

Carney, Judithand Michael Watts (1990) "Manufacturing Dissent: Work, Gender and the Politics of Meaning in a Peasant Society," *Africa* Vol. 60, No.2

Carney, Judith and Michael Watts (1991) "Disciplining Women? Rice, Mechanization and the Evolution of Gender Relations in Senegambia," *Sings,* Vol.16, No.4.

Carney, Judith (1993) "Converting the Wetlands, Engendering the Environment: The Intersection of Gender with Agrarian Change in the Gambia," *Economic Geography* Vol. 69, No.4.

Cao, Jingqing (2000)(China along the Yellow River)(*huang he bian de zhong guo)*, Shanghai: Shanghai Literature and Art Publishing House.

Cartier, Carolyn et al (1999) "Empowering the 'Victims'? Gender, Development, and Women in China under Reform," *Journal of Geography*, Vol. 98, No.6.

Cohen, Myron (1993) "Cultural and Political Inventions in Modern China: The Case of the Chinese 'Peasant'," *Daedalus* Vol. 122, No.2

Croll, Elisabeth (1981) *The Politics of Marriage in Contemporary China.* Cambridge: Cambridge University Press.

——(1984) "The Exchange of Women and Poverty: Marriage in Post-Revolutionary China," Renee Hirschon (ed) *Women and Property-Women as Property*, London: Croom Helm.

——(1994) *From Heaven to Earth: Images and Experiences of Development in China,* London and New York: Routledge.

——(1995) *Changing Identities of Chinese Women: Rhetoric, Experience and Self-Perception in Twentieth Century China*, London: Zed Books Ltd.

Croll, Elisabeth, Huang Ping (1997) "Migration for and Against Agriculture in Eight Chinese Villages," *China Quarterly,* Vol.149.

Davin, Delia (1995) "Women, Work and Property in the Chinese Peasant Household of the 1980s," *Male Bias in the Development Process* (second edition) Diane Elson (ed.) Manchester and New York: Manchester University Press.

Davison, Jean (1988) (ed.) *Agriculture, Women and Land: The African Experience*, Boulder and London: Westview Press.

Deckers, Wolfgang (2004) "China, Globalization and the World Trade Organization," *Journal of Contemporary Asia*, Vol.34, No.1.

Dwyer, Daisy, Judith Bruce (1988) (eds.) *A Home Divided*, Stanford, CA:

Stanford University Press.

Economy, Elizabeth (n.d.) "China's Go West Campaign: Ecological Construction or Ecological Exploitation," *China Environment Series*, Issue 5.

Edmonds, Richard Louis (1994) *Patterns of China's Lost Harmony: A Survey of the County's Environment*, London: Routledge.

Elson, Diann (1995)*Male Bias in the Development Process* (2nd edition), Manchester and NY: Manchester University Press.

Entwisle, Barbara and Gail Henderson (2000) *Re-drawing Boundaries: Work, Households and Gender in China*, Berkeley, London: University of California Press.

Escobar, Arturo (1995) "Power and Visibility: Tales of Peasants, Women, and the Environment," *Encountering Development: the Making and Unmaking of the Third World*, Princeton, New Jersey: Princeton University Press.

Elvin, Mark and T. Liu (1998) *Sediments of Time: Environment and Society in Chinese History*, Cambridge: Cambridge University Press.

Elvin, Mark (1998) "The Environmental Legacy of Imperial China," *The China Quarterly*, No.156, special Issues: China's Environment.

Fangbin Qiao et al (2003) "Producer Benefits from Input Market and Trade Liberalization: the Case of Fertilizer in China," *Australian Journal of Agricultural Economics*, Vol. 85, No.5.

Fei Xiaotong (1990) *Threes Villages in Yunnan (yunnan san cun)*, Tianjin: Tianjin People's Publishing House.

——(1947)(1992) *Form the Soil: The Foundations of Chinese Society*: A *Translation of Fei Xiaotong's Xiangtu Zhongguo*, Introduction and Epilogue by Gary G. Hamilton and Wang Zheng, University of California Press.

Ferguson, James (1994) *The Anti-Politics Machine:"Development", Depoliticization, and Bureaucratic Power in Lesotho*, Minneapolis and London: University of Minnesota Press.

Folbre, Nancy (1986) "Hearts and Spades: Paradigms of Household Economics," *World Development*, Vol.14, No.2.

Friedman, Edward (1978) "The Politics of Local Models, Social Transformation and State Power Struggles in the People's Republic of China: Tachai and Teng Hsiao-p'ing," *The China Quarterly,* No.76

Friedman, Edward, Paul G. Pickowicz and Mark Selden (1991) *Chinese Village, Socialist State,* New Haven & London: Yale University Press.

Fraser, Nancy (1989) *Unruly Practices: Power, Discourse and Gender in Contemporary Social Theory*, Minneapolis: University of Minnesota Press.

Gates, Hill (1996) *China's Motor: A Thousand Years of Petty Capitalism*, Ithaca, New York: Cornell University Press.

Gibson, Clark, Margaret Mckean, Elinor Ostrom (2000) (eds.) *People and Forests: Communities, Institutions and Governance*, Cambridge, MA: The MIT Press.

Goetz, Ann Marie (1997) (ed.) *Getting Institutions Right for Women in Development*, London and New York: Zed Books.

Greater Ao Village (GYV) (2003a) *Nian zhong sheng chan tong ji bao biao* (The Year-end Production Statistics Forms).

Greater Ao Village (GYV) (2003b) *Ao cun jing ji fa zhan gui hua 2003-2005 (Greater Ao Village Economic Development Plan, 2003-2005).*

Guijt, Irene, Meera Kaul Shah (1999) (eds.) *The Myth of Community: Gender Issues in Participatory Development*, Intermediate Technology Publications.

Guyer, Jane (1988) "Dynamic Approaches to Domestic Budgeting: Cases and Methods from Africa," Daisy Dwyer, Judith Bruce (eds.) *A Home Divided*, Stanford, CA: Stanford University Press.

Hanson, Susan and Robert W. Lake (2000) "Needed: Geographic Research on Urban Sustainability," *Economic Geographic*, Vol.76, No.1.

Haraway, Donna (1991) "Situated Knowledges: The Science Question in Feminism and the Privilege of Partial Perspective," Donna Haraway *Simians, Cyborgs, and Women: The Reinvention of Nature,* New York: Routledge.

Hardin, Garrett (1968) "The Tragedy of the Commons," *Science*, Vol.163, No.3859.

Hart, Gillian (1991) "Engendering Everyday Resistance: Gender, Patronage, and Production Politics in Rural Malaysia," *The Journal of Peasant Studies*, Vol.19, No.1.

Hartman, Betsy and James Boyce (1983*) A Quiet Revolution: View From a Bangladesh Village*, Food First Books, Oakland, USA.

Hershatter, Gail (2002) "The Gender of Memory: Rural Chinese Women and the 1950s," *Sings*, 2002, Vol.28, No.1

Hinton, William (1990) *The Great Reversal: The Privatization of China, 1978-1989*, Monthly Review Press.

——(1998) "The Importance of Land Reform in the Reconstruction of China," *Monthly Review*, Vol.50, No. 3.

Ho, Peter (2000a) "The Myth of Desertification at China's Northwestern Frontier: The Case of Ningxia Province 1929-1958," *Modern China*, Vol.26, No.3.

——(2000b) "China's Rangelands under Stress: A Comparative Study of Pasture Commons in the Ningxia Hui Autonomous Region," *Development and Change* Vol. 31,No.2

——(2001) "Rangeland Degradation in North China Revisited? A Preliminary Statistical Analysis to Validate Non-equilibrium Range Ecology," *Journal of Development Studies,* Vol.37, No.3.

Honig, Emily (2000) "Iron Girls Revisited: Gender and the Politics of Work in the Cultural Revolution, 1966-76," Barbara Entwisle (eds.) *Re-drawing Boundaries: Work, Households, and Gender in China,* Berkeley, University of California Press.

Hsiung, Ping-chun (1996) *Living Rooms as Factories: Class, Gender and the Satellite Factory System in Taiwan,* Philadelphia: Temple University Press.

Huang, Shu-min (1989) *The Spiral Road: Change in a Chinese Village Through the Eyes of a Communist Party Leader,* Boulder: Westview Press.

Huang, Philip C. (1985) *The Peasant Economy and Social Change in North China*, Stanford, California: Stanford University Press.

——(1990) *The Peasant Family and Rural Development in the Yangzi-Delta 1350-1988*, Stanford: Stanford University Press.

Hu,Yukun (2002) *Mainstreaming Gender in the Rural Water Supply and Sanitation Project: A Preliminary Field Research,* Central Project Management Office, Ministry of Water Resources, P.R. China, supported by funding from the UK Department for International Development.

Jacka, Tamara (1997) *Women's Work in Rural China: Change and Continuity in an Era of Reform*, Cambridge University Press.

Jackson, Cecile (1995) "From Conjugal Contracts to Environmental Relations: Some Thoughts on Labor and Technology," *IDS Bulletin*, Vol. 26, No.1

Jackson, Cecile, Molly Chattopadhyay (2000) "Identities and Livelihoods: Gender, Ethnicity and Nature in a South Bihar Village," Arun Agrawal, K. Sivaramakrishnan (eds.)*Agrarian Environments: Resources, Representations, and Rule in India*, Durham and London: Duke University Press.

Jagchid, Sechin and Paul Hyer (1979) *Mongolian's Culture and Society*, Boulder,

Colorado: Westview Press.

Jankowiak, William (1988) "The Last Hurrah? Political Protest in Inner Mongolia," *The Australian Journal of Chinese Affairs*, No.19-20.

Jacobson, Jodi (1992) *Gender Bias, Roadlock to Sustainable Development,* Washington, D. C., USA: World Institute.

Jikun Huang, Ninghui Li, Scott Rozelle (2003) "Trade Reform, Household Effects and Poverty in Rural China," *American Journal of Agricultural Economics*, Vol.85, No.5.

Jones, Christine (1986) "Intra-household Bargaining in Response to the Introduction of New Crops: A Case Study from North Cameroon," Joyce Moock (ed.) *Understanding Africa's Rural Households and Farming Systems*, Boulder and London: Westview Press.

Johnson, Kay Ann (1983) *Women, the Family and Peasant Revolution in China,* Chicago: University of Chicago Press.

Judd, Ellen (1989) "Niangjia: Chinese Woman and Their Natal Families," *Journal of Asian Studies,* Vol. 48, No.3.

——1994 *Gender and Power in Rural North China*, Stanford, CA: Stanford University Press.

Kabeer, Naila (1994) *Reversed Realities: Gender Hierarchies in Development Thought*, London and New York: Verso.

Kabeer Naila, Ramya Subrahmanian (1996)"Institutions, Relations and Outcomes: Framework and Tools for Gender Aware Planning," *IDS Bulletin Paper* # 357.

Azizur Rahman Khan and Carl Ruskin (2001) *Inequality and Poverty in China in the Age of Globalization,* Oxford, Oxford University Press.

Kung, James K.S. and Louis Putterman (1997) "China's Collectivisation Puzzle: a New Resolution," *Journal of Development Studies*, Vol.33, No.6.

Kerkvliet, Benedict (1990) *Everyday Politics in the Philippines: Class and Status Relations in a Central Luzon Village,* Berkeley: University of California Press.

Lan Township People's Committee (LTPC) (1960) *A History of Lan Township Development* (*Lan xiang fa zhan shi)*.

Leach, Melissa, Susan Joekes, Cathy Green (1995) "Editorial: Gender Relations and Environmental Change," *IDS Bulletin*, Vo.26, No.1.

Leach, Melissa (1994) *Rainforest Relations: Gender and Resource Use among the Mende of Gola, Sierra Leone*,Washington, DC: Smithsonian Institution Press.

Leach, Melissa, Robin Mearns, Lan Scoones (1999) "Environmental Entitlements: Dynamics and Institutions in Community-based Natural Resource management," *World Development,* Vol.27, No.2.

Lee, Ching Kwan (1998) *Gender and the South China Miracle: Two Worlds of Factory Women,*Berkeley: University of California Press.

Liu, Jingtang (1989) *Aohan Grain Records* (*Aohan liangshi zhi*).

Li, Hui (1991) (ed.) *Aohan Population Records* (*Aohan renkou zhi*) .

Li, Rose Maria (1989) "Migration to China's Northern Frontier, 1953-1982," *Population and Development Review*, Vol.15, No.3.

Li, Zongmin (1999) "Changing Land and Housing Use by Rural Women in Northern China," Irene Tinker (eds.) *Women's Rights to House and Land: China, Laos, Vietnam,* Boulder and London: Lynne Rienner Publishers.

Liu, Xin (2000) *In One's Own Shadow: An Ethnographic Account of the Conditions of Post-reform Rural China*, Berkeley and London: University of California Press.

Ma, Rong (1987) *Migrant and Ethnic Integration in Rural Chifeng, Inner Mongolia Autonomous Region, China,* (Dissertation, Brown University).

Moore, Richard and Robyn Russell (1990) "The 'Three North' Forest Protection System-China,"*Agroforestry System*, No.10.

Mosse, David (1994) "Authority, Gender and Knowledge: Theoretical Reflections on the Practice of Participatory Rural Appraisal," *Development and Change,* Vol.25,No.3.

Momsen, Janet (2000) "Gender Differences in Environmental Concern and Perception," *Journal of Geography* Vol.99,No.2.

Muldavin, Joshua (1996a) "The Political Ecology of Agrarian Reform in China: the Case of Heilongjiang Province," Richard Peets, Michael Watts (eds.) *Liberation Ecologies: Environment, Development and Social Movement*, London and New York: Routledge.

——(1996b) "Impact of Reform on Environmental Sustainability in Rural China," *Journal of Contemporary Asia,* Vol.26, No.3.

——(1997) "Environmental Degradation in Heilongjiang: Policy Reform and Agrarian Dynamics in China's New Hybrid Economy," *Annals of the Association of American Geographers* Vol. 87, No.4.

——(2000) "The Paradox of Environmental Policy and Resource Management in

Reform-Era China," *Economic Geography* Vol.76, No, 3.

Murphey, Rhoads (1967) "Man and Nature in China," *Modern Asian Studies,* Vol.1, No.4.

Netting, Robert McC. (1993) *Smallholders, Householders: Farm Families and the Ecology of Intensive, Sustainable Agriculture*, Stanford, CA: Stanford University Press.

North, Douglass C. (1990) *Institutions, Institutional Change and Economic Performance*, Cambridge: Cambridge University Press.

O'Brien, Kevin J., and Lianjiang Li (1995) "The Politics of Lodging Complaints in Rural China," *China Quarterly* Vol. 143.

Oi, Jean (1990) *State and Peasant in Contemporary China: The Political Economy of Village Government,* Berkeley: University of California Press.

——(1999) *Rural China Takes Off: Institutional Foundations of Economic Reform,* Berkeley and Los Angeles: University of California Press.

Ong, Aihwa (1987) *Spirits of Resistance and Capitalist Discipline: Factory Women in Malaysia*, Albany: State University of New York Press.

——(1988) "Colonialism and Modernity: Feminist Re-presentation of Women in Non-Western Societies," *Inscriptions,* No.3/4.

Ong, Aihwa (1995) "Women Out of China: Traveling Tales and Traveling Theories in Postcolonial Feminism," Ruth Behar, Deborah Gordon (eds.) *Women Writing Culture.* Berkeley: University of California Press

Owen, Lattimore (1962) *Studies in Asian Frontier History Collected Papers 1928-1958,* London, Oxford University Press.

Patai, Daphne (1991) "U.S. Academics and Third World Women: Is Ethical Research Possible?" Sherna Berger Gluck, Daphne Patai (eds.) *Women's Words: The Feminist Practice of Oral History,* New York: Routledge

Parish, William and Martin Whyte (1978) *Village and Family in Contemporary China,* Chicago: University Press.

Peet, Richard and Michael Watts (eds.) (1996) *Liberation Ecologies: Environment, Development and Social Movement*, London and New York: Routledge.

Perkins, Tamara (2002) *Village, Market and Well-Being in a Rural Chinese Township,* New York: Rouledge.

Putterman, Louis (1993) *Continuity and Change in China's Rural Development: Collective and Reform Eras in Perspective*, New York and Oxford: Oxford

University Press.

Potter, Sulamith Heins, and Jack Potter (1990) *China's Peasants: The Anthropology of a Revolution*, New York: Cambridge University Press.

Rai, Shirin and Zhang Junzuo (1994) "Competing and Learning: Women and the State in Contemporary Rural Mainland China," *Issues and studies*, Vol. 30, No.3.

Richardson, Dennis (1990) *Forests and Forestry in China*, Washington, DC: Island Press.

Rozelle, Scott et al (2000) *China: From Afforestation to Poverty Alleviation and Natural Forest Management,* Washington, D. C.: the World Bank.

Rozelle, Scott (1996) "Stagnation without Equity: Changing Patterns of Income and Inequality in China's Post-Reform Rural Economy," *China Journal,* Vol.35.

Rocheleau, Dianne (1995) "Gender and Biodiversity: A Feminist Political Ecology Perspective," *IDS Bulletin*, Vol.26, No.1.

——(1998) "Sustaining What for Whom? Differences of Interest within and Between Households," Sinclair and M. Swisher (eds.) *Sustainability in Managed Ecosystems: the Mesoamerican Experience*, Oxford and New York: Oxford University Press.

Rocheleau, Dianne, Thomas-Slayter Barbar, Esther Wangari (eds.) (1996) *Feminist Political Ecology: Global Issues and Local Experiences*, London and New York: Routledge.

Rocheleau, Dianne, David Edmunds (1997) "Women, Men and Trees: Gender, Power and Property in Forest and Agrarian Landscapes," *World Development*, Vol.25, No.8.

Rocheleau, Dianne, Laurie Ross etal (2001) "Complex Communities and Emergent Ecologies in the Regional Agroforestry of Zambrana-Chacuey, Dominnican Republic," *Ecumene*, Vol.8, No.4.

Rozelle, Scott et al (2000) *China: From Afforestation to Poverty Alleviation and Natural Forest Management,* Washtington, D. C.: the World Bank.

Ruf, Gregory (1998) *Cadres and Kin: Making a Socialist Village in West China, 1921-1991*, California, Stanford University Press.

Sachs, Carolyn (1996) *Gendered Fields: Rural Women, Agriculture, and Environment,* Boulder, Colo.: Westview.

Schroeder, Richard (1999) *Shady Practices: Agroforesty and Gender Politics in the Gambia*, Berkeley:Los Angeles: University of California Press.

Scott, James (1985) *Weapons of the Weak: Everyday Forms of Peasant Resistance,* New Haven: Yale University Press.

——(1990) *Domination and the Arts of Resistance: Hidden Transcripts*, New Haven and London: Yale University Press.

——(1998) *Seeking Like a State: How Certain Schemes to Improve the Human Condition Have Failed*, New Haven: Yale University Press.

Scott, Joan (1988) *Gender and the Politics of History,* New York: Columbia University Press.

Sen, Amartya (1990) "Gender and Cooperative Conflicts," Irene Tinker (ed.) *Persistent Inequalities: Women and World Development*, New York: Oxford University Press.

Shapiro, Judith (2001) *Mao's War against Nature: Politics and the Environment in Revolutionary China,* Cambridge: Cambridge University Press.

Shue, Vivienne (1980) *Peasant China in Transition: The Dynamics of Development Toward Socialism, 1949-1956,* Berkeley: University of California Press.

Siu, Helen (1989) *Agents and Victims in South China: Accomplices in Rural Revolution,* New Haven: Yale University Press.

——(1993) "The Reconstitution of Brideprice and Dowry in South China," in Deborah Davis and Stevan Harrell (eds.) *Chinese Families in the Post-Mao Era*, University of California Press.

Sneath, David (1994) "The Impact of the Cultural-Revolution in China on the Mongolians of Inner-Mongolia," *Modern Asian Studies* Vol. 28, No.2.

Smil, Vaclav (1984) *The Bad Earth*. Armonk, N. Y.: M.E. Sharpe.

——(1993) *China's Environment: An Inquiry into the Limits of National Development*, M. E. Sharpe, Armonk, NY.

——(1998) "Who Will Feed China?" *The China Quarterly,* No.143.

Slocum, Rachel, Lori Wichhart, Dianne Rocheleau, Barbara Thomas-Slayter (1995) (eds.) *Power, Process and Participation: Tools for Change*, Intermadiate Technology Publications.

Stacey, Judith (1991) "Can There Be a Feminist Ethnography?" in Sherna Berger Gluck, Daphne Patai (eds.) *Women's Words: The Feminist Practice of Oral History,* New York: Routledge.

Stephanie Hemelryk Donald and Robert Benewick (2005) *The State of China*

Atlas: Mapping the World's Fastest Growing Economy, Berkeley, California: University of California Press.

Thomas-Slayter, Barbara (1992) "Politics, Class and Gender in African Resource Management: The Case of Rural Kenya," *Economic Development and Cultural Change*, Vol.40, No.4.

Thomas-Slayter, Barbara Dianne Rocheleau (1995a) *Gender, Environment, and Development in Kenya: A Grassroots Perspective*, Boulder and London: Lynne Rienner Publishers.

Townsend, Janet (1995) *Women's Voices from the Rainforest,* London and New York: Routledge.

Tsing, Anna Lowenhaupt (1993) *In the Realm of the Diamond Queen: Marginality in an Out-of-the-Way Place*, Princeton, New Jersey: Princeton University Press.

United Nations (1996) *The Beijing Declaration and the Platform for Action: 4th World Conference on Women,* Beijing, China, New York: Dept. of Public Information.

Visweswaren, Kemala (1994) *Fictions of Feminist Ethnography,* Minneapolis: University of Minnesota Press.

Watson Rubie (1986) "The Named and the Nameless: Gender and Person in Chinese Society," *American Ethnologist* Vol.13, No.4.

Watson, Rubie and Patricia Buckley Ebrey (eds.) (1991) *Marriage and Inequality in Chinese Society*, Berkeley: University of California Press.

Whitehead, Ann (1981) "I'm Hungry, Mum: The Politics of Domestic Budgeting," Kate Young (eds.) *Of Marriage and the Market: Women's Subordination Internationally and Its Lesson*, London: Routledge and Kegan Paul.

Williams, Dee Mack (1996) "The Barbed Walls of China: A Contemporary Grassland Drama," *Journal of Asian Studies*, Vol. 55, No.3.

——(2002) *Beyond Great Walls: Environment, Identity and Development on the Chinese Grasslands of Inner Mongolia,* Standford: Standford University Press.

Watts, Michael (1991) "Entitlements or Empowerment? Famine and Starvation in Africa," *Review of African Political Economy,* Vol.51.

Wolf, Diane (ed.) (1996) *Feminist Dilemmas in Fieldwork*, Boulder, Co: Westview Press.

Wolf, Margery (1985) *Revolution Postponed: Women in Contemporary China*, Stanford, California: Stanford University Press.

Woon, Yuen-fong (1991) "From Mao to Deng: Life Satisfaction among Rural Women in an Emigrant Community in South China," *The Australian Journal of Chinese Affairs*, No.25.

World Bank (1992) *China Environmental Strategy Paper*, Washington DC.

World Bank (2001) *Agenda for Water Sector Strategy for North China*, Vol.1, Summary Report, the World Bank, Washington D. C.

World Bank (1997) *China 2020-Sharing Rising Incomes,* Washington DC: the World Bank.

World Commission on Environment and Development (1987) *Our Common Future*, Oxford and New York: Oxford University Press.

Xu, Cheng, Han Chunru and Donald Taylor (1992) "Sustainable Agricultural Development in China," *World Development*, Vol.20, No.8.

Yan, Yunxiang (1996) *The Flow of Gifts: Reciprocity and Social Networks in a Chinese Village*, Stanford, CA: Stanford University Press.

Yin, Runsheng (1994) "China's Rural Forestry Since 1949," *Journal of World Forest Resource Management*, Vol.7,No.2

——(1998) "Forestry and the Environment in China: the Current Situation and Strategic Choices," *World Development*, Vol.26, No.12.

Zhang, Weiguo (2000) "Dynamics of Marriage Change in Chinese Rural Society in Transition: A Study of a Northern Chinese Village," *Population Studies* Vol.54, No.1.

This book is the result of a co-publication agreement between China Social Sciences Press (China) and Paths International Ltd (UK)

Title: Man and Nature in China: Gender, Natural Resources Management and the Chinese State in an Inner Mongolia Village
Author: Hu Yukun
ISBN: 978-1-84464-600-5
Ebook ISBN: 978-1-84464-601-2

Paths International Ltd
www.pathsinternational.com
Published in the United Kingdom

CPSIA information can be obtained
at www.ICGtesting.com
Printed in the USA
LVHW050827270123
737654LV00004B/111

9 781844 646005